Plato's *Republic*

Plato's *Republic* has proven to be of astounding influence and importance. Justly celebrated as Plato's central text, it brings together all of his prior works, unifying them into a comprehensive vision that is at once theological, philosophical, political, and moral. These essays provide a state-of-the-art research picture of the most interesting aspects of the *Republic*, and address questions that continue to puzzle and provoke, such as: Does Plato succeed in his argument that the life of justice is the most attractive one? Is his tripartite analysis of the soul coherent and plausible? Why does Plato seem to have to *force* his philosopher-guardians to rule when they know this is something that they *ought* to do? What is the point of the strange and complicated closing Myth of Er? This volume will be essential to those looking for thoughtful and detailed excursions into the problems posed by Plato's text and ideas.

MARK L. MCPHERRAN is Professor of Philosophy at Simon Fraser University. He is the author of *The Religion of Socrates* (1996) and of numerous articles on ancient philosophy.

CAMBRIDGE CRITICAL GUIDES

Other titles published in this series:

Hegel's Phenomenology of Spirit
DEAN MOYAR AND MICHAEL QUANTE

Mill's On Liberty
C. L. TEN

Kant's Idea for a Universal History with a Cosmopolitan Aim
AMÉLIE OKSENBERG RORTY AND JAMES SCHMIDT

Kant's Groundwork of the Metaphysics of Morals
JENS TIMMERMANN

Kant's Critique of Practical Reason
ANDREWS REATH AND JENS TIMMERMANN

Wittgenstein's Philosophical Investigations
ARIF AHMED

Kierkegaard's Concluding Unscientific Postscript
RICK ANTHONY FURTAK

PLATO'S
Republic
A Critical Guide

EDITED BY

MARK L. McPHERRAN

CAMBRIDGE UNIVERSITY PRESS
Cambridge, New York, Melbourne, Madrid, Cape Town,
Singapore, São Paulo, Delhi, Mexico City

Cambridge University Press
The Edinburgh Building, Cambridge CB2 8RU, UK

Published in the United States of America by Cambridge University Press, New York

www.cambridge.org
Information on this title: www.cambridge.org/9781107681224

© Cambridge University Press 2010

This publication is in copyright. Subject to statutory exception
and to the provisions of relevant collective licensing agreements,
no reproduction of any part may take place without the written
permission of Cambridge University Press.

First published 2010
Third printing 2012
First paperback edition 2013

A catalogue record for this publication is available from the British Library

ISBN 978-0-521-49190-7 Hardback
ISBN 978-1-107-68122-4 Paperback

Cambridge University Press has no responsibility for the persistence or
accuracy of URLs for external or third-party internet websites referred to in
this publication, and does not guarantee that any content on such websites is,
or will remain, accurate or appropriate.

For my wife, Neda

Trojan, Anchises' son:
The descent into Avernus is easy.
All night and all day long the doors of Hades stand open.
But to retrace the path, and come up to the sweet air of heaven,
That is the task, that is the toil.
Some few whom God was right to love
Or whose innate virtues singled them out from the common run
Have done so.   *Aeneid* 6.10

Contents

Acknowledgments		*page* ix
List of contributors		x
List of abbreviations		xiii
	Introduction	1
	MARK L. MCPHERRAN	
1.	Socrates in the *Republic*	11
	G. R. F. FERRARI	
2.	Platonic ring-composition and *Republic* 10	32
	RACHEL BARNEY	
3.	The Atlantis story: the *Republic* and the *Timaeus*	52
	JULIA ANNAS	
4.	Ethics and politics in Socrates' defense of justice	65
	RACHANA KAMTEKAR	
5.	Return to the cave	83
	NICHOLAS D. SMITH	
6.	Degenerate regimes in Plato's *Republic*	103
	ZENA HITZ	
7.	Virtue, luck, and choice at the end of the *Republic*	132
	MARK L. MCPHERRAN	
8.	Plato's divided soul	147
	CHRISTOPHER SHIELDS	
9.	The meaning of "*saphēneia*" in Plato's Divided Line	171
	J. H. LESHER	

viii *Contents*

10. Plato's philosophical method in the *Republic*: the Divided
Line (510b–511d) 188
HUGH H. BENSON

11. Blindness and reorientation: education and the acquisition of
knowledge in the *Republic* 209
C. D. C. REEVE

12. Music all pow'rful 229
MALCOLM SCHOFIELD

Bibliography 249
Index of passages 261
Index of names and subjects 270

Acknowledgments

This book began to take shape in July, 2007 when Hilary Gaskin, the philosophy editor at Cambridge University Press, and I began to discuss the possibility of there being a Cambridge Critical Guide to the *Republic* in that new series of Guides. The timing was ideal, since I was then laying plans for the Thirteenth Annual Arizona Colloquium in Ancient Philosophy, whose exclusive focus was to be Plato's *Republic*. The Colloquium was subsequently held February 15–17, 2008, at the University of Arizona, Tucson. I wish to thank Julia Annas and Rachana Kamtekar, and, in particular, the Colloquium Assistant, Michelle Jenkins, for their invaluable assistance in arranging the details of our very productive meeting. I want to give special thanks as well to the Chair of the Department of Philosophy at the University of Arizona, Christopher Maloney, for his enthusiastic support of the Colloquium over its fifteen years of existence. The volumes' contributions by Julia Annas, Rachel Barney, Hugh H. Benson, Zena Hitz, Rachana Kamtekar, J. H. Lesher, C. D. C. Reeve, Malcolm Schofield, and Nicholas D. Smith are based on versions of papers they presented at that Colloquium. I was lucky to be able to secure later contributions from G. R. F. Ferrari and Christopher Shields. My own essay on the Myth of Er was at that point in the planning stages and is the seventh entry contained herein.

Besides all the above, I want to thank my student Jennifer Liderth, for her preparation of the Bibliography and indices, Hilary Gaskin for her support of this project, Nicholas Smith for our many years of collaborative friendship, and all those others in ancient philosophy who have helped me along in my joyous and sometimes rough sojourn in this *agōgē biou*. My gratitude, finally, to Simon Fraser University for its generous assistance, and to Dennis Bevington, Nicholas Smith, and David Zimmerman for their comments as this project developed.

Contributors

JULIA ANNAS is Regents Professor of Philosophy at the University of Arizona; she has also taught at St Hugh's College, Oxford and Columbia University. She is the author of *The Morality of Happiness* (1993), *Platonic Ethics Old and New* (1999) and *Intelligent Virtue* (2011), as well as *An Introduction to Plato's* Republic (1981), introductory books on Plato and ancient philosophy, translations and editions. She has published over a wide range of ancient philosophy, and for the last few years has concentrated on ancient ethics and also contemporary virtue ethics.

RACHEL BARNEY is Canada Research Chair in Classical Philosophy at the University of Toronto, in the Departments of Classics and Philosophy. She received her BA from Toronto in 1989 and her PhD from Princeton in 1996. Her publications include *Names and Natures in Plato's* Cratylus (2001), "A Puzzle in Stoic Ethics" (2003), and "Aristotle's Argument for a Human Function" (2008). She is also interested in the sophistic movement, Neoplatonic commentary, and the relation of form and style to philosophical method in ancient philosophy.

HUGH H. BENSON is Professor and Chair of the Department of Philosophy at the University of Oklahoma. He was a Samuel Roberts Noble Presidential Professor from 2000 to 2004. He is the editor of *Essays on the Philosophy of Socrates* (1992) and *A Companion to Plato* (2006), and author of *Socratic Wisdom* (2000). He has also written various articles on the philosophy of Socrates, Plato, and Aristotle.

G. R. F. ("JOHN") FERRARI is Professor of Classics at the University of California, Berkeley. He is editor of the *Cambridge Companion to Plato's* Republic (Cambridge University Press, 2007), and has also edited a translation of the *Republic* by Tom Griffith in the series Cambridge Texts in the History of Political Thought (Cambridge University Press, 2000). He is the author of *Listening to the Cicadas: A Study of Plato's* Phaedrus

List of contributors xi

(Cambridge University Press, 1987) and *City and Soul in Plato's* Republic (2003; rpt. 2005).

ZENA HITZ is Assistant Professor of Philosophy at University of Maryland, Baltimore County. She received her PhD in 2005 from Princeton University's classical philosophy program and works on a range of topics in ancient moral and political philosophy. She is currently writing a book on the function of law in Plato and Aristotle.

RACHANA KAMTEKAR is Associate Professor of Philosophy at the University of Arizona. She has published a number of papers on the psychology, ethics, and politics of the *Republic*. At present, she is writing a book entitled *The Powers of Plato's Psychology*.

J. H. LESHER is Professor of Philosophy at the University of North Carolina at Chapel Hill. He is the author of *Xenophanes of Colophon* (1992); *The Greek Philosophers: Greek Texts with Notes and Commentary* (1998); *Plato's* Symposium: *Issues in Interpretation and Reception*, co-edited with Debra Nails and Frisbee Sheffield (2006); *Essays on Aristotle's* Posterior Analytics: *Papers from the 2009 Duke–UNC Conference* (forthcoming); and more than fifty articles on topics relating to ancient Greek philosophy.

MARK L. McPHERRAN is Professor of Philosophy at Simon Fraser University. He is the author of *The Religion of Socrates* (1996), and numerous articles, including: "Socratic Religion," in *The Cambridge Companion to Socrates* (forthcoming); "Medicine, Magic, and Religion in Plato's *Symposium*," in *Plato's* Symposium: *Issues in Interpretation and Reception* (2006); "Platonic Religion," in *A Companion to Plato* (2006); "The Piety and Gods of Plato's *Republic*," in *The Blackwell Guide to Plato's* Republic (2006); and "Socratic Piety in the *Euthyphro*," *Journal of the History of Philosophy* 23 (1985). He is currently the Director of the Annual Arizona Colloquium in Ancient Philosophy.

C. D. C. REEVE is Delta Kappa Epsilon Distinguished Professor of Philosophy at the University of North Carolina at Chapel Hill. His books include *Philosopher-Kings* (1988; reissued Hackett, 2006), *Socrates in the* Apology (1989), *Practices of Reason* (1995), *Aristotle:* Politics (1998), *Plato:* Cratylus (1998), *The Trials of Socrates* (2002), *Substantial Knowledge* (2003), *Plato:* Republic (2005), *Love's Confusions* (2005), and *Plato on Love* (2006).

MALCOLM SCHOFIELD is Director of Research in the Classics Faculty at Cambridge, where he has taught for close to forty years, following positions at Cornell University and Balliol College, Oxford. He is co-author (with xii *List of contributors*

G. S. Kirk and J. E. Raven) of *The Presocratic Philosophers*, 2nd ed. (1983), and has published widely on many areas and periods of Greek and Roman thought. He has been working mainly on ancient political thought since *The Stoic Idea of the City* (1991), and is co-editor (with Christopher Rowe) of *The Cambridge History of Political Thought* (2000). His latest books are *Plato: Political Philosophy* (2006) and (with Tom Griffith) *Plato: Gorgias, Menexenus, Protagoras* (2010), in the series 'Cambridge Texts in the History of Political Thought'.

CHRISTOPHER SHIELDS is Tutor and Fellow of Lady Margaret Hall and Professor of Classical Philosophy in the University of Oxford. He is the author of *Order in Multiplicity: Homonymy in the Philosophy of Aristotle* (1999), *Classical Philosophy: A Contemporary Introduction* (2003), *Aristotle* (2007), and, with Robert Pasnau, *The Philosophy of Thomas Aquinas* (2003). He is the editor of *The Blackwell Guide to Ancient Philosophy* (2002) and the forthcoming *Oxford Handbook of Aristotle*. Also forthcoming is *Aristotle's De Anima, Translated with Introduction and Notes*.

NICHOLAS D. SMITH is the James F. Miller Professor of Humanities in the Department of Philosophy at Lewis and Clark College. He has published numerous books and articles with Thomas C. Brickhouse, including *Socrates on Trial* (1989), *Plato's Socrates* (1994), *The Philosophy of Socrates* (2000), the *Routledge Philosophy GuideBook to Plato and the Trial of Socrates* (2004), and most recently, *Socratic Moral Psychology* (2010). In addition to his work with Brickhouse, he has published numerous articles on Plato, Aristotle, contemporary epistemology, and virtue theory.

Abbreviations

I. PLATONIC TEXTS

Ap.	*Apology*
Chrm.	*Charmides*
Cri.	*Crito*
Criti.	*Critias*
Euthyphr.	*Euthyphro*
Euthyd.	*Euthydemus*
Grg.	*Gorgias*
Lys.	*Lysis*
Phd.	*Phaedo*
Phdr.	*Phaedrus*
Pol.	*Politicus (Statesman)*
Prt.	*Protagoras*
Rep.	*Republic*
Smp.	*Symposium*
Soph.	*Sophist*
Theag.	*Theages*
Tht.	*Theaetetus*
Ti.	*Timaeus*

II. ARISTOTELIAN TEXTS

E.E.	*Eudemian Ethics*
Meta.	*Metaphysics*
N.E.	*Nicomachean Ethics*
Pol.	*Politics*

Introduction

Mark L. McPherran

The first sentence of Plato's *Republic* recounts how Socrates went on a journey of descent – a *katabasis* – leaving the secure walls of Athens in order to celebrate the introduction of a new worship:

> I went down yesterday to the Piraeus with Glaucon, the son of Ariston, to say a prayer to the goddess [Bendis], and because I was also curious to see how they would conduct the festival, since this was its inauguration. (*Rep.* 327a1–3)

With this opening metaphor of descent – and continuing on through its central books of ascent to the final mythical *katabasis* and revelatory reascent (*anabasis*) of the Myth of Er (614b–621d) – Plato's *Republic* announces itself to be an original and revolutionary journey toward the truth, passing through extraordinarily mysterious terrain. This opening also suggests what the text goes on to confirm, namely, that the purpose of the *Republic* is to introduce a new cult outside the walls of the traditional dispensation. The divinity of this sect proves not to be a Thracian night-goddess, however, but the Reality of the Form-world, and its new worship involves not nocturnal horse races (328a), but the intellectual activity of philosophizing whose sacrificial rewards are threefold: wisdom, happiness, and the assurance of immortality.

Plato's text has more than lived up to its author's aims: the *Republic* has proven to be of astounding influence and importance, setting down in a very real sense the central agenda of the Western philosophical enterprise – and everyday undergraduate education as well – up to the present moment. Although other Platonic texts supersede the *Republic* in some aspect or other (for example, the challenging argumentation of the *Parmenides* and *Theaetetus*) it nevertheless brings together all of Plato's prior work, ranging over everything from moral psychology, philosophy of education, aesthetics, and comparative political science to epistemology and supra-sensible metaphysics – unifying them into a comprehensive vision that is at once theological, philosophical, political, and moral. The *Republic*, then, is justly celebrated as Plato's central text, and scholars continue to regard it as Plato's *magnum opus*. It remains a basic text in Western education in a variety of disciplines (in particular, philosophy, psychology, political science, classics, religious studies, education, and history) – from high school through graduate education – and continues to attract the attention of the very best scholars in a variety of disciplines. The issues scholars target are also not simply historical ones, despite the antiquity of the text. Some moral philosophers, for example, still think they can discern in the eudaimonistic moral theory it traces out a plausible answer to the live and vexing question "Why be moral?"

The essays that follow are the products of scholars such as these, and thus represent the current state of scholarship on key issues in the interpretation of the *Republic*. These issues are constituted by such questions as: Does Plato succeed in his argument that the life of justice is the most attractive one? Is his analysis of the soul as having three parts – appetites, *thumos*, and reason – coherent and plausible? What exactly is the epistemology/ metaphysics of the *Republic* and what are its merits and pitfalls? Why does Plato seem to have to *force* his philosopher-guardians to rule his Kallipolis when that task is something they know that they *ought* to do? What is the point of its strange and complicated closing Myth of Er? These questions and numerous others continue to puzzle and provoke, and in what follows we see some of the field's leading scholars come to terms with these Platonic provocations.

This Critical Guide, then, is not a preparatory book or synopsis for those planning to read the *Republic* for the first time. There are many fine introductions available to that sort of reader, usually accompanied by a translation of the text.[1] Rather, as part of the Cambridge Critical Guide series, this book is for veterans of the text who are looking for thoughtful, detailed excursions into the problems Plato's text and ideas pose. Its aim is to give a state-of-the-art research picture of the most interesting and discussable aspects of the *Republic*, by offering a series of critical, reflective essays rather than providing systematic and comprehensive descriptive coverage of that text. On to our essays then.

We begin with an investigation of the central dramatic character of the *Republic*, Socrates. G. R. F. Ferrari asks how far the Socrates of the *Republic* differs from the Socrates of the aporetic dialogues – those relatively small-scale dialogues in which Socrates questions an interlocutor on his views about virtue, or about a particular virtue, or about some other aspect of how one should live, and which invariably end with their key issues unresolved. At least since Schleiermacher, the *Republic* has been a key exhibit for the argument that Plato's thinking and purpose changed as he wrote the dialogues, whether from being open-ended and provocative to being more explicit and self-contained, or from sticking close to the model of the historic Socrates to inaugurating a new philosophical movement.

Although Ferrari does not set out to dismantle these scholarly accounts, he does mark his distance from them by paying close attention to how Plato in the *Republic* distinguishes his narrative control as philosophical author from that of his philosophic character Socrates, the work's internal narrator. It is typical for interpreters of the *Republic* to think of the character Socrates as holding its argument in a tight intellectual grip. Ferrari argues that it is rather his author Plato who does this, because Socrates in the *Republic* is a man beset by the demands of his interlocutors. For example, as he narrates his earlier discussion to an unknown audience at the house of Cephalus, he gives that audience to understand that he himself was taken by surprise at moments structurally crucial to the *Republic's* ever-expanding argument, which we readers can see in retrospect, but Socrates at the time could not. The Socrates that Ferrari offers cuts a considerably less controlling figure than the politic, ironic Socrates of the aporetic dialogues. For, as Socrates's author, Plato depicts him as achieving *more subtle, surreptitious* control over the interlocutors of the *Republic*. Ferrari contends that in this work Plato has fashioned at the level of large-scale conversational construction an equivalent of the small-scale manipulations that shaped the earlier Socratic questioning. As a result, Ferrari's account finds no doctrinal implications in the contrast between the Socrates of the aporetic dialogues and the Socrates of the *Republic*, but rather a difference in dialectical *approach* to doctrinal substance.

Turning to the overall structure of the *Republic*, Rachel Barney argues for a reading of Plato's *Republic* as being systematically ring-composed. The argument proceeds in five steps. First, she explains "ring-composition" (with particular reference to Books 1 and 24 of the *Iliad*) and introduces some terms useful for discussing it. Second, she briefly sketches a range of instances of ring-composition in other Platonic dialogues (notably the *Cratylus, Theaetetus*, and *Sophist*). Third, she lays out the five themes or topics that we can detect as (somewhat blurry and interleaved) rings in the *Republic*, from the outermost in: *katabasis*, death, justice challenged and vindicated, the development/degeneration of a just city, and the critique of art. Fourth, she briefly suggests that ring-composition may in Plato be an expression of the "method of hypotheses," or what Aristotle describes as argument to and from first principles – that is, of a mode of argumentation that moves from lower-level postulates to higher (namely, logically prior and more explanatory) principles and back down again through the former with the deduction of their consequences. Fifth, she offers a reading of the Book 10 critique of art as an example of ring-composition, showing in some detail the ways in which it functions as a "resolution" of the earlier discussion in Books 2–3, and draws some general methodological morals.

Julia Annas next offers us a reading of the *Republic* that connects it to Plato's other works. Annas claims that the Atlantis story in the *Timaeus* and *Critias* is, as many have argued, fiction rather than an account, at many removes, of fact. But Plato often opposes fiction and finds little value, even harm, in concentration on particular facts and finding them important. What is the point, for him, in writing such a narrative? Annas argues that the story presents in narrative form a core message of the *Republic*, namely, that virtue is to be sought for its own sake and not for the sake of its results. The Atlantis story thus has the same kind of point as Plato's myths, presenting an intellectual message in narrative form in a way that is designed both to present "ancient Athens" as an ideal from which contemporary Athens has declined, and to discourage identification with a glorious past on the part of his Athenian audience.

Rachana Kamtekar goes further into the details of the Platonic conception of virtue by observing that although Glaucon's challenge to Socrates to show the intrinsic value of justice for its possessor and Socrates' defense both concern *individual* justice, 61 out of a total of 85 Stephanus pages in *Republic* 1–4 are devoted to *politics*, to describing the city and its coming-to-be. To wit: its origins in mutual need and the division of labor for efficient production of necessities, the expansion of this simple city to cater to the desire for luxuries, and especially the education of its guardians to purge these unnecessary desires. Why are these political proposals so extensive if Plato is only interested in the city as an analogue for the individual soul? And how does Socrates' definition of political justice as obtaining when each class performs its own function engage Thrasymachus' and Glaucon's specifically political claims about justice (that the laws that define justice in any constitution serve the interests of the rulers, that justice is the result of a social contract among the weak to neither harm nor be harmed)? Or if it does not engage these claims, then why not?

Kamtekar argues that the account of the ideal city in Socrates' defense of justice plays the role of connecting justice as a structural condition of the soul and just behavior. She shows that a proper appreciation of the role of the ideal city in the defense allows us to reply to Sachs' famous charge that Socrates' defense of justice is irrelevant; then, she raises a new worry that the defense is question-begging, but goes on to show why it is not. Finally,

Introduction 5

Kamtekar draws attention to the methodology of Socrates' defense and its relevance to the controversy in Plato scholarship about the relative roles of ethics and politics in the argument of the *Republic*.

Focusing more on the political concerns of our text, Nicholas D. Smith begins by noting that those who have escaped from Plato's cave and seen the world outside are very reluctant to return to the gloomy world below, but Plato insists that the requirement that they do so is a "just order to just people" (*Rep.* 7.520e1). Their reluctance is an indication of the fact that they do not regard ruling in the state as something desirable in itself – thus proving how different Plato's rulers are from those in command in unjust states. But their reluctance also creates a problem for Plato: One of the main arguments of the *Republic* provides a defense of justice that is supposed to show that justice is always preferable to injustice. Yet when justly required to return to the cave, the returners are reluctant. But are the returners not Plato's philosopher-rulers, who most of all should be aware that justice is always preferable? Whence, then, their reluctance?

Many scholarly attempts to solve this problem (sometimes called the "happy philosopher problem") have been offered in the literature, but in this essay Smith argues that none of those offered thus far adequately handles all of the aspects of the problem. After reviewing others' proposals and indicating what he sees as their flaws, Smith provides a novel interpretation which preserves Plato's claim that justice is always preferable to injustice and explains how and why the reluctance of the returners does not indicate any counterexample to this general rule. The keys to his interpretation are in maintaining, on the one hand, a psychological conception of justice of the sort Plato provides in Book 6, and, on the other, noting that those asked to return to the cave have not yet completed their education. Instead, they are only at the very beginning of a phase (to last the next fifteen years) in which they will be asked to perform services to the state under the supervision of the mature rulers – a time in which their judgments of these particular matters is not represented as inerrant.

Going further in a political direction, Zena Hitz examines the often-neglected catalogue of degenerate regimes in *Republic* Books 8 and 9 and presents them as a philosophical response to fifth-century BCE political struggles in Athens and the rest of Greece. Oligarchy, democracy and tyranny are all "appetitive" regimes for Plato, regimes that involve in key ways the use of desire and pleasure as a standard for political decision-making rather than knowledge or honor. As such, their treatment late in the *Republic* echoes and clarifies Thrasymachus' immoralism (Book 1) and images like the Ship of State (Book 6). In Books 8 and 9, the regimes

6   MARK L. McPHERRAN

(with timocracy) are distinguished from one another by their dominant ends or guiding ideals. These ideals are all self-undermining: the ideal of honor leads to the base pursuit of wealth, oligarchic wealth to poverty, democratic freedom to tyranny and slavery. It is unclear, however, why degenerate ideals are unsuccessful: whether the problem is that they justify too much (as the democratic ideal of liberty also may justify lawless or tyrannical actions) or whether the claim is psychological and historical (that is, that these ideals, given human nature, lead inevitably to certain consequences). Hitz speculates that both claims are in play, and that *Republic* Books 8 and 9 accordingly work as both a philosophical analysis of bad regimes and as an explanation of real historical developments such as the oligarchic revolution in Athens in 404 BCE.

The *Republic* famously ends with a consideration of the previously dismissed question of the instrumental rewards of justice by first proving the soul's immortality (608c–612a) and then arguing for the superiority of the just life in what appear to be purely consequentialistic terms. In my contribution to this volume, I observe that happy as this account proves to be, critical readers often find it a silly bedtime story – or worse – lacking in philosophical depth and charm. One reason for this reaction is that in the context of the *Republic*'s project as a whole, Book 10 can appear to be "gratuitous and clumsy" (Annas 1981, p. 335). This is particularly true because of the way Book 10 spells out the post-mortem rewards of justice by deploying the odd story of Er's near-death experience, a myth whose "vulgarity seems to pull us right down to the level of Cephalus, where you take justice seriously when you start thinking about hell-fire" (Annas 1981, p. 349). It is this myth and this sort of sensible reaction to its contents that I consider. Worse than its vulgarity, I point to elements of Er's description of the life-choice lottery that can appear to undermine Plato's entire moral theory by threatening to eliminate our own moral responsibility for our bad choices while simultaneously convicting the gods of immorally tampering with our fates – contrary to the myth's explicit motivation and Plato's own theology. This essay exposes those elements and offers a first, tentative response to these worries.

The *Republic*'s tripartition of the soul is a perennial concern, and on this topic Christopher Shields opens by noting that the *Republic* requires an isomorphism of soul and state: as the ideally just state of Kallipolis comprises three harmoniously integrated parts – Rulers, Soldiers, and Workers – so the just man joins together three roughly analogous psychic parts – Reason, Temper, and Appetite – into a well-structured and unified whole. In terms of the overarching argument of the *Republic*, the partition of the state receives

Introduction

no direct argument and is expressly introduced as a kind of macrocosmic illustration of the microcosm of the soul: its heuristic function is thus subordinate to the ultimate task of helping make clear how we should best conceive the fully just soul (*Rep.* 368c–369b). In contrast with the condition of the state, the division of the soul does receive an extended treatment from Plato, who motivates his contention by means of a complex, two-phased argument (*Rep.* 437b–439e and 439e–441c). Although the consequences of this argument for Plato's moral psychology have been widely examined, comparatively little has been done on the seemingly prior question of Plato's metaphysics of soul, and still less on the form of mereology established by the argument he deploys. Upon closer examination, it emerges that the argument does not establish anything like three *essential* parts of soul, with the result that tripartition, though real and hardly illusory, emerges as an *accidental* feature of the soul, a feature in fact shed by the perfectly just man who is Plato's paragon. In consequence, the moral psychology of the *Republic* cannot plausibly be regarded as *requiring* any such division. This lack of essential division, though, is precisely as Plato contends in the last book of that work (Book 10), in a passage perforce disregarded by those expecting the argument for tripartition to prove more than it does.

Turning to the *Republic's* epistemology and metaphysics, J. H. Lesher observes that in *Republic* 6 Socrates directs Glaucon to draw a line whose four segments are said to represent different degrees of *saphēneia*. Although "*saphēneia*" is commonly translated as "clarity" it is implausible to suppose that the different levels Socrates identifies can be correlated with differing degrees of clarity. Images, for example, are not inherently less clear than physical objects, nor are inquiries that make use of visual diagrams inherently less clear than those that do not. Yet the alternative renderings of "*saphēneia*" as "truth," "precision" (or "exactitude"), and "knowledge" also encounter difficulties. Lesher's review of the use of "*saphēs*" and its cognates by Plato and his predecessors establishes that "*saphēneia*" designated a "full, accurate, and sure awareness," typically gained by means of direct observation of the relevant circumstances. Viewing "*saphēneia*" in its historical context thus enables us not only to understand the point of Plato's line simile (that is, showing what must be done in order to achieve a full, accurate, and sure awareness of the realities), but also to appreciate that Plato's restriction of "*saphēneia*" to the unchanging objects of thought represented a sharp departure from the broadly empirical view of knowledge held by many of his predecessors.

The literature devoted to Plato's image of the divided line is, of course, enormous. To help us further on this "line of thought," Hugh H. Benson notes that this literature is particularly devoted to speculating on the objects of the third section of the line. Despite the attention that these objects of *dianoia* have received, however, Plato's text does not distinguish the top two sections of the line by objects, but rather by methods – the dianoetic method (which leads to *dianoia*) and the dialectical method (which leads to *epistēmē* or *nous*). *Republic* 510b–511d indicates that both of these methods fall under the general rubric of the hypothetical method introduced in the *Meno* and *Phaedo*. The key to understanding the distinction lies in seeing the difference between the methods as being more a matter of degree than of kind. The methods as described in the Divided Line passage are at the two extremes. The dianoetic method makes no attempt to confirm the hypotheses it employs but goes straight to a conclusion, while the dialectical method successfully confirms its hypotheses by means of deriving it from first principles and checking it against all possible counterexamples. When Plato depicts Socrates practicing the method in the dialogues (in, for example, the *Meno*, the *Phaedo*, and the *Republic*) it always falls between these extremes, as one might expect.

Concerns about method typically lead to questions about education, and to this topic the *Republic* devotes more of its pages than to any other: the ideal city Kallipolis described in it is in many ways primarily a school – an institution for producing citizens with the requisite levels of virtue or excellence, the requisite types of character. C. D. C. Reeve explores this vast territory, noting that in the *Republic* education is the craft concerned with "turning the soul around, not of putting sight into it" (518d). Here the key element of the soul that needs turning is reason (*logos*) or the rational element (*to logistikon*) (580d). Together with appetite (439d6–7), spirit (439e2–3, 581a9–b4), and perhaps a few other elements (443d7–8), it constitutes the embodied human soul. Consequently, education cannot accomplish its task of reorienting reason without reorienting the whole soul, any more than an eye can be turned around except by turning the whole body (518c6–8). Primarily targeted on the reason, Platonic education is thus forced to extend its purview to appetite and spirit. Hence, Plato's views on education promise illumination on every aspect of his thought: the methods employed illuminate his psychology, since it is presupposed in their design; the subjects studied illuminate his epistemology and ethics/politics since they are designed to produce wisdom and the other virtues of character – courage, temperance, and justice; and epistemology and ethics; and this in turn illuminates Plato's metaphysics and ontology.

Introduction   9

Much of interest has been written recently about specific topics – for example, about the role of mathematics in the higher education of the guardians or about the good and bad effects of art. But neither the *Cambridge Companion* nor the *Blackwell Guide* to the *Republic* has chapters specifically on education. Their neglect is in no way unusual. It is hard to find a good single discussion of what we are to make of Kallipollian education as a whole. Reeve's essay provides precisely that. Beginning with the vexed question of what sort of education the producers are to receive, and ending with the dialectic that is reserved for philosophers alone, he cashes out in good detail the aforementioned promise of illumination.

Giving us more on educational issues, Malcolm Schofield observes that studies of Plato's treatment of the arts in the *Republic* are typically preoccupied with his critique of poetry and his expulsion of the poets from Kallipolis. His much more positive discussion of music, which gives it a central role in shaping individual and society, is comparatively neglected in English language scholarship on the dialogue. Schofield looks first at some of the key passages in Book 3 where Socrates explains the importance of music *in senso stretto* for fostering our cognitive responses to beauty and capacity for philosophy. Schofield then turns to Socrates' discussions of what *sort* of music is appropriate for training the city's guards and how musical *mimēsis* works. Learning to sing and play in appropriate rhythms and modes will gradually shape the soul by assimilation into concordant structures, which will constitute courage or *sōphrosunē* as the case may be, virtues that will then find expression in such music.

But why is it that poetry looms much larger than music in most accounts of the dialogue's teaching on art and culture? One answer is that Socrates simply has much more to say about poetry than music. Turning to this topic, Schofield devotes particular attention to the treatment of *mimēsis* in Book 10's critique of poetry as imitation, and to ways in which it diverges from the treatment in Book 3. Book 10 is undoubtedly preoccupied with poetry, particularly Homer and tragedy, with music barely getting a mention. Its critique can leave the reader with the impression that only bad art is really art, and only bad art has the power of art, gratifying the emotions by its exploitation of the appearances of things. The idea that art might stimulate the learning-loving capacity of the soul is entirely absent.

The role of music in the later *Laws* is something seldom mentioned or discussed when people think about Plato on art. But here Schofield shows that the *Laws* clearly develops further the cultural agenda of the *Republic*, and in doing so leaves Plato's view of the critical importance of music and musical *mimēsis* for the health of society in no doubt whatsoever.

The chapter concludes with a passage from R. L. Nettleship's *Lectures on the Republic of Plato* which summed up the argument advanced here 125 years ago.

The editor trusts that readers who invest themselves in these essays will find their own journeys through the *Republic* to have been enriched. Although this volume's authors study the *Republic*'s many facets in ways that vary – sometimes widely – from one another, they all share the view that a close and careful reading of this work always repays the effort. It is my hope that with their work, a new generation of readers will come to Plato's text with that same conviction. It has been a pleasure and a privilege to work with these authors on the production of this volume.

Simon Fraser University
October, 2009

NOTES

1. I take this opportunity to recommend C. D. C. Reeve's comprehensive introduction (and translation) of his *Plato, Republic* (2004). For more seasoned readers, I recommend G. R. F. Ferrari's *Cambridge Companion to Plato's Republic* (2007), including his fine Introduction. The new essays here add fresh voices to the perennial discussion of the *Republic* and there is almost no overlap with Ferrari's volume (so rich is the *Republic*), and even in those rare cases where the topics do overlap, the chapters on those topics in this volume offer new insights on subjects that can never be discussed too much.

CHAPTER I

Socrates in the Republic

G. R. F. Ferrari

Not only is Socrates one of the fictional characters in the *Republic*, he is also its fictional voice. The character Socrates speaks every word of the work, retelling a discussion that developed at the house of Cephalus on the preceding day; and it is a discussion in which Socrates himself played a leading role. To the modern narratologist, Socrates is the *Republic*'s "internal narrator."[1] External narrators, by contrast, are not themselves characters in the stories they tell, even if, on occasion, they refer to themselves in the first person. From their vantage point above the fray, external narrators are free to record the private thoughts and feelings of their characters. Internal narrators, at least those who present themselves realistically, do not enjoy the same privilege. For them, a distinction obtains between their private thoughts, plans, and reactions and the thoughts, plans, and reactions of the other characters in the story. An internal narrator may, if he so wishes, describe his private thoughts directly; the thoughts of others he can (or should) only surmise. If he does decide to make the audience for his story – the "narratee" – privy to his thoughts, he can achieve with that audience a degree and a range of intimacy, or its appearance, that is generally unavailable to the external narrator.

Socrates in the *Republic* avails himself of this opportunity for intimacy at several points. Any dicussion of his role in the *Republic* should take into account his descriptions of his private thoughts, and it is with these descriptions that I begin.

Three other Platonic dialogues are, in their entirety, internally narrated by Socrates: the *Lysis*, the *Charmides*, and the *Lovers*. (Even if the *Lovers* was in fact written by a close imitator of Plato, its usefulness for comparison with the *Republic* is not diminished.)[2] The private thoughts that Socrates vouchsafes in these dialogues have much in common with those that we find in the *Republic*: there are admissions of difficulty as the argument reaches an impasse;[3] there are expressions of admiration or pleasure;[4] sometimes Socrates reveals to the narratee a motive that he did not declare at the time – for example, when he admits that his reason for saying something is to provoke a discussion;[5] at other times he makes it clear that he had been paying silent attention to his surroundings, as, for example, when he mentions that he had taken note of Thrasymachus' behavior in advance of the latter's opening sally into the conversation;[6] he often records the blushes of those with whom he speaks;[7] and he does not hold back from shrewd analysis of their pomposity, hypocrisy, evasiveness, mischievousness, and the like.[8]

More tellingly, some types of private thought that show up in those other dialogues are not to be found in the *Republic*, and vice versa. Socrates in the *Republic* never remarks on having privately and spontaneously realized that he was in error, and having redirected the discussion for that reason, as he does at *Lysis* 218c or *Lovers* 133c. He never describes to his narratee a private (because successful) effort at self-restraint, as he does, famously, at *Charmides* 155c–e (when he became aroused by a view inside the young man's robes), or again, though less colorfully, at *Lysis* 210e (when he held back from admonishing Hippothales). Socrates in the *Republic* never admits to having said something at the time for no better reason than to save a discussion from paralysis (as at *Chrm.* 169d, *Lovers* 135a); nor does he ever mention that he took advantage of someone's unexpected intervention, finding that it fits with his larger plans for the discussion (as at *Lys.* 213d, *Lovers* 132d). With interventions such as those, contrast the moment in the *Republic* when Glaucon breaks in to complain about the "city of pigs" that Socrates and Adeimantus have just finished discussing (371c–d). The need for Guardians in the ideal city can be traced back to this intervention. It marks a major turning-point in the work, yet Socrates says nothing to his narratee about having seized upon it to move the discussion along. He says nothing at all of his private thoughts at this point. Rather, he simply represents himself, to Glaucon, as yielding to Glaucon's apparent desire to discuss a more luxurious city (372e).

Unexpected interventions are, in fact, plentiful in the *Republic;* and they are sometimes connected with a private thought of Socrates' in a way that has no parallel in the other three dialogues for which he serves as internal narrator. The connection is made whenever Socrates represents himself to the narratee as having been stymied in his plans by an unexpected objection. The two most significant instances come at the very begining of Book 2 and of Book 5.

Having polished off Thrasymachus in Book 1, Socrates mentions thinking at the time that he was done with discussion, only to discover that

Socrates in the Republic 13

what had been said so far was merely a "proem" (*prooimion*, 357a) – a technical term used of musical preludes, short hymnic poems, and the introductions to rhetorical speeches. By using a term appropriate to complex artistic composition, Socrates here becomes a medium for his author, who, in effect, announces that the remainder of the work, Books 2–10 of the *Republic*, will take their impetus from Glaucon's bold protest at this point. Again, at the opening of Book 5, Socrates tells the narratee that he had something in mind – not, this time, to quit the discussion, but rather to proceed to the topic he had promised to deal with next. He is prevented from fulfilling his intention, however, by a rebellion of his conversation partners, who demand to hear more on a topic they feel he had passed over too quickly. And again, the diversion is massive, and marks a structural pivot in the work as Plato conceives it: Socrates will deliver himself of all of Books 5–7 before he is able to return in Book 8 to the topic announced before the interruption.

Contrast the intervention that brings the *Lysis* to a close. Socrates tells his narratee that he had a mind to get one of the older fellows at the wrestling-school talking, when some of the boys' tutors broke in and caused the whole group to disband (*Lys.* 223a–b). Not only is Socrates at an impasse at this point, and has no particular line of argument to pursue; this is also a discussion-ending diversion rather than one which, as in the *Republic*, signals a continuation of discussion by bringing a completely new subject or range of subjects into play; nor are those who interrupt attempting to control the substance of the dicussion.[9]

A pattern in the portrayal of the character Socrates unites these scattered contrasts between the *Republic* and the other dialogues internally narrated by him. In those dialogues, what he reveals of his private thoughts suggests a man intent on keeping a discussion afloat and on controlling it while it is afloat. This task may include painstaking control of himself. Others' interventions are occasions to bring skillful management and argument-directing improvisation into play; his own mistakes, a motor to further discussion. In the *Republic*, however, Socrates is a man buffeted by the demands of interlocutors, who gives the narratee to understand that he was taken by surprise at moments that we readers, in retrospect, can see – but Socrates at the time could not – to be structurally crucial to the *Republic*'s ever-expanding argument.

These revelations of the narrating Socrates fit with a quality that he displays within his narrative rather than comments on as narrator, and which becomes thematic in the work: his reluctance to speak. As with the unexpected objections from his conversation-partners, this reluctance tends to emerge at structurally significant points in the *Republic*, including both of those already considered in Books 2 and 5.

When presented with Glaucon's challenge at the start of Book 2, Socrates is diffident about accepting it, concerned that he may not do a satisfactory job of defending the thesis that justice pays. He is diffident enough that the whole company feels the need to join with Glaucon in his request (368b–c). The intervention at the opening of Book 5 produces a still more elaborate display of diffidence. Socrates requires of the company nothing short of a full pardon in advance for possible error, before he will agree to address the issue of women and childrearing among the Guardians (450a–451b). He declares that he would have been happy to get away with having the sketchier version of his claim, which was accepted earlier on, remain undisturbed (450b). (Compare 457e, where he tells Glaucon he had hoped to escape having to prove that the sharing of wives and children was not only feasible but also optimal.) A third structural pivot of the *Republic*, Socrates' proposal to make philosophers kings, is introduced by a surprise attack from an interlocutor and a display of reluctance on the part of Socrates in every way similar to the previous two, except that Socrates does not comment on his surprise to the narratee (471c–473b).

Such reluctance to speak is uncharacteristic of the Socrates we know from other dialogues. There, he is instead the indefatigable questioner and discussant, always ready to drop whatever else he may be doing if the opportunity for intellectual conversation presents itself (*Phdr.* 227b); talking late into the night until his partners fall asleep (*Smp.* 223d); driving victims of his interrogation to make their escape while he is still eager for more (*Euthphr.* 15e); delighted even by hostile interventions, provided they promise to prolong discussion (*Grg.* 486d).

The contrast cannot be explained by attributing Socrates' diffidence in the *Republic* to the fact that the proposals he hesitates to reveal are highly controversial. No less counter-intuitive are the claims that Socrates makes in the *Gorgias* (e.g. that wrongdoers are happier if punished than if they get away with their crimes), yet he defends them without hesitation, indeed with relish (see *Grg.* 474a–c). Rather, the contrast is part and parcel of the portrait of a Socrates who is less assured, less in control of the proceedings than in the typically "Socratic" dialogues – those which have bequeathed the famously ironic Socrates to intellectual history, the Socrates who puts youngsters or authority-figures to the test.

Nevertheless, it is more usual for interpreters of the *Republic* to think of the character Socrates as holding its argument in a steely intellectual grip. And this is true of them over a range of interpretive traditions.

Socrates in the Republic

Three traditions in particular stand out in this respect. It is customary among those who treat dialogues featuring Platonic Forms, including the *Republic*, as a foil to the "Socratic" dialogues – whether the foil is chronological or thematic or both – to emphasize the *Republic*'s positive, constructive quality. Here, at last, they feel, is a Socrates who provides definitions that hold up, offers answers more than he poses questions, and arrives at a positive conclusion. If they focus on this Socrates as a fictional character rather than as a mere spokesman for Plato, they are likely to emphasize his authoritativeness.[10]

Those writing in the tradition of Leo Strauss, on the other hand, have no truck with the practice of counting Socrates' constructive pronouncements as so much Platonic doctrine; yet they too, in their way, treat Socrates in the *Republic* as a controlling, authoritative figure. They do so by focussing on his pedagogic mission. Their Socrates is a politic conversational strategist, who, though he may work deviously, has the interests of his interlocutors, Glaucon's in particular, always in mind. Their Socrates is a grandmaster at conversational chess.[11]

Oddly similar, though for quite different reasons, is the Socrates of the Tübingen School, who gives his interlocutors only so much philosophy as he thinks they can handle, holding back from them the fullness of the Unwritten Doctrines. Unlike the Straussian Socrates, he does not resort to subterfuge or irony when dealing with interlocutors of good will such as Glaucon and Adeimantus are; but he does at all times – here resembling the Straussian Socrates – have their limitations in mind. And his control of what they get to receive is absolute: "When Socrates tackles an issue," writes Thomas Szlezák, "it comes to a definite result – the discussion takes no false turns, leads down no blind alleys." Socrates' occasional self-deprecations, on this interpretation, are so much coquetry.[12]

It would be idle to deny that Socrates' behavior in this dialogue is that of a man who has already given much thought to the subject under discussion and who looks ahead as the discussion develops. Socrates admits as much himself, when he describes to the interlocutors, in retrospect, how his account began by "veiling its face" (503a) on the matter of women and childrearing among the Guardians, as well as on the detail that those Guardians must be philosophers; and explains that he acted in this way because he anticipated and was seeking to avoid the further tangles of a lengthy and controversial argument.[13]

But this gives us no reason to assume that Socrates is anything other than sincere when, by contrast, he professes to be unsure of himself, is tentative about the direction the discussion is taking, or expresses surprise – whether to his discussion-partners at the time or to the narratee.

So, for example, when Socrates chooses to take up Glaucon's challenge by considering first what justice is in a city, before asking what it is for an individual to be just, he describes this proposal in retrospect, addressing the narratee, as one in which he was saying "what I thought best." And he picks the phrase up, it seems, from the address he made to his discussion-partners at the time, when he was expressing the limitations of their collective discernment. "I think it best," he says to them at that point, to look first at justice written in big, city-scale letters, rather than in the small print of the individual (368c).[14]

By turning here from the moral to the political, Socrates takes a fateful detour. We could trace the *Republic*'s future place on the bookshelves of political science libraries to this decision of his. But how much of that destiny can Socrates foresee? Let his move be strategic, motivated not only by the strategy that he himself makes plain (namely, that he seeks to take an indirect approach to a difficult issue), but also, given his later admission about the account having veiled its face, by a desire not to plunge headlong, in such company, into the most controversial issues that a discussion of justice might raise – issues which he has pondered before but would be content, on this occasion, to let ride. Let some such strategy as this, or others that a reader might conceive, be in the character Socrates' head at this point; still, he cannot plausibly anticipate that Glaucon will intervene down the road to complain of the "city of pigs," nor that Polemarchus and Adeimantus will mount their mock-rebellion over the issue of women and childrearing. He cannot, that is to say, anticipate the events that will end up determining the large-scale structure of the book that we know as the *Republic*. And the fact that Plato structured his book by visiting these and other surprises on the character Socrates is an indication to us, the readers, that we should not rest our interpretation of the work on the hypothesis of a consummately calculating Socrates, endowed with freakish strategic power. The sharp-sighted one here is not Socrates, but his author.

A reader who assumes that Socrates always knows exactly where he is going with his argument might feel, to take a second telling example, that the extended horseplay in Book 4 (432c–433a), as Socrates launches a metaphorical hunt for the definition of justice in the city, is all an elaborate tease. Socrates invites Glaucon to join him as he rousts justice from a shadowy thicket; shouts as he comes upon its tracks; berates himself for not seeing it sooner. These shenanigans, such a reader might think, could be intended to pique Glaucon's interest in the outcome, or to contribute to the cause of Socratic self-deprecation. But what is this reader to make of Socrates' comment to the narratee when he describes himself coming

Socrates in the Republic

upon justice's tracks? "And then I caught sight of it. 'Aha! Over here, Glaucon,' I cried."

Socrates, who has not hesitated, when narrating the encounter with Thrasymachus, to make the narratee privy to thoughts he had in Thrasymachus' regard that would have undermined the civil front he was maintaining had he voiced them publicly, could have done so here also, had he in fact been stringing Glaucon along. (Or he could have left his true thoughts unexpressed.) Instead, he is at pains to confirm to the narratee that he was indeed discovering his answer about civic justice for the first time, in just the way he gave Glaucon to understand that he was.[15]

If we take Socrates at his word, a different type of explanation for the teasing quality of this passage suggests itself, one which refers the tease to the author Plato rather than to the character Socrates. It is not as if the thought that justice is "doing what is one's own" has never before occurred to Socrates; he points out, in fact, that he has often heard it spoken of in this way, and spoken of it in this way himself (433a). But what he here sees for the first time is how to connect this thought to the account of the just city that he has developed, at considerable length, in concert with Glaucon and Adeimantus. And what Plato here allows the reader to see for the first time is how carefully he laid his plans back in Book 2, when he planted, with what seemed at the time a simple principle of social efficiency ("one man, one job"), the seeds of the definition that emerges here. Socrates says of this definition that "it was rolling under our feet from the start," and means the words ruefully ("we have been slow on the uptake"). But Plato is anything but rueful about the slow and indirect progress of the discussion, and writes these words with a teasing application to the reader. For it is hard to imagine any first-time reader who could have seen this definition coming. The dark and impenetrable thicket from which justice unexpectedly emerges is the elaborate account of the ideal city that has occupied the reader for the best part of three books of the *Republic*. And the luxuriant hunting analogy is Plato's self-congratulation for a writerly coup.

Against taking Socrates at his word, the following objection may be raised. If Socrates is capable of being discreet with his discussion-partners at the time, not revealing to them all that he is thinking, why should this discretion cease to operate when he presents the discussion to a new audience, the narratee? What if Socrates were not at all reluctant to be developing a large-scale account of the ideal city and its philosopher-kings, had in fact seized every opportunity to amplify it, knew where he was headed with it at all times, and is simply perpetrating on his narratee the same ploys that he used on Glaucon and Adeimantus the day before?

Two arguments make such a view implausible. The first is this. In none of the dialogues internally narrated by Socrates does the narratee step forward as a personal character. Not only are these narratees external rather than internal – that is, they play no role in the narrated events – but they are given neither names nor qualities. Indirect argument may yield scattered inferences about them, as, for instance, that the narratee of the *Charmides* seems to be expected to know who Chaerephon is without being told (*Chrm.* 153b), and is addressed with some familiarity or wryness when Socrates tells of his peek into Charmides' robes (*Chrm.* 155c, d). But such characterization is never better than vague (the example just given is, in fact, the best on offer). It never comes close to exhibiting the degree of individual personality possessed by any of the interlocutors in those internally narrated dialogues. And without this kind of individuality in an addressee, Socratic pedagogy loses its point. Unable to construct a plausible scenario in which Socrates' narrative duplicates on its narratee the pedagogy that it supposedly narrates, we would be left attributing to the narrator Socrates the omniscience of the author Plato – a duplication that seems arbitrary, and whose point would be difficult to discern.

The second argument derives from comparison with the *Euthydemus*. This dialogue shows us the resources Plato had at his disposal when he really did wish to make his Socrates an unreliable narrator. It encloses a dialogue internally narrated by Socrates within a frame of direct dialogue between Socrates and a named character, Crito, who is fully personalized within the dialogue and is, in any case, a regular member of the Platonic repertory company. Lest we forget his presence as narratee, he interrupts the narrative a little more than halfway through to question Socrates' narrative reliability (290e). And what Socrates tells Crito directly in the *Euthydemus* with regard to the amazing wisdom of the charlatans Euthydemus and Dionysodorus differs not at all, in its irony, from the praise that he narrates himself bestowing upon them at the time.[16] Socrates never breaks cover in this dialogue. By fully characterizing the narratee, Plato makes the situation clear. It is a technique quite different from the one he employs for the narrative in the *Republic*.

Plato, we can begin to see, is at pains in the *Republic* to distinguish his narrative control from that of Socrates, its internal narrator. Plato is the author of a fiction on an epic scale, who must bear in mind the complex structure of the whole as he writes, and who can weave into its web not only grand themes but also smaller motifs that may recur over long intervals, knowing that he writes for readers who can study and re-read his work. (The point remains valid even if Plato's ancient "readers" were mostly listeners; for they could request a re-hearing, as portrayed at *Phdr.* 263e–264a.)

The character Socrates, on the other hand, is neither relating a fiction, nor is he even engaged in artistic speech. He is presenting to an unnamed person or persons a philosophic conversation that he had the day before – as we ourselves might convey to an acquaintance the substance of a recent conversation by reporting the actual words, interspersed with many a "and then I said . . .," "and then he goes . . ." (That the scale of Socrates' report would be simply preposterous in real life is a topic I shall come to presently.) His situation is quite different from that of the disciples who self-consciously rehearse Socratic conversations from the past in order to preserve them – Apollodorus in the *Symposium*, Antiphon in the *Parmenides*, Eucleides in the *Theaetetus*. This is a point brought home to the reader by the *Republic's* opening sentence, in which Socrates mentions that the conversation he is narrating took place only "yesterday." (The same brief time-lag is mentioned in the first sentences of the *Charmides* and *Euthydemus*.) Socrates' situation differs also from that of, say, the Phaedrus who seeks permission in the *Phaedrus* to reproduce, as best he can remember it, the speech on love he had heard Lysias deliver that morning (*Phdr.* 228d); for this is a case of one would-be artistic speaker attempting to rival another. No: in Socrates' case, neither the original fictional conversation nor its subsequent fictional narration is an artistic event.

But although it is not itself artistic, Socrates' narrative does include a presentation of what amounts to the earliest extended theory of narrative artistry in the Greek intellectual record – a theory that relates in a surprising way to his situation as internal narrator. It occurs in Book 3, when discussion of the education appropriate for the Guardians turns to the issue of narrative form. Plato flags the novelty of the issue by having Adeimantus fail to understand, at first, any of the terms in which Socrates draws the distinctions he considers relevant (392c–d).

A poet may present his story, says Socrates, using any of three different narrative means: simple narrative, imitation, or a combination of the two. Adeimantus' incomprehension compels Socrates to fall back on an example to explain his meaning. Take the opening of the *Iliad*, he says. Homer begins by speaking as himself, the poet; he makes no attempt to have us think the voice we hear is other than Homer's own. Then he brings the priest Chryses into the story and gives the actual words of the priest's appeal to the Greeks. In so doing, Homer does his best to make us believe the voice we hear is no longer Homer's but that of his character Chryses. This is what it is for a narrative to combine simple narrative (Homer speaking as himself) with narrative through imitation (Homer imitating the voice of Chryses). Socrates proceeds to recast the entire opening scene of the *Iliad* as simple narrative (what we would call indirect discourse) in order to make his meaning clear (393a–394a). The passage concludes by mentioning examples of narrative that use only one form throughout, whether that of narrative through imitation, as in tragic and comic drama, or that of simple narrative, as in certain kinds of lyric poetry (394b–c).

Socrates' analysis may seem both technical and exhaustive; but his use of the Homeric example – a recourse he acknowledges to be the substitution of a part for the whole (392d) – does indeed prove to be fatally limiting. There is one narrative form that escapes the alternatives he has proposed: the narrative form of the very work in which he himself, the fictional character Socrates, is speaking. For whereas the *Republic* is narrated by an internal narrator, Homeric epic is narrated by an external narrator – a narrator who is not himself a participant in the events he narrates. And were we to protest that the *Republic* does at least resemble Homeric epic in respect of being a mixed narrative, one that uses both simple narrative and imitation, we would find ourselves unable to press the comparison without modifying the terms in which Socrates presents his theory.

Socrates has defined the simple narrative component of mixed narrative as a form in which the poet speaks (or the writer writes) as himself, in his own voice. And he has defined its imitative component as a form in which the poet speaks as if he were someone else. The character Socrates might seem to be telling his tale through a mixture of simple narrative and imitation, as Homer does; but although he takes on the voices of others, he also imitates his own voice, quotes his own contributions to the discussion – an act which violates his definition of imitation, and something which Homer, as an external narrator, never does. And besides, Socrates is a fictional character; he is not, as Homer is, the very poet who composed the work that his own voice narrates. So we cannot say that Socrates employs simple narrative either. (It seems significant, then, that Socrates, presenting his prose-version of the *Iliad*'s opening scene, should make a point of saying that he is no poet, 393d.)

Are we to claim, perhaps, if we wish to save Socrates' theory, that the *Republic* is, in its entirety, a narrative through imitation? The whole thing, after all, could be thought of as a single, enormous speech of the character Socrates, whose voice is taken on by the author Plato.[17] But such an approach would be out of line with Socrates' own presentation of the category. He presents purely imitative narrative as a narrative in which the author's voice has been subtracted from between the speeches, so as to leave only the direct exchanges between the characters. Hence Adeimantus immediately concludes that tragic drama would count as an example (394b). Socrates' way of presenting the category fails, then, to anticipate the kind of imitative narrative that is the *Republic*, in which the author's voice has been subtracted not from between the dialogue, but, as it were, from around the edges of a single monologue. And in any case, it is evident enough that the *Republic* does not read as monologue, any more than Homer reads as a monologue issuing from its poet; it reads, to use the Socratic terms, as a mixed narrative that consists in very large part of narrative through imitation.[18] Yet, technically speaking, it is no such thing. It is something different.

It is, in fact, something quite new in the history of Greek literature. Not only the epic poets such as Homer and Hesiod but also the lyric and choral poets – Sappho, Pindar, and the like – mean themselves, the poets, when they write the equivalent of "I" or "me." (Call this their poetic "persona," if you wish; the contrast with Plato remains.) The same applies to the fictional prose of Plato's contemporaries Xenophon and Isocrates. Prose fictions written in a first person different from the author were composed before Plato, but they consist of monologue attributed to mythological or otherwise hypothetical characters – Gorgias' *Palamedes*, for example, or Antisthenes' *Ajax* and *Odysseus*, or Antiphon's *Tetralogies*, or the *Eroticus* attributed to Lysias as a result of its inclusion in Plato's *Phaedrus*.[19] As that last example helps show, such fictions are nothing like the first-person narrative of dialogue by one of its fictional participants. Internally narrated dialogue was invented, it seems, specifically for the new genre of Socratic dialogue.[20]

No wonder, then, that Socrates fails to include internally narrated dialogue in his narratological schema: at the dramatic date of the dialogue in which he comes up with his theory, the genre of internally narrated dialogue simply did not exist! But of course, Plato could very easily have allowed Socrates to prophesy its advent, in much the way he allows him in Book 7 to peer into the future and anticipate the new results in solid geometry that Theaetetus and others were achieving in Plato's Academy (528a–b). That he chooses not to do so, when the topic is narrative form, amounts to a declaration of Platonic poetics – instruction to the reader on how to read the narrative that is the *Republic*. It is as if Plato were saying, "My character Socrates, as you see, is blind to the narrative form of the very work for which I have made him narrator. His theory is incomplete. If you wish to appreciate, in its fullness, the narratology that I am proposing, you should consider not only what I make Socrates say, but what I am doing

22 G. R. F. FERRARI

when I make him, and others, say what they say. And you should do so not just when reading this discussion of narratology, but throughout. Never forget that Socrates sees only what I allow him to see."

By comparison with other internally narrated dialogues, the *Republic* is inordinately long. Greek literature before Plato contains only one internal narrative of remotely comparable length: Books 9–12 of Homer's *Odyssey*.[21] In these books, Odysseus, speaking in the first person, recounts to an audience at the court of King Alcinous his adventures during the return from Troy. Not that the narrative form of the *Odyssey* as a whole furnishes any precedent for the narrative form of the *Republic*: Odysseus' internal narrative is a story within a story, embedded in Homer's much larger external narrative. But Plato nevertheless seems intent on turning the reader's thoughts toward the parallel between Socrates' and Odysseus' narratives; for the *Republic*, as many have noted, is replete with thematic reminders of the *Odyssey*. These range from its opening "descent" to the Piraeus (as Odysseus descended to the underworld) to Socrates' closing insistence that the myth he is about to tell, the myth of Er, is "no Alcinous-story" (614b) – using there the collective title by which Books 9–12 of the *Odyssey* came to be known.[22] And Socrates is, unwittingly, correct to insist; for it is not when he externally narrates a myth of the afterlife that Socrates is telling his Alcinous-story; it is when he internally narrates the previous day's adventures in the Piraeus. Socrates is no poet, any more than Odysseus is a poet; Socrates, like Odysseus, is a hero telling a story; like Odysseus, a man known for his skill with words. The poet is Homer; the poet is Plato.

One thing that Plato achieves through this Odyssean parallel, then (that is, through Socrates' obliviousness to it), is to assert his narrative control over the character Socrates. But another is to acknowledge the epic scale of the *Republic*. Odysseus engages his audience through four entire books of the *Odyssey*. Although he is not himself a poet, he is speaking in the place and at the hour at which the bard would entertain Alcinous' court, and is, in effect, and at Alcinous' invitation, substituting for the bard. To string out a spellbinding yarn at such length is a heroic task, but appropriate enough to its teller and the situation. Hence Homer can interrupt Odysseus in Book 11 to return us temporarily to Alcinous' court and to the realism of the framing narrative. By contrast, for Socrates to be taxing his audience, in one continuous feat of memory, with the reproduction of a discussion ten books long – this strains not only good manners, but the reader's credulity.

It is unsurprising, then, that Plato should concentrate Socrates' reports of his private thoughts and reactions in the early books of the *Republic* (Book 1 contains more of them than the rest of the work put together), since it is only these reports that make the reader conscious of the narratee's presence. He allows them to come to a halt for good at the opening of Book 5, with Socrates' report of how Polemarchus' and Adeimantus' rebellion prevented him from proceeding with his account in the order he had intended.[23] From that point forward, Socrates' narrative voice ceases to obtrude. Apart from speech tags, he offers three brief descriptions of Glaucon's reactions to something that he said, but gives no further insight into his private thoughts and reactions on the original occasion.[24]

Plato's timing of this disappearance is hardly accidental. For the beginning of Book 5, as we have seen, is the point at which the progress of the discussion slips definitively from Socrates' control, and the *Republic* takes on a complexity of structure that can only be the creation of its writer, not its narrator. Socrates' voice recedes as Plato makes his presence violently felt.[25]

I have claimed that the character Socrates is not engaged in artistic speech when he narrates the discussion held on the previous day at the house of Cephalus. To this it may be objected that Socrates does not simply report that discussion, but edits it for smoothness. Take the opening scene of the work. Socrates reports that when Polemarchus caught sight of himself and Glaucon "from afar," he told his slave to run and catch them, and bid them wait (327b). Clearly, Socrates could not have heard Polemarchus giving his slave the instructions. (When Socrates turns back to look, he cannot even see where Polemarchus is.) He inferred this act in retrospect. Yet he does not say something like "Polemarchus must have told his slave to catch up with us, since . . ." He skips the inference, and narrates only its results – sounding in this respect like an omniscient narrator.[26]

The bulk of Socrates' retrospective editing, however, is directed at Thrasymachus. For one thing, Thrasymachus is the only interlocutor in the *Republic* to have some of his replies reported indirectly (as in "he agreed, reluctantly," 342e), rather than quoted. More saliently, Socrates twice points out that his narrative of the discussion has been proceeding more smoothly than Thrasymachus allowed at the time. When Thrasymachus breaks in on Socrates and Polemarchus at 336b, Socrates sees fit to mention that he had already tried to break in several times, but had been restrained by the others, who wanted to hear Socrates' questioning of Polemarchus through to the end. And at 350d, reporting Thrasymachus' blush, Socrates alerts the narratee to the recalcitrance Thrasymachus had displayed throughout the preceding argument – how he had not agreed "in the way that I am speaking now, easily."

24 G. R. F. FERRARI

That Socrates' editing is brought to our attention in Book 1 of the *Republic* is undeniable. But there is something that those scholars who take note of this editing[27] fail to see. This is that it is brought to our attention only in Book 1, and never in later books. Socrates' reports of his private thoughts continue, to be sure; but these imply no narrative omniscience, nor do they import a distinction between the chronological order of the "actual" events and the sequence in which they are narrated. Furthermore, Socrates' editing in Book 1 is almost wholly concentrated on his conversation with Thrasymachus; and Thrasymachus is also the only interlocutor whose behavior is subjected to disparaging analysis by Socrates in his private assessments.[28] Thrasymachus accuses Socrates of treating him with irony (337a); Socrates' private thinking, declared to the narratee, show that Thrasymachus had a point.[29]

These two characteristics of the Socrates we meet in Book 1 – his penchant for editing, and his irony – are connected. And the connection brings me to a much-discussed topic in the interpretation of the *Republic*, which bears directly on the contrast developed at the outset of this study between the politic, controlling, ironic Socrates of the "Socratic" dialogues, on the one hand, and, on the other, the less controlling figure he cuts in the *Republic*. That topic is the contrast between Book 1 of the *Republic* and the remaining books. For of course, even one who finds Socrates a less controlling figure in the *Republic* must acknowledge that the contrast between an assured, ironic Socrates and a less controlling Socrates is present in the *Republic* itself.

The Socrates of Book 1 is the figure familiar from the "Socratic" dialogues, who puts his interlocutors to the test and finds them wanting. Like those dialogues, Book 1 ends aporetically, its questions unresolved. And as in those dialogues, Socrates adopts an ironic stance toward the conversation.[30] All this changes in subsequent books. Socrates begins Book 2 with the thought that his role in the discussion now seemed at an end; in reality, it is only the controlling Socrates whose role in the discussion is now at an end. Hence it is entirely appropriate that the editorial Socrates, the overt controller of the narrative, should find that his role, too, has come to an end.

One group of Plato scholars (or an element among them) finds large doctrinal implications in the contrast between Book 1 of the *Republic* and the books that follow it. Let us pass once again in review the three positions that I cited earlier for their shared belief in a Socrates who holds the entire argument of the *Republic* in a steely intellectual grip. Among those who emphasize the difference that Platonic Forms can make, we find some who see Book 1 as a farewell to the inquisitorial Socrates, and the turn to constructive theory in Books 2–10 as contributing to a more dogmatic and systematic phase of (or approach within) Plato's philosophical thought.[31] The other two positions – those of the Tübingen School and of writers in the tradition of Leo Strauss – do not draw doctrinal consequences directly from the contrast between Book 1 and the rest. Rather, both draw on a contrast between the respective interlocutors of these books in order to reinforce, indirectly, their views about Plato. Thomas Szlezák focusses on the contrast between the hostility of Thrasymachus in Book 1 and the good will of Glaucon and Adeimantus in subsequent books; notes that Socrates withholds information even from the good-willed interlocutors, despite paying them the compliment of unironic handling; and finds support here for his general thesis about the limits Plato imposed on transmission of the Unwritten Doctrines.[32] Strauss ascribes a different strategy to Socrates when he is dealing with the Athenian gentlemen Glaucon and Adeimantus than when his interlocutors are the foreigners and metics of Book 1. Strauss emphasizes, however, that this is a strategy nonetheless, and one which casts suspicion on the sincerity of many of Socrates' recommendations for the ideal city, if taken at face value.[33]

My reader will perhaps be prepared by now for an approach to the contrast between Book 1 of the *Republic* and subsequent books that differs from all three of these positions by its focus on Plato's task as writer of the work – in particular, his writerly task of composing Socratic dialogue on an epic scale. Unlike the first of the three positions, my approach finds no doctrinal implications in the contrast; unlike the second and third, its focus is not on the strategy of the character Socrates, but on the strategy of Plato as author of the character Socrates.

To appreciate Plato's strategy, it is best to begin from a distinction between the dialectic that Socrates employs in Book 1, and that which he employs in later books. By "dialectic," I mean the technique of constructing an argument through question and answer that was a component of philosophical training in the Academy and whose rules were later formalized by Aristotle in the *Topics*. In the formal contest sketched by Aristotle, a questioner constructs the refutation of a thesis from steps conceded by the respondent, who has elected to defend the thesis. In order to secure the necessary concessions, the questioner conceals the progress of his argument by taking a variety of indirect or circuitous paths to his conclusion (*Topics* 155b29–157a7).[34]

This inquisitorial type of dialectic has much in common with Socrates' practice in the "Socratic" dialogues in general, and Book 1 in particular.[35]

26   G. R. F. FERRARI

Take, for example, his interrogation of Polemarchus. Socrates' first move is to convert the moral injunction cited by Polemarchus from the poet Simonides into a formal definition of justice, in order to give Polemarchus, as respondent, a proper thesis to defend. At the point where the definition has attained the intermediate form "justice is giving to each what is appropriate," Socrates shifts his ground:

"Heavens, then," I said, "Suppose someone were to ask him: 'By giving what that is due and appropriate, Simonides, and giving it to whom, does an art come to be called medicine?' What answer do you suppose he would give us?" (332c)

He then asks the same question of cookery, before asking it of justice.

Commentators note that Socrates' hypothetical question smuggles into the discussion the assumption that justice is an art – a controversial assumption that will prove key to the difficulties Socrates goes on to make for Polemarchus. Commentators do not also note that this gambit is a fine example of the kind of indirection that Aristotle recommends to the dialectical inquisitor.

The smuggling itself is a case of "drawing the opponent into the kind of statement against which we will have abundant avenues of attack," something Aristotle calls "a sophistic move" (*Topics* 111b32–33). Once Socrates has enticed Polemarchus into defining justice as a particular kind of art, the way is open for him to create difficulties about what its artistic domain might be – a technique of which he is fond.[36] The examples within which he cloaks the claim that justice is an art are, for their part, an instance of "getting answers through similarity." Aristotle commends this technique on two grounds: that it carries conviction, and that it enables "the universal to get by more readily" (*Topics* 156b10–11). It is harder for Polemarchus to resist treating justice as an art when the question concerning justice comes third in a series of questions treating it as analogous to arts, than if Socrates had asked the question directly. As for the universal getting by: Socrates need never make explicit the universal claim underlying his examples, namely, that all arts give to their objects what is appropriate. Had he done so, he would have drawn unwelcome attention to the important role played in his argument by the concept of art. Still less does he need to face the preliminary issue of whether everything that gives what is appropriate to the object of its concern need be an art.

Space precludes mention of the several other examples of Aristotelian technique that occur in the argument with Polemarchus. But the upshot is this: Socrates is out to win this argument. He wants Polemarchus' vehemence in support of the idea that harming enemies is the natural counterpart to helping friends to seem to the young man, in retrospect, as the pride that goes before a fall (332a–b, with 334b, 335e–336a). Socrates does not scruple at using dialectical tricks to ensure that Polemarchus loses; for if Polemarchus is ever to be enlightened, he must first be chastened.[37]

Of course, the inquisitorial dialectic between Socrates and Polemarchus, however much it has in common with Aristotelian dialectic, is not the formal contest played by strict rules, and before judges, that Book 8 of the *Topics* describes. Socrates poses more open questions to Polemarchus, and elsewhere in his inquisitorial dialectic, than would be permitted by the Aristotelian rules. But this is only to say that Plato thought the record of a formal dialectical "moot" (Ryle's word) would make for dull reading.[38] The discrepancy does not invalidate the comparison with Aristotelian dialectic.[39] Socrates is an *Über*-Inquisitor, who requires no time to prepare his case, and can grant his respondent the rope needed to hang himself, relying on his powers of improvisation to cope with whatever replies may come his way. He stands to the school dialectician as Sherlock Holmes to the shoe leather detective, and for the same reason: because the audience wants no humdrum reality in its fictions.

With Glaucon and Adeimantus in Books 2–10, Socrates does not suddenly lose his power to improvise in the face of surprises and objections; but he no longer improvises in order to win against a conversational opponent.[40] And again a comparison with Aristotelian dialectic is revealing.

In formal inquisitorial dialectic, the respondent does not defend his thesis with arguments of his own (although he may challenge the questioner on various grounds); rather, he attempts not to concede what he believes the questioner is trying to get him to concede. The situation of Glaucon and Adeimantus, however, is quite different. Although they elect to defend a thesis that Socrates will have the task of refuting (the thesis that justice does not pay), all their defending is delivered up front, in long speeches from which, as devil's advocates, they explicitly dissociate themselves. Indeed, they are defending the thesis, they say, only because they are keen to see Socrates refute it (358c–d, 367a–b). And from that point on, being brought to concede what Socrates is trying to get them to concede is precisely what they desire.

In response to this desire, Socrates becomes more didactic as well as more openly investigative in Books 2–10 than he had been in Book 1.[41] Although he continues to pose questions, and although at all times, even when directly stating his view, he continues to await his interlocutors' agreement before moving on, Glaucon and Adeimantus behave as Socrates' followers, who join him in his investigation, rather than as respondents looking to maintain a position. They will make comments such as, "I'm following; just speak" (when Socrates invites them to move with him to the next topic, 445c), or ask "What's next on the agenda?" (484b). They go so far as to satirize the method of question and answer, and their own acquiescence in the process: "And I, of course, think the same as you" (500a); "Do you know by how much the life of the tyrant is less pleasant than that of the king?" "I'll know if you tell me" (587b); "Listen, then; or rather, answer." "Ask away" (595c).[42]

On the other hand, as we have seen, they are capable of offering strenuous objections, of a kind that radically diverts the path of discussion. And the reason such a diversion can occur is that Socrates no longer needs to maintain the strict control over his respondents required of a man who is out to assemble a refutation from their concessions.

However paradoxical it may seem, when Socrates turns from the inquisitorial dialectic of Book 1 to the didactic-cum-investigative dialectic of Books 2–10, he becomes less authoritative, not more. This has nothing to do with his elaborate protestations of uncertainty, which merely continue the theme of Socratic ignorance familiar from the inquisitorial dialogues.[43] Nor is the point affected by the long stretches of argument and exposition in which Socrates seems to know exactly where he is headed (e.g. when he elaborates the analogies of Sun, Divided Line, and Cave; or confronts the "three waves" of Book 5; or argues the "three falls" of Book 9). Socrates becomes less authoritative in the sense that he is no longer concealing his moves from his interlocutors. He is holding back from them at various points, to be sure; what he allows them to learn is determined, to a considerable extent, by what their protests are able to extract from him; but he is not surreptitiously controlling them.

Surreptitious control over the speakers of this dialogue is rather what Socrates' author exerts himself to achieve. It is Plato, not Socrates, who holds the progress of the discussion in his steely intellectual grip; and his control is surreptitious in the sense that it emerges only when the reader asks what Plato is doing – behind the scenes, as it were – by making his characters say what they say. (This we saw when considering Socrates' narratology in Book 3.) It makes no difference to Plato as author, and should make none to us as readers, whether his Socrates is the controlling inquisitor of Book 1 or the hero buffeted by the winds and waves of protest in subsequent books. The full sense of Plato's writing can only come across to us by the same surreptitious means in either case.

Socrates in the Republic

It makes a considerable difference to Plato's chances of success in constructing so massive a dialogue as the *Republic*, however, that he should borrow from a different type of dialectic than the inquisitorial, using a different type of interlocutor, when the time comes to portray the ideal city and its philosopher-kings. The *Gorgias* probably represents the outer limits of Plato's ability to construct a lengthy dialogue with a positive outcome while still basing his construction on inquisitorial dialectic. And the technique he employs to build it, interleaving long, constructive speeches with passages of destructive inquisition, is one that we may well find a good deal patchier in its effect than the narrative drive of the *Republic*. Relaxing Socrates' control as character is one way, and a good way, for Plato to increase the scope of the material he can control as author.[44] Rather than permit Socrates to take the indirect and circuitous path to a preordained conclusion recommended by Aristotle to the aspiring dialectician, Plato in the *Republic* steps out himself along the digressive, circuitous path of large-scale narrative construction.

NOTES

1. De Jong 2004, pp. 1–2; Morgan 2004, pp. 361–64.
2. See Pangle 1987, pp. 1–20.
3. *Charmides* 169c, *Lovers* 135a, *Republic* 375d.
4. E.g. *Charmides* 158c, *Lysis* 213d, *Republic* 329d, 367e.
5. *Lysis* 223a, *Lovers* 135a, *Republic* 329d; for the general case: *Lovers* 132d, *Republic* 336d.
6. *Republic* 336b, d; cf. *Charmides* 162c, *Lysis* 207a.
7. *Charmides* 158c, *Lysis* 204b–c, 213d, 222b, *Lovers* 134b, *Republic* 350d.
8. *Charmides* 162c, 169c, *Lysis* 207b, 211a, *Lovers* 132b, *Republic* 336b, 338a, 343a, 344d.
9. This last point applies also to the calling-away of Menexenus at *Lysis* 207d. No interventions that Socrates describes as having disrupted his plans occur in the *Charmides* or *Lovers*.
10. See e.g. Cooper 1997b, p. xvi; Blondell 2002, p. 209 (with references to earlier scholarship on this theme on p. 210, n. 150).
11. Strauss 1964, ch. 2; compare Bloom 1968, Brann 1989–90, Benardete 1989, Rosen 2005.
12. Szlezák 1985, p. 302 (translation mine).
13. Other references to these tangles: 450b, 453c, 543d–544a.
14. *eipon oun hoper emoi edoxen . . . dokei moi, ēn d' egō . . .*
15. Szlezák 1985, p. 302, with n. 81, who takes the whole passage as a case where Socrates engages in irony at his own expense, fails to consider Socrates' comment to the narratee.
16. Compare e.g. *Euthydemus* 303a–c with 304b–c.

30   G. R. F. FERRARI

17. So Clay 1994, p. 47; cf. Morgan 2004, n. 7, Blondell 2002, pp. 238–39.
18. It is revealing, in this regard, that when Proclus declares the *Republic* a mixed narrative, he treats Socrates as its author, temporarily forgetting that Socrates is himself a character in the work (Proclus *In Platonis Rem Publicam*, ed. Kroll, pp. 14.26–15.11).
19. Aristotle, *Rhetoric* 3.17 (1418b28), tells us that Archilochus wrote two of his poems in character. Again, this would have been the monologue of a single character. Hippias' *Trojan Dialogue*, acknowledged by Plato in the *Hippias Major* (286a), has been lost; from the description of it there, however, it seems unlikely to have been internally narrated.
20. We cannot be certain that Plato himself originated the form. Aeschines of Sphettos, a contemporary of Plato, also used the form for his Socratic dialogue *Alcibiades*, whose exact date of composition is unknown. On Aeschines, see Kahn 1996, p. 19. Halperin 1992, p. 95 notes, but does not develop, the general contrast between internally narrated Platonic dialogue and the external narration common to Homer and the historians.
21. Blondell 2002, p. 17 n. 46, also notes the parallel.
22. Full accounts of Odyssean themes in the *Republic* can be found in Howland 1993, Brann 1989–90, and O'Connor 2007.
23. Here is the full list of such reports up to that point: In Book 1, 327a–c, 328b, 329d, 336b, 338a, 342c, 342d, 342e, 343a, 344d, 350d; in Book 2, 357a, 362d, 367e, 368c, 375d; in Book 3, none; in Book 4, 432d.
24. Glaucon's reactions are described at 451b, 508c (which I take to be more a description of the jocular quality of Glaucon's outburst than of Socrates' response to it), and 608d. Socrates' remark at 487d, "And when I had heard this, I said . . ." marks the importance of the moment, but reveals nothing private.
25. A further consequence of this timing is worthy of note: Plato puts an end to Socrates' private thoughts after four books of the *Republic*, the same number as for Odysseus' internal narrative in the *Odyssey*. (This is to assume, first, that the division of the *Odyssey* into its traditional books occurred in the time of Pisistratus, and second, that the division of the *Republic* into ten books was Plato's own. An argument can be made for both claims; but neither of them is uncontested.)
26. Benardete 1989, pp. 9–10 also notes this narrative sleight of hand.
27. In addition to Benardete (previous note), see Blondell 2002, p. 43, Morgan 2004, p. 363.
28. See the references in n. 8 above.
29. See Blondell 2002, p. 184.
30. My understanding of Socratic irony in the aporetic dialogues is set out in full in Ferrari 2008b.
31. Let Vlastos 1991, esp. ch. 4, be the synecdoche for this widespread position. For fuller discussion and references see Blondell 2002, pp. 209–10.
32. Szlezák 1985, p. 301 with n. 74.
33. Strauss 1964, esp. p. 85.

Socrates in the Republic

34. See further R. Smith 1997, pp. xiii–xxi. For a systematic description of the dialectical bout, see Moraux 1968.
35. For comparison of Socratic practice in Plato's dialogues with Aristotelian dialectic see Thionville 1983 (1855), pp. 77–85, Frede 1992, Ostenfeld 1996.
36. See e.g. *Charmides* 165c–166b, *Laches* 194e–195c, *Ion* 539d–541a.
37. Compare the purificatory rationale given for "noble sophistry" at *Sophist* 230b–d, and note the mention of Polemarchus' conversion to philosophy at *Phaedrus* 257b.
38. I borrow Ryle's term in order to turn it against him; for he speculated that the dialogues featuring the inquisitorial Socrates were culled from the minutes of actual moots (Ryle 1966, ch. 6).
39. *Pace* Stemmer 1992, p. 136.
40. On the element of improvisation in Books 2–10 cf. Blössner 1997, pp. 32–37.
41. Aristotle mentions didactic and investigative ends among those to which dialectic could be put, but says too little about them for us to be sure how far Socrates' practice in Books 2–10 resembles either.
42. Cf. Blondell 2002, p. 201.
43. See 354c, 368b, 450e–451a, 506c, 517b, 533a.
44. We might wonder why, in that case, he takes the trouble to include inquisitorial dialectic at all, by writing Book 1. One answer: because he wishes to mark his first foray into writing dialogue on a massive scale and its departure from an earlier (or, if you prefer, an alternative) pattern of brief, inquisitorial dialogue. In addition, as many scholars have noted, he contrives in Book 1 to introduce and to motivate important themes in subsequent books (see e.g. Blössner 1997, p. 40, with n. 89; Stauffer 2001, *passim*; Barney 2006). The contrast of dialectics helps to set the introductory book apart.

CHAPTER 2

Platonic ring-composition and Republic *10*

Rachel Barney

In Book I of the *Iliad*, anger and social rupture are transmitted in a chain reaction: from the grieving father Chryses to Apollo, from Apollo to Agamemnon and Achilles, from Achilles to his mother Thetis, and from Thetis to Zeus and the other gods. In Book 24 acceptance and reconciliation flow in the other direction, from the divine to the human. In Book 1, the aged Trojan priest Chryses travels to the Greek camp to ransom his daughter, and his pleas are rejected; in 24, the elderly Trojan king Priam travels to the Greek camp to ransom his dead son, and his pleas are accepted. In Book 1, Achilles quarrels publicly with his leader Agamemnon and rejects his role as warrior; he appeals to his divine mother Thetis, who appeals to Zeus on his behalf. In Book 24, Zeus directs Thetis to appeal to Achilles, who then reconciles privately with his enemy Priam and accepts his fate.

In short, the first and last Books of the *Iliad* are mirror-images of each other. Similar, though less marked, mirrorings structure Books 2 and 23, and to a lesser extent 3 and 22. The *Iliad* is thus structured by *ring-composition*, so that the work as a whole has the pattern ABCDCBA.[1] Smaller ring-structures pervade it as well, most notably in the famous Homeric similes (in which, for instance, a warrior is likened to some force of nature, usually in an ABA pattern) and many of the important speeches.

Homeric ring-composition is never pressed to the point of rigidity or artificial display. There are profound differences between even Book 1 and Book 24 – for instance, there is no real correlate in Book 1 to the mourning for Hector which ends the *Iliad* as a whole. The resonances are just quietly powerful enough to give the reader a sense of order, harmony, and completion. The ring-structure also seems to have a *cognitive* import: it is part of the reason that in reading Book 24 we feel we are learning something fundamental about human life as the *Iliad* has been depicting it all along. Ring-composition makes it possible for the culminating insights and conclusions of a work to be experienced as moments of *recognition*. It

Platonic ring-composition and Republic *10* 33

is impossible to discuss its aesthetic function without being reminded of the famous lines from T. S. Eliot's *Four Quartets*:

> We shall not cease from exploration
> And the end of all our exploring
> Will be to arrive where we started
> And know the place for the first time.[2]

I

Ring-composition is found in every kind of temporally extended artistic composition, on every scale, and in a bewildering variety of patterns: ABA, ABBA, ABCBA, ABCCBA, and so on indefinitely. *Beowulf* is ring-composed;[3] so is Meleager's self-referential *Garland*;[4] so is almost any movie told in flashback form. The standard sonata form, used for first movements of symphonies, sonatas and chamber works since the mid-eighteenth century, is a kind of ring-composition. I will adopt musical terminology and speak of *exposition* and *recapitulation* for the rings found in the opening and closing halves of a work respectively.

One useful distinction we can draw is between what I will call "bookend" and "pyramid" forms of ring-composition. By "bookends," I mean a form in which the closing part gestures back to the beginning, without any rings being discernible in between – an ABA in which the great bulk of the work falls into the central B. Most movies in flashback form follow this pattern; so does a poem in which the last line repeats or rhymes with the first. A pyramid structure (one might also think of a coastal shelf, or a Russian doll) is more elaborate and pervasive, with a regress of multiple rings: e.g., an ABCDCBA structure.

We can also distinguish between various kinds of recapitulation. The obvious distinction here is between simple repetition, as when a musical motif from a work's opening is reiterated, and *mirroring*, in which the order of events is reversed as in *Iliad* 24, creating a kind of chiasmus or *husteron proteron*. But perhaps a more important distinction is between *mere* repetition and the kind of transposition we find in *Iliad* 24 (and most uses of sonata form), where the reappearing content is transposed – even inverted – in ways which add meaning. Instead of a live daughter, Priam ransoms a dead son; instead of a public quarrel with his allies, Achilles shares a private meal with an enemy; instead of anger being transmitted from the human to the divine, reconciliation is passed on in the other direction. I will call this kind of transformed recapitulation a *resolution*, and will represent such ring-structures as ABB'A': the point is again to suggest the musical term, since the effect is often that of a dissonance resolved. The "Eliot" experience of recognition tends to be the mark of a certain kind of resolution.

In truth the distinction between resolutions and other recapitulations is a matter of degree, for even in a limerick *pure* repetition is rarely to be found:

> There was an Old Person of Hurst,
> Who drank when he was not athirst;
> When they said, "You'll grow fatter,"
> He answered, "What matter?"
> That globular Person of Hurst.[5]

Here the first and last lines are bookends, and the repetition is reinforced by the rhyme scheme; but the "globular" in the last line is a significant addition, giving the upshot of the intervening lines. In more sophisticated works, exposition and resolution may differ dramatically, and the ring-structure may be very messy and incomplete. The only *perfectly* ring-composed work is a palindrome: in high art, asymmetries, blurring, partial melding and interleaving of rings are all par for the course, whether the composition is a Pindaric ode or a Beethoven sonata. None of this prevents the ring form, and the resolution in particular, from serving its structural, aesthetic, and cognitive functions.

II

Ring-composition is characteristic of some major works in elevated style with roots in oral tradition: the *Iliad, Beowulf,* parts of the Pentateuch, some Sanskrit epic and drama, and the Zoroastrian Gathas.[6] Scholars have inferred that it is a marker of oral composition;[7] but ring-composition of various kinds is pervasive in later Greek literature as well, including Pindar, Herodotus, Thucydides, and various orators and epigrammatists.[8] It has tended to go undetected in philosophical texts – or perhaps to be ignored as philosophically insignificant. My aim in this chapter is to remedy this partially for the case of Plato, and the *Republic* in particular. We can warm up by noting some other instances of ring-composition in Plato and Aristotle – though to do so will require dogmatizing about some endlessly controversial texts.

(1) Bookending is present in several Socratic dialogues. The *Charmides* reverts near the end to the opening topic of Socrates' Thracian charm (155b–157c; 175a–176a); the *Meno* ends with an answer to Meno's opening question (70a; 99e–100b); in an amusing "transposed" resolution, the

Platonic ring-composition and Republic *10* 35

Laches opens with the question of how the young (the sons of Lysimachus and Melesias) should be educated and ends with the subject of how the *old* (Socrates and his friends) might yet be (179a–180a; 200a–201c). In these cases the bookending serves to prompt reflection on how far the opening questions of the dialogue have been answered by the intervening dialectic – and perhaps hints that Socrates and his interlocutors have in some sense ended up where they began. Mark McPherran has also argued that both the *Phaedo* by itself and the suite *Apology–Crito–Phaedo* should be counted as ring-compositions, though I cannot go into his argument here.[9]

(2) The dialectic of the *Theaetetus* is also quietly bookended. Theaetetus' first attempt at a definition of knowledge consists in a list of *epistēmai* (146c–d); Socrates objects that this is as if one were to define "clay" by listing "potters' clay," "brickmakers' clay," and so on (147a). This is obviously doomed: "a man who does not know what knowledge is will not understand 'knowledge of shoes' either" (147b).[10] At the close of the dialogue, the last definition of knowledge Socrates considers is that knowledge consists in correct judgment together with an account of the differentiating feature of an object. But this is ambiguous: is mere judgment of the differentiating feature required, or *knowledge* of it? The latter option provokes an objection which is the same as Socrates' first: "it is surely just silly to tell us, when we are trying to discover what knowledge is, that it is correct judgment accompanied by *knowledge*, whether of differentness or of anything else" (210a). In short, both the first and last definitions are vitiated by inclusion of the term to be defined – that is, by being *circular*. This circling back to circularity reinforces the aporetic character of Socrates' conclusion: the dialectic of the *Theaetetus* as a whole ends where it began.

(3) The *Sophist* has a pyramidal structure, though two steps are more or less fused in the first half.[11] We work through (A) preliminary definitions of the sophist (217a–236e); (B and C) the puzzles raised by false statement and by any kind of thought or speech about Not-Being (237a–241d); and (D) the puzzles raised by Being (241d–251a). The recapitulation revisits the same topics in mirror order, resolving the puzzles raised in the first half: (D′) Being and the other greatest kinds are explained as distinct but interacting forms (251a–256d); (C′) Not-Being is identified with the form of Difference (256d–259e); (B′) false statement is explained and shown to be possible (260a–264b); and (A′) the final definition of the sophist is produced (264d–268d).

(4) The *Cratylus* has both bookends and a somewhat messy pyramidal structure.[12] The bookending is through a small motif: at the start, Cratylus denies that "Hermogenes" is really the name of Hermogenes (383b, 384c); at

the end, Socrates hands Hermogenes' name back to him by calling on him to escort [*propempsei*] Cratylus to the country, as a son of Hermes *pompaios* would do (440e).[13] The name "Hermogenes" is also discussed more extensively near the mid-point of the dialogue (407e–408b): as Mary Douglas notes, ring-composed works often have a marked "turn" at mid-point tied to the outermost rings in some way.[14] The pyramid is shaped roughly as follows (pairing exposition and recapitulation rings): (A) Cratylus and Hermogenes are introduced as being at odds (merged with the exposition of conventionalism) (384a–385e), then later (A′) they are reconciled, or at any rate sent off together by Socrates (440e); (B) the stability of things is accepted as a necessary assumption by Hermogenes (385e–387b), then later (B′) argued for by Socrates (439b–440d); (C) truth and falsity in *logoi* are said to depend on truth and falsity in naming, and thus on the possibility of false names (385b–d, following Schofield 1972 in shifting 385b2–d1 to follow 387c5, though even on this reading there is some interleaving of rings in the recapitulation),[15] then later (C′) the possibility of false names is shown to make truth and falsity in *logoi* possible (432e); (D) conventionalism is rejected (387d–391a), then later (D′) rehabilitated, in connection with the understanding of names as pictures (433a–435e). All this is oriented around a kind of twofold dialectical core, (F) the account of natural correctness (391c – or perhaps 387b–427d) and (G) its critique (427d–433a).

(5) Its authenticity is a matter of perennial dispute, but for whatever it is worth the Platonic *Seventh Letter* is also ring-composed. It centres on a philosophical "digression" (341a–45c) surrounded on both sides by historical autobiography; and that digression is itself ring-composed. It progresses through (A) references to Plato's conversations with Dionysius (341a–b; with extended criticisms in (A′), 344d–345c); (B) criticism of writing (341b–c; (B′) at 344c); (C) affirmation that dialectic alone can lead to knowledge (341c; (C′) at 343e–344b); (D) the difficulties of communication (341d–e; (D′), 343c–d); and at the core, (E) an exposition of the metaphysics of the "five" and a critique of language itself (342a–343b).

(6) Before turning to the *Republic*, a few words about Aristotle by way of comparison. First, both the *Nicomachean Ethics* and *Eudemian Ethics* exhibit marked "bookending": this falls out so naturally from the flow of Aristotle's dialectic that it hardly registers as a *formal* feature at all, but it is exceptional – whether by authorial design or not, most of Aristotle's works seem to follow a strictly linear trajectory, with nothing of significance at the end reverting to the start. But in the *N.E.*, both the first and last books are concerned with the nature of happiness, the "choice of lives," and the roles of excellence and external goods. Book 10 reverts to these opening themes in

order to give conclusive answers to the questions posed (and addressed in a preliminary way) by Book 1, answers informed by the account of the virtues (and pleasure, friendship, etc.) given in the intervening books. It is of course enormously controversial *exactly* what those answers are, and how *exactly* the various claims of Books 1 and 10 fit together. But it should be uncontroversial that the *general* relation of Book 10 to Book 1 is one of ring-compositional resolution. And this structure is no accident if, as seems likely, the *N.E.* is in many ways Aristotle's answer to and replacement for Plato's *Republic*, which (as we will see) is strongly ring-composed itself.[16]

The *Eudemian Ethics* likewise reverts at the end to its opening themes. The ring-composition here is both more exact and, because of the superficially chaotic nature of *E.E.* 8, harder to spot. But the *E.E.* opens in 1.1 with (A) the question of the relation of the good, the beautiful, and the pleasant, and turns immediately to (B) the question of whether happiness comes from nature, teaching and knowledge, divine inspiration, or chance and good luck – Meno's question, rephrased as a question about happiness rather than virtue. Book 8 returns to this list of candidates ((B′), 8.1–2). Aristotle first considers puzzles raised by his opting for a version of "knowledge" as his answer to Meno's question; the solution is to distinguish *wisdom* from mere knowledge (8.1, cf. esp. 1246b31–35). Second, in 8.2, he considers again the roles of good fortune, divine influence, and chance, asking whether these in turn could be due to nature – in other words, he reverts to the rival candidates of (B), and confirms their rejection (8.2). The *E.E.* then closes in 8.3 with a reversion to the outermost ring (A). Here Aristotle gives a final accounting of the relation of the good, the noble, and the pleasant: the highest life, that of the "noble and good," is one in which all three converge ((A′), 8.3).[17]

In section III I will suggest that this sort of ring-composition expresses a conception of philosophical method common to Plato and Aristotle. Yet, given the size of the *oeuvres* of these two philosophers, the examples I have listed are relatively few – which should at least quiet fears that I have defined ring-composition so broadly that it could be found anywhere. So my claim is not that ring-composition is a *pervasive* feature of Platonic composition. In some cases he even seems to duck obvious occasions for it, perhaps to preserve an air of lifelike spontaneity: for instance, the introductory frame of the *Theaetetus* and the regress of narrators which opens the *Symposium* are not resumed at the end of those dialogues (apart from a few passing references to Aristodemus, *Smp.* 223b, d). But the instances I have noted are none the less real for that, and it is striking that the most interesting cases – the *Cratylus*, *Theaetetus*, and *Sophist* – come from a group of

38   RACHEL BARNEY

dialogues closely related in themes and probable order of composition. The *kind* of ring-composition we find in the *Sophist*, and more murkily in the *Cratylus* (and the *Seventh Letter* as well), is also of particular interest. For in these cases literary form follows philosophical function: the ring-composition is an expression of a dialectical strategy in which one problem or hypothesis leads to another more basic one, which leads to another; the solutions and explanations then unfold in reverse order, from prior to posterior, after a dialectical core articulating the principles which make the solutions possible. And the *Cratylus*, *Theaetetus*, and *Sophist* are all plausibly read as composed not long after the *Republic*, which I will now argue is ring-composed in much the same way.

III

That the *Republic* is structured by ring-composition seems to belong to the common folk wisdom of Platonic scholarship, in a way which (so far as I can discover) outruns anything reflected in the published literature. The copy of the OCT *Republic* which I used for undergraduate courses at the University of Toronto in the 1980s has "ring composition" written in the margins at various points – alas I failed to give any references, though J. M. Rist must have been the principal direct source.[18] In a recent account of the structure of the *Republic*, Georges Leroux cites the oral tradition rather than any published precursors: "cette structure en forme de 'grande voûte,' pour reprendre une expression de Jacques Brunschwig."[19] Platonic ring-composition has also been noted under various guises in works by Eva Brann ("concentric circles"), Holger Thesleff ("pedimental" or "two-level" composition), Kenneth Dorter, and, in his discussion of Plato on mimetic art, Myles Burnyeat.[20] Burnyeat uses the general claim to bring out a point which I too mean to argue for in section IV: "Book X . . . is designed to be consistent with Book III and to give a retrospective, theoretical commentary on its major claims."[21] No two scholars carve up the *Republic* in exactly the same way, and I will not here be concerned to compare and assess the different analyses on offer; but the "rings" are for the most part evident enough, running roughly as follows:

(A) and (A′) Katabasis and Return: *Katebēn* is the first word of the *Republic*, which begins with Socrates' going down to the Piraeus (327a); the Myth of Er with which it closes depicts a more literal katabasis to the underworld (though Er himself remains in an intermediate-level limbo, 614b–d), ending in a return to the light by both Er himself and the other souls (617d, 621b). As Mary Douglas has noted, ring-composed works often reinforce the outermost rings at the "mid-turn";[22] it cannot be a compositional accident that at the dialectical mid-point of the *Republic*, we have another descent in the Cave allegory. (Strictly speaking what is depicted there is an ascent *followed* by a descent on the part of the prisoner; but the reader surely *experiences* the description of the cave and ascent as a *katabasis* and return.)

(B) and (B′) Death: The first topic of discussion between Socrates and Cephalus is how we should face the end of life (328d–331b); Book 10 ends with a vision of the afterlife in the Myth of Er (614b–621d).[23]

(C) and (C′) The Challenge and the Answer: The impetus for the argument of the *Republic* is the challenge to the value of justice presented by Thrasymachus in Book 1 and reformulated by Glaucon and Adeimantus in Book 2. Glaucon's central demand is that Socrates explain why justice is in itself a good thing, leaving out its "rewards" (358b). Books 9 and 10 revert to this challenge in systematic stages. First, Socrates reintroduces the "choice of lives" trope (580a–588b, cf. 360d–362c), arguing that the just philosopher is happiest. An allegory of the soul (588b) is used to bring out that it is absurd to suppose that injustice could be beneficial to the doer, however far the appearances may diverge from the reality (the guiding theme of Glaucon's opening challenge). Finally, in Book 10, the rewards of justice are restored.

(D) and (D′): The City: Development and Degeneration: Socrates meets Glaucon's challenge by sketching the stages by which a city might develop into a maximally just one, beginning with a "first city" which harbours only moderate appetitive motivations. In Books 8–9 he sketches the stages by which the just city might degenerate into a maximally unjust one, in which only the most immoderate appetitive motivations have any sway. The two accounts belong to the same genre, presenting analyses of permanent psychological and political forces in the manner of genetic myths (rather than being historical or even pseudo-historical accounts of particular cities).

(E) and (E′): Poetry and the Arts: Blurring together with (D) (and recapitulated out of order in Book 10 – i.e., (E′) is interleaved between (B′) and (C′)) is an account of the appropriate standards for poetry and the other arts, as needed for the education of the "guardian" class in the just city. This is recapitulated in Book 10 when Socrates returns to give a more fully grounded account of art, one explicitly based on the intervening discussion: I will return to this account in section IV.

So much by way of an outline of the "rings." It should be obvious that the recapitulation steps here ((A')–(E')), presented in more or less mirror order, are a matter of "resolution" rather than mere repetition. In the case of (B') and (C'), we might say that the relation of exposition to resolution is one of question and answer: How should we face death? Is it advantageous to us to be just or not? And, to state the crashingly obvious, the answers given in (B') and (C') are informed by the intervening core of the work. The relation of (A) to (A') calls for a somewhat different kind of analysis, and I am not sure quite how to describe the philosophical import of the *katabasis* motif. The relation of (D) to (D') seems different again: in addition to their being symmetrical as narratives of progress and decline, I would suggest that among other things (D') *corrects* the earlier exposition, being based as (D) was not on the true tripartite psychology.[24]

That resolution can take the form of correction is clear from a small-scale example. Though it makes a mess of my divisions (by belonging to all of (A'), (B'), and (C')), the "choice of lives" depicted in the Myth of Er (617d–621b) clearly stands in a ring-relation to Glaucon's Book 2 speech and the myth of Gyges' ring in particular (C) (359c–360d). As Sarah Broadie has noted, both passages are images of "context-free choice," the selection of a destiny in a magical absence of social constraints and moral convention.[25] In choosing his next life in the Myth of Er, a nameless person who "participated in virtue through habit without philosophy" (619c–d) throws his moral habituation aside to lunge at tyranny: "in the next world, where no impediments surround us, what had been a fantasy becomes an automatically self-fulfilling choice."[26] Now the Gyges story was presented by Glaucon to show that, freed of social constraints, *anybody* will gravitate to his most selfish desires, of which tyranny is the perfect expression. When the Myth of Er revisits this claim, it is to specify that it holds only for the unreflective person; and to show that he will not be happy with his choice. The genuinely virtuous person, who understands the necessity of justice for happiness, will not even feel tempted by such a mistake. So it seems fair to say that the Myth of Er serves to (among other things) *correct* the Ring of Gyges story, showing that it only depicts human nature in its uneducated state and thus misrepresents the powers of justice. But this correction is (like most philosophical resolutions, I would think) not exactly a matter of contradicting or rejecting the earlier account. The Gyges story is not simply wrong: for one thing, it is right empirically about how most people would behave. But as initially presented it is at best a half-truth. Socrates' correction is thus a matter of clarification – of *relocating* Glaucon's insight, we might say, putting it in

Platonic ring-composition and Republic 10

its place as only half the story, and showing that if properly understood it points the opposite of the moral initially intended.

I will turn in section IV to consider another, more obvious and large-scale instance in which Book 10 operates as a resolution of an earlier discussion, namely its critique of mimetic art. But first it is worth trying to say something about how the ring-structure I have noted relates to the dialectical methodology of the *Republic*. So far as I can see the pyramidal "steps" of the *Republic* end at (E)–(E′), with no further rings internal to the dialectical core of Books 4–7. But there is at the same time a shape to Books 4–7 which harmonizes with the ring-structure in which it is placed, if only at rather a high level of abstraction. For we begin in Book 4 by establishing that the city, being good, must be ruled by wisdom (427e–429a); and we end Book 7 with, for the first time, a full understanding of what wisdom entails and *how* exactly it qualifies its possessors to rule. We end where we began, knowing the place for the first time: here too there is what we might call a structure of *explanatory regress*, though just how best to spell it out is a tricky question. Now I think that we can see ring-composition in Plato and Aristotle, and explanatory regress more generally, as expressing a distinctively Platonic–Aristotelian conception of philosophical method. Aristotle alludes to that conception in *Nicomachean Ethics* 1.4:

> Let us not fail to notice, however, that there is a difference between arguments from and those to the first principles. For Plato, too, was right in raising this question and asking, as he used to do, "Are we on the way from or to the first principles?" There is a difference as there is in a race-course between the course from the judges to the turning-point and the way back. For, while we must begin with what is better known, things are so in two ways – some to us, some without qualification. Presumably, then, we must begin with the things better known to us (*N.E.* 1.4, 1095a–b, trans. W. D. Ross in Barnes 1984, with minor changes)

The phrase "arguments from and to first principles (*archaî*)" recalls (if it is not an outright allusion to) the Divided Line in *Republic* 6, where the highest level of thought, *noēsis*, is contrasted with the kind of mere thinking (*dianoia*) used by mathematicians. The difference between the two lies in their different relations to hypotheses. *Dianoia* proceeds from hypotheses as unquestioned assumptions and relies on sensible particulars as images; but *noēsis* works its way "up" from those hypotheses, without treating them as assumptions and without the aid of images. Philosophical dialectic "does not consider these hypotheses as first principles but truly as hypotheses – i.e. as stepping stones to take off from, enabling it to reach the unhypothetical first principle (*archē*) of everything" (511b4–6). Then, "having grasped this principle, it reverses itself and, keeping hold of what follows from it, comes down to a conclusion without making use of anything visible at all, but only of Forms themselves, moving on from Forms to Forms, and ending in Forms" (511b6–511c2).[27]

The obvious precursors to this dialectical *noēsis* are the kinds of "hypothetical method" discussed in the *Phaedo* and *Meno*.[28] In the *Phaedo* the Forms are themselves to be adopted as hypotheses in order to prove the immortality of the soul (100b); in the *Meno*, it is by adopting a hypothesis that Socrates hopes to answer Meno's question whether virtue is teachable (86d–87c).[29] Neither passage is terribly informative about the method, and inasmuch as the hypotheses seem to be treated as assumptions we are presumably at the level to be distinguished in the *Republic* as *dianoia* rather than *noēsis*. But the *Phaedo* does gesture vaguely towards a complementary "upwards" path:

> when you must give an account of your hypothesis itself you will proceed in the same way: you will assume another hypothesis, the one which seems to you best of the higher ones until you come to something sufficient, but you will not jumble the two as the debaters do by discussing the hypothesis and its consequences at the same time... (101d6–101e2, trans. G. M. A. Grube)

The *Phaedo* does not envisage a transformation of reasoning from hypothetical into demonstrative by way of an *unhypothetical* first principle. But it does here adumbrate the *Republic* by distinguishing "upwards" and "downwards" lines of argument, and insisting on the importance of the distinction. Socrates' language here is almost as abstract as in the Line, but I think it is possible to get some sense of how the two directions differ. Upwards reasoning to a hypothesis will be a matter of finding non-deductive reasons to adopt some principle as "strongest" (*errōmenestaton*, 100a4) or "sufficient" (*hikanon*, 101d8): presumably this is a matter of both explanatory power and inherent plausibility. And we may advance upwards indefinitely, in each case adopting a "higher" hypothesis which will serve to explain (we would find it natural to say "ground") a lower one. Downwards reasoning from a hypothesis then takes the form of deducing its consequences and testing them for coherence, presumably by taking the hypothesis in conjunction with plausible auxiliary assumptions.

Variations on this pattern are to be found, I believe, in a number of Platonic dialogues.[30] In the *Republic*, the upwards path operates as a dialectical progression from practically immediate but posterior questions to more general and prior ones. Q: In what spirit should we face death? A: It depends on where we stand in relation to justice. Q: But is justice really a good thing? A: To know that, we need to know what justice really is. If

Platonic ring-composition and Republic *10*

justice is common to the just person and the just city, perhaps we can grasp the former by seeing the latter. Q: But what makes a city just? A: A just city is plausibly one in which what is appropriate is rendered to each – i.e., each class does its own work, so that it is ruled by the wise. Q: But who are the wise? A: The philosophers: those who have been well educated. Q: But what is a good education? A: One which leads us to know and love the Good. A: But what is the Good, and what does it mean to know it? Dialectically, the buck stops here: whatever exactly is being claimed for it in the Divided Line, the Good *does* function in the *Republic* itself as an unhypothetical first principle, in the sense that our questions about it are answered, not by a further explanatory regress, but – if at all – by evocative allegories and analogies.

So the rings of the *Republic* are united to the inner dialectical core by this shared, more general pattern of explanatory regress, which becomes visible as a ring-structure in the outer zones. And the latter, recapitulation half of the *Republic* covers much of the terrain we might expect from "downwards" argument, retracing the "upwards" steps and putting to work the principles established in the dialectical core. The higher education of the Guardians sketched in Book 7 is explicitly informed by the account of the Forms in Books 5–7, as the earlier account of their early education could not be. The depiction of corrupt constitutions and psychological types in 8–9 is explicitly informed by the tripartite theory of the soul in Book 4, as the earlier account of the first city and its successors could not be. The final choice of lives in Book 9 brings together the Book 4 psychology and the Book 6–7 metaphysics to establish that the life of the philosopher is happiest and most pleasant, in answer to and correction of Glaucon and Adeimantus in Book 2. This same combination of "core" principles is brought to bear in the Book 10 account of the arts: I now want to give this a closer look, as a case study of ring-composition in action.

IV

Socrates' critique of mimetic art in Book 10 is explicitly presented as a resolution of his earlier exposition in 2–3. That is: he announces both that his discussion will reaffirm the earlier account and that it will draw on the principles articulated in the intervening discussion, and the partition of the soul in particular:

Indeed, I said, our city has many features that assure me that we were entirely right in founding it as we did, and, when I say this, I'm especially thinking of poetry.

44   RACHEL BARNEY

What about it in particular? Glaucon said.

That we didn't admit any that is imitative (*mimētikē*). Now that we have distinguished the separate parts of the soul, it is even clearer, I think, that such poetry should be altogether excluded. (595a–b)

His conclusion, addressed to the defender of poetry, reiterates this claim to consistency: "Then let this be our defense – now that we've returned to the topic of poetry – that, in view of its nature,[31] we had reason to banish it from the city earlier, for our argument compelled us to do so" (607b).

That the intervening arguments do invoke the principles of the dialectical core – the theory of Forms as well as the tripartition of the soul – is obvious and uncontroversial. But the exact machinery and import of the argument here have been the subject of enormous interpretive controversy. I cannot engage with this fully here, and will offer only a brief and somewhat dogmatic sketch of my own reading: my aim is simply to take seriously Socrates' presentation of his account as a resolution, and show how it operates as such. I will proceed from what seem to be the clearest points to ones which are more problematic:

1. In its general upshot, it is easy to read the Book 10 account as a resolution of the discussion of art in Books 2 and 3. For the earlier account is (again, in its general upshot) an argument for the expulsion of tragedy and comedy from the well-run city (394d, 397d–398b, 568a–c).[32] That is why Socrates recalls the ban as one not on *mimēsis* as such, or *mimēsis* of bad models, but poetry "insofar as it is mimetic" (595a5). The reference here is to the *type* of poetry distinguished as "narration through imitation" at 392d–4d, i.e. dramatic poetry; whether the results extend to the third class distinguished there, the *partially* mimetic poetry of Homer, is left an open question (394d). And this is just the question taken up in Book 10. Hence the strong and otherwise puzzling focus on Homeric poetry and in particular on *Homer as a tragedian*, at 595c ("the first teacher and leader of all these fine tragedians"), 598d ("tragedy and its leader, Homer"), 605c ("Homer or some other tragedian"), and in Socrates' peroration:

    And so, Glaucon, when you happen to meet those who praise Homer and say that he's the poet who educated Greece, that it's worth taking up his works in order to learn how to manage and educate people, and that one should arrange one's whole life in accordance with his teachings, you should welcome these people and treat them as friends, since they're as good as they're capable of being, and you should agree that Homer is the most poetic of the tragedians and the first among them. But you should also know that hymns to the gods and eulogies to good people are the only poetry we can admit into our city. If you

Platonic ring-composition and Republic *10*   45

admit the pleasure-giving Muse, whether in lyric or epic poetry, pleasure and pain will be kings in your city instead of law or the thing that everyone has always believed to be best, namely, reason. (606e–607a)

Now that we are in a position to see what mimesis really is, we can also see that its defining and objectionable features are, alas, equally (or even more) present in the work of the greatest of poets.

2. The principles drawn on for the resolution are, as Socrates tells us at 595a–b, to do with the partition of the soul. This claim might seem surprising or incomplete, since the first of his arguments, to the effect that the products of imitation are "third from the truth," actually depends on the theory of Forms and the accompanying epistemology sketched in Books 5–7. However, the concluding arguments of the Book 10 discussion *are* psychological, and do indeed draw on the analysis earlier of the lower parts of the soul. So what Socrates' allusion suggests is that we are to read what follows *as a single continuous argument*: the metaphysical and epistemological principles introduced in its early stages are salient because of their implications for human psychology.

3. So read, as a continuous chain of argument, the trajectory of the Book 10 discussion is in broad outline clear. It runs as follows (cf. Socrates' recap, in mirror order, at 605b): (i) Mimesis is the creation of objects at a "third" remove from the truth (596a–8b); (ii) the imitator should not be presumed to have knowledge of the truth, and cannot be trusted (598b–600e); (iii) the imitations created by poets are actively misleading, like optical illusions (601a–602b); (iv) such illusions persuade, appeal to, and gratify the lower, irrational parts of the soul (602c–605c); (v) when we experience empathetic emotion and aesthetic pleasure at Homeric poetry, we are indulging and strengthening the lower parts of our soul at the expense of reason, which can only be a dangerous and corrupting course ("the most serious charge," 605c–607a).[33] Exactly how each of these steps leads to the following one is a complex and difficult question which I cannot properly address here; on the face of it, each seems to establish a crucial necessary condition for the following claim, which is further elaborated and supported by independent argument. An important point to note is that only the final argument, (v), is presented as a warrant for the expulsion of the poets. Plato is not worried about the presence in his just city of ontologically low-grade entities as such – there is no hint that painting, which is equally mimetic, is to be banned (let alone that the Guardians are to fret over the presence of shadows and reflections). The point of the earlier stages of the argument is rather to clarify *what mimēsis is* (argument i) in order to establish *that* (ii–iii)

and show *how* (iii–v) mimetic poetry in particular is able to do the damage it does.

4. The crucial turning point (and greatest source of interpretive difficulty) is thus the claim in (iii) that mimetic poetry is inherently deceptive, as in the optical illusion analogy: it is here that Plato pivots from the comparatively straightforward claim that the poet is as such ignorant (ii) to the damning argument that his work is actively harmful (iv–v). This part of Plato's argument has been the subject of enormous controversy, and raises a number of issues I cannot go into here. But the basic move is easy to grasp so long as we do not shrink from taking Plato at his word. When we take Ajax for a hero, enjoy weeping with him, and form false moral beliefs accordingly, it is because *something primitive and irrational within us takes him as a real hero*, and takes the poet's representation of him as true in a literal and straightforward sense.[34] To find this absurd or incredible is to miss the point of Plato's analysis of the tripartite soul, which shows how irrational emotions and magical thinking can coexist with a rational self which "knows better." Our rational part does of course "know better" than to think that the tragic Ajax is a real hero, just as it does in cases of optical illusions. But what makes tragedy so dangerous is that, through pleasure, it puts our rational part off guard, and encourages it to give in to our irrational selves. Tragic poetry is a kind of state-sponsored akrasia; and tragedy includes epic.

5. Now we still might well wonder how the Book 10 account so understood can function as a resolution of Books 2–3. For the account given in 2–3 was of "mimesis" understood as *oratio recta* within poetry, not as representation in general (393d–394b). And the *objection* to *mimēsis* so understood was that (unless restricted to good models) it corrupted its practitioners – not its audience (394d–398b). So it might seem that Plato's two discussions are really saying quite different things *about* different things, even if the two can be misleadingly lumped together as "critique of *mimēsis*" – less an exposition and resolution, then, than a bait and switch. The general question this raises is the delicate one of how a philosophical resolution can complete and correct the correlative exposition without either simply contradicting it or replacing it as irrelevant. One way it can do so – and this is, I think, the answer in the present case – is by interlocking with the earlier argument in a complementary way. Here the crucial point to note is that, according to the Book 10 account, epic and tragedy corrupt *by stimulating the very emotions they depict*. When I take pleasure in Achilles' lamentation,[35] I share his sufferings (*sumpaschontes*): I take seriously what he does, and

feel grief as a result (605d); I may even weep as he does. In other words, *poetry makes imitators of its audience*. (Obviously I do not *pretend* to be Achilles when I weep with him; but I do make myself *like* him, which is what counts (cf. 393b–c).) So the Book 2–3 argument, that the activity of imitation corrupts, turns out to have a far wider reach than we might have thought – and the problem is not one which could be solved by outsourcing dramatic performance to non-citizens. At the same time, the analysis of the tripartite soul now enables us to see *why* this experience of imitation is corrupting: it indulges and strengthens the power in us which forms false opinions and low desires, and which is, not by coincidence, what poets specialize in depicting.[36]

In sum, the Book 10 account of poetry serves as a resolution to the Book 2–3 exposition in a number of ways. It *reaffirms* its central result, the banning of tragedy qua mimetic poetry. It *clarifies* and makes precise the scope of that result, by showing that tragedy properly understood includes Homeric epic. It *grounds* the earlier argument by deploying the principles set out in the dialectical core, i.e. the analysis of the tripartite soul, to show how mimetic poetry has its effect. And in doing so it circles back to and *supports* the earlier line of argument, by showing both how imitative activity is harmful for the imitator and how poetry, through empathy, makes imitators of its audience.

v

I have argued for five claims.

First, the *Republic*, along with certain other works of Plato and Aristotle, is structured by ring-composition, with a "pyramid" structure surrounding the dialectical core of Books 4–7.

Second, this is not just an aesthetic and formal strategy, part of Plato's appropriation of and competition with Homer: it also expresses a Platonic philosophical method marked by "upwards and downwards paths" of argument to and from first principles, or at any rate highest hypotheses.

Third, the recognition of ring-structures, and their methodological functions, can help us to solve interpretive puzzles large and small. This is a weak claim: obviously we need to figure out *as much as we can* about the design of Plato's works in order to get their content right. And inasmuch as structure expresses philosophical method, structure *is* content.

Fourth, by way of a case study, the discussion of mimetic art in *Republic* Book 10 needs to be read as a resolution corresponding to the expository discussion in Books 2 and 3, just as Socrates tells us at 595a.

And fifth, the cases I have discussed here show that resolution is a complex and variable business. In philosophical works, we should expect a resolution to answer open questions, correct provisional hypotheses, relocate half-truths and revise earlier arguments on the basis of intervening principles – *not* merely to repeat points which could have been made the first time around. To work out which of these complex operations are being performed in any given case, and exactly how, is the hard part: to recognize a philosophical work as ring-composed is the beginning of interpretation, not the end.

In *Thinking in Circles*, Mary Douglas argues that ancient ring-composed works are chronically misunderstood and underrated by modern readers not attuned to their form.[37] It would sound odd to call the *Republic* underrated: but seeing just how far it is ring-composed should, I think, shift the reader's expectations in a salutary way. For to read a philosophical work as ring-composed is to approach it with the *expectation* that earlier topics will be reverted to later on, and with the presumption that the earlier discussion is provisional while the later one is complementary, principled, and authoritative. To ask whether the critique of the arts in *Republic* 10 is "consistent" with Books 2–3 (or, I would suggest more provocatively, whether *N.E.* 10 is "consistent" with *N.E.* 1) is thus to put the question too simply, if not to ask the wrong question altogether. The relation between beginning and end in such works will be complicated in all the ways that it is in the *Iliad*, and the point of the ring form is at bottom the same. It is that at the end of our exploring we may return to the place where we started, and – like the philosophers returning to the Cave – know the place for the first time.

NOTES

1. The *locus classicus* for Iliadic ring-composition is the work of van Otterlo 1944, which also reviews earlier applications of the concept to Greek texts, and 1948. A fascinating discussion in English is Whitman 1963; for a more recent account, cf. Schein 1997, pp. 345–59. Douglas 2007, pp. 101–24, devotes two chapters to the *Iliad*, emphasizing the symmetrical pattern of days and nights over which the events are distributed. Cf. also Myres 1932. Ring-composition in the *Odyssey* is discussed by Tracy 1997, pp. 360–79.
2. Eliot 1944, "Little Gidding," lines 239–42.
3. Tonsfeldt 1977.
4. Cf. Höschele 2010, pp. 172–76.
5. E. Lear 1862, p. 21.
6. For the Pentateuch and the Gathas, see Douglas 2007, pp. 2–5, 12–16, 43–71 and 6–7 respectively; for *Beowulf*, Tonsfeldt 1977.

Platonic ring-composition and Republic 10

7. Notopoulos 1951, p. 98; but the further claim that ring-composition died out early in the history of Greek literature ("it is a stylistic device which terminates with the fifth century," p. 97) is clearly false. In fairness, much of the early scholarship on ring-composition, Notopoulos' paper included, focusses on the small-scale rings used to structure speeches and digressions in epic and tragedy, not the larger structures I am concerned with here.

8. For Pindar, see Race 1997, vol. 1, pp. 20ff. and Kirkwood 1982; for "pedimental" structure in Herodotus, Myres 1953, ch. 4; for Thucydides, Hornblower 2004, pp. 271, 282–83, 315, 328, 338, 346–47; 349; for the orators, Worthington 1991 and 1993; for the Hippocratic corpus, Wenskus 1982; for epigrammatists, Höschele 2010, n. 4.

9. McPherran 2003, esp. pp. 80–82.

10. Quotations from the works of Plato are by the various hands in Cooper 1997b, including the translation of the *Republic* by G. M. A. Grube revised by C. D. C. Reeve, in some cases with revisions.

11. Cf. Notomi 1999 for the *Sophist* as ring-composed (p. 41), in the context of an interesting broader discussion of "digressions" in late Plato (pp. 27–42).

12. Cf. Barney 2001a, p. 17 n. 25.

13. Barney 2001a, p. 160.

14. Douglas 2007, pp. 31–32, 37.

15. Schofield 1972.

16. For the structural parallels between the *Republic* and the *N.E.*, see Sparshott 1982.

17. For what it is worth, the other Aristotelian work with the strongest suggestions of ring-composition is the *Metaphysics*. For Books M and N revert to some of the topics of A, at times to the point of being a "doublet" text. Since (in part for this very reason) it is very hard to believe that the *Metaphysics* as we have it is a work completed by Aristotle, all formal bets are off: but I suspect that the *Metaphysics* should be seen as (incompletely and abortively) ring-composed, with ZHΘ (or an intended account of metaphysical principles for which they serve as a place-holder) as the dialectical core, and Λ and MN (ditto) working through its positive and critical implications, thus resolving the opening aporiai (B).

18. Likewise, my talk of the upwards and downwards paths in this section is indebted to the teaching of Stephen Menn.

19. Leroux 2002, p. 30.

20. Brann 2004, pp. 93ff., 116ff. with chart of concentric circles at p. 117; Dorter 2006, pp. 3ff. with chart at p. 7; Thesleff 1993; and Burnyeat 1999. Burnyeat remarks, "The structure of *Republic* II–X is, in broad outline, a ring composition: poetry/city and soul/Forms/city and soul/poetry," while "Book I stands outside the structure" (p. 288 with n. 8). This is very different from how I would identify the "rings," but it enables Burnyeat to be unusually appreciative of how closely Book 10 relates to the earlier discussions.

21. Burnyeat 1999, p. 319.

22. Douglas 2007, pp. 31–32, 37.

50   RACHEL BARNEY

23. Tae-Yeoun Keum has also drawn my attention to a number of respects in which the Myth of Er is *internally* ring-composed, though I cannot explore these here.

24. I have argued that the psychology presupposed by the "first city" of Book 2 is false in Barney 2001b.

25. See Broadie 2005, pp. 100–04 with p. 111 n. 25.

26. Broadie 2005, p. 102.

27. As Annas 1982a has pointed out, the imagery which comes naturally to us here is the reverse of Plato's: we think of proceeding downwards to foundations where he speaks of a movement *upwards* to a first or governing principle, *archē* (p. 104 n. 21).

28. On the method of hypothesis, the state of the art remains Robinson 1953, now joined by Hugh Benson's essay in this volume.

29. Exactly which proposition(s) here count as hypotheses is very controversial. I discuss these texts and the method of hypothesis more fully in another paper currently in preparation, "Socrates, Virtue and the Method of Hypothesis."

30. I cannot make the case for this here, but other instances I have in mind include the *Theaetetus* and *Gorgias*, where the positions of Theaetetus–Protagoras–Heraclitus and Gorgias–Polus–Callicles represent a kind of explanatory regress of *false* higher hypotheses.

31. Literally "being such," *toiautēn ousan*, picking up the introductory *hoia tugchanei onta*, "of what sort it is" in the introduction of the critique (595b7). It is only in Book 10 that we find out what poetry as such is: the Book 3 discussion thus was necessarily hypothetical and provisional, as are all attempts to determine the qualities of an object without first defining its nature (cf. Socrates' strictures in the *Meno*, 71a–c, 86d).

32. Cf. Burnyeat 1999.

33. These last two, allusively presented steps leave any number of residual puzzles, including: how exactly does an imitative representation register as *normative* – why does the audience admire and sympathize with Achilles and not with Thersites? And what exactly is the role of *pleasure* in mimetic poetry? Plato seems to present it as an important factor in the capacity of poetry to rouse emotion and deceive, but how exactly does this work?

34. In the terms of Belfiore 1983, the "veridical mistake" is mediated by the "ontological mistake." For after all, "doesn't your soul, in its enthusiasm, believe that it is present at the actions you describe, whether they're in Ithaca or in Troy or wherever the epic actually takes place?" (*Ion* 535c). When I suspend disbelief, I turn over my thinking, including my formation of evaluative judgments, to a part of me too foolish and childish to distinguish between appearance and reality. I then take Ajax for a real warrior, and it is *because* I do so that I take his virtues "in the fiction" to be real ones. Once the play is over, the first mistake is shrugged off; the second remains (cf. the ancient accounts of actual reactions to tragedy noted by Stanford 1983, pp. 1–10).

35. Cf. the chain reaction described in the *Ion* (535a–536d). It is very helpful to Plato's argument in Book 10 that he uses pity, i.e., sorrow at the sufferings of

Platonic ring-composition and Republic *10*

another, as the case at hand. For one thing, its evocation is important common ground to Homeric and tragic poetry (cf. Stanford, "the supreme tragic emotion" (1983), 23). For another, were the argument to focus on any other emotion, Plato would have to face the objection that even our strongest emotional reactions to art need not resemble the representations which cause them. It is not so obvious that Achilles' anger makes the listener angry, or that fear on stage (as opposed to the sight of the fearful) provokes it in the audience. Also, as the canonical cause of weeping, pity is an emotion which has a demonstrable physical effect on the audience (cf. Gorgias, *Helen* 8–9): it is all the more plausible that it can affect our beliefs and our character as well.

36. How exactly the two conceptions of *mimēsis* are connected remains a tricky question. Briefly, my answer would be to note, first, that the Book 3 and Book 10 senses are never confused or conflated; and second, that *neither* captures exactly the sense in which both Book 3 and Book 10 are properly described as critical of "mimetic poetry." Rather, Socrates uses "mimetic" (and, in Book 10, "tragic") as shorthand for "poetry which is bad in the way that tragedy is standardly bad": the two discussions work together gradually to define the salient kind by identifying its distinctive features and fixing its scope. What really defines such poetry, as it turns out, is that it strengthens the lower parts of the soul against reason. The fact that *all* artistic representation is ontologically defective and causally independent of any wisdom in its creators explains how this vicious poetry is possible (cf., perhaps, the way in which the ontological defectiveness of all language explains how false statements are possible (*Cratylus* 428d–433b)). That irrational, unstable behavior is better suited than the opposite to pleasure-giving poetic depiction then explains why tragic and epic poetry tend to fall into the vicious class more or less inevitably and universally.

37. Douglas 2007, pp. ix–x, 1, 11, 125–26, 139–48.

CHAPTER 3

The Atlantis story: the Republic *and the* Timaeus

Julia Annas

The *Republic* is linked to the *Timaeus* by the latter's preface, and also by the appearance in the *Timaeus* of the Atlantis story, which continues in the unfinished *Critias*. There are problems, well-known to scholars, with the link provided in the preface by the references to the *Republic*. Socrates in the *Timaeus* summarizes a speech he gave "yesterday" – but he is at a different festival, in entirely different company. He refers back to the ideal state in the *Republic*, but in a strikingly selective way. He touches on the communal life of the Guardians in Book 5 of the *Republic*, but he elides the *Republic*'s distinction between the Guardians and the Auxiliaries, and, most strikingly, makes no mention at all of the point that the rulers of the ideal state are to be philosophers.[1]

Some scholars have taken these divergences to indicate that we are not meant to think here of the whole *Republic* as we have it,[2] but this does not solve any problems, since, as we shall see, the link between the dialogues provided by the Atlantis story requires us to bear in mind the *Republic*'s main argument about virtue as well as the part about the ideal state. I have no solution to the anomalies in the preface beyond the rather obvious suggestion that Plato wants to link the argument of the *Republic* with the cosmological project of the *Timaeus*, and does so by means of selective reference to the *Republic* in a new context, one in which he refers only to the ideal state in Book 5. As we shall see, this sets us up for the Atlantis story.

In this chapter I will be focussing on the Atlantis story and its links to the main argument of the *Republic* and the cosmology of the *Timaeus*. I take it that the Atlantis story is fiction, something which I cannot argue fully for here, but has been convincingly established by scholarly work.[3] It is a story invented by Plato, drawing on mythical materials, which is intended to carry an ethical message.[4] It is told among serious and philosophically minded people like Socrates, Timaeus, and Critias,[5] and so the potential problems involved in representation, so stressed in the *Republic*, do not

52

The Atlantis story

apply here (*Ti.* 19c8–20b7). It has a message like those of Plato's myths in other dialogues, but here there are features which make it reasonable to regard it as, in our terms, a fictional story rather than a myth.

For a start, the story insists on its own truth, something which is a familiar feature of fiction. It has a long roundabout account of how the story came into the possession of the present teller, another familiar feature of fiction, which often starts with the "discovery" of a long-lost manuscript or the like.[6] It develops the picture of ancient Athens and Atlantis at length and with circumstantial detail which is itself not needed for the ethical message, but serves to build up an imaginary world that appeals to the reader's (or hearer's) imagination. This, again, is quite standard in fiction. It has been objected that Plato did not have a concept of fiction available,[7] but this is not a decisive objection, since the Greeks never developed a theoretical notion of fiction as a genre, despite later having many examples of fiction in ancient novels.[8] A society lacking our developed concept of fiction can still have a conception of fiction if it recognizes the convention of storytelling: the expectation that a narrative presented emphatically as true, and with much circumstantial detail, is not to be accepted as true. (This is especially so if it contains exotic details like the elephants and other wonders of Atlantis.) It is not assuming much to think that Plato's readers could work with this convention.

What is, however, the point of the Atlantis story? It may well, of course, have more than one point, but here I want to bring out something that suggests itself when we think of the story's linking function between the two dialogues.

As the story is announced in the *Timaeus* introduction, we are told that the ideal state did once exist in the world, in the form of ancient Athens. It did many great deeds, but its greatest was its successful repulse of a great invasion by Atlantis. The rulers of Atlantis, a huge island outside the Mediterranean, had extended their rule inside that sea, as far as Italy to the north and Egypt to the south. Then they invaded the Greek world; ancient Athens first led a coalition, then was left isolated, but defeated Atlantis on her own, not only preventing further "enslavement" of Mediterranean countries but freeing those that Atlantis had already "enslaved."

The reference here to the Persian empire, its invasion of Greece, and the battle of Marathon could hardly be clearer. Athenians, of course, never forgot Marathon, and regarded it as their finest hour. And, while Plato is scornful of facile patriotism, as we can see from the *Menexenus*, he thinks that the values and way of life of the generation of the Persian wars are worthy of respect. In a passage in *Laws* 3 he explicitly praises the response of Athenians at that time, ascribing their unflinching virtue to their strict obedience to their laws (something undermined later by excessive freedom).[9] So far it looks as though virtuous ancient Athens, nobly repelling an unjust imperialist attack, is being evoked via thoughts about historical Athens and her noble stand against the Persians at Marathon.

But we are in for a surprise in the *Critias*, one which presumably comes as a shock to Plato's Athenian audience, who will have been expecting identification with the heroes of the Atlantis story. The description of ancient Athens turns her from a sea power into a land power, giving her wider land boundaries than historical Athens, and a layer of fertile agricultural soil. Ancient Athens is a city based on a surrounding area of rich farming land, with a separate warrior class living off a class of farmers, with modest buildings constructed for living and not for show, and a communal lifestyle; she comes to look utterly unlike historic Athens, and very like her enemy, historic Sparta. After this shock we then have a repetition of the point that the institutions of ancient Athens were ideally just, for they resembled those of the Guardians in the ideal state (*Cri.* 110c3–d4). Plato is here obviously distancing his Athenian audience from identification with the heroes of his story. He has other things in mind also; his Sparta-like ancient Athens foreshadows Magnesia of the *Laws*, with its blend of Athenian and Spartan institutions. But expectations that ancient Athens would resemble historic Athens of the Marathon period have been radically upended.

Ancient Athens, then, resembles historic Sparta. And as the description of it is built up, it is Atlantis which comes to resemble historic Athens – the Athens in fact of Plato's own youth, the period of a very different war, the Peloponnesian War. The Atlanteans have abundance of everything they need. But they are restless and seek to go beyond what they have. They build bridges and dig canals to join their city to the sea; they build docks and harbours and become traders, till the great harbour is full of the din of merchant ships coming and going. Their temples are massive and ostentatious. At first they obey their laws and hold virtue to be more important than wealth, but in time are led by greed and their power to subordinate virtue to wealth and show. We know from the earlier description that they used their sea power to conquer and dominate other people. Critias comments that they seemed at the height of fortune to people ignorant of the true nature of happiness, while to those who do judge rightly they were most wretched. Here it is obvious that Plato is thinking of the Athens of the fifth century, which became a great naval power and turned her allies into subjects, making them tributaries who paid for ostentatious buildings like the Parthenon and the Long Walls joining Athens to its seaport. The

Gorgias contains a similar protest in the mouth of Socrates: it is virtue, not wealth, which renders a city happy, and so Athens' proud temples and harbours, built on injustice, are "rubbish," not a cause for pride (*Grg.* 518d–519b).

We are told what is going to happen in the Atlantis story: Atlantis invades the Greek world and is utterly defeated by ancient Athens, losing even her former Mediterranean possessions. Again, there is a clear reference to the outcome of the Peloponnesian War, when Athens' hubristic expedition to Sicily ended in complete disaster and ultimately her own utter defeat, in which she lost her former tributary subjects. So much is clear not just from the obvious parallel, but from the presence in the dialogue of Hermocrates, the Syracusan general who was the main mover of opposition to the apparently invincible Athenians, and organizer of their destruction. Plato is, to say the least, making no concessions to Athenian patriotism of his day.[10]

The idea that the Atlantis story should be read as evoking both the Persian and Peloponnesian wars, but doing so in a way that identifies her with Atlantis while simultaneously foiling the identification of historic Athens with ideal ancient Athens, is of course not new; it has been influential among scholars (though not, as we will see, the broader culture) since the work of Vidal-Naquet and Gill. But what is Plato driving at with this elaborate layering of historical stories? Some have thought that he intends a detailed political message to Athens, a warning against renewed imperialist ambition in his own day.[11] It might also look like a recommendation to return to the "good old days" of Marathon and the "ancestral constitution" of Athens at that time, in contrast to Athens' contemporary democracy, blamed for Athens' sea-power imperialism and consequent defeat.[12] We can't exclude the idea that these messages are intended.[13] But the contrast of ancient Athens and Atlantis is introduced in the *Timaeus* in order to show the *ideal* state in action, so Plato would have failed to achieve his own aim if such specific messages are all that the story bears.

We might get some help here from the *Republic*. As the ideal state is introduced, it is famously as the "large letters" which will make justice in the individual soul easier for us to read (*Rep.* 368c7–369b4). Much of the description of the ideal state consists of only those details about it that we need to know in order to see the analogy between state and soul. Other aspects are described which illustrate the principle that it is knowledge alone that entitles someone to rule. There is one section of Book 5, however, which cannot be accounted for in this way. It begins at 466e1 with, "As for war, it's clear that this is how they will wage it," and continues with accounts

56   JULIA ANNAS

of children being taken to view battles, behavior to enemies and the like, until 471c3. This aspect of the ideal state – how it will wage war – has no analogue in the smaller letters of the individual soul; it is circumstantial detail in a picture of the ideal state itself. It is this passage, I suggest, which is uppermost in Socrates' mind when in the *Timaeus* he desires to see static figures from the *Republic* in motion: he wants, he says, a story of the ideal state in combat with other states in a way that shows how superior its character and education is to theirs (*Ti.* 19b–c). It is as if Plato had recognized the potential for fiction of the description of the ideal state, especially those aspects of it that have no analogue in the individual soul.

There is one crucial feature of the story, often underplayed. After Atlantis' defeat, the whole island is destroyed by earthquakes and sinks in the sea (*Criti.* 108e4–109a2). But the same cataclysm utterly destroys ancient Athens too (*Ti.* 25c6–d6). (That is, the Guardians are all destroyed; there are a few surviving farmers for historic Athenians to be descended from, but there are no written records, and so no cultural continuity.)[14] But the defeat of Atlantis is the greatest and finest of the many great deeds of ancient Athens. It is Zeus' punishment for the greed and injustice of the Atlanteans. Moreover, the victory has good results both on the ordinary level (ancient Athens frees the lands previously conquered by Atlantis) and on the ethical level (Zeus punishes the Atlanteans to improve them, making them more disciplined and orderly) (*Ti.* 24d6–e1, 25c3–6; *Criti.* 121b7–c2). The destruction equally of ancient Athens and Atlantis seems to make the great victory look alarmingly pointless.

There is a feeble response to this: Plato needs the story to end with general destruction so that the story can be lost, even to the ancient Athenians' descendants, until it is discovered by Solon, and hence by us. Plato, however, could have handled this mechanism of transmission differently if he had felt that having the general destruction follow the great victory rendered the latter pointless or detracted from it. As it is, the general destruction is introduced twice before Critias begins the story (*Ti.* 25c6–d6, *Criti.* 108e4–109a2), so our knowledge of how the story ends colors our hearing of it. Plato is not just "giving away the ending" but ensuring that we read the whole story knowing that ancient Athens perishes just as does Atlantis. This emphasis indicates that the general destruction is for him an important aspect of the story. It's reasonable, then, to ask what the point of it is in the story, rather than to dismiss it as merely a mechanism for the transmission of the story.

Here we can, I think, find a link with the *Republic*. The ideal state in the *Republic* is a state of virtuous people in an ideal society which encourages the formation of virtuous people. In the main argument of the book Socrates undertakes to show that it is better for you to be virtuous even in the worst possible circumstances than wicked in the best possible circumstances. Glaucon presents him with the virtuous man who is misrepresented as well as ruined and tortured, and the wicked man who has a reputation for virtue and all worldly advantages; Socrates argues that even so it is better to be virtuous. Thus virtue cannot be recommended because of any of the advantages which normally come from it; it must be valuable and choice-worthy for itself alone.[15] Virtue is worth having for itself, not because it brings you wealth, or power, or the reputation for being virtuous; it is worth having even when it brings you none of these, indeed the opposites of all of them.

The people of the ideal state (at least the Guardians; in this context Plato forgets about the producers, and cares less about the division into Guardians and Auxiliaries) are virtuous people whose virtue is sustained by their society, unlike us. When we see them in action, in the Atlantis story, we see them acting virtuously without thought of gain or reputation. They stand alone against Atlantis because that is the virtuous thing to do. They do not take any advantage of their victory to get spoils, or power; they are not interested in money or gold, which are the concerns of the Atlanteans, and they free Atlantis' conquests instead of keeping them for themselves. (In this they are conspicuously unlike historic Athens after the Persian Wars.)

Among the things that being virtuous brings is usually a reputation for being virtuous; thus ancient Athens rightly got a reputation for bravery, like historic Athens after Marathon. But ancient Athens' deeds were lost and forgotten after the general destruction. We know from the main argument of the *Republic*, however, that reputation is one of the things whose loss makes virtue no less choiceworthy. It is irrelevant to the virtue, and so happiness, of the ancient Athenians that all knowledge of their great victory perished. Virtue is its own reward, even if other people are unaware of it.[16] There is a moral here for contemporary Athenians who are so proud of Marathon. Plato presents a world in which there will be periodic destructions of Greek societies, so one day Marathon will be as forgotten as the defeat of Atlantis was. But this is nothing for the fighters at Marathon to regret. People who fought at Marathon in order to achieve lasting fame were, Plato thinks, fighting for the wrong reason.

What of the Atlanteans? If their defeat merely made them greedier and more aggressive, then destruction would be good for them, saving them from further degeneration. But if, as Zeus hopes, defeat made them wiser and disciplined them, the general destruction seems to cut them off from

58   JULIA ANNAS

improvement.[17] Perhaps Plato thought that the punishment of injustice that happens when ancient Athens defeats Atlantis is a good in itself, unaffected by loss of knowledge of it, and doesn't raise the question of the Atlanteans' reaction to it. But it remains an awkwardness in the narrative.

I have suggested that the Atlantis story links to the *Republic* in that the general destruction following ancient Athens' great defeat of Atlantis can reasonably be seen as illustrating the main *Republic* argument: it is better for you to be virtuous even when virtue brings none of the usual rewards. What of a link to the *Timaeus*? This is less obvious, and indeed some have thought that Timaeus' speech does not really fit in its frame. There is, for example, the notorious clash between Timaeus' view of females as the result of males degenerating, and the ideal state in Socrates' introduction, where, as in the *Republic*, they are to share the education and activities of men (*Ti.* 18 c1–4; 42b3–d2, 90e6–91d6). Yet we can see a clear way in which the Atlantis story fits well into the *Timaeus'* cosmology.

The *Timaeus'* account of the cosmos gives humans a notably small part; they do not even get to be created by the Demiurge, only by the "created gods." Nonetheless, we humans are the best placed beings in the cosmos to understand it, if we can only get our rational soul to conform its movements to those of the cosmos, thereby returning to their natural (circular) form the motions that have been crushed in the perceiving body. Doing so is achieving the human *telos* of the best life, set before us by the gods (*Ti.* 90d1–7).

This might seem a remote kind of goal for humans living everyday lives, and it is clear from the passage that it is open only to the person who devotes himself in earnest to love of learning and true understanding; he will have immortal and divine thoughts insofar as he grasps truth, sharing in immortality insofar as mortals can. Such a person will be supremely happy, having taken proper care of the divine aspect of himself.[18] He will grasp the nature and workings of the cosmos and of his own part in it. He will understand that humans are a very small part of the cosmos, and that most of them are unruly and badly ordered, but that the cosmos as a whole is not only good, but as good as it can be. The best life for humans lies in developing their reason so that they conform to the ordered rationality of the cosmos.

How does this relate to the story of Atlantis? Only in the most general way in the *Timaeus* itself, and we have to remember that we have an unfinished trilogy, where perhaps the third part was intended to relate Timaeus' cosmology more closely to human actions, in something of the way we find in the *Laws*.

In the *Laws* we find it explicit that humans are very puny and insignificant in relation to God; and should feel humble about this.[19] We find in Book 10 that the world as a whole is as good as it can be, and misfortunes to particular people do not falsify this. The person who complains that bad things happen to good people is told two things. First, he is only a small part of the universe, which did not come about for his sake; rather the reverse. What is best for the entire universe is in fact best for him, since he is a part of it (*Laws* 903b4–d3). Second, the divine economy does judge rightly in terms of what matters, namely virtue and vice, so that good and bad people are rewarded and punished appropriately; this comes down to changing their "place" in the cosmos, the virtuous living with the virtuous and the vicious with other vicious people. Hence, nothing bad does actually happen to good people. Their virtue or vice is appropriately rewarded, and what happens to them, apart from what they do to make themselves virtuous or vicious, is part of the good workings of the universe, which it would be childish and misguided to resent (*Laws* 904c6–905c4).

I am not of course claiming that we can read these ideas back into the *Timaeus* itself. Rather, they are the kind of ideas appropriate to its cosmology when we think about humans and how they relate to good and bad fortune. The *Timaeus* itself is more interested in the details of the cosmos and its structure; the relation of humans to the cosmos waits to be spelled out until the *Laws*.[20] The *Timaeus* and *Laws* present these ideas in a cosmological setting rather than that of the ideal state of the *Republic*; but at a not too strenuous level of generality we can reasonably see that they take the same view about the happiness of the virtuous. Only virtue is relevant for living happily; so the virtuous do not lose, as people normally think they lose, when their city is destroyed and their actions forgotten.[21]

Insofar as we can reconstruct Plato's aim in writing the Atlantis story, as I have tried to do, we can see that it has links to both the *Republic* and the *Timaeus*. Ancient Athens is virtuous, and its citizens act virtuously even though all credit for their deeds is wiped out. The *Republic* argues for the value and benefit of virtue in a person's life even in the worst conditions of the actual world. In the *Timaeus* Plato creates a cosmology in which the goodness of the gods, insisted on in the *Republic*, is seen in the good ordering and construction of the whole cosmos, in which virtue and vice get the appropriate reward despite appearances.

In both dialogues, those who complain that bad things happen to good people are shown to be mistaken about what truly is good and bad. The *Timaeus* gives us a world-view which forms the background to this thought. Happiness is achieved by bringing one's thoughts into tune with the rationality of the universe, from which perspective it can be appreciated that what is good for the whole is good for the parts, despite appearances. Hence, even where periodic destructions are part of our world, they do not diminish the goodness available to us. The people of the ideal city of the *Republic* are ideally virtuous. When they are seen "in motion" they act virtuously and do not lose anything by the destruction of their city, or by their actions being forgotten by others.

Plato, however, never completed the Atlantis story. We do not know why, especially since the unfinished *Critias* was considered important enough to be preserved. The ancients were no wiser than we are as to why it was never finished.[22] Clearly we would be ill-advised to make firm claims here, but I think we can see, from the nature of the Atlantis story as I have set it out, some reasons that may have given Plato pause about his new literary project.

The idea of Atlantis enjoys wide recognition in Western culture; indeed the Atlantis story has achieved wider fame than anything else Plato wrote (something that philosophers may easily miss).[23] Interestingly, Atlantis figures in our culture in two entirely different ways.

The first way is as a real place, a lost continent which can be discovered. This idea has a long history, one which picked up pace in the early modern period as Europeans began to explore distant parts of the world. The idea of discovering a lost civilization is exciting, particularly so if one can find links to it which promote one's own culture and show its ancestor to be the source of Western civilization. The siting of Atlantis in different parts of the world reflects to more or less extent the claims and self-image of the discoverers. To give only one example, the distinguished seventeenth-century Swedish scientist Olof Rudbeck spent years "proving" that Plato's Atlantis was actually Gamla Uppsala, prehistoric remains near his university town, thus placing the source of Western civilization in the north of Europe at a time of Swedish supremacy.[24] There has in fact been quite a competition to have Atlantis as the geographical or cultural ancestor of one's country. It is interesting that this competition is undeterred by the fact that Atlantis is the villain in Plato's story, the state which, in contrast to the ideal goodness of ancient Athens, falls because it becomes corrupted.

The advent of underwater archaeology has done nothing to dent the enthusiasm of Atlantis discoverers. Definite proof that there is no massive sunken continent in the Atlantic has merely encouraged discoverers to drop the requirement that Atlantis be west of the Mediterranean, and it has been located at Troy, and the Greek island of Thera,[25] as well as Bolivia and Britain.[26] In 2004 alone a US researcher "definitely" found Atlantis off the

The Atlantis story 61

coast of Cyprus, French researchers identified it with Spartel, a tiny sunken island near Gibraltar, a German researcher claimed that satellite images located Atlantis in southern Spain, and geographer Ulf Erlingsson identified it with Ireland. "I am amazed no one has come up with this before," Erlingsson remarked. "It's incredible."[27]

There is another role for Atlantis in our culture, that of a fantasy which recurs in science fiction novels and movies (including one by Disney) as part of plots involving a wondrous lost civilization, usually underwater. To the best of my knowledge Atlantis has not inspired any good literature, but if you skim the "Fantasy" and "Science Fiction" shelves in your local book-store, it doesn't take long to find "Atlantis" in the titles. Caesar's Palace casino in Las Vegas has an Atlantis show.

One of the Strip's newest entertainment features unleashes the wrath of the gods on the city of Atlantis. Fire, water, smoke and special effects combine into an extravaganza as animatronic characters Atlas, Gadrius and Alia struggle to rule Atlantis. Surrounded by a 50,000 gallon saltwater aquarium, the mythical sunken continent rises and falls before our eyes. Shows are daily on the hour, beginning at 10.00 am.[28]

Needless to say the plots of these movies, novels, and shows bear no relation to Plato's; people at Caesar's Palace would not be very entertained by virtuous ancient Athens.

I don't think it's a very bold counterfactual to say that Plato would have been extremely displeased by the factual role of Atlantis in contemporary culture. Trying to find the real Atlantis under the sea, or at Troy, or in Sweden, focusses attention on a particular place, and thinks of it as having a significance, which no particular item, even if it existed, could have. Plato's own interest in the Atlantis story is in telling a story about two cities which will illustrate a philosophical truth in narrative form. Apart from this role, concern with Atlantis itself, taking it to be an actual place with walls, harbours, canals, and so on, can only be a futile and even harmful use of our time and attention, which should be devoted to more philosophical activities.

Nor would Plato be any warmer towards the fantasy role of Atlantis. The objections he makes to artistic imitations in the *Republic* would all hold of stories and movies in which we are encouraged to enjoy the fantasy as mere entertainment. This is especially true where we are encouraged to enjoy the Atlantis fantasy in the absence of any ethical lesson about the Atlanteans' corruption coming from their greed for riches and material goods. In the *Timaeus* and *Critias* the story is carefully presented as a narrative which

JULIA ANNAS

supports philosophical ideas, presented among a select group of experts who will appreciate it for its contribution to the ideas presented in the *Republic*. But what has actually appealed about the story is the fantastic and exotic aspect of Atlantis, which is enjoyed with virtuous ancient Athens dropping out.

It is no accident that Atlantis has come to have both these roles for us. The story as we have it is an engaging narrative which draws us into its imagined world, full of circumstantial realistic detail about harbours, canals, and walls. Moreover, it is an exotic world. In Atlantis everything is lavish and luxurious; there are hot and cold baths, for example, and an abundance of all kinds of produce. Moreover, everything is of massive size; the temple of Poseidon, covered in silver and gold, is three times the size of the Parthenon. Despite its being in the west, Atlantis clearly has oriental features, such as elephants,[29] presented in an "orientalizing" way. It is a world which is described in realistic detail and yet is excitingly unlike ours. It seems no accident that the Atlantis story has lived on in genres that fuse realistic detail with the exotic, like fantasy novels and movies (and water shows at Caesar's Palace). Plutarch remarks of the unfinished story that its introductory features, which he calls "porches and surrounds and courts (*prothura, periboloi, aulai*)," are "like those of no other *logos* or *muthos* or *poiēsis*" (Plutarch, *Life of Solon* 32). There is, we might say, a tremendous build-up to the story.

Having created something unprecedented, Plato may well have thought that there was a mismatch between vehicle and message. The point of the story is to illustrate the *Republic*'s message about virtue by putting it in a cosmic setting of the kind that the *Timaeus* will give a philosophical and scientific account of. If Plato worried that the details and exoticism of his story would encourage the wrong response to it – a fascination with Atlantis itself, its location, canals, temples, and elephants – we can only say that, judging from the story's afterlife, he was right. Huge numbers of people find Atlantis a riveting subject of fact or fantasy, in ways that ignore, and draw attention away from, ancient Athens and its wholehearted devotion to virtue.[30]

NOTES

1. As though to underline these points, we find the term *philosophos* used at 18a5 in a way clearly pointing to the *Republic*'s "philosophical dog" at 375d–376b, rather than the philosopher-rulers of Book V, and the term *epikouros*, at 18b3, used not of a separate class but of the Guardians themselves in their capacity as paid "mercenaries."

The Atlantis story

2. It would surely be a mistake to think that this must be an "earlier version" of the *Republic*. Plato is capable of using his work in different ways in different settings.

3. Gill's articles deal with the issue of fictionality from various perspectives. Clay 1999 has an interesting survey of ancient reactions to the story, some regarding it as fiction (notably Aristotle) and some as factual; it influenced later "utopian" writings.

4. See Vidal-Naquet 1964, 2008; Gill 1980, especially pp. xii and xiii; Clay 1999.

5. Is Hermocrates philosophically as well as practically and politically well-equipped? There is too little of him in the dialogues as we have them for us to conjecture what his role was meant to be (other than the obvious significance of his presence, reminding us of the disaster overtaking the hubristic Athenian expedition to Syracuse).

6. In modern fiction this device is by now regarded as over-obvious, and is found less in "serious" novels than in genre novels like detective stories. The long account of how the story came to be preserved also serves another function; see below, p. 57.

7. Gill 1993.

8. Feeney 1993. Greek novels, very clear examples of fiction, were very popular (we have a number of them, Jewish and Christian as well as pagan), but literary criticism never developed any theoretical account of them.

9. *Laws* 698a–701e. Plato there praises the men of the Persian War period, not just Marathon; but shortly afterwards (707b–d) claims that the land battles of Marathon and Plataea improved the Greeks, while sea battles like Salamis made them worse.

10. We can see from the satirical *Menexenus* that Athenians of Plato's day dwelt endlessly on Marathon while skimming over the embarrassingly total defeat of the Peloponnesian War (in the *Menexenus* the "spin" with which the latter is presented is highly comic).

11. Morgan 1998 develops this idea, examining the fourth-century context of the story.

12. See Gill 1980, pp. xvii–xx for this idea.

13. And the passage in Book 3 of the *Laws* mentioned above shows that Plato was willing to subscribe to something like this view.

14. *Timaeus* 23b6–c3. We are told that all the soldier class (*to te par'humōn machimon pan*) were destroyed (25d1–2).

15. I am referring to the "two figures" of *Republic* 360e1–361d3 rather than the more tangled passage about three kinds of good. The "two figures" passage presents the challenge which Socrates accepts.

16. In the story this creates the transmission problem: we, the readers, have to be aware of it to appreciate this point. This creates the need for the long story about Solon and Egyptian priests, which underlines the unlikelihood of ancient Athens' deeds being discovered.

17. As is suggested by Broadie 2001, p. 6, where she suggests that ancient Athens was saved by the destruction from the degeneration that occurs in the ideal

64 JULIA ANNAS

state of the *Republic*. "More likely the Atlantideans were the unlucky ones, since they were cut off probably before they could absorb the moral lesson of their defeat."

18. *Timaeus* 90b6–c6. Plato plays on the idea of the *eudaimon* having a properly cared-for *daimon*.

19. The most extreme statement is to be found at *Laws* 804a4–c1.

20. Of course there are differences between the cosmological thought of the *Timaeus* and the *Laws* – the absence of the Demiurge in the latter, for example. But these differences are not relevant to the present point, that humans are placed in a cosmos which as a whole is ordered as well as it can be, and that virtue, and so happiness, reside in appreciating this.

21. There are adumbrations of this idea in the *Republic* itself, at 604b3–d6 and 486a1–b2. I owe these references to Tony Long.

22. Plutarch (*Life of Solon* 32) claims that Plato died before completing the Atlantis story. He does not cite any sources, and the claim parallels his claim (31, cf. 26) that Solon failed to finish his poem on Atlantis because of old age, not because of distraction by public affairs, as Plato claims.

23. A friend sends me Atlantis stories from the headlines of supermarket checkout magazines. Like more serious uses of the Atlantis idea, they reflect contemporary concerns – for example, concern about growing obesity rates is reflected in the "discovery" that Atlantis sank because the Atlanteans got too heavy (*Fatlantis, World Weekly News*, October 22, 2002). It is hard to imagine references to other Platonic works selling magazines at checkouts.

24. King 2005, although a superficial book, gives a riveting account of obsession (and university politics) revealing the blend of serious scientific endeavor and obsession in Rudbeck. His multi-volume *Atlantica* for some time received international respect.

25. Thera sprang into prominence after the discovery that it is the remains of a massive prehistoric volcanic eruption. See Rowe 1999, and Gill 1980 for discussions of the Troy and Thera claims.

26. In 1997 BBC News reported a British exploration to find Atlantis in Lake Poopo, an inland Bolivian lake, at the same time as a Russian expedition to find it in Little Sole Bank, a hundred miles off Land's End in Cornwall.

27. Sources here are BBC News Web page, June 7, 2004 and Reuters, August 6, November 15 and 16, 2004.

28. Flier for Caesar's Palace Forum Shops, 2003.

29. Elephants establish the setting as exotic. Rushdie 1996, p. 87, exploits this point, in promising his readers elephants at a point in the book where he imagines them complaining that the setting is insufficiently exotic. Presumably Atlantis discoverers who place it in northern countries have to invoke an earlier hot climate to accommodate the elephants.

30. I am grateful for comments from my audience at the Arizona Plato conference, where an earlier version of this chapter was read, and especially to my commentator, Tony Long.

CHAPTER 4

Ethics and politics in Socrates' defense of justice

Rachana Kamtekar

I. INTRODUCTION: WHY SO SO MUCH POLITICS? DEFENSE OF JUSTICE

In the *Republic*, Socrates argues that justice ought to be valued both for its own sake and for the sake of its consequences (358a1–3). His interlocutors Glaucon and Adeimantus have reported a number of arguments to the effect that the value of justice lies purely in the rewards and reputation that are the usual consequence of being seen to be just, and have asked Socrates to say what justice is and to show that justice is always intrinsically better than is acting contrary to justice when doing so would win you more non-moral goods. Glaucon presents these arguments as renewing Thrasymachus' Book 1 position that justice is "another's good" (358b–c, cf. 343c), which Thrasymachus had associated with the claim that the rulers in any constitution frame laws to their own advantage and call these laws' prescriptions "justice" (338d–339e); Glaucon picks up this claim in his account of the founding of the terms of justice by social contract (359a–b). In reply, on the assumption that the justice in the soul is the same sort of thing as the (more abundant or at any rate more visible) justice in the city (368e–369a), a claim he will later justify in the Book 4 argument for the tripartition of the soul, Socrates first describes a city based on need and specialization (369b–372d), then introduces and elaborates the musical and physical education of the citizens (376c–402a, 403c–412b), and then identifies the four virtues, which he assumes he will find in such a city (427e). (Socrates assumes that justice is a virtue, a good-making feature, of a city;[1] however, this leaves open the question of the goodness of justice for the agent who acts justly.) According to Socrates, the city's wisdom consists in the rulers' knowledge of what is good for the whole, its courage in the military's preservation of true beliefs about what is to be feared and what is not, its moderation in the classes' agreement that the rulers should rule; and so its justice – the remaining virtue – in the fact that in it, each class does its

65

own job (433c).[2] After arguing that the individual soul is relevantly like the city in the number and character of their parts (435c–441c), Socrates concludes that the wisdom, courage, moderation, and justice of the individual soul are analogous in structure to those of the city; in particular, individual justice is the condition in which each part of the soul does its own job: reason ruling with knowledge of what is best for each part and the whole, and spirit obeying and allying with reason in the rule over appetite (441c–442b). This condition of justice turns out to be the healthy condition of the soul, which is intrinsically valuable, sufficient for the non-performance of unjust actions, and brought about by the performance of just actions; conversely, injustice is the soul's ill-health, a condition brought about by the performance of unjust actions (442e–443b, 444c–445b).

This summary of *Republic* 2–4's ambitious and elaborate argument in defense of justice may mask how much of that defense is devoted to politics, to describing the city and its coming-to-be: its origins in mutual need and the division of labor for efficient production of necessities, the expansion of this simple city to cater to the desire for luxuries, and especially the education of its guardians to purge these unnecessary desires, together occupy 61 out of a total 85 Stephanus pages of text. Why are these political proposals so extensive if Plato is only interested in the city as an analogue for the individual soul? And how does Socrates' definition of political justice as obtaining when each class performs its own function engage Thrasymachus' and Glaucon's specifically political claims about justice (that the laws that define justice in any constitution serve the interests of the rulers, that justice is the result of a social contract among the weak to neither harm nor be harmed)? Or if it does not engage these claims, then why not?

Scholars divide over the importance of politics in the *Republic*. To take only a few recent examples,[3] Annas (1999, p. 88) reasons that while the ideal city is supposed to illuminate virtue, the overall argument's conclusion, that virtue is sufficient for happiness, does not depend on the city, "since the conditions of the ideal state do not form part of what the virtuous person needs to be happy." She concludes that the city's political details are "imaginative constructions rather than ... serious matter for political discussion, never mind practical proposals" (p. 91). It seems true that if the account of the ideal city is to deserve the space Plato devotes to it in the *Republic*, it must play another role in the overall argument than that of claiming that the ideal city would facilitate the happiness of the just.

On the other side, Schofield's *Plato: Political Philosophy* (2006) takes the *Republic* as its central political text on the grounds that "the dialogue contains most of Plato's most striking ideas in political philosophy" (p. 9),

Ethics and politics in Socrates' defense of justice 67

which are taken seriously by Plato's later writings and by subsequent writers on politics, ancient as well as modern (pp. 9–13). Menn (2006) argues that the very title of the *Republic*, *Politeia* (already used by Aristotle), puts it in an established genre for describing the ideal constitution (or *polis'* way of life), and points out that the challenge to justice that sets the stage for Socrates' defense is Thrasymachus' claim that constitutions always serve the interests of the rulers,[4] a claim with roots in the sophistic thought (voiced by Glaucon) that justice is society-relative or conventional. But we can grant all these points and observe that *Socrates* explicitly subordinates the political to the ethical argument when he gives as his reason for introducing the city that they will see justice more easily in the city and then be able to say what it is in the individual (368e–369a).[5] Similarly, the tempting thought that individual and society shape one another,[6] while clearly something Plato believed in (the account of the degeneration of societies and individual characters in Books 8 and 9 attests to this), does little to explain the particular use to which Plato puts the city in the argument of the *Republic*.

This chapter argues that the account of the ideal city in Socrates' defense of justice plays the role of connecting justice as a structural condition of the soul and just behavior. Having just reviewed Socrates' defense of justice in Books 2–4, in section 2 I revisit a classic worry that the defense is irrelevant and show that a proper appreciation of the role of the ideal city in the defense allows us to reply to it; then, in section 3 I raise a new worry that the defense is question-begging and show why it is not. Finally, in section 4, I draw out some methodological implications relevant to the controversy in Plato scholarship about the relative roles of ethics and politics in the argument of the *Republic*.

2. THE FALLACY OF IRRELEVANCE

In his classic paper "A Fallacy in Plato's *Republic*," David Sachs (1963, pp. 152–54) argues that in response to Thrasymachus' and Glaucon's and Adeimantus' demand that Socrates show the intrinsic value of just action, Socrates gives the irrelevant reply that it is intrinsically valuable to have a harmonious soul, which he claims is a just soul, assuming without argument that having a just soul suffices for the performance of just and only just actions, and not even bothering to claim that the person who performs just actions has a just soul.

We may begin by observing that Socrates does not hold that the person who performs just actions thereby has a just soul, and that is why he doesn't bother to claim it – although he does claim that performing actions of a certain character accrues that character to the soul, thereby giving an indirect and psychologically plausible reason why unjust actions are not preferable to just actions. Further, as Sachs acknowledges, Glaucon and Adeimantus don't only challenge Socrates to show that it's better to act justly than unjustly; they also express an interest in the value of being just, i.e., of having a just disposition (cf., e.g., 358b, 361e). Still, Sachs is owed an explanation of what licenses Socrates' assumption that the harmonious-souled person will perform just actions and not unjust ones, and most scholarly responses to Sachs in Plato's defense have attempted such an explanation.

One explanation appeals to the psychology of virtue developed in the *Republic*. Socrates claims that strong desires for one type of thing result in correspondingly weaker desires for other things; thus, the lover of knowledge has little desire for the bodily goods that might motivate unjust actions (485b–487a). To this may be added that the lover of knowledge, upon seeing the harmonious arrangement of the Forms, will desire to imitate that arrangement; this would give him a positive incentive to behave justly (rather than merely to refrain from unjust actions) – not only because he wishes to accrue justice to his soul, but also because one is moved to imitate and reproduce what one loves (500c–d) (Kraut 1992, p. 328). Or, drawing on the motivational account in the *Symposium*, one might argue that reproducing what one values is the way one pursues immortal possession of the good, and what a harmonious- or just-souled person reproduces is just actions.[7]

A second explanation appeals to the content of the education a just person must have had. On this view, a proper education, such as the sort provided by the city Socrates is constructing in the *Republic*, is both necessary for one's soul-parts each to do its own thing, and sufficient for one to behave justly – as prescribed by the law.[8] However, this response to the Sachs fallacy fails, because having education (especially the pre-rational education of *Republic* 2–3, which is likened to stamping an impressionable soul with beliefs, 377a–b) be the guarantor that the just person doesn't commit unjust actions raises Glaucon and Adeimantus' challenge to the rational choiceworthiness of just actions all over again. Why wouldn't a just person looking back on the education that made her psychologically unable to break the law at least wish that such an inhibition had not been inculcated in her? It's also worth noticing that this response conflates the dialectical context – in which Socrates must answer the challenge about the intrinsic choiceworthiness of justice – and the political construction being used to examine the question. An upshot of this conflation seems to be that justice is not available to those who are not citizens of Plato's ideal city, that is, to all of us. Yet Socrates' defense of justice does not take the form "Establish the ideal city that you or your children may finally acquire a just soul and thus happiness!" Instead, when he is asked to comment on the possibility of the just city's coming into being (471c–472a), he replies that they investigated justice in the city in order to discover what justice is like, and that we will be happy insofar as we are most like the just person (472b–c), adding at the conclusion of Book 9 that a person of understanding will direct his efforts to attaining a just state of soul, which includes pursuing justice-promoting studies, *avoiding* politics unless his city's constitution is like his or divine luck intervenes (591b–592b).

But explanation appealing to the developed psychology of virtue is not without difficulties either, for that says why the just-souled person has reason to act justly rather than unjustly, and that the just soul everyone has reason to acquire is acquired by engaging in just actions. Yet what about Thrasymachus' worry that the actions we call just are simply those in accordance with the laws established by the rulers to their own advantage? At the end of Book 4 Socrates adduces conventionally unjust actions (*ta phortika*) to confirm (*bebaiōsametha*) his account of psychic justice as one in which each part does its own; his claim is that the psychically just person will not steal from temples, commit adultery, and so on; this he takes to confirm that it is still justice that the account transferred from city to soul is an account of (442e–443b). But Socrates' appeal to such easy cases doesn't seem sufficient, and certainly not sufficient to address Thrasymachus' concern. What if the temples are used to store wealth the rulers have expropriated by force from citizens? What if the prohibition on adultery conflicts with marriage practices that would produce better offspring for the city?

On Sachs' report, and in much subsequent scholarship, the ordinary unjust actions of 442e appear to be some kind of *deus ex machina*. This appearance arises out of Sachs' diagnosis of Plato's strategy in the *Republic*, according to which Book 1 shows that any definition in terms of action-types fails in the face of counterexamples, following which, subsequent books take justice to be a character-trait – which, fatally for the defense, Plato fails to connect adequately to just actions (157–58).

However, on examination it turns out that the Book 1 definitions of justice do not all fail because of counterexamples. Some do: for example, justice cannot be returning what you have borrowed, because in the case that the friend who loaned you a weapon and is now asking for it back is insane, returning what you have borrowed will harm him – but it can't be just to harm your friend (331e–332a). Similarly, justice cannot be helping friends and harming enemies, for in the case that your friends are people you mistakenly believe to be good and your enemies people you mistakenly believe to be bad, justice would have to be the cause of your helping unjust people and harming just people – but how could justice be the cause of helping unjust people or harming just people (334b–e)? But to the reformulated definition – justice is (knowingly) helping friends who are good and harming enemies who are bad – Socrates objects that the harming clause would make justice be the cause of harming someone, that is, of making him worse in terms of human virtue, in a word, unjust, whereas surely justice can't be the cause of injustice (335b–d). This is not a counterexample; rather, the definition has failed because of the wrongness of the harming clause. If that clause is dropped, then the remainder, "Help friends, where friends both are and are seen by you to be good," survives. There is no sign that this rule admits of exceptions; its deficiency rather seems to be that it provides no guidance with respect to non-friends, and that even towards friends, it is too abstract to guide action (a similar problem obtains for the action-type definition of civic justice proposed by Socrates himself, i.e., doing one's own). The lack of guidance problem could be addressed by going into the reasons why the just person acts as he does towards friends and non-friends. A final point about the allegation that Plato retreats from action-types to character-traits in order to avoid counterexamples: counterexamples may also be avoided by specifying the contexts in which action-types are just.

Sachs' explanation for Socrates' change in focus from action-types to character-traits in giving an account of justice (i.e., this allows him to avoid the counterexamples he believes any definition in terms of action-types must face) is unduly uncharitable. The change is well-motivated by the fact that action-types leave out agents' reasons for action, which are crucial to whether their actions are virtuous or only compatible with virtue. Evidence of Socrates' view that virtuous actions must be performed for the right reasons is found at 430b–c, where he contrasts the motivations underlying the law-abiding behavior of slaves and animals, on the one hand, and the (politically) courageous guardians of the ideal city, on the other (cf. *Phaedo* 68c–69a). While the former obey the law out of fear of punishment, the latter do so as a result of their education. It is true that the final definition of individual justice is a condition of the soul that makes no reference to action-types. But that definition can have been shaped all along by the consideration of just and unjust action-types, for our judgments that such-and-such an act is just or unjust are likely to be less controversial and more accurate than our initial accounts of what justice is.[9]

Ethics and politics in Socrates' defense of justice

When we read the pages of Socrates' defense of justice in the light of Sachs' account of it, we should be struck by how much Socrates has to say about which action-types are just and unjust, and in general virtuous and vicious. For example, Book 2–3's censored stories about gods and heroes say what actions are virtuous and vicious. Some of the stories of Homer, Hesiod and the other poets, such as Hesiod's account of the parricidal succession of Ouranos by Cronus and Cronus by Zeus, are rejected on the grounds that the image they give of the gods and heroes is false, i.e., not at all like god, who is entirely good and unchanging (377d–e, 378d–e, 379a, 380c, 383a). But Socrates also appeals directly to the stories' effects on citizens' beliefs about human virtue, including human justice: about Hesiod's succession story, he says: "it shouldn't be said to a young listener that he would surprise no-one by committing the worst injustices or by punishing his unjust father in every way, but he would only be doing what the first and greatest of the gods did" (378b). Again, he says that if young people think stories of gods lamenting are serious and do not ridicule them, they will not consider lamenting unworthy of themselves (388d); stories of heroes speaking impertinently to their superiors or overvaluing food will not encourage self-control in young people (390a–b); hearing about the misdeeds of gods and heroes will make young people excuse their own misdeeds (391e). These stories make up the greater part of civic education, the education that trains citizens to behave in ways that result in the city's virtues; so if the city's justice consists in each class doing its own work, we must suppose that the non-performance of ordinarily unjust actions (and perhaps the performance of ordinarily just actions) is not only the effect, but also the cause, of each doing his or her own.

Notice that by placing these virtuous and vicious action-types in a narrative, Plato is placing them in a context, which facilitates judgment about what actions are just or unjust. Further, when Socrates specifies the arrangements in the city, he is specifying the contexts in which certain action-types are just and unjust. For example, it is required by justice for philosophers to rule in the city that has educated them – but not in cities where they have grown up "on their own" (520a–c). Again, in the city, it is just to do one's (socially-determined) job – but it does not follow that this is just outside the city. (What *would* one's job be outside the city?) Still more obviously, in the city Socrates is describing, it is just for citizens to share their spouses and children – but Socrates is not urging his interlocutors to mate with their neighbors' spouses and rear their neighbors' children. So it is not only in the confirmatory passage at the end of Book 4, but also in the course of city construction, that Socrates presupposes some things about what actions are just. And of course, he must do so for city construction, since justice in the city has to involve laws and institutions that regulate the conduct of citizens.

It's worth noting, finally, that although Glaucon thinks (and seems to have been followed in this by Sachs) that the defense of justice is complete by the end of Book 4, Socrates does not. After arguing that justice is a harmonious condition of soul and that just actions promote this condition, Socrates says, "it remains, it seems, to inquire whether it is more profitable to act justly, live in a fine way, and be just, whether one is known to be or not, or to act unjustly and be unjust, provided that one doesn't pay the penalty and become better as a result of punishment" (444e–445a, tr. Grube–Reeve). When Glaucon protests that he has already shown this, Socrates says he will show it "most clearly" by examining the kinds of vice. The ranking of constitutions and characters from the least to the most vicious in Books 8 and 9 depicts many kinds of unjust actions. And the identification of the perfectly just person with the philosopher in Books 5–7 (which explains the just person's lack of incentive to commit acts of injustice by his absorption in the goods of intellect, 485d–486b) prepares for Book 9's rebuttal of Thrasymachus' claim that the just person is a dupe, in the argument that the philosopher's superiority in experience, reason, and argument guarantees that his judgments are authoritative (582a–e). Thus just actions will also turn out to be most pleasant.

My proposal, then, is at once a response on Socrates' behalf to the irrelevance charge and an explanation of why Socrates elaborates (in such detail!) the city when his topic is individual justice: the account of justice in the city ensures that the justice in the soul Socrates is going to describe remains connected to the justice of actions. In other words, while Socrates defines justice in the city and in the soul in terms of the internal harmonious relations of the parts, he does not leave behind just action-types. And as for the Thrasymachean point that the exemplary just and unjust actions used to guide the definition are so-called because it serves the interests of the rulers, as we shall see, this is addressed by Socrates' stipulation that the law in the ideal city aims at the good of the whole city rather than only at the good of the rulers (420b, 519e–520a).

3. BEGGING THE QUESTION: A NEW FALLACY?

In the course of constructing the ideal city, Socrates interrupts his description of the virtue-inculcating education citizens of the ideal city are to receive, and asks,

Ethics and politics in Socrates' defense of justice

> Now, isn't there a kind of story whose content we haven't yet discussed? So far, we've said how one should speak about gods, heroes, daemons, and things in Hades. . . . Then what's left is how to deal with stories about human beings. . . . But we can't settle that matter at present. . . . Because I think we'll say that what poets and prose-writers tell us about the most important matters concerning human beings is bad. They say that many unjust people are happy and many just ones wretched, that injustice is profitable if it escapes detection, and that justice is another's good but one's own loss. I think we'll prohibit these stories and order the poets to compose the opposite kind of poetry and tell the opposite kind of tales. Don't you think so? . . . But if you agree that what I said is correct, couldn't I reply that you've agreed to the very point that is in question in our whole discussion? . . . Then we'll agree about what stories should be told about human beings only when we've discovered what sort of thing justice is and how by nature it profits the one who has it, whether he is believed to be just or not. (392a–c, translation Grube–Reeve)

In describing the stories that guardians may be told during education, Socrates is responding to Adeimantus' side of the brothers' challenge to justice: the poets and our other educators, when they speak in praise of justice, only tell us of the good consequences of being seen as just, thereby undermining our commitment to be rather than to appear just; you, Socrates, must tell us why justice is good for its own sake (362e–367e). Socrates, for his part, is in this passage pointing out that to earn the right to say what should be the content of stories about human justice – in particular about the goodness of justice for the agents that engage in just behavior – he must first explain how justice is intrinsically good for its possessor.

But has Socrates not already implicitly claimed that just actions are good for the agents that perform them in the course of describing the content of early education? For consider: the grounds for adopting or rejecting any given traditional story about the gods and heroes are its truth or compatibility with the truth and its effects on the beliefs of young citizens about what behavior is worthy or unworthy of them (377d–383a). It seems that the whole educational programme of Books 2 and 3 has been directed by the assumption that individual justice is a virtue – an excellence, and therefore good for its possessor. So what is the point now of refraining from discussing the admissible content of stories about human beings?

One might reply on Socrates' behalf that he is assuming that the other virtues of an individual (courage, moderation, etc.) are good for their possessors, but leaving open the question whether *justice* is; perhaps he has introduced the stories about the gods *as* affecting citizens' courage-, moderation-, and piety-related beliefs, not their justice-related beliefs. But this is not plausible, given how closely the beliefs about courage, moderation, and piety are related to the beliefs about justice. Take for instance the beliefs about piety. In addition to Hesiod's succession story, Socrates censors stories about the gods fighting their family and friends on the grounds that this is necessary if citizens are to believe that it is most shameful to hate fellow-citizens (378c). Although these stories are censored as antithetical to piety, it's clear that they also violate at least a couple of common conceptions of justice: helping rather than harming your friends, and not injuring those who have not injured you. Socrates says that the censored line "Gifts persuade gods; gifts persuade revered kings" (390d–e) attributes a lack of moderation to gods and kings, but surely giving and taking bribes is also unjust (later on, Socrates discloses that loving money is itself a condition of injustice and leads to unjust actions). Yet again, consider Achilles' words to Apollo: "You hurt me, far-shooting, most destructive of all, | And I would pay you back, if I had the power" (391a). Although officially banned as impious, these words are also indicative of injustice, as not observing the proper hierarchy between gods and heroes.

To make matters worse, the *Republic* does not include piety in its list of the virtues of city and individual, which would suggest that it somehow folds piety into one of the other virtues, and the most likely candidate for piety to be folded into is justice. The *Euthyphro* suggests taking piety to be that part of justice that pertains to our relations with the gods (11e–12e, cf. *Protagoras* 331a–b). If the stories permitted and prohibited in early education introduce the content of justice, only by another name, then Socrates' worry about begging the question of the value of justice by determining which stories about human justice may and may not be told applies to the whole account of early education – in particular, to the stories about gods and heroes.

Has Socrates, after all, begged the question of whether or not justice is intrinsically valuable to its possessor? I do not think so, but determining how he might avoid begging the question illuminates his defense of justice.

One way for Socrates to avoid short-circuiting the process for defining and evaluating justice first in the city and then by analogy in the soul is by maintaining that just action is strictly distinct from pious action, moderate action, etc. This can only become clear once Socrates has defined justice as "doing one's own" – as long as this is not taken too loosely – for the stories considered and banned are not about the violation of this principle. The banned stories may show violations of justice as that is commonly conceived, but not on Socrates' "doing one's own" account. This proposal requires us to understand the *Republic*'s various claims that such-and-such is "just" in terms of doing one's own job. So, for example, when Glaucon says

Ethics and politics in Socrates' defense of justice

that the philosophers will agree to rule the city because Socrates' speech urging them to rule is saying just things to just people (520d–e), we should read this to mean: ruling is their job, and they are just-souled people, whose soul-parts each do their job, so they will do their job of ruling.[10]

Here is another way of putting the proposal. In the first two chapters of *Nicomachean Ethics* 5, Aristotle distinguishes two closely related senses of justice and injustice: in the general sense, justice is the lawful, comprising the whole of virtue in relations with others, and injustice is the unlawful; in the specific sense, justice is the equal or fair, comprising one part of virtue distinct from courage, moderation, and wisdom, and injustice is the unequal or unfair.[11] According to the strategy being explored here, political justice in the *Republic* would be restricted not only to Aristotle's specific, distributive, sense, but to the fair distribution of citizens' jobs; justice would be silent on the fair distribution of social benefits.

Is this restriction of the sense of "justice" plausible? On the one hand, it is striking that throughout his description of the ideal city, Socrates does not use the term "just" to characterize either the laws governing its social organization, or obedience to these laws, or even the principle guiding the construction of the city, namely that the founders and the law aim to make the city as a whole and not only one particular class as happy as possible. Instead, he says that making the city as a whole as happy as possible is "what we were looking to in establishing the city (*touto blepontes tēn polin oikizomen*)."

On the other hand, rescuing Socrates' defense of justice from the fallacy of begging the question by narrowing the content of justice comes at the cost of indicting it of a Sachs-style fallacy of irrelevance, this time in the case of political justice. For while in the individual case, each part doing its own *is* a harmonious, hence intrinsically valuable, condition of the individual, surely "doing one's own" understood as narrowly as I have taken it is deeply disappointing as an account of political justice. Above all, political justice should include the distribution not only of society's work but also of society's goods, but "doing one's own" ignores the latter.[12] In the city, each class's doing its own seems to stand in need of further social arrangements that would distribute the social product (e.g., education) according to some principle such as, "to each according to his capacity for benefit." One might suppose that Plato intends rulers doing their own job to entail such distribution, because he says that the rulers will ensure that each has his or her own (433e–434a); however, the mention of lawsuits (*dikas*) in this passage suggests that what Plato has in mind here is corrective, rather than distributive, justice. Further, "doing one's own," "*ta hautou prattein*," is a partisan conception of justice, an aristocrat's slogan expressing opposition to political participation by non-aristocrats[13] – participation that is commended, e.g., in Pericles' Funeral Oration. Would a democrat agree that "doing one's own" is justice? And, since "doing one's own" turns out to require depriving the ruling class of private property, would an oligarch agree that this is justice? Finally, the narrowing strategy is in tension with the elaboration of the city giving behavioral content to justice, for it would seem that actions that are not job-related may be just or unjust, but "doing one's own" would be silent about them. These difficulties seem to me to be serious enough that we should seek out another strategy for avoiding question-begging.

Let's return again to the passage about education in which Socrates cautions against begging the question about the value of just behavior to the just agent. He excludes, not stories about justice, but "stories about *human* beings" (392a, my emphasis). So the answer to the fallacy-threatening question (i.e., don't the stories about divine and heroic virtue and its benefits determine, on grounds of truth and desirable behavioral consequences, what beliefs the citizens in the ideal city should have, and how they should behave, and thereby settle the content of human virtue, including justice?) may be: yes, the stories told so far do determine the content of human justice, but Socrates is leaving it open whether the results of this shaping are *good for the citizens* who have been shaped, or merely good for the city. He *has* to leave this open to avoid begging the question of his defense of justice – and if the virtues are inter-entailing, he has to leave open the value-to-the-possessor for all the human virtues.[14]

When Socrates deprives the guardians of the city of private property, Adeimantus protests that he is depriving them of happiness (419–20a). Socrates replies that although he wouldn't be surprised if they turn out to be happiest in this condition, he isn't aiming to make any group in the city outstandingly happy, but to make the whole city as happy as possible. He goes on to compare his construction of the city to the painting of a statue, and says that just as a painter who painted the eyes purple (the most beautiful color) wouldn't be painting eyes at all, so too, if he gave the guardians the kind of happiness Adeimantus is talking about, he would make them other than guardians. Students of Plato's political thought have asked: what is Socrates saying about the relationship between this happiness of the city and the happiness of the citizens? Does the happiness of the city consist in the happiness of its citizens?[15] Or does the happiness of the city float free of the happiness of its citizens?[16] Or is the happiness of the city related in some more complex way to the happiness of its citizens?[17]

Ethics and politics in Socrates' defense of justice

But Socrates follows his statement that he is aiming to make not one group, but the city as a whole, as happy as possible, with the explanation that he is doing this *for the reason that*[18] he expects to find justice most easily in such a city (*ōiēthēmen gar en tēi toiautēi malista an heurein dikaiosunēn*, 420b–c, cf. 369a, 371e, 372e, 376d). We now have an explanation for why the text of the *Republic* is so elusive on the question of whether the often-mentioned happiness of the city is independent of, or constituted by, or causally related to, the happiness of all, most, or the dominant citizens. It is not because only the guardians are really happy, and Plato wants to bury this politically embarrassing point, nor is it because he simply assumes that the happiness of the city consists in the happiness of citizens. Rather, Plato has given Socrates two dialectical constraints: first, in response to Thrasymachus he has to display justice in a city where the laws are not designed to serve the interests of the rulers (as he repeatedly reminds Glaucon and Adeimantus), and second, in response to Glaucon and Adeimantus, he has first to say what justice is and then to show that it is good for the just person. But saying what justice is – not just as a harmonious condition of city or soul, but also what sorts of actions are just – requires spelling out many details of the city, and it would beg the second question, of justice's value, to say that these just citizens are happy.

These two dialectical constraints explain features of the two other passages in which Socrates discusses the happiness of the guardians. First, at 465e–466b, referring back to the passage I've just discussed, Socrates says that *then* their concern had been to make the guardians true guardians and the city the happiest they could, rather than to make any group particularly happy; now, however, he is free to add that the guardians'/auxiliaries' (*epikourōn*) life is better (*kalliōn kai ameinōn*) even than an Olympic victor's. He is free to do so now because the case for the intrinsic goodness of justice for its possessor has been made at the end of Book 4. (The case for the superiority of the just life to the unjust no matter what the external circumstances will not be complete until the end of Book 9, but in this passage, Socrates is comparing the specific external circumstances of guardians and Olympic victors.) Second, in response to Glaucon's complaint that he is doing the philosophers an injustice by requiring them to rule when they do not want to (519d), Socrates repeats that the aim of the law is not to make any class in the city outstandingly happy but to spread happiness throughout the city by bringing the citizens into harmony with one another by persuasion or compulsion and by making them share with each other the benefits that each can confer on the community (519e–520a). Recalling Thrasymachus' claim that everywhere in cities rulers establish laws that serve their own interests helps us understand Socrates' reference to "law" in this passage: Socrates has been designing a city in which the law's goal is the city's happiness rather than the rulers'.

4. THE STATUS OF SOCRATES' DEFENSE

I have argued that the role played by the city in Socrates' defense of justice is that of illustrating not only the structure of justice in the individual soul, but also what actions are just and unjust. In this respect, Plato clearly subordinates the politics of the ideal city to the ethical argument for the preferability of the just life to the unjust. However, what Socrates tells us in the *Republic* about the correct method for investigating a question suggests that for the city to play this illustrative role, he must be relatively strongly committed to his political claims. Of course, as we saw in section 3, Socrates has to observe the dialectical constraints he has set up on what political claims he can make, given that what is up for examination is the value of justice. Still, the political claims have at least the status of a most plausible hypothesis, with the ethical claims being their consequences. This calls for some explanation.

In the middle books of the *Republic*, Socrates lays out the very intellectually demanding conditions for knowledge of what justice is – which involve knowledge of the Good itself, a knowledge he himself lacks (504b–c, 506c). Despite his lack of knowledge, he is able to give three images of what the Good itself is like (it is, like the sun, a source of illumination as well as the cause of the things illuminated), what are the grades of cognition (in the divided line), and how education affects the soul (it frees those who did not even know they were imprisoned in a cave). Socrates' remarkable ability to illustrate what he does not know is likened, by the divided line, to the practice of geometers, who use drawn images in order to prove theorems about intelligible objects they hypothesize without fully knowing them (510b–511a). Throughout his defense of justice, Socrates has been sketching, or constructing, an image of justice in the city.

The divided line also says what are the limitations of this kind of reasoning: the consequences are only as good as the hypotheses on which they are based, and this kind of reasoning is not capable of going on to prove the hypotheses themselves. Doing that – and doing that finally on the basis of knowledge of the Good itself – is a very necessary task, but it is left to dialectic.[19] It is not Socrates' task in the *Republic* to investigate the sort of object dialectic investigates, i.e., "the being itself of each thing" (532a, cf. 402c). First, the defense of justice involves no claims about what

Ethics and politics in Socrates' defense of justice 79

Justice itself is: the accounts of the city's and soul's justice Socrates provides in *Republic* 4, namely "each part doing its own job" (433a–b, 441d–e), are not presented even as approximate answers to the question "What is justice?" (although presumably they might inform such an inquiry) but instead to the more modest questions, "What is justice in a city?" and "What is justice in the individual soul?" Given Socrates' view that it is necessary to know the Just itself to know as accurately as possible justice in its various instantiations (cf. 520c, 402c), it is not surprising that he should remind us that the treatment of justice he has been able to give is only relatively adequate (504a–b). On the other hand, the defense makes it clear that knowledge of Justice itself is not necessary for an adequate enough grasp of individual justice to prove it more beneficial to its possessor than individual injustice.

Second, even when it comes to investigating justice in the individual by way of its civic analogue, Socrates says little to justify his assumption that the city that he has constructed is an ideally happy and virtuous city. He starts out simply constructing *a* city on the bases of mutual need and specialization of labor, and it gradually becomes "the good and correct constitution" (449a). But it is only because Thrasymachus implicitly agrees that this city's laws have been established to make the whole city happy that it is a better city than the tyrannies, democracies, and oligarchies that Thrasymachus says establish laws to serve their rulers' interest.

Perhaps the ranking of constitutions in Books 8 and 9 goes some distance towards justifying the claim of the city of Socrates' defense to be an ideal city. Or perhaps it is the better-than-Laconizing arrangements (educating women, abolishing the biological family, rule by philosophers) showcased in Book 5. Or perhaps Plato does not try too hard because Socrates' dialectical situation has kept him from giving the true justification: that it is the best city because its citizens are the happiest (*Laws* 743c). In any event, he will consider the merits of the political arrangements proposed for the *Republic*'s ideal city in other works.[20]

NOTES

1. The assumption may seem reasonable on the grounds that from the perspective of any individual – whether that individual himself conforms to the norms of justice or not – it is good to live in a just city on the grounds that the general upholding of the norms of justice affords the individual security against becoming the victim of others' injustice. (Irwin 1995, p. 184, suggests that Glaucon overlooks this point in favor of justice.) But such reasoning is not uncontroversial: Glaucon (or the *Gorgias*' Callicles) might argue that a super-strong individual would prefer to live without the norms of justice being generally upheld;

80 RACHANA KAMTEKAR

Thrasymachus might object that "justice" creates systematic disadvantages for the ruled that are far worse than any security it provides. As we shall see, Socrates' assumption is innocent because he blocks direct inferences from "good for the city" to "good for the individual."

2. Although Socrates supposes that cities get their characters from the characters of the individuals that make them up (435d–436a, 544d–e), this relationship is not always straightforward, since he is also clear that for a city to possess a given virtue, it is not necessary for all or most of the individuals in the city to possess that virtue. Thus the wisdom of the tiny ruling class suffices for the city to be wise, and the military's obedience to rational pronouncements concerning what is fearful and what is not suffices for the city to be courageous. The cases of moderation and justice are more complicated: these virtues belong to the city in virtue of certain relations among the classes, i.e., the classes each doing their own job of ruling, guarding, and producing, and agreeing that the rulers of the city ought to rule. For all that the accounts of civic virtue tell us, a city may be moderate and just without any of its citizens being moderate and just.

3. This division among readers of Plato's *Republic* was already noted by the Neoplatonist Proclus, according to Schofield 2006, p. 30.

4. Strictly speaking, Thrasymachus begins with an exposé of what is called "justice" in cities, but concludes that prudence commends a policy of *individual* "injustice" (343c–344a).

5. Ferrari 2003, p. 92, suggests that the reason is that the individual is capable of philosophy, whereas the city is at most capable of having its superior members rule the inferior. But I don't see how the relative greatness of individual excellence explains the subordination of city to individual in the argumentative structure of the *Republic*.

6. Argued for in Lear 1992 and against in Ferrari 2003, pp. 52–53 and 65–75.

7. Irwin 1995, pp. 298–317. Irwin's particular concern is with the just-souled person's acting for the sake of the good of others.

8. This is argued in Brown 2004.

9. Burnyeat 1977 observes that in Socratic dialectic, examples are brought up after, and as tests of, definitions rather than before, and as guides to, these definitions – as I am claiming. While this is correct as an account of what Plato makes explicit in elenctic contexts (and Burnyeat himself so restricts his account, p. 384), Plato also shows a keen awareness in the *Statesman* that examples guide the process of definition whether we are explicitly aware of it or not (267c–275c). Burnyeat also points out that in Socratic dialectic examples are not the last word because definitions are supposed to settle questions about whether a given example (of, e.g., piety) is indeed a real example (p. 386). In light of this, I find it interesting that the cases of just and unjust behavior considered in Books 2–4 are relatively uncontroversial, but once Socrates has given his definition of justice he is able to unveil highly controversial behavior legislated by the ideal city such as the holding of women and children in common.

10. Rather than that they will rule because it is commanded by the law, as is argued by Brown 2000.
11. Vlastos 1971 holds that justice in the *Republic* is the whole of social virtue (p. 60) because "doing one's own" applies to the whole of one's life (pp. 80–81), and so to all one's dealings with others. But just because the boundaries of "one's own" are vague it doesn't follow that the scope of "one's own" is the whole of one's life. Vlastos infers this from the absence of a private sphere unregulated by the state (pp. 77–78), but the inference from the state regulating the whole of life to justice regulating the whole of life is invalid.
12. In Kamtekar 2001 I argued that the *Republic* captures this aspect of justice under the rubric of "the happiness of the whole." But I never found a satisfactory explanation of why Plato should carve up justice and happiness in this way.
13. For evidence, see Adkins 1971.
14. I think I am in agreement here with Ferrari 2003, p. 80, when he says that the account of the city enables Socrates to say more about justice and injustice understood conventionally than would seem to be allowed by Glaucon's and Adeimantus' exclusion of justice's consequences. I also think that what I have to say here about avoiding question-begging justifies Ferrari's insistence that the city–soul analogy be treated as an analogy rather than a psychodynamic account. However, I do not share Ferrari's sense that we need to read away the two passages in which Socrates asserts that cities have the characters they do because of the characters of their citizens (435d–e, 544d–e). Socrates clearly believes this (otherwise, why would he suppose that the educational programme resulting in wise rulers and courageous guardians would make the city wise and courageous?) and clearly uses it to justify the city–soul analogy. Ferrari's acute observations of Socrates' elaboration of the analogy between city and soul rather than of the causal relations between them need to be taken into account. But I think I can do so and at the same time explain why Plato is writing in this way.
15. This view is taken by, for example, Vlastos 1977, p. 15; and Annas 1981, p. 179.
16. This view is taken by Popper 1962, p. 169; for Popper, this follows quite naturally from Plato's thinking of the state as a "superorganism" which is something over and above and superior to its citizens (pp. 79–81). Williams 1973, p. 197, reasons that just as a statue may be beautiful without its components being beautiful, so too a city may be happy without its citizens being happy.
17. In Kamtekar 2001 I suggested that the happiness of the city is the happiness of the citizens when the city's institutions are the cause of the citizens' happiness (pp. 205–06); similarly, Donald Morrison (2001) argues that the happiness of the city consists in the goodness of its structure, i.e., in its virtue, but that the goal of this structure is "to promote the greatest possible well-being of the individual citizens," with the result that the "maximal happiness of the city is ... definitionally dependent on the concept of the well-being of the citizens" and "the happiness of the city is ... causally dependent on the happiness of the

82   RACHANA KAMTEKAR

       citizens, because unless many of the citizens possess a considerable degree of
       virtue, the overall structure of the city will be unsound" (p. 7).

18. The *gar*, 420b8, is not translated by Grube–Reeve or Griffith, but is by Shorey
       and Reeve.

19. Benson 2006 argues that dialectic (by which he means Plato's preferred
       method of investigation in any work) in the *Republic* (as in the *Phaedo* and
       Meno) is a two-stage process in which a hypothesis is introduced, its conse-
       quences worked out, and then the hypothesis itself is justified. According to
       Benson, Socrates only practices the first of these two stages in the *Republic*, but
       this is no reason to think that he is practicing *dianoia*, for two features of
       dianoia distinguish it from the first stage of dialectic: it uses sense-experience
       when dealing with hypotheses and supposes these hypotheses to be confirmed –
       whereas dialectic does neither (pp. 96, 98). But notice that the sun is very much
       a sensible image for the Good itself, and I would venture that the city is a
       sensible image for the soul. As for treating hypotheses as in need of confirma-
       tion or already confirmed, that seems to me to be up to the individuals doing
       the investigation – if it characterizes the practice itself, then both the first stage
       of dialectic and *dianoia* have the same deficiency, of not having justified their
       hypotheses by going all the way back to the unhypothetical first principle.

20. For comments on previous drafts, I am grateful to audiences at the Arizona Ancient
       Philosophy Colloquium and the University of Chicago Ancient Philosophy
       Workshop, and especially to Eric Brown, commentator extraordinaire.

CHAPTER 5

Return to the cave

Nicholas D. Smith

I. INTRODUCTION TO THE PROBLEM

In the beginning of Book 2 of the *Republic*, Glaucon challenges Socrates to show that it is "better in every way"[1] to be just than unjust (2, 357b1–2). Socrates responds to the challenge by telling Glaucon, "I want truly to convince you ... if I can" (2, 357b3). Later in the *Republic*, however, it appears that those who should be the best qualified to realize that justice is always preferable – the philosophers of the *kallipolis* – find themselves in a situation in which they do *not* prefer to be just. Once they have "seen" the Form of the Good, they reach a point where, Socrates tells Glaucon, they are "unwilling to occupy themselves with human affairs" (7, 517c8–9). And yet, occupying themselves with human affairs is precisely what they *must* do, as their training has always ultimately been aimed at preparing them for their role in the state as leaders:

It is our task as founders, then, to compel the best natures to reach the study we said before is the most important, namely, to make the ascent and see the good. But when they've made it and looked sufficiently, we mustn't allow them to do what they are allowed to do today.

What's that?

To stay there and refuse to go down again to the prisoners in the cave and share their labors and honors, whether they are of less worth or of greater. (7, 519c8–d7)

Glaucon is disturbed by the sacrifice this appears to require: "Then are we to do them an injustice by making them live a worse life when they could live a better one?" (7, 519d8–9). Socrates' reply to Glaucon appears actually to confirm Glaucon's worry:

You are forgetting again that it isn't the law's concern to make any one class in the city outstandingly happy but to contrive to spread happiness throughout the city by bringing the citizens into harmony with each other through persuasion or compulsion and by making them share with each other the benefits that each class can

84   NICHOLAS D. SMITH

confer on the community. The law produces such people in the city, not in order to allow them to turn in whatever direction they want, but to make use of them to bind the city together.

That's true, I had forgotten. (7, 519e1–520a5; see also 4, 419a1–420c4, 5, 465e4–466c5)

The problem I address in this essay, sometimes called "the happy philosopher problem,"[2] is, then, that one of the main arguments of the *Republic* was supposed to show that justice is always preferable to injustice, for the agent, whereas doing what is just is *not* preferable to those who must return to the cave,[3] who would be happier shirking their duties and remaining uninvolved with the dirty business of politics. So it appears that, in the case of the returners, Plato provides a counterexample to his claim that justice is invariably preferable to injustice.[4]

I will attempt to solve this famous problem by trying to become clear, first, about what conditions are required for a solution to count as successful.

II. CONDITIONS FOR A SATISFACTORY SOLUTION TO THE PROBLEM

The problem for the returners seems to be that the prospect of returning to the cave is, to say the least, not an attractive one. Indeed, it is central to their qualifications for political office in Plato's *kallipolis* that they regard the life to which they are being compelled to return with utter disdain:

Can you name any life that despises political rule besides that of the true philosopher?
No, by god, I can't.
But surely it is those who are not lovers of ruling who must rule, for if they don't, the lovers of it, who are rivals, will fight over it.
Of course.
Then whom will you compel to become guardians of the city, if not those who have the best understanding of what matters for good government and who have other honors than political ones, and a better life as well?
No one. (7, 521b1–11; see also 1, 346e3–347d8)

Our first condition, then, requires suitable recognition of this claim:

(C1) The returners despise the life they are to be compelled into, and have a better life outside the cave.

Their dislike for politics would not create a problem for Plato and his interpreters, were it not for the fact that Plato earlier had Socrates accept

Return to the cave 85

Glaucon's challenge to defend justice as always preferable to injustice, so let us stipulate Socrates' response to Glaucon's challenge as the next condition that a successful solution must meet:

(C2) Being just and acting justly are always preferable to being unjust or acting unjustly.

Let us recall, moreover, what Plato means by "being just and acting justly," on the basis of which account Glaucon agrees that the challenge he presented to Socrates in Book 2 is met:

In truth justice is, it seems, something of this sort. However, it isn't concerned with someone's doing his own externally, but with what is inside him, and what is truly himself and his own. One who is just does not allow any part of himself to do the work of another part or allow the various classes within him to meddle with each other. He regulates well what is really his own and rules himself. He puts himself in order, is his own friend, and harmonizes the three parts of himself like three limiting notes on a musical scale – high, low, and middle. He binds together those parts and any others there may be in between, and from having been many things he becomes entirely one, moderate and harmonious. Only then does he act. And when he does anything, whether acquiring wealth, taking care of his body, engaging in politics, or in private contracts – in all of these, he believes that the action is just and fine that preserves this inner harmony and helps achieve it, and calls it so, and regards as wisdom the knowledge that oversees such actions. And he believes that the action that destroys this harmony is unjust, and calls it so, and regards the belief that oversees it as ignorance. (4, 443c9–444a2)

It is clear, then, that what makes acting justly always choiceworthy is that it "preserves this inner harmony and helps achieve it." It does not follow, however, that acting justly must be preferable for its own sake, but rather, for the sake of what *is* always preferable for its own sake, namely psychic harmony. In some cases, a just agent may have some grounds for preferring not to do what justice requires; however, the fact that an action creates or preserves psychic harmony will trump any other considerations.

While this account of "being just and acting justly" may be compatible with other accounts in various applications (as Plato has Socrates note explicitly at 442d10–443a10), it is *this* account of "being just and acting justly" that must be applied in relation to the justice of the return to the cave:

(C3) "Being just" = being in a condition of psychic harmony, and "acting justly" = acting in such a way as to create or preserve psychic harmony; "being unjust" = being in a condition of psychic *dis*harmony, and "acting unjustly" = acting in such a way as to prevent or destroy psychic harmony.

86 NICHOLAS D. SMITH

Now, Plato sees no requirement to "return to the cave" for those who were not educated by the state (7, 520a9–c3; see also 6, 496a10–e2), so there is no fully general requirement that those who study philosophy must always or everywhere toil in the labors of ruling "in the caves" of wherever they may happen to live. However, those raised and educated in the *kallipolis* are required to return to the cave, and the mandate that they return to the cave is one that is *just* (see 7, 520e1: "We will be giving just orders to just people"). Let us separate these into separate two conditions. First:

(C4) It is just (= creates or preserves psychic harmony) to require the returners to return to the cave.

At this point, there are some questions we should want answered. First, we should ask *for whom* the requirement is just: Is the justice of the command to be associated with the creation or preservation of psychic harmony in those giving the command, in those being commanded, or both? Now, perhaps there are cases in which we might imagine that A could justly command B to do something, but it would not be just for B to do what is commanded, but I think there are good reasons to set this particular worry aside here.[5] At the origin of the state, those issuing the command will be the original law-givers of the *kallipolis* – and these, we may infer from Socrates' persistent use of the first-person plural throughout this passage, include at least Socrates and Glaucon. It may well be that they would promote justice in their souls by making such a command, but I do not think we need to insist that Socrates or Glaucon here are claiming or implying that they have already fully achieved psychic harmony. Once the state has been created, subsequent generations of returners will be given the command by their elders, who will themselves be just people. More likely Plato's intent was for us to see that the justice of the command would apply to the returners themselves, whether at the origin of the state, or in later generations. It seems plain that Plato's whole point is that, as just people, they cannot refuse to do as they are commanded. In other words, because

(C5) The returners are just people (= are psychically harmonious),

they cannot refuse to return to the cave. But *why* can they not refuse? As I said above, it is not that ruling *as such* is a requirement of people like the returners, for justice does not require people like them to rule in unjust cities or in any in which they did not have the same debts as those they bear in the *kallipolis*. But in the *kallipolis*, because of the way in which the city has supported and educated them (see the explanation given at 520a6–c6),

Return to the cave 87

(C6) It is just (= it will sustain their psychic harmony)[6] for the returners to return to the cave, and would be unjust for them not to return.

It follows from **C2** and **C6** that returning to the cave is actually *preferable* for the returners, all things considered. Were *failing* to return to the cave actually preferable, all things considered, then the problem of the returners could have no solution – for it would simply be true that the injustice of failing to return would thereby be proven to be preferable to the justice of returning, and Plato would have provided a counterexample to his defense of justice. Hence, we may now add this as a condition for our solution:

(C7) It is preferable for the returners to return to the cave.

Now, as Plato makes Socrates and Glaucon say quite explicitly, the preferability of the returners' returning to the cave is *not at all* grounded in conceiving of ruling itself as something good. Whatever it is that *makes* returning preferable, for the returners, nonetheless – because preferability had all along been stipulated to be measurable only in terms of conduciveness to *eudaimonia* ("happiness"; see *Rep.* 1. 354c3) – it must be that the returners will be happier, as a result of returning to the cave, than they would be if they refused to return.

(C8) Those returning to the cave will be happier as a result, and would be less happy if they refused to return.

But **C7** and **C8** seem inconsistent with **C1**. Any solution to the problem of the returners, then, will need to explain how these three conditions are actually all consistent.

In addition, the conception and defense of justice Plato has already had Socrates provide makes it clear why returning is preferable (in terms of happiness) for the returners.

(C9) Those returning to the cave will do so *because* they are just (= psychically harmonious) and *because* they will be acting justly (= preserving their psychic harmony), and conversely, were those returning to the cave to fail to do so, they would not be just (= psychically harmonious) and would be acting unjustly (= failing to preserve their psychic harmony).

So already we can now clearly identify one of the most difficult problems associated with the returners: On the one hand, Plato makes it plain that we should regard returning to the cave, for those compelled to do so, as something just. Hence, for them to refuse would be *unjust*. In the account of psychic justice given in Book 4, injustice must be the result of psychic imbalance, but it is anything but clear how refusing to return to the cave

NICHOLAS D. SMITH

would indicate an imbalance in the abdicators' souls – for plainly their preference for intellectual over political pursuits could not plausibly be characterized as the product of an overthrow of reason's rule by spirit or appetite.[7] In the remainder of this essay, I shall call this the "psychic disharmony problem."

Moreover, we can now see clearly what I regard as the other great puzzle of the problem, for Plato gives us many reasons for thinking that those who are to return to the cave *have to be compelled*[8] to do so, and so must fail on their own to recognize that it is preferable for them to rule. It makes no sense to speak so often of compulsion if those being compelled are already independently fully motivated to do what they are compelled to do.[9] So, some explanation of this is also required:

(C10) Those compelled (or persuaded) to return to the cave must be compelled (or persuaded) to do so, and would not be inclined to return to the cave without the compulsion or persuasion.

From **C10**, it plainly follows that those compelled to return to the cave are not immediately aware of, or immediately motivated by, the reasons why it is preferable for them to return to the cave – until these reasons are given to them (see "*eroumen*" at 520a9).[10] This, again, is a most puzzling feature of the problem: How could Plato's philosophers miss this? In the remainder of this essay, I shall call this the "epistemic fault problem." [11] I think, in brief, that the so-called "happy philosopher problem" is simply the conjunction of the psychic disharmony problem and the epistemic fault problem; solve both of these problems, and one will have solved the "happy philosopher problem" once and for all.

III. A BRIEF SURVEY OF SOLUTIONS PROPOSED

Perhaps the easiest way to remove a problem is simply to eliminate or modify one of the conditions that create the problem. In my view, every one of the solutions scholars have proposed uses some version of this strategy – and the authors of such solutions might well complain that I have simply begged the question against their solutions already, by listing as conditions of adequacy for a successful solution one or more claims that their solution rejects. But I suppose it is already plain from what I have said so far that all of the conditions (**C1** through **C10**) that I have given above are evident in the text we are seeking to understand, and therefore that any interpretation that denies Plato's commitment to these claims is the worse for that denial. At the very least, then, the fact that an interpretation makes such a denial creates some awkwardness – some degree of implausibility – for that interpretation. In the end, some degree of such awkwardness and implausibility may be inevitable – it is possible that Plato's own attention to what we come to regard as a problem in his text was less than perfect, or that Plato's position was not as well worked-out (or consistent) as we would like it to be. I will eventually contend, however, that no such awkwardness or implausibility is required in an adequate interpretation of this issue. For now, I intend merely to sketch how the interpretations that have been offered on this problem do create the kind of awkwardness and implausibility I am talking about.

Perhaps the most popular and influential accounts of the problem have sought to resolve it by denying C8, which stipulates that the returners must actually be happier as a result of returning. There have been several versions of this sort of approach, but all of them share the feature of insisting that the young philosophers' exposure to the Form of the Good has created a change to their motivation such that they are now ready to value justice or goodness in a way that is independent of their own happiness.[12] It is certainly awkward for this sort of interpretation that – even after having supposedly abandoned the tight linkage between justice and happiness for the philosophers – Plato manages to reaffirm this exact linkage again at the very end of the *Republic*, by having Socrates assert clearly that "This is the way that a human being becomes happiest (*eudaimonestatos*)" (10, 619a7–b1; see also 9, 580b5–c4). At any rate, supposing the philosophers to abandon their eudaimonistic egoism this seems to me no solution at all to our problem, for if Plato really does concede that – however well motivated by a knowledge of the Good itself – the philosophers of the *kallipolis* really would be personally better off or happier refusing to rule than in ruling, then he has condemned his defense of justice to the dustbin (and with it, our appreciation for how Plato had seemed to answer what has sometimes been called the "ultimate question" of ethics: "Why should I be moral?"), for in fact, it would appear, were these interpretations correct, that there is actually no assurance that the requirements of justice (or morality), if accepted, will lead to the best possible life, measured in the happiness of the moral agent.

Now, most of the critics of the approaches that require the returners to shift away from egoism have labored to provide reasons for defending the very claim the other scholars have denied – again, C8, according to which the returners will actually be better off (in terms of happiness) because they rule. Quite a number of accounts of how this is supposed to work have been offered, and I will here provide just a sampling of interpretations of this sort. It has been suggested, for example, that the philosophers' *erōs* will make them realize that they cannot be truly fulfilled without leaving behind images of the good and beauty they love, in the form of just political institutions.[13] Others have insisted that life in the *kallipolis* itself is so rewarding to the returners that they would scarcely neglect their duties to the state that provides them with such benefits – especially when such benefits are only possible if, indeed, philosophers rule the state.[14] Still others have supposed that the returners can only achieve their goal of comprehending the good by returning to the cave.[15] Yet others have argued that a life of pure contemplation would be humanly impossible for abdicators anyway, because of the requirements of their humanity, with its tripartite psychology and various needs.[16] One recent argument makes a very plausible case that Plato believes that concern for others is inherently a feature of concern for self, from which it would seem to follow that the returners are better off ruling than abdicating because in abdicating they would damage their self-interest via damaging their interests in others with whom they are significantly connected.[17]

All views of this general sort only manage to underscore the difficulty of what I have called the "epistemic fault problem," however, because if any of these reasons why it really is in the returners' interest to rule are correct, then it becomes even more puzzling that *we* can manage to perceive their correctness, but the returners themselves manage at least initially to misjudge or fail to recognize their own interest. If we are to maintain **C8** as a criterion of adequacy for any interpretation, of course, it must actually be in the returners' interest to return to the cave. But in their enthusiasm to explain the returners' interests, scholars have generally neglected the problem that their perceptions of the returners' interests does not match the returners' own perceptions of that interest. Without this aspect of the problem addressed, therefore, we have no adequate solution.

Moreover, it is a puzzling feature of all of these approaches to explicating the returners' benefits that they manage to lend support to the claim that the returners will benefit from their return (condition **C8**) in ways that make no connection at all to Plato's actual defense of justice in response to Glaucon's challenge in Book 2, as something good *in itself*, rather than for its consequences, which intrinsic goodness Plato plainly explains in terms of psychic harmony (**C9**).[18] Whatever other beneficial consequences the returners may enjoy as a result of their return, the psychic disharmony problem must be addressed. For even if we suppose that the returners would sacrifice some benefits by refusing to return, these accounts all fail to explain why the loss of such benefits would be psychically destructive to them.

Now, some few interpreters have actually been more sensitive to the psychic disharmony problem, and have attempted to resolve it by recalling the connection Plato has Socrates make between the psychic conception of justice he has explicated, and what he calls the "ordinary cases" generally regarded as unjust (at 4, 442d10–443b3). Taking a hypothetical refusal to return to the cave as an instance of "ordinary" injustice (which has come to be called "vulgar injustice" in the literature),[19] scholars have insisted that such a refusal *has to be* destructive to the returners' psychic harmony.[20] But, as the main proponent of this approach notes, the text actually does not supply any clear explication of how this general connection might apply to the specific case of the reluctant returner:

Plato never explicitly *argues* for either the claim that psychological justice requires social justice or the claim that psychological justice requires vulgar justice. It is sufficient, however, for the resolution of the paradox being advanced here [sc. the "happy philosopher problem"] that Plato have only *asserted* the necessity of either social justice or vulgar justice (or both) to the maintenance of psychological justice. It is beyond dispute that Plato does at least assert that each is necessary for the maintenance of psychological justice (441E1–2 and 442D10–443B2, respectively). (Brickhouse 1998, p. 147)

But even if we accept Brickhouse's assertion about Plato's assertions, there is something at best unsatisfying here. For if we find we are at a loss as to precisely how Plato's assertions apply to the specific case of the reluctant returner, we may yet find we have reason to think the problem is not (yet) solved. This worry becomes worse still if we actually suspect, as some have, that the specific connection Brickhouse makes here actually *cannot* be made in the way Plato's psychological account requires.[21]

IV. RETURNING TO THE PROBLEM OF RETURNING TO THE CAVE

The above survey of proposed solutions suffices to show that what I have called the "psychic disharmony" and "epistemic fault" problems remain unresolved. I do not dispute that Brickhouse is correct to insist that anything that Plato is willing to count as a genuine instance of injustice in the social (or vulgar) realm must, if he is to be consistent, also be a case that *can* be accounted for in terms of damage to (or obstruction of) psychic harmony. It is also true that, in explicating the injustice that would be done in a refusal to return to the cave, Plato does not explicitly provide the account that is needed. Instead, he explains the justice of the compulsion to return to the cave in terms of what the city has bestowed upon the returners, particularly in providing them the education they have enjoyed. Since the text does not provide explicitly the required psychological account, if an account can be provided at all, it must be pieced together on the basis of whatever Plato does tell us that might help. It turns out that Plato provides ample assistance, in fact, even if he does not explicitly supply the necessary account itself.

When Plato discusses injustice as psychic disharmony in Book 4, the account requires that each part of the soul must "do its own," and no part may "do the work of another part or allow the various classes within him to meddle with each other" (4, 443d1–3). Were the returner to refuse to return to the cave, Plato makes clear, it would be because he or she prefers intellectual to practical or political activities. So if there is to be psychic imbalance indicated in or resulting from[22] refusing to return to the cave, it cannot be the result of the overthrow of reason by appetite or spirit – the kinds of cases that appear in the most common instances of injustice (those, that is, that Plato surveys as the "ordinary" ones). So we may assume that the sort of injustice the abdicator would commit – and hence, the sort of imbalance that would be indicated in or result from his or her refusal to return to the cave – is of an *extraordinary* sort. In this sense, then, I cannot wholly agree with those who seek to avoid the problem by appealing to the link between the psychological and ordinary (social or vulgar) conceptions of justice and injustice. Even so, if it is nonetheless an instance of imbalance, then it must be a case in which some part or parts of the soul are impeded in its (or their) proper function.

Now Plato actually identifies two distinct ways in which imbalance and disharmony can be created in a *state*. One of these ways is the political analogue to the overthrow of the rational part of the soul by one of the lower parts – where one of the classes of the state usurps the role appropriately performed by a different class (see 4, 434a3–d1). But another way in which imbalance and disharmony can be created in the state is actually indicated by the way Plato characterizes the effects of allowing the returners to abdicate: he says that to permit this would be a case in which they would fail, as lawgivers, to be making the whole city happy, by allowing a single part of the city outstanding or excessive happiness at the expense of the other parts (see 4, 420b5–421c6; 519e1–520a4). If we apply this to the psychic disharmony problem via the analogy of soul and state, then, we may assume that abdication would indicate (or result in) a condition of the soul in which the rational part was afforded an outstanding or excessive share of happiness at the expense of some other part or parts. When the good of the whole state is not taken into account, the form of rule becomes tyranny, and those ruled become "slaves" (5, 463b5). So, too, then, the sort of imbalance we may expect to find in an abdicator – or resulting from abdication – would be one in which the rational part's rule was not aristocratic and kingly, as Aristotle might put it, but tyrannical, and some other part (or parts) of the soul, rather than harmonized in a unity with the rational part, would be stymied and treated merely as slave(s) to the rational part.

So, in addition to the natural and appropriate desires of the rational part of the soul, the returner – to sustain the balance in his or her soul – must also take care to ensure that the natural and appropriate interests of the other parts of his or her soul are also taken care of. Now presumably the decision not to return to the cave would not result in the abdicator ceasing to be able to satisfy his natural and appropriate appetitive desires. Plato does indicate that those who could not or would not perform their duties in the state would no longer be supported by the state (see 3, 407c7–e2; 410a2–3), but even so, there is no reason to think that the abdicator would be incapable of finding adequate food or water elsewhere and by other means than having it provided by the state, and the same for any other appetitive requirements.

I take it as an indication of what function might be impeded, then, that Plato characterizes those who must return to the cave as having "other honors than political ones" that matter to them (*timas allas . . . tou politikou*; 7, 521b9–10). Plato does not go on to indicate precisely what these "other honors" might be – perhaps they are the honors appropriate to superiority in knowledge, to wisdom, or to virtue more generally – but we are reminded in this passage that it is not *merely* contemplation of the Good (or creating instantiations of goodness, for that matter) that matters to the whole soul of the returner. And one range of appropriate interests the returners' souls would continue to have would be those in which the desire for honor and aversion to shame are featured, namely the spirited part of the soul. In explaining why it is not acceptable for the returners to refuse to go back into the cave, Socrates stresses the reasons why it would be dishonorable – shameful – for them to refuse. Were they, then (again *per impossibile*), to abdicate, they would indicate or create a condition in their souls in which their rational part ceased to take into account the appropriate interests of another part: by acting in such a shameful way, they would afford excessive happiness to their rational parts only by starving and tyrannizing their spirited parts. Besotted with the joys of their recent contemplation, the returners are at first reluctant to consider any other way of life – especially one they recognize as having no interest in itself for them. But reminded of the details, the upshot of which is that they cannot honorably refuse the

94   NICHOLAS D. SMITH

requirement to rule, these "just men" will *necessarily* accede to the requirement, for they cannot and would not create the imbalance of tyranny in
their souls.

In Book 4, Plato characterizes the virtue of the spirited part of the soul to
consist in preserving "the declarations of reason about what is to be feared
and not feared" (4, 442c2–3). But we should not suppose that the relation of
spirit to reason is one of absolutely blind compliance, for recall that Plato
argued that the *kallipolis* would be courageous as a result of "a part of itself
that has the power to preserve through everything its belief about what
things are to be feared, namely, that they are the things and kinds of things
that the lawgiver declared to be such in the course of educating it" (4,
429b8–c2). Similarly, the returners have been educated in the *kallipolis* in
such a way as to be habituated to feel a strong "conviction that they must
always do what they believe to be best for the city" (3, 413c6–7), and to
internalize a feeling of shame at violating this norm (which, in other words,
would continue to apply even when one is unobserved by others). The
returners might well feel strongly a desire to remain rapt in contemplation
of the Forms, but when the unjust effect of following this impulse is made
clear to them, we can assume their spirited parts – thoroughly trained always
to do what is best for the city and to desist from anything contrary to that
aim – would resist the impulse to abdicate. Hence, an abdicator would have
to quell this resistance, while providing his or her spirited part no ground for
acquiescence.

If this account is at all plausible, it would appear to provide an appropriately psychological ground for the injustice of abdication. It would follow
that the returners actually do benefit – in psychic harmony and thus in
happiness – from returning to the cave. This account, moreover, does not
run afoul of Plato's description of the life of contemplation as a "better life"
than that of political engagement – for it would remain true that the
contemplative life would always remain preferable to the life of political
engagement all other things being equal. The problem for the returners is
that their debt to the state is such that continuing in rapt contemplation of
the Forms is temporarily not consistent with preserving their psychic
harmony. But when – as it was before they must return, and after they
have served their duty to the state – the contemplative life is compatible
with their psychic harmony, they will always prefer it to the life of political
engagement. This is why they *always* "go to rule as something compulsory"
(7, 520e2), even when they recognize that performing this service to the state
is the only way, in their circumstances, to remain psychically balanced and
happy. Just as no one relishes the prospect of going to the dentist, but

Return to the cave

regards doing so as necessary for one's health, so the returners go back into the cave, which they would never choose to do for any reason other than the preservation of the health of their souls.

Even if this is a plausible tale of why and how abdication would create psychic imbalance, however, it thrusts us squarely into what I have called the "epistemic fault" problem, because it would seem that the returners themselves should surely be able to recognize that refusing to do their duty in the state would be psychologically unbalancing. Now, one way we might hope to avoid the attribution of epistemic fault to the returners is to try to find a way to account for their reluctance that does not require them ever to err or miss that their own interests are best served by returning. But, as others have noted,[23] any such attempt does not seem adequately to confront Plato's emphasis on the fact that the returners must be *compelled*. As I said earlier (in discussing C10), it does not seem plausible to say both that one must be compelled to do something, and also to say that the person is already fully motivated to do what she is compelled to do. So, the compulsion put upon the returners seems to indicate an epistemic fault, for without that fault, they would not require compulsion – or even persuasion – for them to be fully motivated to do what they must.

To my knowledge, only two scholars[24] have insisted that the returners are not already philosopher-kings, and are also, therefore, not to be held to the same high epistemic standards as apply to the latter group. Here is how Brickhouse puts it:

If we read the entire passage, 519B–520E, however, it is clear that when the philosophers apprehend the Good, they do not immediately apprehend that they have an obligation to return to the cave. And there is no reason why they should. Simply because they have come to understand the form of the Good, there is no reason why they must have, thereby, understood all of the actions which doing the good requires. (Brickhouse 1998, p. 149)

Now scholars have disputed Brickhouse's assumption, in this argument, that the returners have actually already apprehended the Good. The returners, recall, have yet to complete the required fifteen years of experience as apprentice rulers (see 7, 539e2–540a4). Having completed all of the other phases of their education prior to apprenticing ("in the cave"), then, they are 35 years old, for they will take over as full-fledged rulers at age 50 (7, 540a4–5). According to Eric Brown, "the philosophers do not grasp the Form of the Good until the age of fifty" (Brown 2000, p. 1, n. 1; see also Reeve 1988, p. 195). The basis for this dissent from Brickhouse's view of the matter is what Plato says at 7, 540a4–b1:

96 NICHOLAS D. SMITH

Then, at the age of fifty, those who've survived the tests and been successful both in practical matters and in the sciences must be led to the goal and compelled to lift up the radiant light of their souls to what itself provides light for everything. And once they have seen the good itself, they must each in turn put the city, its citizens, and themselves in order, using it as their model.

Now, if Brown were right about this, we could explain the returners' epistemic fault quite easily, for it would be plain that the most important element of their philosophical education was still to come.[25] But one can understand this passage Brown's way only if we read it in isolation from what Plato said, earlier in Book 7, about the experience of the young philosophers outside the cave. For Plato had already made clear, in his summary of the activities of the ex-prisoner outside the cave, that a direct apprehension of the Good is the culminating experience one has in one's journey outside the cave:

This whole image, Glaucon, must be fitted together with what we said before. The visible realm should be likened to the prison dwelling, and the light of the fire inside it to the power of the sun. And if you interpret the upward journey and the study of things above as the upward journey of the soul to the intelligible realm, you'll grasp what I hope to convey, since that is what you wanted to hear about. Whether it's true or not, only the god knows. But this is how I see it: In the knowable realm, the Form of the Good is the last thing to be seen, and it is reached only with difficulty. Once one has seen it, however, one must conclude that it is the cause of all that is correct and beautiful in anything, that it produces both light and its source in the visible realm, and that in the intelligible realm it controls and provides truth and understanding, so that anyone who is to act sensibly in private or public must see it. (7, 517a8–c5)

The very next thing Plato has Socrates say after this, moreover, plainly blocks any possibility that he is referring to the mature philosopher-rulers in these lines:

Come, then, share with me this thought also: It isn't surprising that the ones who get to this point are unwilling (*ouk ethelousin*) to occupy themselves with human affairs and that their souls are always pressing upwards, eager to spend their time above, for, after all, this is surely what we would expect, if indeed things fit the image I described before. (7, 517c7–d2)

The mature philosopher will, of course, continue to treat ruling "not as if he were doing something fine, but rather something that has to be done" (7, 540b4–5). But they surely cannot correctly be said to be "unwilling to occupy themselves with human affairs," as Plato describes the philosophers here – for such unwillingness plainly convicts those who feel it of an epistemic fault. As Brickhouse rightly notes, once reminded of their obligation to the state, "any reluctance to rule vanishes" (Brickhouse 1998, p. 149).

So the explanation of the returners' epistemic fault cannot be that they have not yet completed their higher education or apprehended the Good. But Brickhouse contends, nonetheless, that their having done so should not be understood as immunizing them from error, on the ground that they have not yet been trained to recognize accurately all of the specific applications that follow from this apprehension. Although he does not provide much textual support for this understanding of the returners' condition in his article, compelling evidence for Brickhouse's view is easily found in Plato's descriptions of how the returners will function when they first find themselves engaged in judging the images of the Forms they apprehended earlier (that is, while outside the cave, in the realm of originals).

> What about what happens when someone turns from divine study to the evils of human life? Do you think it's surprising, since his sight is still dim, and he hasn't become accustomed to the darkness around him, that he behaves awkwardly and appears completely ridiculous if he's compelled, either in the courts or elsewhere, to contend about the shadows of justice or the statues of which they are the shadows and to dispute about the way these things are understood by people who have never seen justice itself? (7, 517d4–e2, see also 516e3–517a6; 518a1–b4; 520c2–6)

Until the returners become acclimatized to the dimness of the cave, Plato emphasizes, they will fare very poorly in the judging of the "shadows of justice" – so poorly, indeed, that those who remained in the cave would suppose their vision had actually been ruined by their time outside the cave. The time required for the complete habituation of the returners to the gloom of the cave, moreover, will be considerable – as we have seen, their apprenticeship under the watchful guidance of the mature philosopher-rulers will take fifteen years, and during all of this time they will continue to be tested (7, 539e5–540a2) – presumably, because they continue to be vulnerable to epistemic fault during the whole period of their apprenticeship.

Indeed, the very first instance of a "shadow of justice" that the returners encounter, after their upward journey, is the instantiation of justice consisting in their own return to the cave. Not surprisingly, their first reaction to this gloomy particular is that they are blind to its merits. They must be compelled (or persuaded) to do what is right in this instance (and many others like it) for several years to come, perhaps, precisely because they are, as yet, very poor at the task of seeing in the dark.

So it should now be obvious why I earlier insisted on calling those who must be compelled to return to the cave "returners," rather than simply "philosophers," since although the returners have completed their education in dialectic (and may thus rightly be called "philosophers") they remain educationally deficient and require another fifteen years of education and testing before they are able to rule – and require all of the additional time precisely because in the interim they are not immune to epistemic fault. Simply calling the returners "philosophers" tends to obscure the critical fact of the incomplete state of their education, relative to the mature philosophers who must rule the *kallipolis*. For similar reasons (and even more importantly), we should not conceive of the returners as "rulers,"[26] or "philosopher-kings," for they are many years yet from having the qualifications requisite for this role.

V. SUMMARY AND CONCLUSION

The so-called "happy philosopher problem," I have argued, consists in two related problems, which I have called the psychic disharmony problem – according to which it did not seem possible to explain the injustice of abdication by the returner in terms of psychic disharmony – and the epistemic fault problem, which consisted in the puzzle that returning to the cave must be beneficial to the returner, according to Plato's defense of justice, but the returners seem either unaware of that benefit, or inclined actually to misjudge it altogether. I have attempted herein first to explain the textual grounds for these problems, and then to show how and why other discussions of the "happy philosopher problem" have failed to provide fully adequate solutions to the problem, generally because the solutions they offered failed to dissolve either the psychic disharmony problem or the epistemic fault problem, or both. I concluded with my own account of how refusing to return to the cave would be psychically unbalancing, and also of how the incomplete education of the returners could be used to explain their epistemic defects. If I am right, the solution I have given to the two foundational problems of the returners' reluctance provides a complete solution to the "happy philosopher problem."[27]

NOTES

1. Unless otherwise noted, all translations are those of G. M. A. Grube revised by C. D. C. Reeve, from Cooper 1997b. Citations are from the Oxford Classical Text.
2. From the title of Aronson 1972. For reasons that will become apparent later in my discussion, I actually find this name misleading (see next note).

Return to the cave

99

3. For the sake of brevity – and so as not to beg against myself one of the most important questions I seek to answer in my argument – I will henceforth call those who are compelled to return to the cave the "returners," and those who (*per impossibile*, Plato claims – *adunaton*; 7, 520d1) refuse to return as "abdicators."

4. According to some scholars, this is all there is to be said, as Plato gives us this counterexample precisely to emphasize that the philosophical life is incompatible with the political life, and so the problem cannot be solved in the way I propose to do herein. For examples of this view, see Brann 2004, pp. 134–35; Bloom 1968, pp. 407–10; Sallis 1975, pp. 379–80; Saxonhouse 1978; Strauss 1964, pp. 124, 127. Similar views seem to be expressed more briefly in Guthrie 1975, p. 502; Randall 1970, pp. 162–70; Wolin 1960, p. 42. Klosko 1981, p. 370, at first seems to concede that the returners will have to sacrifice some happiness in returning to the cave, but then indicates a reason why they would benefit from doing so (see n. 13, below). Although he rejects the explanation that Plato deliberately undercut his seeming endorsement of the *kallipolis* in this way, Morrison 2007 similarly seems to think that the problem of the returners is insoluble: "the great messy hairball of the issue that is the philosopher's return to the cave has no clear resolution without importing a great deal that is not explicit in the text, so any answer that is put forward by its advocates is speculative" (pp. 242–43).

5. In criticisms of an earlier draft of this essay, Eric Brown cautioned me that I needed to take this concern more seriously. I have tried at least to address the concern more clearly herein, but doubt that Brown will find my treatment wholly adequate.

6. Because of C5, it cannot be that the returning will *create* psychic harmony in their souls, as they have already achieved that condition.

7. Some scholars have regarded this problem as so deadly as to prove that the justice of the return to the cave (and the injustice of a refusal to do so) simply cannot be accounted for via Plato's account of psychic justice. See, e.g., Brown 2000, p. 12: "Plato's account of psychic injustice cannot explain any unjust abdication by a philosopher."

8. There has been some debate among scholars as to whether it is compulsion or only persuasion that must be used to get the returners to return to the cave: see, e.g., Brown 2000; Irwin 1995, p. 299; Kraut 1973 and 1991, pp. 46–47; Mara 1983 (esp. p. 608); Reeve 1988, p. 203; Taft 1982; Vernezze 1998; Wagner 2005. I will not herein engage that particular controversy. On the one hand, Plato manages to use the language of *anankē* some eleven times in describing the reaction to ruling of those best suited to rule: 1, 347c1, 1, 347c3, 1, 347d1, 5, 473d4, 6, 500d4, 7, 519e4, 7, 520a8, 7, 520e2, 7, 521b7, 7, 539e3, 7, 540b5, which seems to underscore that the returners themselves would be inclined to resist the return itself. (I am indebted to Eric Brown and Rachel Singpurwalla for help in compiling this list of passages.) On the other hand, even if we suppose that all the philosophers require is more like persuasion than force, the problem remains: If ruling really is preferable for the returners, why don't they seem to

100   NICHOLAS D. SMITH

recognize this fact? It would seem that those with the utmost knowledge possible for human beings would need *neither* compulsion nor persuasion to be motivated to do what is most preferable for them to do.

9. Of course, one may in fact be compelled to do something one is independently motivated to do – someone might lock me into a room in which I am independently motivated to remain, for example. But were those returning to the cave already fully motivated to do so, Plato's eleven references to compulsion would be rhetorically gratuitous.

10. Even if we assume that the requirement to return to the cave does not become just until the moment it is announced to the returners, it is plain in the text that the justice of the requirement must be explained to the returners. Hence, they must not initially understand or appreciate the justice of the requirement. It seems likely, however, that the returners would have known for some time why they were being trained and what they could expect after each phase of that training was completed.

11. I call the problem one of epistemic fault, because it would appear to require either an error or an oversight on the part of those who are supposed to be immune from either. For various descriptions of this problem, see Aronson 1972, p. 394; Brickhouse 1998, p. 152 n. 11; Dobbs 1985, p. 816; Mara 1983, p. 609.

12. For examples of this sort of approach, see Adkins 1960, pp. 290–92; Annas 1981, pp. 266–71; Aronson 1972; Bloom 1968, pp. 407–08; Cooper 1997a, p. 147; Foster 1936; Kraut 1973 (Kraut revises this aspect of his view in Kraut 1991 and 1992); Miller 1985; Parry 1996, esp. ch. 4; Schofield 2007, p. 152; Waterlow 1972–73, p. 35; and White 1986 and 2002, p. 210. This general approach has been adequately critiqued, in my view, by several critics. See especially Brickhouse 1998 (esp. p. 152 n. 11) and Brown 2000.

13. Vernezze 1998. Similar views are suggested in Dahl 1991, pp. 827–29; Gosling 1973, pp. 70–71; Irwin 1977, p. 237; Kahn 1987, pp. 95–96; Kayser 1970, p. 265; Klosko 1981; Kraut, 1973, 1991, and 1992; Mahoney 1992. Hatzistavrou 2006 finds in the rulers "a strong desire to benefit the city" (p. 110) which would be frustrated by a life of pure contemplation.

14. Cross and Woozley 1964, p. 101; Davies 1968; Hall 1977; Mara 1983; Nettleship 1901, p. 263; Reeve 1988, pp. 202–03; Sedley 2007. One weakness in this sort of approach is that while it may explain why the philosophers should be interested in making sure that *some* philosophers rule, it does not show why a single philosopher opting out of ruling wouldn't be happier as a result. Sedley attempts to resolve this problem by imagining the rulers' agreeing to take turns to rule as a "rational settlement they come to among themselves" (2007, p. 281), which would have the desired result that all rule, but which does not seem to me adequate to explain away the problem of the "free rider." In some versions of this view, arguments are offered for why even a single philosopher's refusal to rule would result in the destruction of the state – for an example of this sort of view, see Beatty 1976b, though see the next note. Contra Beatty, see White 1986, p. 25.

Return to the cave

15. Beatty 1976a, 1976b; Dobbs 1985. One problem unique to this proposed solution is that it appears to contradict Plato's characterization of the returners as having *already* completed the ascent and "seen" the good itself (at 7, 519c8–d1).

16. See, e.g., Adam 1963, vol. 2, note on 520c14; Davies 1968, pp. 125–26; Murphy 1951, pp. 53–54, n. 2; Reeve 1988, p. 203. As Brown has argued, however, this view "sets up a false dilemma between the life of a philosopher-ruler and the life of pure contemplation; left out of the middle is the active philosophical life outside of political office, which would take full account of our tripartite nature" as well as all others related to our mortal, human nature (Brown 2000, p. 7). I will not deny that a life of pure contemplation is possible for a human being, though neither am I committed to this being a possibility. I will affirm, however, that the requirements of psychic harmony require the returner to return. One worry about this sort of account, however, is that Plato thinks that it is possible to be a genuine philosopher in conditions other than the *kallipolis* (see 6, 496a10–e2 and 7, 520a9–c3); so even if a life of pure contemplation might not be possible for an abdicator, a philosophical life would still seem to be possible.

17. Singpurwalla 2006. Singpurwalla does not directly apply her account of interest in others to the case of the returners, and so my application of her view to this particular case is my own. I believe it is implied by her view, however.

18. Others have also made this same criticism. See Aronson 1972, p. 397; Brown 2000, p. 4; Irwin 1995, p. 300; Kraut 1991, pp. 50–51.

19. Following Sachs 1963 and the many responses to the original publication of that paper subsequently published.

20. For an example of this sort of approach see especially Brickhouse 1998, following responses to Sachs 1963 by Demos 1964, Kahn 1972, and Vlastos 1981a. A more recent insistence that the justice of the return must be understood in terms of psychic harmony is given in Sedley 2007, pp. 278–79.

21. As, for example, Brown claims (Brown 2000, p. 12).

22. I have yet to address the epistemic fault problem. If it is an error in judgment that the abdicator must make, to refuse to return, it does not follow that the refusal would *be the result* of imbalance in the soul, for Plato's theory does not require that balance in the soul is a sufficient condition for moral infallibility. However, if wrong action must either cause or be the product of psychic imbalance, then we can assume that even if the refusal is the product of an innocent error of judgment, the effect of the refusal would be damage to the balance of the abdicator's soul.

23. Brown 2000, pp. 5–7.

24. Brickhouse 1998 and Dobbs 1985.

25. Brown himself would not solve the epistemic fault problem in this way, however, as he sees no distinction between the motivations of the philosophers at any stage of their educational development (see Brown 2000, p. 1 n. 1).

26. As, for example, in White 1986.
27. I am indebted to several friends for criticisms of various earlier drafts of this essay: (in alphabetical order) Thomas Brickhouse, Eric Brown, Zina Giannopoulou, Joel Martinez, and Rachel Singpurwalla. All errors that remain are likely the result of my failure to accommodate adequately some criticism one or more of the above has already made of my arguments.

CHAPTER 6

Degenerate regimes in Plato's Republic

Zena Hitz

I. THE CRITIQUE OF INJUSTICE IN THE *REPUBLIC*

This essay concerns the negative end of the political argument of the *Republic*, that injustice – the rule of unreason – is both widespread and undesirable, and that whatever shadows of virtue or order might be found in its midst are corrupt and unstable. This claim is explained in detail in *Republic* 8 and 9. These passages explain recognizable faults in recognizable regimes in terms of the failure of the rule of reason and the corresponding success of the rule of non-rational forms of motivation. I will first look at degenerate regimes as they appear in a less systematic way in the Ship of State passage in *Republic* 6 and in the discussion with Thrasymachus in Book 1. I will then give a general overview of the system of degenerate regimes in Book 8 to examine what exactly goes wrong with them and why, and will explain how the process of degeneration ought be understood as the progressive decay of the rule of reason. Finally, I will argue that a close look at this decay reveals something surprising: that degenerate regimes and characters feature weak versions of virtue, shadow-virtues that are based on appearances and held in place by force. Thus in the end the whole process of degeneration ought be understood as an extended conflict between reason and appetite.

However, since the negative or critical political philosophy of the *Republic* is a relatively neglected topic, it will be useful to begin by sketching its place within its historical context and in the context of the broad political outlook of the *Republic*. Plato grew up in a world riven by violent conflict between supporters of democracy and supporters of oligarchy. Thucydides describes the civil wars instigated all over Greece by Athens and Sparta during the Peloponnesian War and the enormous toll they took both in lives and in civic health.[1] The conflict came home to Athens in the Spartan-sponsored oligarchic coup of 404, when Plato was 23.[2] The band of oligarchs, known as the "Thirty Tyrants," included Plato's relatives Critias and Charmides. The execution of Socrates in 399 after the restoration of democracy is widely thought to be a response to the excesses of the Thirty.[3]

103

The political turmoil of the late fifth and early fourth centuries clearly lies in the background of Plato's *Republic*, taking place as it does in a household destroyed by the Thirty, and featuring in its most famous image – the Cave – a philosopher executed by the majority.[4] Toward the end of the *Republic*, as a lead-up to Socrates' final argument that the just life is superior to the unjust life, Socrates describes a degenerating series of characters and regimes parallel to those characters. The just city they have described makes an error in its marriage ritual, and begins a decline first into a Spartan-style timocracy,[5] then an oligarchy, then a democracy, and finally a tyranny. These regimes are characterized by division, violent conflict, and instability. In light of the dramatic and historical background of the *Republic*, it is natural to think that in these passages Plato means to diagnose and explain the historical conditions of his youth.[6]

What kind of diagnosis of bad politics is the *Republic*? So far as philosophizing about politics goes, it is a very puzzling piece of work. It praises a certain form of political community as best, and describes its educational system in great detail, while saying little about its governing institutions.[7] Furthermore, the just city is not defended against alternatives in the way we might expect. No democrat appears on the dramatic scene of the dialogue to object (as we might well want to object) that the rulers of Kallipolis are not bound by law, or that people ought not to be educated from a single perspective, but rather exposed to a variety of points of view. The great opponent of Socrates in the dialogue, Thrasymachus, is practically silent while the just city is under construction; he speaks up only once, to agree with the other interlocutors that the community of women and children needs more explanation (450a). The interlocutors are so agreeable that one can readily sympathize with the great Neoplatonic commentator Proclus, who reportedly removed the *Republic* from his Platonic curriculum in part since it was "not written in dialogue form."[8]

Likewise, the alternatives to Kallipolis – timocracy, oligarchy, democracy, and tyranny – are presented as instances of evil (*kakia*; 445c) and as aberrations (*hēmartēmena*; 544a) without protest. Their names are mostly conventional, but their general character and their putative overarching goals seem to have little or no basis in history.[9] Aristotle, in his careful catalog of regime-changes in *Politics* 5, releases a battery of historical counterexamples to *Republic* 8: democracies that have changed into oligarchies, oligarchies that have changed into tyrannies, oligarchies with different laws and defining principles (1316a20–b14). He furthermore complains that while the causes of political change are numerous, Socrates has spoken as if there were only one per regime; and that indeed there are many forms

Degenerate regimes in Plato's Republic

of democracy and oligarchy, not just one as presented in the *Republic* (1316b15–27).

Given these difficulties, it is understandable that the political theory of the *Republic* is often dismissed *tout court* by commentators.[10] They point out – correctly – that the main argument of the *Republic* is about the choice of lives for individuals. The just regime and the bad regimes are explicitly constructed to clarify the argument that a just life for an individual is superior to an unjust one (368c–369a; 445a–d; 544a). Accordingly, it might well seem justified to focus, as the existing literature on *Republic* 8 and 9 has overwhelmingly done, on the individual character-types described in those sections rather than the regimes.[11]

That said, to dismiss the political theory of the *Republic* – either the positive view of political justice shown in the construction of Kallipolis or the critical remarks on bad regimes in Books 8 and 9 – is a mistake. While the individual choice of lives is more fundamental to the argument of the dialogue, the discussions of politics are important in their own right.[12] What has caused confusion is a lack of recognition of the distinctive type of political theory that the *Republic* presents. Unlike the *Laws* or Aristotle's *Politics*, it is not a practical guide for legislators and politicians to make improvements in their cities in a variety of circumstances.[13] The *Republic* is not concerned with practical politics, any more than it is concerned with practical morality. The choice of lives is a matter of the choice of a standard. So too the political theory of the *Republic* concerns *political standards*: the ultimate goals around which cities and governments are organized. Roughly speaking, these standards are two, corresponding to the ultimate standards guiding the choice of lives for individuals: the rule of reason and the rule of appetite.[14]

Why are political standards important? According to the political philosophy presented in the *Republic* and the *Laws*, one's political standard ultimately determines the practical choices one makes about political institutions and laws. The decisions about laws and institutions made while constructing Kallipolis are made with an eye to the production of justice. In the *Laws*, a primary concern for the rule of reason determines both institutional structure and specific laws in the hypothetical new colony.[15] Likewise, in the degenerate regimes of the *Republic*, it is the misguided pursuit of a faulty ultimate standard that drives poor choices about political institutions and laws – as for instance when the pursuit of wealth in oligarchy leads the leadership to permit by law the selling all of one's possessions (552a, 555c). Furthermore, knowledge of the correct standard is valuable in its own right – as a means of evaluating existing institutions, as a way to see them as they really are. Knowledge of the objective moral condition of one's political community is useful for making practical changes; but it is also worth having for its own sake.

The rule of appetite, from the perspective of the *Republic*, is by and large the operative standard in existing cities and communities. In this way, Plato's response in the *Republic* to the political turmoil of his surroundings is the wholesale rejection of the terms of conventional politics.[16] Civic conflict, for Plato, is the result of appetitive rule: cities governed by rulers and made up of citizens who consider the objects of appetite to have ultimate value. Justice and civic health, by contrast, involve the rule of reason in rulers and in citizens. The rule of reason is rare – perhaps non-existent – while appetitive rule is widespread.[17] So Socrates' famous slogan turns out to be the central thesis of the political theory of the *Republic*:

Until philosophers rule as kings or those who are now kings and rulers genuinely and adequately philosophize, until political power and philosophy coincide ... there can be no rest from evils, dear Glaucon, in cities nor, I fancy, for the human race either. (473d; translations from Shorey 1930, with frequent modifications)

The background of the thesis is the presence of unrelenting evils in cities and in individuals. Socrates argues first of all that despite this background, the rule of reason and justice – for which philosopher-kings are necessary – is both attractive and possible, given human nature as it is.[18] Second, he argues, the rule of unreason or injustice is both ubiquitous and undesirable – and without the rule of reason, inevitable. Whatever desirable order can be found in non-rational regimes is corrupt and ultimately unstable. This argument is made in terms of the central contrast between the rule of reason and the rule of non-rational forces. Accordingly, these two arguments – the bulk of which are found in Books 4, 8 and 9 – involve constant reference to the tripartite soul.

The possibility of Kallipolis ought not to be confused with the practicality of Kallipolis. Its possibility is explicit in the text (471c–473d): it is the whole premise for the central books of the *Republic*. Socrates and his interlocutors are also explicit that they consider the conditions for the possibility of Kallipolis as unlikely ever to hold (473c, 592a–b). This means that Kallipolis is meant to be possible, at least minimally so, even if it can never be put into practice. As Socrates insists, it ought rather to be understood as a paradigm or standard (472c–e, 544a, 592b). This suggests that Socrates and his interlocutors mean to construct a paradigm or standard for political action with an eye to the best condition human beings are capable of, given their nature.[19]

Degenerate regimes in Plato's Republic

I turn now to the negative end of the political argument of the *Republic*, that injustice – the rule of unreason – is both widespread and undesirable. Before looking at the account of degenerate regimes in *Republic* 8, I want to show how the central contrast between the rule of reason and the rule of appetite is prefigured in earlier, more familiar, and less systematic parts of the *Republic*: the Ship of State image and the argument with Thrasymachus in Book 1.

II. APPETITIVE RULE: THRASYMACHUS AND THE SHIP OF STATE

The degenerate regimes of Book 8 are regimes marked by instability and violent struggle between factions (*stasis*). Their rulers or ruling classes are susceptible to their appetites, and their guiding ideals are wrong-headed and ultimately self-undermining. As such, the Book 8 discussion does not introduce the idea of a degenerate regime, but rather organizes and clarifies earlier discussions: namely, the Ship of State in Book 6, and Thrasymachus' critique of conventional justice in Book 1.

The Ship of State analogy is introduced to explain why philosophers are not held in honor, and so why philosophical rule seems ridiculous (487e7–489c7). In the analogy, sailors, analogous to citizens seeking power, strive for power over an incompetent shipmaster, the city itself.[20] They seek power for the sake of consuming the ship's cargo, with the "drinking and feasting" that that involves (488c4–7). And this striving for power involves conflict and violence: they "struggle (*stasiazontas*) with one another for control of the helm" (488b3–4); they "cut to pieces" anyone who says the art of steering can be taught (488b6–8); they execute and exile others who attain over the city (such as oligarchs, demagogues, and potential tyrants, presumably; 488c3–4). The true navigator, in the meantime, languishes on the sidelines or is mocked as a buffoon (488e3–489a2).

The Ship of State, like the analogy between the demos and the ravening beast that follows it (493a6-c8), is a figure directed at the Athenian democracy in which the interlocutors live, as a way of explaining why, in that context, philosophy is not considered an art of ruling, as something to which power naturally belongs. The image is accordingly of a piece with the image in the *Gorgias* (464d3–465a2) of the doctor and the rhetor competing for the hearts of a band of children: it serves to contrast starkly the democratic status quo, where appetites rule, with a hypothetical ideal of the rule of knowledge. The apparent political good in the Ship of State image is the cargo, represented as the objects of appetites of hunger and thirst, but standing in for the objects of appetite generally including wealth and other appetitive pleasures. This good is zero-sum – more for one means less for others, hence the competition, the violence, and the ensuing instability.[21] The struggles of fifth-century Athens have parallels throughout Greece in the *staseis* Thucydides describes.[22] Accordingly, its central image of appetitive rule is generalized both in Book 8 and Book 1 to apply to any regime where reason does not rule.[23]

It is a strange irony of the *Republic* that if we consider instability, violence, *stasis*, and deference to appetites as cardinal features of conventional regimes, and if we consider Thrasymachus as a critic of conventional justice,[24] we find considerable agreement between Thrasymachus and Plato on conventional politics – how politics is actually practiced – even if the disagreement between them on how politics ought be practiced is stark. The unstable, *stasis*-riddled regimes seen in Books 6 and 8 are just those where the rulers rule for their own advantage, given Thrasymachus' initial implicit understanding of advantage as power and wealth.[25] While Thrasymachus is tripped up toward the end of the argument by pressure from Socrates as to whether advantage is virtue, wisdom, or the exercise of one's proper function, he clearly begins with a much more simple and concrete vision of the political good: it is power, and behind power, wealth. Hence his example of the shepherd who rules for wages (343b); his claim that the just man loses out in business dealings (343d–344a); and his comparison between the tyrant and other lesser, unjust wealth-seekers: temple-robbers, kidnappers, swindlers, and thieves (344b3–5).

I am not here prepared to make claims about the coherence in the details of Thrasymachus' view of politics, nor about the coherence or effectiveness of Socrates' arguments against him.[26] All the same, Thrasymachus has a certain general vision of politics that, taken as a description of the way things are, is not only not incoherent but closely matches the image of conventional politics Plato endorses. According to Thrasymachus, at least before he is pressured by Socrates into admitting other sorts of motivation and types of good, political regimes are characterized by appetitive rule, which is to say, the rule of appetitive people in the service of their own appetites and pleasures. Like the politics of the Ship of State, Thrasymachus' politics is zero-sum – one wins only because another loses;[27] and accordingly, politics should be expected to be competitive, violent, and unstable.

The degenerate regimes of Books 1 and 6 give us some help in explaining what makes a bad regime bad. A regime organized around the appetitive ends of wealth and power will be violent and unstable, since if one faction of the city has more of these things, another has less. This explains at least in

Degenerate regimes in Plato's Republic

part why Plato describes degenerate regimes as susceptible to appetite, and why they are unstable and prone to conflict and violence. In Book 8, the connection between these defects and the non-rational motivations and ends of the rulers is developed in detail. Any political community not ruled by reason will be susceptible to the appetites and so susceptible to conflict, violence, and ultimate collapse.

The general contrast between appetitive rule and the rule of reason presented in the earlier parts of the *Republic* is developed in detail in Book 8. The degenerate regimes of Book 8 are characterized by violence and instability, and they are defined in terms of false conceptions of the good: honor, wealth, and liberty. I will argue that these more general features can be explained in terms of the progressing failure of the rule of reason. The account of degenerate regimes is in its way as idealized or hypothetical as the earlier sections describing the construction of a just city. Just as nothing external to human justice determines the construction of Kallipolis – the city of pigs is not suddenly attacked by a pack of bears, for instance – so nothing external to human injustice or vice determines the deterioration of regimes as described.[28] A city might be destroyed by fire, flood, or conquest; Plato's concern is what a human political community might do or suffer when the guidance of reason alone fails.[29] Thus the decline is organized *anthropologically*: it starts with a human being (and a city) in a natural condition and decomposes it piece by piece.[30]

III. THE REGIMES OF *REPUBLIC* 8: AN OVERVIEW

What characterizes the degenerate regimes of *Republic* 8, and what distinguishes them from one another? The bad regimes share a number of features in common: division or *stasis*;[31] the use of force and violence;[32] and instability. Instability, however, is shared also with Kallipolis; it too inevitably falls apart, although for different sorts of reasons.[33] The just city falls when the rulers miss the mathematically expressed law of good births (546a4–b3), thanks to their use of a mix of reasoning and sense-perception (*logismos met' aisthēseōs*, 546b2).[34] Socrates appeals to a general principle that everything that comes to be must be destroyed (546a); it seems likely that the bad regimes fail for more specific reasons, from some feature internal to themselves.

Division and violence are shared among the bad regimes, then, and perhaps there are forms of instability special to them. How are the regimes different from one another, and what is it that defines a regime as one kind and not another? The name "timocracy" is Plato's novelty, but oligarchy, democracy, and tyranny are conventional ways of categorizing regimes. However, earlier discussions of these regimes differentiate them by the number of rulers: the rule of one, the rule of many, the rule of a few.[35] This obvious distinction in types of institutional arrangement plays little to no role in *Republic* 8. The regime-types are differentiated in two ways: (i) the law defining office-holders, or the ruling class, and (ii) the *dominant end*, the goal around which the constitution is organized.[36]

The timocracy is defined by its exclusion of wise people from office (547e–548a);[37] the oligarchy by its restriction of office to the wealthy (551b); and the democracy by its inclusion of every free man, according to the principle of equality or *isonomia* (557a). The defining characteristic of the ruling class is related to a regime's dominant end. The dominant end of timocracy is honor, rather than the good (548c) – accordingly it restricts (however informally) lovers of wisdom and the good from rule. The dominant end of oligarchy is wealth, and so rule is restricted to the wealthy. In democracy, the dominant end is liberty or *eleutheria*, understood as "doing what one wants" (557b); citizenship and a share in rule is granted to every freeman or *eleutheros*, as in Athens citizenship was granted to every free-born Athenian male.[38] Tyranny is defined by the disregard of law, not only written laws establishing criteria for office, but also unwritten customs forbidding harmful or licentious behavior. Correspondingly, no dominant end is attributed to the tyranny; this marks its place at the lowest extreme of psychic and political degeneration and disorganization.

Political degeneration, Socrates claims to the agreement of his inter-locutors, begins from the top: each regime decays by the decay in character of its ruling class (cf. 545d). Socrates also appeals to the dominant ends of oligarchy and democracy to explain what is wrong with them and why they collapse. Socrates says that oligarchy turns into democracy "by the insatiate desire (*aplēstia*) for that which it sets before itself as the good, the attainment of the greatest possible wealth" (555b). He repeats this claim about oligarchy at 562b and applies it also to the transition from democracy to tyranny: "Is it not the case that the insatiate desire (*aplēstia*) for what the democracy defines as good also destroys it?" and confirms that this defined good is liberty (*eleutheria*; 562b, cf. 557b). Looking backward, it seems that timocracy, too, is assigned a dominant good, when its most conspicuous feature is said to be love of honor and victory (548c). One possibility is that honor, too, is such a self-undermining good, the pursuit of which both defines the regime and destroys it. I suspect, however, that honor is rather undermined by appetite, and that only the appetitive dominant ends undermine themselves. I will explain why this might be the case further on.

Republic 8 and 9 alternate discussion of degenerate regime-types with discussion of the degenerate types of individual that correspond to each regime. A complication that has obscured the importance of the dominant ends is the wide array of special types of motivation that arise in the individual characters. The dominant ends are emphasized in the discussions of regime-types; in the discussions of individual types, we find instead discussion of dominant types of desire. With the timocrat and just man, there is nothing either puzzling or interesting about the connection between dominant motive and dominant end: the dominant ends are the good and honor, respectively; and the dominant motives are desire for the good and desire for honor. But as the decline continues, new types of desire are unleashed in the soul. Certain types of desire are characteristically unleashed in the tyrant and the democrat that ought not to be confused with their dominant desires. Unnecessary desires – desires unconnected to one's own health and preservation – first appear in the oligarchic character, but he is nonetheless ruled by his necessary appetites, and these are the only appetites he indulges (554a). The unnecessary desires are first indulged by the democratic character (561a; I call them "characteristic" of him in the chart below). However, the democratic character is not ruled by these desires, but by a kind of compromise between them and his necessary desires (561b).[39] Likewise, we encounter lawless desires first in the tyrant, but the tyrant is not ruled by these desires, but by single dominating *erōs* (572e, 575a).[40] Thus the connection between the dominant end and the dominant type of motivation becomes looser the further we descend down the degenerative chain. The whole scheme can be summarized as follows:[41]

Individual character	Philosopher-king	Timocrat	Oligarch	Democrat	Tyrant
Constitution	Aristocracy	Timocracy	Oligarchy	Democracy	Tyranny
Characteristic motive	Reason	Spirit (*thumos*)	Necessary desires	Unnecessary desires	Lawless desires
Dominant motive	Reason	Spirit	Necessary desires	Necessary & unnecessary	Eros
Dominant end	the Good	Honor	Wealth	Liberty	–

One key pattern in the decline, seen from the perspective of the dominant ends and motivations, is that appetites play an increasing role. The democracy, oligarchy, and tyranny are all appetitive regimes, and their individual analogues are appetitive characters, in that their dominant ends are appetitive ends. The pursuit of wealth is clearly appetitive: wealth and money are emphasized throughout the *Republic* as a characteristic object – sometimes *the* characteristic object – of appetite (581a). Likewise, the liberty of the democracy and the democrat, understood as "doing what one likes," is an appetitive end: the standard for personal and political action is simply what one happens to desire (557b; 561b–d).[42] The tyrant, while he has no dominant end, is characterized by the rapid and chaotic growth of appetite (571b, 572b, 573e, 574d), which drives him to ever-escalating acts of violence (574d, 566e–567c). The tyrant has, in fact, no internal constraint on his actions: the scope of harm he does depends only on external considerations, namely how numerous the other tyrannical characters are in his city (575b–576a). Thus the degeneration of regimes follows the progress of the appetites and their increase in power over the political leadership in cities.

Furthermore, the appetites play a role in the fall of every regime including Kallipolis. While the appetites are not likely to be the original cause of the fall of Kallipolis,[43] the mistake in sense-perception does cause a decay in the quality of the rulers, which leads those rulers to neglect education, which in turn allows mixing of the classes (546e). This mixing results in the introduction of appetitive characters into the ruling class, which results in a civil war among the rulers with one side seeking money and property (547b). The secret lust for wealth in the timocracy – marked by the political leadership's keeping of secret private treasuries for themselves (548a) – gradually corrupts the leadership until their primary interest is in wealth rather than honor, so bringing about the decline in the regime (548a5–b2, 550e4–551a10). The oligarchy is said to fall because of its insatiate love of wealth (555b); and the democracy hands itself over to the tyrant, it is suggested, the better to confiscate the property of the rich (566a).

Thus human appetite seems to be the main culprit for the instability of political regimes. This reading has the advantage of a unified account of decline, however attenuated it is in the first instance. It has the further advantage of a concrete explanation for the inevitable decline of created human institutions: appetites belong to human beings as necessary conditions of their embodiment, as Socrates suggests in Book 10 (611a10–612a6). But it must be only a partial explanation, as a number of aspects of the text remain mysterious. Why do the appetites progress in the way that they do? Why is it, for instance, that the introduction of private property in the timocracy results in the ultimate corruption of the whole ruling class from the love of honor to the love of money? Why is it that the oligarchy's repressive instruments in the pursuit of wealth are ineffective, and

Degenerate regimes in Plato's Republic

ultimately lead to its dissolution? Why can't democracy's appetitive pursuits stay within the bounds of law? And why, if it is the appetites that drive dissolution and destruction, does Plato bother with categorizing regimes by dominant end, and why does Socrates claim that the dominant ends of oligarchy and democracy are self-destructive? These questions can be answered by seeing a different type of progress in the regimes, corresponding to the growth of appetites, and that is the decline of reason.

IV. THE DECLINE OF REASON

In the remainder of this essay I make two claims about the function of reason in the degenerate regimes and characters. The first (less speculative) claim is that the neglect of reason is the ultimate cause of the decline of regimes. It is the neglect of reason that allows for the growth and fragmentation of appetite – and so ultimately it is what drives the division, violence, and instability found in bad regimes. The second (more speculative) claim is that reason is in fact the source of what order there is in the bad regimes; that it allows them certain shadows of virtue and goodness; and that the continued function of reason is necessary to understand the role of dominant ends in bad regimes. Reason is not dispensed with in the degenerate regimes; rather, it pursues inadequate objects. Rather than seeking what is genuinely good, degenerate reason pursues certain shadowy appearances of the good: honor, constraint, and lawfulness.

First, the less speculative claim: it is the neglect of reason that allows for the growth of the appetites and so for the process of degeneration itself. Here Socrates is quite explicit. The first sign of decay in Kallipolis after the mistake in eugenic arrangements is the neglect of musical education and then education in gymnastics, with the result that the guardians become "less musical" (*amousoteroi*; 546d). The ordaining and regulation of music is the function of reason, or reason's analogue, philosopher-kings. In Book 3, it is said that the education must be preserved by a "permanent overseer" (*epistatēs*; 412a). This is developed in Book 6, when Socrates indicates that the philosopher-kings will amount to the presence of the legislators (Socrates and his interlocutors) in the city (497c). So the neglect of education is a failing of the function of reason in the best city.[44]

This neglect of education results in the growth of the appetites because of its impact on the *thumos* or spirited part of the rulers. The neglect of music *vis-à-vis* gymnastics, it is said in Book 3, results in the crippling of the part of the soul that loves learning: it becomes "feeble, deaf, and blind," since it is "not aroused or nurtured, nor are its perceptions purified" (411d). The result is that the man so educated becomes a misologist, a hater of reason, and "he no longer makes any use of persuasion by speech but achieves all his ends like a beast by violence and savagery" (411d–e).

The deterioration of the use of reason and the corresponding decay in education has precisely this effect on the timocracy. The timocratic ruling class "fears to admit wise men into office" (547d) and it rules by violence and force. The propensity to violence is shown internally, by its subjection of its own people as slaves (547b–c), and externally, by "waging war most of the time" (548a). Furthermore – and most importantly, for its own stability – it represses its love of wealth by force. The following passage is crucial:

> Will they not be stingy about money, since they prize it and are not allowed to possess it openly, prodigal of others' wealth because of their appetites, enjoying their pleasures in secret, and running away from the law as boys from a father, since they have not been educated by persuasion but by force because of their neglect of the true Muse, the companion of discussion and philosophy, and because of their preference of gymnastics to music? (548b)

Their preference of gymnastics to music leads to the incapacity of reason; the incapacity of reason means that the power of persuasion over the appetites is lost; and the use of force over the appetites is manifestly ineffective.

Clearly, to unpack this dynamic in detail would require a detailed analysis of how, exactly, reason persuades appetite: is it by talking to it and so convincing it, for instance, not to love wealth? By satisfying it with its natural object? Or soothing it in a mysterious mechanical way by means of music? There is evidence in the *Republic* for all of these methods,[45] but there is nothing in the discussion of timocracy itself that points one way or the other. All the same, one difference between the rule of reason and the rule of force is suggested, however subtly, by the text: force can only maintain an external appearance of virtue.

The love of wealth in the timocracy is the engine of its decline; it eventually corrupts the ruling class and makes them into oligarchs. How and why does this take place? One thing to notice is that the love of wealth is secret. The timocrats hide their gold and silver in private treasuries and in their homes; they are not allowed to possess it openly; they are lavish in private but stingy in public (548b). This suggests that honor, decency, and virtue, for them, are a matter of appearance.[46] They must look good in public. The overarching value put on honor, and the disdain for wealth, is for them something imposed from outside, by force of law or convention.

Degenerate regimes in Plato's Republic

They force this appearance on themselves and others contrary to their own inclinations.

A practice that Xenophon describes in his account of Sparta illustrates this feature nicely. Boys when they reached adolescence were put under the supervision of older adolescents who would supervise them and set for them various tasks and contests as a part of their training as soldiers. The boys were not fed enough to be satisfied, but it was expected and permitted that they steal food. Nonetheless, if they were caught, they were severely beaten.[47] Plutarch reports that one Spartan boy allowed a stolen fox to disembowel him with its teeth and claws rather than be caught.[48] Xenophon explains this practice as a way of teaching soldiers to survive in the field. But it illustrates in a particularly extreme way what it might mean to pursue virtue only as a matter of appearance. The boys are allowed – indeed encouraged – to be vicious out of sight.

One function of education, then, and one thing that it means for reason to "persuade" appetite, is to produce virtue, to the extent that it is possible, from within, because one wants or desires it. In Book 3, this control of reason over the love of wealth is described in two ways: first of all, the guardians are told a story about gold and silver, that it exists in their own souls and so they have no need of metals; and they are told that metallic gold and silver are connected to "many impious deeds" (416e–417a). Reason (understood as embodied in the legislator) furthermore gives a law (*themis*) forbidding the guardians from any contact with gold and silver (417a). This combination of (alleged) persuasion and restriction on reason's part allows the avoidance of wealth to be holistic, internal as well as external, and not a mere imposition from without.[49] This law is overturned when the timocracy establishes private property for the ruling class.

The neglect of reason, the rule of force, and the preoccupation with appearing virtuous in public also play a prominent role in the discussion of oligarchy. The oligarchic character esteems wealth above everything "because he has never turned his thoughts to education" (554b). Because of his "lack of education" (*apaideusia*) drone-like appetites spring up in him (554c), appetites which we later learn are the unnecessary appetites that can be trained by discipline or practice. The discipline in question seems to be the sort administered by reason in the soul or by legislative educators in the city. Likewise, in the oligarchic city, Socrates says that the presence of the class of impoverished and sometimes criminal drones is on account of "lack of education and bad upbringing" (*kakē trophē*; 552e). The oligarchic person's forcible restraint of his dronish appetites is mirrored by the oligarchy's forcible restraint of the impoverished drone-classes.

In oligarchy, however, there is a twist: the emergence of unruly appetites and their forcible restraint is all in the service of an appetitive end, the acquisition of wealth. The oligarchic rulers impoverish their subjects by allowing citizens to sell their entire net worth, reducing some to penury while increasing the wealth of others (552a). They then forcibly restrain the impoverished criminals (552e), rather than removing the root cause of their poverty. Here the criminal law is doing double duty: under the guise of restraining petty injustice such as thievery and temple-robbing (552d), the oligarchic rulers maintain a legal structure which enriches them.

The use of the appearance of virtue for appetitive purposes is yet clearer in the oligarchic individual. While he will privately abuse orphans, or commit other injustices (554c), he will maintain an outward appearance of decency in order to transact business: in his "contractual obligations (*sumbolaioi*), where he enjoys the reputation of a seemingly just man (*eudokimei dokōn dikaios*)" he forcibly suppresses his evil desires (554c–d). It is presumably his reputation for decency which allows him to make his profitable loans, and so he maintains it carefully and forcefully.[50] His appearance of virtue, in other words, is in the service of his pursuit of wealth through destructive loans, and his enforcement of the law is in the service of protecting his unjustly acquired wealth from theft. This is, I think, the sense in which his reason and *thumos* are at the service of his appetitive love of wealth. The supervisory capacities of the city and the individual are dedicated to the promotion of wealth and wealth alone.

What happens when we turn to the democrat and the democracy? The democracy not only neglects education, but considers it something inferior (558b), which suggests that it abandons to some extent even holding up the appearance of virtue as a standard. Force and violence are replaced, by and large, with tolerance, laxity, and the liberty to do what one likes, as seen most clearly when Socrates claims that there is no compulsion to hold office if one doesn't want to; one can hold office if forbidden by law; and convicted criminals wander freely (557e–558a).[51] Here, however, the suggestion is not that force and violence have been replaced by persuasion in virtue, but rather that the standard of virtue has been at least partially abandoned. The appetites nurtured in the neglect of reason and held in forcible constraint by the previous two administrations have been set loose.

Nonetheless, on Socrates' portrayal, the democracy is still concerned with a certain kind of restraint and with the projection of a certain kind of appearance. This can be seen in part by looking backward from the tyrant. The tyrant alone unleashes his lawless appetites, the desires that drive violent injustices such as theft and murder. What has kept the democrat and the democracy from this sort of indulgence? The democratic character settles a compromise between his necessary and unnecessary appetites, under something like a law of equality (572b10–d3). In doing so, the democratic character imagines he is being moderate. The rule of equality or compromise, in other words, a kind of lawfulness, is the source of order in the democratic character, a source of order he pretends is something lofty and virtuous. But since he refuses to evaluate his desires on their content, by his total commitment to his desires as a standard for action, the democrat has no real grounds to oppose the pursuit of lawless desires. As Nettleship puts it, he has made the absence of principle into a principle.[52] In this way the democrat, like the oligarch and the timocrat, nurtures appetites hostile to his own values while pretending to himself – and perhaps to others – that he is in fact safe from them.

The self-deception of the democratic individual has a political analogue. When Socrates describes the degeneration of the democracy into tyranny, he emphasizes the deception of the farming demos by the drone-demagogues and ultimately by the tyrant. The demagogues seek to extract wealth from the rich – but the people will not support this program if it is described to them as a way to get more money. They must be deceived into believing that the rich are already attacking the existing order (565b–c). To that extent they consider themselves bound by law. On the other hand, they have pursued "liberty" to the point of denying the most basic kinds of authority – the authority of age, wisdom, and most memorably, species (562e–563c) – and so they themselves lay the ground for the eventual destruction of the laws which constrain tyrannical behavior. Furthermore, they are perfectly happy to exploit the rich, it is suggested, under other pretenses (565a).[53]

I have shown, I hope, that the rise of appetite in degenerate regimes ought to be understood as caused by the neglect of reason and education. Without the rule of reason, the political and psychological elements that are hostile to order can only be constrained by force. In place of rulers who persuade and educate with an eye to the real good, we find rulers who constrain their subjects under the auspices of a false good, a good determined by how things look to oneself or to others. Sometimes the rulers endorse this good sincerely and sometimes with an eye to deception. Regardless, the false appearance of good functions as a sort of mask, under which the appetites or other elements dangerous to the regime are inadvertently nurtured.

However, something strange has emerged from a close look at the decline of reason in the bad regimes. We find forms of order in the bad regimes that are set against genuinely harmful elements: honor versus the pursuit of wealth in timocracy; the orderly acquisition of wealth versus the pursuit of self-indulgent desire in the oligarchy; and lawfulness versus the pursuit of violent injustices in the democracy. These forms of order are incomplete – they are based on the presentation of appearances – and they are helpless against the forces arrayed against them and that they inadvertently nurture. I will argue in my final section that these forms of order are residual functions of reason, and that they are the key to understanding how the dominant ends define regimes.

V. REASON AS A SOURCE OF ORDER

It is to my knowledge an almost entirely neglected fact about the degenerate regimes and characters that they contain weak versions of virtue, versions of virtue that are based on appearances.[54] The failings of this type of appearance-based virtue by comparison with real virtue should not be underestimated. On the other hand, it must be acknowledged that Socrates often speaks of these "shadow-virtues" as if they are real virtues. The shadow-virtues are the function of the corrupted and weakened rational elements in both degenerate individuals and degenerate regimes.

The clearest evidence of the presence of valuable, if limited, shadow-virtues is in the discussion of the oligarchic man. Consider the passage where Socrates describes the oligarchic character's restraint when making business deals: it says that he keeps down his bad desires "by something decent in himself" (*epieikei tini heautou*; 554c). In explaining the collapse of the oligarchy, Socrates says that the regime falls because the love of wealth is ultimately incompatible with the possession of *sōphrosunē*, moderation, which implies that the oligarchy had moderation to begin with (555c).[55] Finally – and I think most convincingly – the transition from the oligarchic to the democratic character unmistakably assumes that certain virtues are in place until the destructive influence of the democrat's drone-friends comes into play. The democratic character comes very near to the ultimate collapse of all constraint and pretense of virtue, and to the actual reversal of the dictates of reason. The democratic character when young is torn between the oligarchic constraint of his father and the freedom and license of his drone-friends. The outcome of the struggle can be oligarchy (at which point, Socrates says, "a certain reverence or shame (*aidōs*) is engendered in the soul of the young man and it is once again set in order" (*katekosmēthē*; 560a)). Or the drone-desires win out, "seizing the *akropolis* or citadel of the man's soul." Since the citadel is empty of learning and study, the drone-desires fill it with demagogue-like speeches and rename the virtues, calling *aidōs* or shame foolishness and

Degenerate regimes in Plato's Republic

sōphrosunē unmanliness, putting in their place *hubris* (renamed "good education"), *anarchia* or lawlessness (renamed "freedom (*eleutheria*)"), and lack of shame (renamed "manliness") (560b–e).[56]

This total overturning of any shadow of the rule of reason is only temporary; the tumult dies down, and the democratic character settles into a quasi-orderly compromise, admits back into his soul some of the "oligarchic" desires and puts all of his desires, oligarchic and drone-like, under the law of equality, *isonomia* (561b). All the same, the implication is unmistakable that the democratic child of the oligarchic father, before coming under the influence of the drones, has some version of *aidōs* and *sōphrosunē*, shame and moderation. If this were not the case, or if there were no value whatsoever in the oligarchic versions of the virtues, the whole drama of the decline into the democratic character would be meaningless.

It is important to see that these shadow-virtues do not meet Book 4's criteria for full virtue.[57] The oligarch's *sōphrosunē* does not amount to all parts of the soul agreeing that reason ought to rule – the oligarch is a deeply conflicted person. At best, he is like Aristotle's continent person: someone who is good only by constraint and strength of will. The timocrat's unruly and suppressed desire for wealth puts him in a similar position: he succeeds in moderation, to the extent that he does succeed, only by force. Accordingly, we find inconsistent behavior: the timocrat's wild parties (548a), the oligarch's abuse of orphans (554c). Such inconsistencies, whether caused by sincerely felt inner conflict or simply by social pressure, would be a constant danger for these characters. The oligarch, since his restraint is motivated by greed, ought to be considered in a yet worse position than the timocrat.

That the virtues attributed to the oligarch and oligarchy are *aidōs* and *sōphrosunē*, and not, say, courage or wisdom, is also significant. We can assume, I think, that wisdom is impossible in the degenerate regimes, from the moment that the timocracy excludes wise people from ruling (547e). Although no virtues in particular are explicitly ascribed to the timocracy or the timocrat, the *stasis* that brings down the timocracy is described as a struggle between the forces of virtue (*aretē*) and the love of wealth (550e–551a). Further, the focus of the regime and character on war and competition suggests that at least some sort of courage is retained. This point is bolstered by the emphatic loss of the warlike virtues in the oligarchy and the oligarchic character. The oligarchic state "will be unable to wage war," because it fears the people (551d–e). Likewise, the oligarchic character is "a feeble competitor" on his own, and avoids any kind of civic contest (555a). So it seems that we can trace the decline in regimes as a progressive decay in virtue: first wisdom is lost; then courage – whatever kind is possible without wisdom – and then moderation.

How then ought we to understand the situation of democracy and the democratic character? Socrates' narrative is vague on this point: after the destruction of virtue in the democratic character's soul, he allows that a real democratic character will emerge when he "receives back a part of the banished elements [*aidōs, sōphrosunē*, etc.]" and "establishes ... all his pleasures on the footing of equality (*eis ison*)" (561b). Some of the quasi-virtuous elements such as shame or moderation return. In the later discussion of the decay from the democratic character into the tyrannical one, Socrates disparages the moderation in question as something that the democratic character "supposes" (572d); it is suggested that it consists simply in the avoidance of lawlessness, or violent injustice. On the other hand, when the dominant *erōs* is instilled in the tyrannical character, it is said that the *erōs* purges any remaining opinions or desires "capable of shame" and also expels "moderation" (*sōphrosunē*) (573b). This final purge of any remaining good motivations by the tyrant is the individual analogue of the political tyrant's purgation of any good or virtuous characters remaining in the city, removing the best and leaving the worst (567c).

The tyrant's final purgation of any trace of goodness, and his aggressive pursuit of violent injustice, theft, murder, and temple-robbing, mark him out as the furthest extreme of moral and rational degeneration. To understand the shadow-virtues of the democrat, then, I suggest we look to the source of order in the democratic soul and the democracy. Socrates implies that the democrat's "moderation" consists in lawfulness: his avoidance of behavior that is violent (such as theft or murder) or grotesque (such as lying with one's mother; 571d). This orderliness is the defining structure of the democratic character, and it is mimicked by the constraint of *nomos* or law in the political democracy. The democracy, whatever its faults, distributes political power according to law, the principle of equality or *isonomia*. The equal share in office is the defining law of democracy (557a), just as the wealth-qualification is for oligarchy. Just as the wealth-qualification is indiscriminate to the actual capacity for ruling (551c), so also the principle of *isonomia* assigns "a kind of equality to equals and unequals alike" (558c). All the same, it formally prevents the absorption of political power into one person as we find in the tyranny.

One considerable advantage of emphasizing the passages about the shadow-virtues is that it brings the degenerate regimes into closer contact with the historical regimes that they are meant at least partially to capture (see note 9). As I noted earlier, commentators often complain that neither

Degenerate regimes in Plato's Republic

the democracy nor the oligarchy of *Republic* 8 seems grounded in historical reality. The importance of law as a key feature of democratic ideology has been widely attested.[58] By contrast, liberty understood as "doing what one wants" is only attested among critics of democracy, unless one counts the patriotic contrasts with austere Sparta in wartime speeches in Thucydides.[59] If we see that the definition of democracy in the *Republic* and its source of order is the shadow-virtue of *isonomia*, we can see that Plato meant to take real-life Athenian ideals into account.

The difficulty of historical correspondence would seem even more serious with the oligarchy, since while there is some evidence that liberty or *eleutheria* was some kind of democratic ideal, the historical proponents of oligarchy did not any of them seem to endorse the pursuit of wealth. Rather, they considered themselves and promoted themselves as proponents of virtue and traditional values.[60] If we take seriously, however, the attribution of some kind of moderation and decency to oligarchs and oligarchy, this complaint about Plato's account seems unjustified. Indeed, Plato takes pains, in describing the shadow-virtues, to explain just this fact: that the oligarchs call themselves virtuous. In part, this is a deceptive appearance used to issue loans that enrich themselves at the expense of others. And in part, it has some truth: the oligarchs do indeed constrain and moderate their desires, if only by force and if only for corrupt purposes.[61]

If this interpretation is correct, then attribution of the dominant ends of "wealth" and "liberty" to the regimes ought to be understood as involving a critical judgment, a sort of debunking of the ideals that the real-life regimes espouse. In this way, it might be compared to similar attributions in contemporary political rhetoric: that proponents of radical Islam, under the guise of promoting "virtue," in fact hate freedom; or that, under the guise of "freedom," American capitalists seek their own aggrandizement at the expense of the working peoples of the world. Such attributions criticize the ends or goals that the regimes criticized pursue in practice, by contrast to the loftier ideals they lay claim to in self-justifying rhetoric.

One might question this reading simply because the ugly, repressive greed of the oligarch and the silly, licentious liberty of the democrat are by far the most memorable passages of the whole sequence of characters and regimes. Their rhetorical importance is unquestionable, and one can't help but think that it is these images that do most of the persuasive work in determining the place of oligarchic and democratic characters in the final ranking in Book 9. However, we must also remember that we read this book twenty-five centuries from its original context. It is not far-fetched to think that the democratic ideal of *isonomia* and lawfulness, and the corresponding oligarchic ideal of virtue and a return to old-fashioned values, would have been foremost in the minds both of the hypothetical interlocutors and the fourth-century audience of the *Republic*. The conventional ideals, then, which the *Republic* keeps in the background and treats as shadowy, are simply taken for granted in the discussion. It is only from this further distance that exegesis is needed to eke them out.

VI. CONCLUSIONS: DOMINANT ENDS, THE ROLE OF REASON, AND APPEARANCES

Two points of crucial interest thus emerge from tracing the loosening hold of reason over the degenerate regimes. As reason loses its grip, and the appetites gain, so do we also find a decrease of order and structure. One natural thought – borne out by evidence of shadowy and defective virtues – is that reason is the source of that structure. Consider the oligarchic character, which is (unfortunately) the only place where the role of reason is at all clear or explicit. Reason is subjugated to appetite; it calculates and considers "only" how to gain wealth. The single-minded pursuit of wealth is also the oligarchic character's source of order: it is what justifies the forceful repression of unnecessary appetites. This is indeed just what it means to have wealth as a dominant end: it means to organize one's life around that end. A dominant end is an organizing principle, a source of order set against some source of disorder. As such, it is a rational structure, a function of reason.

Politically speaking, the dominant end functions not only by its influence on the character of the rulers, but also by laws and institutions. The dominant end of wealth determines the qualifications for office (property) and laws governing the exchange of property. The dominant end of liberty also determines the qualifications for office (equality, or "being a free-born citizen"), and more broadly it promotes a culture of tolerant lawfulness.

If these speculations are correct, then we have available to us a much more attractive view of how the dominant ends attributed to the regimes work. They have a double structure. In one respect, they are the end (or an end) associated with a particular part of the soul, honor for *thumos* and the timocracy, wealth and the lower appetitive pleasures for oligarchy and democracy. Considered from this angle, the ends are not self-undermining. The pursuit of honor in timocracy is not undermined by the pursuit of honor itself, but by the conflicting pursuit of wealth. Likewise, the pursuit of wealth in oligarchy is not undermined, strictly speaking, by the pursuit of wealth: after all, both the democracy and the tyranny show considerable

Degenerate regimes in Plato's Republic   123

wealth-seeking behavior. Rather, the oligarchy is undermined by the pursuit of liberty, and the democracy by the pursuit of lawlessness.

In another respect, however, the ends are also shadow-virtues. They are courage (without wisdom) in timocracy, moderation (understood as constraint) in oligarchy, and justice (reduced to lawfulness) in democracy. These shadow-virtues give the regimes definition and structure, and make a regime one type and not another. So it seems reasonable to conclude that it is the corrupt rational structures of the degenerate regimes that are destroyed by the advance of appetite. In the case of oligarchy and democracy, where these rational structures are set up for appetitive ends, the shadow-virtues are pursued by the deception of oneself and others, masking the inadvertent encouragement of elements that will undermine them. In this respect these two regimes are self-undermining.

What conclusions can we draw about why the regimes collapse? The first is that the conflicts that bring them down ought to be understood, not as conflicts among the multifarious appetites, all competing for first place, but as conflicts between weak rational or lawful structures and appetitive forces, personal or political.[62] In this way the whole process of degeneration can be viewed as an extended conflict between reason and appetite.

The second conclusion is that part of the weakness of what I have called rational structures is their reliance on *appearance*. Without the rule of reason, one has no ability to weigh appearances critically and to make decisions based on those critical evaluations.[63] The timocrat seeks courage, the oligarch moderation, and the democrat lawful freedom by the criterion of how these things *look*. They are interested in projecting an image in public. This image may be self-deceptive – as I think it must be in the case of individuals – or it may be manipulative, as may be the case in the political contexts, or it may be both. However, authentic virtue must take concern for the internal, for shaping the real motivations of individuals in particular ways. Only then can virtue produce behavior that can endure changes in social circumstance – or even behavior that presents direct opposition to social pressure – as the virtue of Socrates did. This is why neglect of education is so emphasized in the discussion of regime collapse.

It is thus not surprising in the stories of degeneration in *Republic* 8 that Socrates emphasizes what the various characters *perceive*, especially in their social surroundings.[64] Every one of the degenerate characters degenerates because of social influence: the timocrat and oligarch because of their fathers' low social status (549d–550a, 553a–b), and the democrat because of the influence of his drone-friends (559d–e). One's values, in the *Republic*, come from the outside – unless, that is, one determines them by reason and has the means to impose them. Once one has renounced or lost rational rule – the power to criticize appearances and to enforce those criticisms – one is carried along willy-nilly to whatever things present themselves as appealing in one's social surroundings.

While an honor-governed regime may partially or temporarily succeed in putting vice out of sight, the appetitive regimes always have variety and division. This means that the social context does not determine any coherent value, and so a socially determined appetitive end will be particularly unstable. Hence the haplessness of the degenerate characters: none of them succeed in their aims, since their aims are shadow-virtues, appearances that are subject to being replaced by other appearances. Without the guidance of reason, human beings and human communities ultimately do not have the power to resist these appearances, no matter how evil or base they might have judged them initially.

Whether Plato is correct in his account of his own historical context – or whether he is more generally correct about the forces of evil and degeneration in regimes – is outside the scope of this essay. All the same, it ought to be clearer what exactly that account amounts to. And one can often find insights at a different level of generality, whatever the disagreements between Plato and ourselves. For example: what ought human beings to do, who find themselves in fragmented political cultures, characterized by conflict and violence, where virtues are sought via their appearances and so are susceptible to corruption or collapse? The *Republic* offers one alternative: to use reason to determine, as best as one can, what justice for human beings could look like; and to use the conclusions so gathered to look clearly at one's surroundings, the better to distinguish the apparent from the real.[65]

NOTES

1. See especially the discussion of civil war in Corcyra: Thucydides 2.81–85 and discussion in Balot, 2001, chs. 5 and 6.
2. See Xenophon, *Hellenica* 2.3–43 and Aristotle, *Athenian Constitution* 35.
3. The orator Aeschines makes the claim that Socrates was executed for educating Critias (*Against Timarchus* 173); see discussion in Schofield 2006, pp. 22–23.
4. For more on the historical context of the *Republic*, see the vividly written and thorough introduction to the *Republic* in Ferrari and Griffith 2000, as well as Menn 2006; Balot 2001, esp. ch. 7; Schofield, 2006, chs. 1–3. I should add that if James Wilberding's (2004) interpretation of the Cave is correct, it is the demagogues and political leaders who execute the philosopher, not the majority.
5. The timocracy is explicitly called Laconian or Spartan (545a). A constitution called "timocracy" is Plato's invention. Sparta in the Peloponnesian War was

Degenerate regimes in Plato's Republic

considered an oligarchy. I discuss the difficulties in mapping the degenerate constitutions of Book 8 onto historical constitutions below.

6. Annas claims on the contrary that "Athenian politics of the fifth and fourth centuries do not actually shed any light on the *Republic*" (Annas 1999, p. 77; see discussion pp. 73–78). Her argument against the use of sketchy ancient biographies of Plato seems to me fair enough. But there is abundant evidence within the text of the *Republic* (and bolstered by the *Apology, Gorgias,* and *Protagoras*) of Plato's critical response to Athenian politics. Her other charges – that Kallipolis is based on first principles rather than historical regimes, and that the degenerate regimes of Books 8 and 9 have no basis in real regimes – are addressed in this essay.

7. It is true that *politeia* has a different and broader meaning in Plato's time and place than "constitution" does for us, and referred to individual ways of life and political culture as well as to institutional arrangements (Schofield 2006, pp. 30–35). It is also true that the two *Politeiai* attributed to Xenophon praise or blame particular cities (Athens and Sparta), with special reference to their cultural life rather than their political instutions (on which see Menn 2006). All the same, I am not convinced that complaints about the lack of institutional detail in the *Republic* are thereby provincial or anachronistic. After all, constitutions are discussed in terms of institutional arrangements in authors as early as Herodotus 3.80–82, in Thucydides 8.97, and of course in later literature such as the *Laws* and Aristotle's *Politics*. The broad meaning of *politeia* is not enough to explain the strangeness of the *Republic*.

8. So cites the anonymous author of the sixth-century *Prolegomena to Platonic Philosophy* 26.6–7. It is not clear what Proclus meant by saying that the *Republic* (and the *Laws*) were not written *dialogikōs*. Proclus would certainly not complain about a dialogue being dogmatic, but he may have thought that the *Republic* was ill-suited for pedagogical purposes because of its dogmatism combined with its political focus. It is not clear to which text of Proclus the anonymous commentator is referring, and neither the adverb *dialogikōs* nor the adjective *dialogikos* seem to have been standard ways for Neoplatonists to describe particular dialogues as opposed to others.

9. See Annas 1999, pp. 77–78; Frede 1996, pp. 260–66; Schofield 2006, pp. 104–05.

10. Annas 1999, ch. 4; Frede 1996, pp. 259–69; Blössner 2007, pp. 366–72. I agree with both Frede and Blössner that the emphasis in these passages is on ultimate values rather than on political systems or institutions; I disagree that the treatment of values does not count as serious reflection on history and politics, and so not as serious political theory.

11. As for example does Irwin 1995, pp. 281–97.

12. As Ferrari 2003, p. 59, points out, it is very hard to believe that the political structures are only introduced as an analogy.

13. Both of those later books provide much more extensive catalogs of (a) existing or historical political constitutions and (b) many more recommendations for institutional arrangements. In the case of the *Laws*, it seems likely that these recommendations are meant to be adapted to different circumstances (see Laks

126   ZENA HITZ

2000). In the case of the *Politics*, this is explicit. To take one example, Aristotle's catalog of types of regime-change in *Politics* 5 culminates in a series of recommendations as to how to maintain stability in regimes in different circumstances (*Politics* 5.8–12). Aristotle regularly addresses "the lawgiver" or *nomothetēs* and it seems reasonable to think he is addressing lawmakers and politicians in a variety of circumstances (on which see Bodéüs 1993). By contrast, there is only one point in *Republic* 8 and 9 that might count as a widely applicable generalization: the condemnation of the oligarchy's failure to ban by law the selling of all one's possessions (552a, 555c). The only "lawgivers" mentioned in the *Republic* are Socrates and his interlocutors, constructing the just regime (see n. 44 for references).

14. The failings of the rule of *thumos* in timocracy are closely tied to its failure to control appetite. I discuss this in detail below.

15. See for example *Laws* 713e on the rule of law and the rule of reason.

16. See Schofield 2006, p. 103, for a similar point.

17. So, at least, in the framework of the *Republic*. It is possible that the limited praise of law-governed regimes in the *Statesman* (291b–303c) indicates a change in view as to how rare the rule of reason is. However, the standard of the rule of reason is so far lowered in this passage in the *Statesman*, and the praise so mixed (as for instance when the rulers of such regimes are called *stasiastikoi*, leaders of faction (303c)), that it is not obvious that the law-governed regimes exclude, say, the oligarchy or democracy of *Republic* 8.

18. As Stephen Menn (2006, p. 34), puts it, Plato wants a just city that is "psychologically possible."

19. Seeing Kallipolis as the minimally possible just regime compatible with human nature makes sense of some of the puzzling features of the text I mention above. The interlocutors interrupt the construction of the best city, not to raise objections with a view to alternative cities, but to indicate the distance between the city as constructed and their own desires. The response to these interruptions is either to adapt the city to those desires or to give further explanation so that the objectionable feature seems attractive. When Glaucon complains in Book 2 that the just city they have described is "a city of pigs," Socrates responds by introducing classes of people and practices that will produce the luxury Glaucon requires (372c–e). When all of the interlocutors stumble on the community of wives and children, further explanation and defense is given (449c). When a question is raised at the end of Book 5 about whether the ideal city is practicable, Socrates introduces the notion of the philosopher-king, and to produce such rulers he devises a new program of education for the guardians of the previously described city (471c–473e). When the constructed city is adapted to their needs, this is a concession to human nature. When the constructed city is defended against their complaints, their subsequent persuasion (e.g. 445a–b, 471c–e) is evidence that such persuasion is possible, and so that the distance between desire and ideal can be met.

20. My interpretation of the details of this passage (for which I am indebted to Alexander Nehamas) is controversial, and the points of controversy are not

Degenerate regimes in Plato's Republic 127

important for the general gist: the contrast between appetitive rule and rational rule is clear either way. The traditional interpretation, as given by Aristotle (*Rhetoric* 1406b25), followed by the anonymous author of *Prologomena to Platonic Philosophy* (221.29), is that the shipmaster is the demos. But this does not make sense of the sailors' praise of "bad pilots" as the ones who are most successful in persuading or compelling the shipmaster to let them rule. Rather, it seems that the bad pilots are demagogues or politicians, and that the sailors are the demos. Furthermore, the sailors' hostility to those who say that the art of steering can be taught seems to parallel democratic hostility to the sophists, as depicted in Anytus in *Meno* 91a–94e and described by Socrates in *Protagoras* 319a–320b. This interpretation also alleviates the tension between the image of the demos as a helpless, half-deaf idiot here and the image almost immediately following of the demos as a greedy, immensely powerful beast (493a6–c8, cf. 492a1–c8; Benardete 1989, p. 147 points out the tension). The greedy, violent sailors, by contrast, fit quite well with what follows. My interpretation does face difficulties of its own: if the shipmaster is the city itself, what is the ship? For a very useful discussion of the passage (although it follows the traditional interpretation of the shipmaster), see Keyt 2006.

21. That appetitive goods are zero-sum and so cannot be shared is also pointed out by Blössner 2007, pp. 364–65. He claims that honor also cannot be shared, since a superior person requires an inferior. While this would explain some things, for instance, why the timocracy is a slave-state, it also creates difficulties. For one thing, honor can certainly be shared among soldiers and citizens: while a victory may require someone else's loss, that loss need not be sustained *within* the city. Moreover, competition over honor in the timocracy is not portrayed as destructive, unlike the portrayal of competition over appetitive goods in the other bad regimes. Accordingly I am not sure that honor ought to be counted as a zero-sum good in the *Republic*.

22. See n. 1. This may be why Socrates suggests that the struggles of Athens can be imagined as taking place "on many ships, or on one" (488a).

23. Timocracy, while violent and divided, is not organized around appetitive goods and so is an exception to this general principle. See discussion below (and n. 21).

24. Cf. the illuminating discussion of Thrasymachus in Barney 2004, pp. 4–8.

25. Cf. Menn 2006, p. 14, Barney 2004, p. 6.

26. On which see Barney 2006 in addition to Barney 2004.

27. Cf. Barney 2004, p. 6.

28. Taylor 1939, p. 27 puts a similar point somewhat differently.

29. That the regimes track the failure of reason is suggested by Frede 1996, p. 261.

30. For another moral decline with an anthropological structure, see Paul, *Romans* 1.18–22.

31. Division or *stasis* in timocracy: 547a–b; in oligarchy, 551d; in democracy, 564c–565a; in tyranny, 566a, 567b–c, 569a. Contrast the just city, whose unity is constituted by agreement as to who should rule (431d–432a).

32. Timocracy, 547b–c; oligarchy, 551b–c; democracy, 557a; tyranny 565d–566a, 566e–567c.

128   ZENA HITZ

33. Accordingly Frede 1996, p. 261, cannot be quite right in saying that Plato's point is to show the inherent instability of the bad regimes without the rule of reason. The rule of reason is also unstable.

34. What exactly have they gotten wrong, and why? The end result of their failure is the decline of the ruling class and the ultimate mixing of the social classes (546c6–547a5), which suggests the possibility that the ruling class misapplies the rule on account of its being misled by its own sexual appetites. (For a related view, see Roochnik 2003, who argues that the just city falls because the regulation of *erōs* is impossible (cf. especially p. 46, ch. 2).) This possibility, however tempting, is very unlikely. For one thing, there is no suggestion of wayward appetite in the text; *aisthēsis* alone is suggested as the human failing involved. For another, the eugenic discussions generally speak as if the rulers are organizing marriages for others, not themselves (e.g. 458e–461e). Lastly, since the rulers cannot even contemplate Forms until the age of 50, and rule only after some such contemplation (540a–c), they have been for the most part educated past the ordained age of child-begetting. Women rulers, forbidden to beget past 40, are certainly ruled out; men rulers have until 55, which gives them a very short window at best in which they could both rule and beget (459a–461a). The remaining scenario – that the rulers are led astray by their own appetites while arranging marriages on behalf of others – seems farfetched.

35. Number of rulers seems to distinguish monarchy, oligarchy, and democracy in Herodotus 3.80–82, although the oligarchy is also clearly meant to be an aristocracy or rule of the best. A similar distinction with a similar assumption is found in Pindar, *Pythian* 2.86. The number of rulers also plays a role in the taxonomies of constitutions in Plato's *Statesman* 302b–303b as well as Aristotle's *Nicomachean Ethics* 8.10 and *Politics* 3.5, although it is not the sole distinguishing criterion in these passages.

36. As Frede notes, using the term "characteristic value" (Frede 1996, pp. 266–67); see also Blössner 2007.

37. Unlike the democracy or oligarchy, there is no suggestion that this is a legal exclusion.

38. Cf. Aristotle, *Politics* 1317a40–1317b17.

39. Reeve 1988, pp. 47–48, claims wrongly that the democratic character is ruled by unnecessary desires. Furthermore, the distinction between necessary and unnecessary desires is clearly meant to be a division only within the appetites, and not, as Reeve claims, one that cuts across desires of reason and spirit (pp. 44–47; *Republic* 558d–559d).

40. Reeve claims on the contrary that the tyrant is ruled by lawless desires (Reeve 1988, p. 47).

41. My schema differs from that found in Reeve not only on some interpretive points (see previous two notes) but also because of differences in emphasis and interest: (1) it is meant to summarize only Books 8 and 9, and not the whole *Republic*, and (2) I emphasize the dominant end over the type of motivation, and treat the finer-grained distinction in dominant ends found in *Republic* 8 as

Degenerate regimes in Plato's Republic 129

more significant than the broader division in Book 9 between lovers of wisdom, honor, and money (Reeve 1988, p. 43).

42. The question of whether the democrat and the democracy are ruled by appetite is a different question from the question of whether all of the democratic character's motivations are appetites. Cooper 1984 argues that they are all appetites; Scott 2000 claims that the democratic character features rather a mixture of motivations. The passage at 572c where the democratic character is said to draw equally from his necessary and unnecessary appetites supports Cooper; the famous description of the democrat pursuing everything that strikes his fancy, including soldiering and philosophy (561c–d), supports Scott. I think that the passages can be reconciled by simply assuming that the democrat's primary focus is the appetites (as described at 572); that not all of the democrat's motives are appetites (as seen at 561c–d); and that he is to be considered "appetitive" or "ruled by appetite," since his ultimate standard is his desires or what he happens to want. This ultimate standard vitiates any good motivation and renders its goodness powerless. The same is true in the political analogy; although democracy contains a variety of characters (557b–d), a wise and good man such as Socrates is powerless in the Athenian democracy. According to the account at *Apology* 32b–c, Socrates is ordered to act unjustly both by the democracy and by the Thirty, and so faces either the compromise of his goodness or prosecution resulting in execution or expulsion. So, I suggest, we ought to think of the function of better characters in democracies and the better motivations in the democrat; the democrat's interest in philosophy cannot attain knowledge, and his flirtation with soldiering cannot produce courage.

43. See n. 34.

44. Socrates describes what he and the interlocutors are doing as *nomothetein*, legislating, at various points in the text (398b3, 403b4, 409e5, 417b8, 456b12, 459e5, 463c9, 525b11, 534b8, 534e1); he also three times calls Glaucon *nomothetēs*, the lawgiver (429c2, 458c6, 497d1).

45. Talking to it: 416e–417a; satisfying it with its natural object: 586a–587a; soothing it in a mysterious way by music: 390a–b. Moss agrees that the education in music is meant to educate both appetite and spirit (Moss 2008, pp. 43–44).

46. I am indebted to Caroline Wekselbaum (2006) for pointing out the importance of public appearance in degenerate regimes.

47. Xenophon, *Constitution of the Lacedaimonians* 11.5–9; cf. Plutarch, *Lycurgus* 17.1–4.

48. Plutarch, *Lycurgus* 18.1.

49. The combination of persuasion and compulsion in the law described here seems to me a clear anticipation of the doctrine of preludes in the *Laws*.

50. See Wekselbaum (2006, p. 28) for the point.

51. Frede 1996, p. 263, complains that this is without historical basis; Schofield 2006, pp. 118–19, finds otherwise, citing Adam's example of Crito's assumption that Socrates can walk away even though he has been sentenced to death.

130 ZENA HITZ

52. Nettleship 1897, p. 310, cited by Adam 1902, p. 244.
53. Shorey 1930, p. 316, notes parallel accounts of the exploitation of the rich in Athens.
54. A 1915 paper by F. V. Merriman is the exception: Merriman makes the claim that one can trace the decline through the progressive loss of the virtues (cf. especially p. 13).
55. See the parallel account of the shifting balance between *aretē* and greed in the timocracy (550e–551a).
56. This passage has an obvious parallel in Thucydides' account of the shifting virtues during the plague at Athens (3.82).
57. It is possible that timocratic courage is an exception, especially given the qualifications put on Book 4 courage as "civic courage" (430c).
58. See Ober 1989, pp. 291–304; Vlastos 1981a.
59. Aristotle, *Politics* 1317a40–1317b17; Thucydides 2.37, 7.69. I discuss this in my 2005 review of Kurt Raaflaub's *The Discovery of Freedom in Ancient Greece*.
60. See Schofield 2006, pp. 104–05, with references.
61. This is not to say, of course, that Plato's analysis of historical democracy and oligarchy is correct. It is only to say that it is more sophisticated than it looks at first appearance, and so evaluating its correctness is more complex than it might have seemed.
62. This is supported by recent work by Hendrik Lorenz 2006 on the division of the tripartite soul. Lorenz argues – to my mind, entirely convincingly – that rational functioning can never be attributed to the lower parts, appetite or *thumos*, and that appetites do not directly conflict with one another (Lorenz 2006, part I). Accordingly, mental conflict is always between soul-parts. On his reading of the oligarchic character, for instance, the conflict in his soul is not between different types of appetite, but between weak and corrupt rational desires and strong appetitive ones (pp. 41–52).
63. I have been much influenced by the arguments of Moss 2008. She argues that Plato's division of the soul ought to be understood as a division between (i) reason as an active calculator and evaluator of appearances and (ii) non-rational parts passively affected by appearances and closely associated with sense-perception.
64. The timocrat arises from hearing (*akouein*) his mother's complaints about his father's status (549c), and "sees and hears" the same things (repeated twice), while also "seeing and hearing the words of his father" (550a). The timocratic leadership "observe" (*horōn*) and emulate one another and decay accordingly (550e). The timocrat turns into an oligarch after seeing his father ruined, and after "seeing and suffering these things" (*idōn tauta kai pathōn*), he turns to the pursuit of wealth (553b). The oligarchy falls when the rich and poor "observing" (*theōmenoi*) one another at a public event see that the one class is weaker than the other (556c–d). The democratic man arises from the oligarch by being exposed to certain pleasures (559d). The misleading speeches of the demagogue-drones are the means to overturning democracy (564d–566b).

65. I thank the audience at the 2008 Arizona Colloquium and my commentator Nils Raahut for a very helpful discussion; thanks also to Cristina Ionescu, Liz Irwin, Patrick Miller, and Rachel Singpurwalla for valuable comments on a previous version. I have learned a great deal from many conversations with many people about *Republic* 8 over the past several years, and I gratefully dedicate this essay to them: my fellow-students, teachers, colleagues, and friends.

CHAPTER 7

Virtue, luck, and choice at the end of the Republic

Mark L. McPherran

> Human life occurs only once, and the reason we cannot determine
> which of our decisions are good and which bad is that in a given
> situation we can make only one decision; we are not granted a second,
> third, or fourth life in which to compare various decisions.
>
> (Milan Kundera, *The Unbearable Lightness of Being*)

The *Republic* famously ends with a consideration of the previously dismissed question of the rewards of justice by first proving the soul's immortality (*Rep.* 10, 608c–612a) and then arguing for the superiority of the just life in what appear to be purely consequentialistic terms. Plato begins by affirming Adeimantus' story (362d–363e) that the gods reward just souls and punish the unjust during the course of their earthly lives (612a–614a), and then – just as Cephalus feared (330d–331a) – the gods do the same in the afterlife (614a–621a).[1] In the world as it is, the *reputation* of being just – though often ill-accorded – correctly reaps the external rewards that it typically does; but regardless of one's earthly reputation, the gods are fully aware of who is just and who is not, always loving the former and always hating the latter (612d–e; cf. 2, 362e–363e). Hence, although we might believe that those who are actually just are neglected in favor of those who are only seemingly just on those occasions when the actually just are visited by conventional evils (e.g., poverty, disease), these events must be understood to be only apparent evils: they are either beneficial punishments for previous errors or they assist the recipient in some other fashion. Besides such disguised benefits, however, the gods visit easily-recognizable goods on the just person insofar as he or she resembles the gods by being good (612e–613b).

Happy as this account is, critical readers often find it a silly bedtime story – or worse – lacking in philosophical depth and charm. For in the context of the *Republic*'s justice-advocating project as a whole, Book 10 can appear to be "gratuitous and clumsy," to quote Julia Annas.[2] This is particularly true because of the way Book 10 spells out the post-mortem

Virtue, luck, and choice at the end of the Republic

rewards of justice by deploying the odd story of Er's near-death experience, a myth whose "vulgarity seems to pull us right down to the level of Cephalus, where you take justice seriously when you start thinking about hell-fire."[3] It is this myth and this sort of sensible reaction to its contents that I want to consider here.

The Myth of Er provides a last glimpse of the *Republic*'s gods as they dispense justice in the hereafter, but it is difficult at best to know how to view this particular story in light of Plato's categorical denigration of mimetic writing.[4] It is, however, in both theme and detail similar to Plato's other eschatological myths that display a willingness to use pain and pleasure as inducements to virtuous behavior for those non-philosophical individuals who are not yet prepared to pursue virtue for its own sake (*Phd.* 107c; *Grg.* 523a–527e; *Phdr.* 245c–257b). These are myths that are to be taken as true in their essentials (e.g., *Grg.* 522b–523a, 526d–527c); each is an allegory – a *hyponoia* (*Rep.* 2, 378d–e) – and, as such, has an "underthought" that might be revealed. Moreover, in this particular case, Socrates also emphasizes the need to *heed* the message of Er's story, whatever it might be (621b–d; and see 618b–619a). Nevertheless, its complex portrait of the long-term rewards for striving after justice is, again, often found to be depressing, not reassuring.[5] For although there are tenfold rewards for the just and tenfold punishments for the unjust, there are also non-redeeming, everlasting tortures for those who, because of their impious and murderous behavior, have become morally incurable (615c–616b; cf. *Grg.* 525b–526b). True to the theological principle established in Book 2 that "God is not the cause of all things, but only of the good things" (whatever it is that causes bad things, that cause is not divine; *Rep.* 2, 380c6–10; 3, 391e1–2), Plato then explicitly attempts to relieve the gods of all responsibility for the future suffering we might experience in our next incarnation by means of two insulating episodes. First, there is a lottery that determines one's order of choice in picking that new life, and then one is offered the chance to browse through and select from a range of future lives (619e; cf. *Odyssey* 1.32–41). An individual soul's choice of what will prove to be a happy life of justice depends both on the apparently random fall of the lots (617d–618b, 619c–d) and on that soul's ability to select its next life wisely. Unfortunately, it is unclear if the lottery is rigged in some fashion, and a soul's degree of practical choice-making wisdom is constrained by its prior experiences, experiences that were in turn the result of even earlier, seemingly chancy, and relatively ignorant choices. Hence, even the souls that have lived lives of just action – but performed their actions out of habit rather than genuine understanding – will arrive at the lottery having forgotten the sufferings that preceded the narcotic, memory-erasing rewards they received in Heaven. As a result, most of these souls will make hasty, unfortunate choices in picking their next incarnations and so will suffer further torments in the future (617d–621b). Particularly noteworthy on this score is the first soul in the life-choice line. Despite – or perhaps because of – the rich variety of lives laid out before him, he rashly chooses the life of a man who is fated (*heimartos*; 619c1) to eat his own children (619b–c).

Finally, aside from the apparently random work of the lottery, Plato has never adumbrated the many sources of evil mentioned in Book 2; sources against which even the gods are powerless and which might – for all we know – thwart the expected happiness of our next lives.[6] So although the last lines of the *Republic* encourage us to race after justice so that we may collect our Olympian rewards (621b–d), it is understandable that some might still find Thrasymachean short-cuts a better moral strategy in the choice-insistent here and now.

It is exceedingly hard to determine how Plato meant for us to read this myth: perhaps all its details of colored whorls and lotteries are only entertaining bits of window-dressing, not to be taken as contributing to a philosophically coherent eschatology.[7] This is poetry, after all, and it is, again, composed within the framework of a dialogue that disdains poetry. On the other hand, it may be possible to read Er's tale as alluding to the beneficial initiations of Eleusis, but now connected to the true initiation and *conversion* provided by philosophical dialectic.[8] There are also reasons to suppose that the Myth's display of whorls, Sirens, and Necessity are symbolic of the metaphysical elements of the *Republic*'s middle books, and are thus meant to impress on each soul prior to its next choice of life and its drink from the River of Forgetfulness (620e–621c) the message of those books, namely, that the happiest life is the life of Justice and the Good, and so ought to be chosen for that reason alone.[9]

The essential message that Plato intends does seem to come through loud and clear, however: no god or *daimōn* can be blamed for whatever fix we may happen to find ourselves in when we put down Plato's text. Moreover, by fixing the determinates and outcomes of our present choices in the lap of the gods of past choice (Lachesis) and future necessity (Atropos) – and whether Plato intends this effect or not – readers can find themselves put off by all such *dei ex machina* and thus inclined to recall the truly pious aspirations of philosophy developed over the preceding nine books. If so, they will perhaps find themselves encouraged and emboldened to dismiss the cheap motivations of carrot and stick outlined in Book 10, seemingly for the benefit of the vulgar many.[10] The end of the *Republic* can thus be read as

Virtue, luck, and choice at the end of the Republic

returning us to the stern Socrates of Book 1 who urges us to choose the path of justice *simpliciter*, and damn the consequences (cf. *Cri.* 48a–49e). To this, however, his pupil has now added in eight books of subsequent argument a more rigorous moral and religious message that grounds that choice in a transcendental aspiration and assimilation to an unseen perfect Justice apprehended by collegial, all-good gods.[11]

With this happy albeit speculative solution to the place of the Myth in the philosophical economy of the *Republic*, we must, however, face as best we can the problem it poses for Plato's own conception of moral responsibility (and the attached Problem of Evil).[12] That is, Plato clearly intends to keep the gods clear of any responsibility for *our* wrongdoing and consequent suffering, but the muddled insulating mechanisms he installs to place such responsibilities in our laps call into question the *Republic*'s entire project of adumbrating a theory of justice: for, one wonders, how can there be any sort of human justice without our possessing real, coherent responsibility for the character from which our actions – for whose consequences we will later pay – spring? Moreover, how can the *Republic* make any legitimate impact on its readers, if its readers cannot be held morally responsible for their reactions to that very text? Do we not generally forgive our own freshmen when they recoil from their first encounter with Kallipolis, finding it an anti-Spring Break dystopia?

The pivotal section of the *Republic* generating our concern runs as follows:

Now when ... [the souls] arrived they were straightway bidden to go before Lachesis, and then a certain prophet (*prophētēs*; 617d2–3) first marshaled them in orderly intervals, and there took from the lap of Lachesis lots and patterns of lives and went up to a lofty platform and spoke, "This is the word of Lachesis, the maiden daughter of Necessity. 'Souls that live for a day, now is the beginning of another cycle of mortal generation where birth is the beacon of death. Your *daimōn* will not be assigned to you by lot; you will *choose your own daimōn*. Let him to whom falls the initial lot first select a life to which he shall be bound by necessity (*anagkē*; 617e3). But virtue knows no master; each will possess it to a greater or less degree, depending on whether he values it or disdains it. The blame is his who chooses. God is blameless' (*anaitios*; 617e5)." So saying, the prophet flung the lots out among them all, and each took up the lot that fell by his side, except himself [Er]; him they did not permit. And whoever took up a lot saw plainly what number he had drawn. And after this again the prophet placed the patterns of lives before them on the ground, far more numerous than the assembly. They were of every variety ... But there was no determination of the quality of soul, because *the choice of a different life inevitably (anagkē; 618b3) determined a different character.* But all other things were commingled with one another and with wealth and

136   MARK L. McPHERRAN

poverty and sickness and health and the intermediate conditions. (*Rep.* 10, 617d–618b; my emphasis)

Every commentator on the Myth of Er has rightly understood Plato's insertion of the initial lottery to be his way of initially absolving the gods of moral responsibility for each soul's choice of a life and the consequences that accompany that choice. Blame for one's placement in the choice-queue will then be placed on *tuchē*, commonly translated as "luck" or "chance" (619c–d). Any doubts on that score can be settled by looking at Book 5, 460a, where the marriage lottery – albeit a "sophisticated" lottery, meaning a "fixed" one – is introduced with the explicit aim of deflecting blame from the guardians onto *tuchē*. It is also possible to suppose that the lottery is introduced as a mechanism that will ensure as fair a distribution of life-choices as is practically possible (although such a supposition would appear to undermine the gods' providential power and goodness). We are, then, to understand the mysterious prophet to cast out in one throw a collection of markers with numbers or other indicators of the sort we moderns find in large delicatessens and government offices, with the assembled souls then each simply *choosing* the marker closest to them in order to determine each of their places in the life-choice queue. Interestingly, Plato does not explain why no soul attempts to acquire a lower-numbered marker that falls near another (as might happen in a jostling, big city deli, especially if Plato's would-be tyrant of 619b–c were there). The solution to this puzzle is evident, however. Lachesis is a deity – the goddess of lots – and that deity has implicitly ordered each soul to choose the closest marker. But then this scenario seems to offer the souls less choice than we might have thought.

Once confronted with the final selection of a life, each soul inspects a series of life-paradigms and picks one. The life-experiences that are the consequences of choosing that life-paradigm will reconfigure the ordering of that soul's three component parts, thereby deciding whether it will be driven primarily by its appetites, spirited part, or intelligence in a human or non-human form. This, however, seems often a purely reactive, emotionally driven selection, and so not a relatively unconstrained choice. For example, and in what is perhaps a last slap at the poets, Plato tells us that the soul "that had once belonged to Orpheus" adopted the life of a swan in order to avoid being conceived by and born to the kind of being – a female human – that had caused his previous death (620a). The choice of a life, we are meant to see – at least for non-philosophers – is a somewhat automatic *reaction* to the kind of suffering experienced in one's previous incarnation. It is clear that Plato means to emphasize this fact, for otherwise he would not

Virtue, luck, and choice at the end of the Republic   137

go on at length, offering one example after another of famous and relatively intelligent individuals who – despite their rich experiences of life – make choices that have all the appearance of being "on the rebound" selections (619e–620d). For example, besides the case of Orpheus, we are told that both Ajax and Agamemnon chose animal lives – the life of a lion and an eagle respectively – because of what they suffered at the hands of other humans (620a–b). But as we saw above, this account then seems to result in an infinite regress of states of moral responsibility, since every choice of a life springs from the character of a soul whose condition is the result of the consequences of its presumably constrained prior choice, and so on (Dorter 2003, p. 131). Worse yet, the sketchy model of deliberation we are given makes a mystery of the disembodied soul, for if it is not *Orpheus* who chooses to become a swan but *the soul* that once was Orpheus, we are left to wonder concerning the identity and nature of this soul-in-itself prior to and subsequent to its incarnation into swanhood.[13] The most plausible account of it in view of Plato's remarks at 618d would identify it with our reason alone – a reason that is able to deliberate and choose a new life – but do we or Plato really want to credit the souls of birds and beasts with the same rational faculty that *we* possess?[14] And if here the soul *is* pure reason, then what sort of pleasures and pains could this purified soul have experienced during its previous thousand years of reward and punishment? That is, if the soul in the afterlife is reason alone, how can it possess lower-level appetites or desires to reward or thwart? This problem may explain why Plato does not spell out these rewards and punishments in any degree of satisfying detail (see n. 23).

Despite all this, some commentators have chosen to accept Plato's story at more or less face value, and so find him in the cosmic context he mythologizes to be advocating the idea that even if " ... our choices are always determined by an infinite regress of previous choices, at least this chain of causality is not an empty, meaningless, blind necessity, but follows from the rational nature of the universe."[15] For although the rewards and punishments of Tartarus and Heaven might on many occasions influence the appetitive and spirited parts of a particular soul, it remains possible for each soul's rational part to choose its next life wisely and to then prevent it from drinking too deeply from the River of Unheeding (619b, 619e; 621a).[16] And while our reason may itself be structured and strongly influenced by its prior life choices, the pick of a particular life by a soul's reason is free in a sense compatible with causal determinism. After all, goes this line of thought, this choice is made by our truest self, namely, Reason.[17] However, I remain unconvinced by this sort of approach, although that does also leave me at this juncture with not much more than a "record of honest perplexity" (to recall Gregory Vlastos's view of the first part of the *Parmenides*).[18]

The problem, as I see it, begins with the casting of lots. Here we must ask why Plato employs a prophet, and why he fails to name him. The best answer to this second query is, presumably, that any identification of the prophet would make suspect the prophet's motivations, and this would then cast doubt on the apparent randomness of his throw. Next, we have to have a *prophet* because Plato requires a divine being of some kind – this is a non-mortal Realm (whether it be extraterrestrial or not), after all, and so Plato requires an immortal of some sort to do the job of lot-casting and soul-instruction. However, a full-blown divinity would thwart the entire purpose of insulating the gods from any responsibility for our next-life suffering; hence, Plato adopts a lesser divinity for the job. Is this move successful? The answer, alas, has to be "no."

Plato mysteriously undermines his insulation project by describing the lot-caster as a *prophet*, thus as a being who can in theory know in advance the outcome of his toss. The semi-divine prophet could, then, influence his toss in a non-random way. But, still, it might be objected that we cannot be sure that the prophet does anything more than the minimum a prophet might be expected to do, namely "speak on behalf, or under the influence, of divine authority/inspiration."[19] So, our prophet might not know the outcome of his toss, or even if he does, that need not mean that he would influence that toss.[20] But although this point does blunt the force of the worry that Plato's use of the term "prophet" causes, it does not entirely dissipate it. For a reader is bound to notice that the prophet does more than merely *speak* for the god Lachesis: he *acts* as well – and if, then, the point is to insulate the gods thoroughly from any moral responsibility for our bad choices, why label this being a "prophet" in the first place? Why not just call him "the tosser" or "the croupier," or why not install a lottery tumbler or other device that might better reassure us that random, non-intentional forces and not divinities are at work in the arrangement of the life-queue?

More worrisome, perhaps, is the fact that for the audience Plato has the prophet address – the disembodied souls *and* Plato's own ancient readers – the casting of lots (*klēroi*) was not a way of making a decision *via* a random selection; rather, it was a way of allowing *the gods* to decide an issue.[21] Moreover, the meaning of "*tuchē*" cited at 619c5 as a force the tyranny-choosing-soul will blame is easily construed as "divine providence" and not the random, contingent, spontaneous, and indeterminate chance that was recognized (if not endorsed) by the early atomists and others (e.g.,

Virtue, luck, and choice at the end of the Republic 139

Thucydides [perhaps], Jocasta in Soph. *Oedipus Tyrannus* 977–78, and Euripides [*Helena* 267–69; *Troiades* 469–71]).[22] So, then, it seems that on a deeper reading the ordering of the life-choice queue is not random, but takes place through a Providence Plato is unwilling to expose and explain (and, in addition, results from Lachesis' implicit order to pick the closest marker). Still, we might be reassured by this reading, precisely because it *does* implicate wise(r) beings in the process of our future life-choices. On the other hand, though, one would expect that, if the lottery is being manipulated, the first choice would go to a *philosophical* soul, not one who was virtuous merely through habit and who thus goes on to make a monumental, child-abusing error.

A graver stumbling block appears once we arrive at the head of the queue, where each soul in that cohort is presented with a collection of life-outlines. These paradigms have inscribed on them the major, more or less *external* life-events with which one would have to cope, such as the fact that one will be well-born or not, and whether one will at some point in that life become wealthy or poor, healthy or ill, and so on (617e–619b). To the gods' credit, the prophet announces that it is possible for even the very last soul in the queue to discover a life-token that would yield a satisfactory life-experience, if that life were to be lived with serious intent (619b). However, we should worry that, since at any one moment there are many more non-philosophers than philosophers on the earth, the souls will be selecting out of a pool of lives that includes a large number of non-philosophical life-tokens and only a few philosophical ones (617e–618a). Moreover, their choices will occur in a haphazard and/or reactive way, and hence, the chance of one's having a maximally happy future life is directly proportional to one's place in the suspiciously organized queue.

In any event, we are at least told that the assembled souls are warned to choose a life only after a careful, deliberative inspection of the outlines before them (619b). But despite this warning, some souls are stubbornly negligent and thus choose lives without sufficient rational consideration, lives that cause them grave unhappiness – as, again, illustrated by the first unfortunate soul in the queue (who rashly chooses the life of a child-eating tyrant [619b–c]). When we wonder how this individual could have overlooked such a glaring, painful, evil episode, Plato explains that this overhasty soul was one of those whose previous life had been virtuous merely through habit, and hence, was someone still under the spell of his pleasure-filled thousand-year rewards (619c).[23] In this tranquilized state he is overcome by foolish, blind greed (*laimargia*; 619c) and so snatches up what seems to be an attractive life of power and luxury. The problem here, of course, is that this story requires that the externals of the life one chooses – such as riches and political power – when allied to a particular sort of soul, *necessitate* a particular character-state that then *necessitates* the performance of an action that one ought not to perform both absolutely and in terms of consequentialistic self-interest (618c–d, 619b–c, 620a). One is stuck choosing one's *future* choices in a state of relative ignorance. This is especially true, given that souls commonly drink too deeply from the River of Unheeding (under their new *daimōn*'s influence?), forgetting all the educational conversations they had with their fellow souls during their previous week of leisure in the Meadow (614d–616b; 621a–b). To avoid a completely deterministic system, however, Plato posits that the soul's rational part – *if* that soul is ruled by that part and *if* that part possesses a knowledge of how external factors such as wealth will affect its future character-states and actions – *will* allow that soul to overcome its past habits and so constrain its *thumos* and appetites (e.g., mastering its fears: see 616a), and can thus choose its next life wisely.

One solution to this dismal picture might perhaps be this: the necessity that Plato speaks of at 617e3, 618b3, and 619c1 may also be a contingent one. That is, the fateful requirement that the first soul who chooses a tyrant's life eat his own children might be a necessity that comes into play only after *that* particular soul picks *that* particular life. On this interpretation, the soul selects a tyrannical life-token that contains no clear signs of what will come to pass if that particular soul does pick that particular token. But subsequent to that choice the factors that necessarily attend a tyrannical life – those a more philosophical soul might have spotted more readily – come into play and thus make inevitable its grisly family dinner.[24]

Unfortunately, readers of Plato know that he endorses the asymmetry of good and bad character states, that is, that "the voluntary acquisition of a bad character is no more possible than the voluntary performance of a bad action," and that he thinks that an action that flows from a character state is voluntary if and only if that character state is voluntary.[25] However, Plato also holds that no one acts unjustly except in a fashion contrary to his or her rational will (*Prt.* 345e; *Laws* 731c–d, 860d–861b). As the *Timaeus* has it, for example, "no one is willingly evil. A man becomes evil, rather, as a result of one or another corrupt condition of his body and an uneducated upbringing" (*Ti.* 86d–e; see also 87b). The result is a more detailed version of the vicious circle I alluded to earlier in this essay. Plato wants to absolve the gods of any responsibility for our suffering, but the cost is that he must embrace an apparently deterministic eschatology according to which the choice of a life by a non-philosopher dictates the sort of character state that then

Virtue, luck, and choice at the end of the Republic   141

dictates – or at least severely influences – courses of action that mandate that soul's future suffering or rewards that then dictate its subsequent choice of a life-paradigm, and so on.

Still, we might suppose that although the myth postulates that various external features of a life such as health and wealth can mould a non-philosopher's character, this influence need not follow a rule of causal necessity in every case. We might, for example, take the myth to claim that there are regular and predictable effects of such external influences that are not wholly deterministic, although they allow for prediction and *post hoc* explanation. So when Plato says that evil actions are involuntary, we need not understand him to hold that we cannot do other than what we do when we act badly, as a determinist would have it. What he could mean is that we violate our own deepest will and preferences when we act in such ways, and yet still maintain a degree of responsibility over how our characters are formed.[26]

Now, it is true that Plato does hold out this possibility of free deliberation and consequent responsibility for the truly philosophical souls gathered before the Throne of Necessity. They can "reason out which life is better" (618d) and so choose the best, most just life. Plato makes this alleged possibility vivid by contrasting the first, unsatisfied, soul to choose with a glimpse of the last soul to choose, namely, that of Odysseus.[27] In confirmation of the prophet's earlier claim that even the last soul in line will be able to descry a satisfactory life, Odysseus is able to find the life-token of an ordinary private individual; one that he says he would have picked even if he had been first in line. Socrates explains in what appears to be a laudatory tone that this Odysseus had been relieved of his prior love of honor by his earlier sufferings – presumably those portrayed in the *Odyssey*. Odysseus the Cunning, it seems, has been transformed into a more virtuous and philosophically reflective individual[28] by means of the purification that suffering and punishment provide (see, e.g., *Grg.* 523a–527e). He thus looks "for a long time" (620c) for the life-token of a private individual who "did his own work" (620c) – the very definition of justice the preceding books of the *Republic* had adumbrated. True to Socrates' stern advice to Glaucon at 618b–619b, by choosing the mean over the extremes Odysseus has found a life token that will lead him to live a life that will increase his justice, and thus his overall happiness.[29]

Still, though, while it's all very well to *postulate* that such souls can escape the causal chains the Myth employs, one is still left to wonder how a non-philosophical soul could ever make the sort of choice that would convert it into a philosophical soul.[30] Yet if the Myth of Er is to offer intelligent but non-philosophical souls such as Thrasymachus a motive for becoming truly just by becoming philosophical, it must at least make some attempt to address this bootstrapping problem. As it is, we seem to be left almost where the *Meno* ends: our souls might become virtuously philosophical by means of Kallipolis' educational program, but we will choose such a life in the afterlife only by means of some fortuitous, providential *theia moira* (cf. *Rep.* 6, 492a, 492e–493a).[31] In the case of Odysseus, this *theia moira* takes the form of his being third only to Zeus and Athena in his possession of wisdom, and a man who faces ten years of seafaring sufferings, imposed by the god Poseidon. But this then suggests that the gods are back in the hot seat of a responsibility from which Plato wanted to unseat them.

It will not do, then, to hold simply as Dorter (2003) does that all the souls' choices are free in a sense because they are "made by our truest self, namely, reason," since the ability of that very element to make something we would want to call a "choice" – a choice significantly unencumbered by the influence of not only *thumos* and appetite but character (one's degree of ignorance, intellectual habits, and so on) as well – appears to have been too severely compromised by the sorts of prior experiences that Er spells out. It seems that for Plato we simply are not free in the fashion that he himself requires.

Still, perhaps I am misreading the real function of the myth. Jonathan Lear, for example, has argued that those who are disappointed by the Myth because they take it to be a sign that Plato is admitting argumentative defeat are misplacing their disappointment (Lear 2006, pp. 40–42). He contends that "Plato has used myth not to argue for an actuality, but to cover the universe of possibilities," of which there are three: (1) nothingness; (2) death as removal to another sphere of existence, or (3) death as removal to another sphere of existence followed by reincarnation.[32]

One way or another, these are the ways things have to be – unless, that is, there is a fourth possibility: namely, that the world is essentially a bad place, an occasion for despair. In this world there would be an afterlife in which the just would be mocked and tortured by malevolent gods. Virtually all of the rhetorical power of the *Republic* – the allegories and myths, the arguments and images – is designed to cure the reader of the temptation to think this is a real possibility. Reality and intelligibility itself are structured by the Good. Thus while there may be grounds for *pessimism*, there can never be grounds for *despair*.[33]

I have, unfortunately, provided an argument that Lear's confidence in this last claim is itself misplaced. If the third alternative for the afterlife as spelled out by Plato is in fact a true allegory, then in light of that possibility

Virtue, luck, and choice at the end of the Republic

I might well despair of ever getting off the many-thousand-year wheel of painful incarnation Plato has thus set in motion. Where, then, does this leave us?

I suggest that although it is hard to determine Plato's designs at this point, we are supposed to be left with the strong impression – whether it is founded in a genuine Platonic commitment to the myth's reality or not – that we must still in the here and now continue to believe that we are forced to make morally significant choices in a hurry, that these choices have long-term consequences that extend beyond this present life, and that since more future pains are guaranteed for the unjust than for the just, we have instrumental reasons for being just in the present moment. For if nothing else, pain interferes with the ready acquisition of the wisdom we require to be truly happy. We can then understand the Myth of Er as an allegory of the lives we are already leading. Its motif of a prenatal life can then be interpreted as "a stark emblem of the inescapably self-forming consequences of ethical agency, a magnified image of how at every moment ... the individual soul/person is intrinsically responsible for what matters most about its existence."[34] At the very best, we can live in hope of modeling ourselves after Plato's reformed Odysseus, and thus hope that in the furnace of personal suffering our prior conceits will be eradicated. At the worst, we will hurt our children and then blame *Tuchē*, the gods, or the uncaring universe. But, Plato has warned us, the choice – such as it is – is ours alone ... so far as we can tell, at any rate. Ancient readers who thus understand Plato's picture of the afterlife as having disguised and not solved the problems of morally responsible choice and evil are thus left with reasons for performing what still *appear* to be unconstrained rational choices.[35] Modern readers can then both admire and commiserate with Plato on the size of the problem he raised but did not solve. And if the master can write dialogues that are aporetic, then perhaps it's acceptable for us to write aporetic conference papers. And if philosophy begins in wonder, then perhaps it's acceptable now and again to end there as well.[36]

NOTES

1. See J. Lear 2006, p. 39.
2. J. Annas 1981, p. 335.
3. J. Annas 1981, p. 349.
4. See J. S. Morrison 1955, and J. A. Stewart 1905, for detailed discussion of the Myth. M. L. Morgan 1990, p. 152, notes that the precise sources of the Myth "are beyond our grasp. There are doubtless Orphic, Pythagorean, and traditional elements" (cf. Stewart 1905, pp. 152–69). K. A. Morgan 2000, p. 208, claims that

144 MARK L. McPHERRAN

the Myth has the sort of correct form that Plato thinks he can use to replace traditional myth in his reformed Kallipolis.

5. E.g., Annas 1981, pp. 350–53.
6. The role of chance that seems implicit here, though, suggests that Plato may have had his later *Timaeus* view of the causes of evil in mind, causes that he locates in the disorderly motions of matter (see H. Cherniss 1971); cf. *Phdr.* 248c–d. The *Republic* does at least make clear that human evil is a consequence of our having souls that are maimed by their association "with the body and other evils" (10, 611c1–2; cf. 611b–d, 1, 353e; *Phd.* 78b–84b; *Tht.* 176a–b; *Laws* 896c–897c); e.g., not even the *Republic*'s rulers are infallible in their judgments of particulars, and so Kallipolis will fail through the inability of the guardians to make infallibly good marriages (given their need to use perception; *Rep.* 8, 546b–c). Such imperfection is, however, a necessary condition of human beings having been created in the first place, a creation that Plato clearly thought was a good thing, all things considered.
7. Annas 1981, pp. 351–53.
8. M. L. Morgan 1990, p. 150.
9. See Johnson 1999 for this reading.
10. Annas 1982a appears to come to this view of the effect of the myth, moderating her assessment in Annas 1981, pp. 349–53. This, however, raises the issue of the intended audience of the *Republic*, on which see below.
11. However, note Else 1972, who distances Plato from the authorship of Book 10.
12. Dorter 2003, p. 132; Stewart 1905, p. 169, holds that with the Myth of Er Plato is attempting (for the first time in Western philosophy) to "reconcile Free Will with the Reign of Law."
13. Thayer 1988, pp. 372, 378; Halliwell 2007, pp. 458–63.
14. I suppose Plato can maintain that animal souls possess the same rational faculty as we do, but that their diminished rational capacities result from their souls having taken a very deep drink from the River of Unheeding (619b, 619e; 621a).
15. Dorter 2003, p. 135.
16. But then here Dorter seems to think that the soul has all three of its parts present to it, but this seems at odds with the evidence that we have just seen that only the rational part of the soul is present during the period in which it makes its life-choice (see above).
17. Dorter 2003, pp. 137–38.
18. Vlastos 1954, p. 343.
19. Halliwell 1988, p. 183.
20. Thanks to Mark Ralkowski for this point. Of course, if the prophet does know the potential outcome of the toss, then it might seem incumbent on him to influence his toss for the greater good.
21. See, e.g., *Laws* 690c; 756e–758a; cf. *Ti.* 34b–36d; 46c–47e.
22. See Berry 1940, pp. 26–27. As he notes (p. 8), in its original sense *tuchē* had little to do with chance in causality, but always designated a result that found its cause in divinity. In Pindar's *Olympian* 12, for example, we are told that "saving Fortune" is the "child of Zeus the Deliverer" (12.1–2; cf. 8.67); in

Virtue, luck, and choice at the end of the Republic 145

Aeschylus *Agamemnon* 661–80 "*tuchē*" designates the work of an unknown god, while at *Libation Bearers* 59–60 we read "Among mortals good fortune (*eutuchia*) is a god and more than a god." Only later did "*tuchē*" begin to be used to mean "chance" by those who might postulate wiggle room in a cosmos otherwise under the causal thumb of divinity (Berry 1940, pp. 8–9). Halliwell 2007, p. 470, n. 37, observes that "*Tuchē* is glimpsed only in the margins of the *Republic*: see esp. 492a–c, 579c, 592a, 603e."

C. C. W. Taylor 1999, pp. 185–87, discusses Democritus' and Leucippus' assertion that all things do not happen by chance but for a reason (the Principle of Sufficient Reason) and by necessity (see, e.g., DK 67 B1), and its relation to other evidence that would allow random chance to play a causal role (e.g., Ar. *Physics* 196a24–28). A. A. Long 1977, pp. 63–88, argues that the later atomists' (e.g., Epicurus' and Lucretius') references to chance and the atomic "swerve" "do not imply . . . that sheer contingency or spontaneous events play a part in nature along with necessity" (p. 85).

See, e.g., *Rep.* 5, 460a8–10; Ar. *E.E.* 7, 1247b4–9, b28–29; *Physics* 2, 195b36–196a17; and observe that "*tuchē*" can bear the sense of "Fate" or "Necessity" (and see Taylor 1999, esp. pp. 186–88, who comments on Aetius 1.29.7: "Democritus and the Stoics say that it [i.e., chance] is a cause which is unclear to human reason"). Aristotle appears to distinguish two senses of *tuchē* at *Rhetoric* 1, 1361b39–1362a13 – where some events due to *tuchē* can be either in accordance with or contrary to nature – and *E.E.* 7, 1248b3–7, where he distinguishes divine (god-caused) good fortune from the irrational sort (at *On Divination in Sleep* 463b12–22, Aristotle uses "*tuchē*" to describe the operation of tossing dice).

23. But here one *must* ask: *Why* does Plato postulate a Heaven that rewards mere habitual virtue (especially if this myth is written for a philosophical audience)? If the point is to make virtue attractive to the non-philosophical many, why mention the later sufferings of those who are virtuous only through habit? If the point is to make philosophy attractive to the non-philosophical, why reward the non-philosophical with anything? And if the point is to spell out the rewards of any old virtuous life to the non-philosopher, why not do so *at length* and in *luscious detail*? We know well what such souls want to hear. For example, when asked about the afterlife, the late Anna Nicole Smith – a figure from popular American culture – proclaimed to a reporter for the *Los Angeles* magazine that "I think heaven's a beautiful place. Gold. You walk on gold floors." Finally, if the point is to emphasize that the just *are* to be well-rewarded, why not make their reward a permanent one, as suggested at the end of the *Timaeus* (though this last worry may simply be a consequence of an overriding commitment to reincarnation on Plato's part)?

24. Thanks to Julia Annas for this suggestion.

25. Ott 2006, pp. 66–68.

26. Thanks to Nicholas Smith for this point.

27. Thanks to Toph Marshall for this point. Note how placing Odysseus last in line brings the tale of Er full circle, back to the mention of the "tale told to

Alcinous" in the *Odyssey* (614a). Halliwell 2007, pp. 447–48, elaborates on the Odyssean motifs of the Myth, such as the Sirens. We see here in the Myth, perhaps, the kind of proper poetry that is to be distinguished from the sort rejected by Plato in Books 2 and 3.

28. *Pace* K. A. Morgan 2000, p. 207.
29. Cf. 621d; O'Connor 2007.
30. Here the puppets of the *Laws* (644e, 803c–804b) come to mind: one might read these texts as suggesting that Plato's final view was strictly deterministic: we just *are* puppets of the gods, gods who "pull *all* of our internal strings." However, a close look at those texts shows that Plato imagines that we might freely employ our "golden string of judgment" in order to rule over those other string-like internal forces.
31. Forster 2007 argues that Socrates understood all his positive moral convictions to be gifts of the gods in some sense.
32. J. Lear 2006, p. 41.
33. J. Lear 2006, pp. 41–42.
34. Halliwell 2007, p. 469; Albinus 1998, p. 99.
35. If we suppose that the intended audience of Book 10 are all philosophers already (or consider themselves so, at least – especially after their having plowed through the first nine books), we have one speculative solution to our initial puzzle: namely, that Book 10 is *not* a proleptic encouragement that employs heavenly rewards to urge its non-philosophical readers to become virtuous by becoming philosophers. Rather, Book 10 would be Plato's way of reassuring his *already*-philosophical readers that all is well *with them*, especially if they should find themselves bothered by the fear of death and the equally lowly but all-too-human worry concerning afterlife payoffs. This would more closely align the Myth of Er with the myth at the end of the *Phaedo* (107c–115a), which is said to serve as a kind of incantation against the fear of death (114d–115a). See also the myth of the *Phaedrus* at 246a–257a (on which, see Griswold 1986, pp. 87–136).
36. Thanks to Sylvia Berryman and Nicholas Smith for their comments on an earlier version of this essay. I am also indebted to Mark Ralkowski for his very useful response to the version of this essay I presented in Tucson, Arizona, February, 2007, to the Twelfth Annual Arizona Colloquium in Ancient Philosophy ("Socrates and Plato on the Nature and Teaching of Virtue"). The essay also benefited from being presented to the Classical, Near Eastern, and Religious Studies Visiting Speakers Programme, University of British Columbia, September, 2007, and the International Plato Society meeting, World Congress of Philosophy, Seoul, August, 2008.

CHAPTER 8

Plato's divided soul

Christopher Shields

I. A SURPRISE IN THE *REPUBLIC*

In the tenth book of Plato's *Republic* (608d2–5), Socrates asks Glaucon an unexpected question: "Haven't you realized that our soul is immortal and never destroyed?" Glaucon, caught unawares, responds rather incredulously: "No, by god, I certainly have not. Yet you find yourself able to assert this?" Although Socrates is confident that he is indeed able to affirm the soul's immortality, Glaucon is reflexively surprised and suspicious.

Glaucon's surprise is understandable on several distinct levels. In addition to the general incredulity Socrates' contention might awaken in a normal Greek of his place and time,[1] his question in *Republic* 10 also occasions two more local forms of surprise. First, by the time Socrates puts his question to Glaucon, we have moved through the great bulk of the *Republic*, a work whose central concern is the care and custody of the soul, finding it to contain only the briefest hints that its author supposes the soul to be immortal (*Rep.* 496c3–e2 , 498d25; cf. 330d1–331a6). Second, and more pointedly, we have to the contrary been given some reason for doubting that the soul could possibly be immortal; and presumably this is at least part of the reason Glaucon wonders aloud how Socrates feels justified in regarding himself as in a position to assert its immortality so baldly. As their exchange develops, in fact, Plato himself draws to our attention this very reason for doubt: "It is not easy," he allows, "for anything composed of many parts and not put together in the very finest way to be immortal – yet this is how the soul appeared to us" (*Rep.* 611b4–6).

In saying that the soul had appeared to the interlocutors of the *Republic* to be composite, Plato is evidently alluding to the argument for the tripartition of the soul in Book 4 of the *Republic*. If so, then he is pointing out that one of the centerpieces of his *Republic* sits poorly with his commitment to the immortality of the soul. Plainly the argument concerning the structure of the soul in *Republic* 4 is central to the entire edifice of the *Republic*; without

147

it, there would be no chance of establishing the isomorphism of soul and state, and so no chance of securing the account of justice in the soul, which is held by Socrates to be univocal with the justice of the state. Yet this is the ultimate end to which the entire apparatus of the state is expressly introduced (*Rep.* 368c–369a). Plato is accordingly right to worry about the consequences of the soul's internal divisions, if any, for the soul's immortality.

The general worry is both severe and easy to state. If we suppose, as Plato had been inclined to suppose in the *Phaedo* (esp. 78c1–4, 80b2), that everything composite eventually resolves into its parts, or more modestly that everything composite is at least liable to resolve into its parts, then if the soul has parts it will eventually go out of existence, or at least becomes liable to go out of existence – in which case we cannot be sure of its immortality. So, even in the best-case scenario, if we have committed ourselves to a divided soul, we cannot also vouchsafe its immortality. Hence Glaucon's justifiable surprise: how can Socrates, who had argued at length for the tripartition of the soul in *Republic* 4, now, much later, in *Republic* 10, regard himself as in any sort of position to allege its deathlessness?

II. AN EXPLANATION IN *REPUBLIC* 10

Socrates might give way to Glaucon's surprise by yielding on the question of the soul's immortality; but this he emphatically does not do. Instead, he steadfastly maintains that the soul "is akin to what is divine, deathless, and it always is" (*Rep.* 611e2). He must, then, confront this dilemma straightforwardly: if composite, the soul is not immortal; but if incomposite, the soul is not isomorphic with Kallipolis, with the result that there is no reason to suppose that one account of justice applies to both.[2]

One might look for an easy resolution by supposing that Plato gives up the thought that the soul is immortal if and only if it is incomposite. This possibility gains some support from the somewhat tentative nature of Socrates' statement of his problem: he says only that it is *not easy* (*ou radion*; *Rep.* 611b4) – not that it is *not possible* – to fathom something both composite and immortal.[3] This contrasts with his less qualified claim in the *Phaedo*, where he pointedly asks Cebes: "Is it not the case that anything that is a composite and compound by nature is liable to be taken apart into its component parts, and only that which is incomposite, if anything at all, is not liable to be taken apart?" (*Phaedo* 78c1–4). Perhaps, then, Plato came to hold that a suitably unified composite soul might yet be immortal.

Tempting though this resolution may be, it is not at all adequate to Plato's actual procedure in *Republic* 10. In fact, the response Socrates offers to Glaucon's surprise is much more challenging and interesting than any such expedient. His view emerges in an elaborate analogy: the situation with the soul, he contends, is akin to what we encounter in the case of the sea god Glaucus, a mortal fisherman who had been transformed into a god by eating an herb able to resuscitate dead fish.[4] Though an immortal god, Glaucus is difficult to recognize: he is besmirched by the sea, barnacle-encrusted, and misshapen in visage. Even so, he has a determinate nature lurking beneath his defilement, a nature discernible by those who study him, even if it is obscured at first and inaccessible to those able to see only his most manifest appearance. So too with our souls, Plato concludes:

> We must not think that the soul – for our argument does not allow it – is in its truest nature (*tēi alēthestatēi phusei*) anything of this sort, that it is full of variation and dissimilarity and difference, taken by itself in relation to itself. (611a10–b2)

Like Glaucus, the soul becomes manifest in essence when cleansed of its sullying connection to the body: "then one might see its true nature, whether it is multiform or uniform, and whether it is such and how" (*Rep.* 612a3–4).

If we trace the analogy with Glaucus even a little distance, then we see that Plato's contention is that the soul is, as he says, "disfigured by its association with the body and other evils" (*lelōbēmenon ... hupo te tēs tou sōmatos koinōnias kai allōn kakōn*; *Rep.* 611b10–c2; cf. *Gorg.* 511a2), just as Glaucus is "completely disfigured by the waves and the shells, seaweeds and stones that have attached themselves to him, so that he looks more like a wild animal than as he is in his nature" (*Rep.* 611d2–4). The result, he contends, is that the general account of the soul in *Republic* is apt, so long as it is borne in mind that that account is limited: "as regards the affections and forms present in human life (*ta en tō(i) anthrōpinō(i) biō(i) pathē te kai eidē*), we have given a serviceable account of the soul" (*Rep.* 612a4–5).[5] To discover its truest nature, he contends, it is necessary to "look elsewhere" (*ekeise blepein*; *Rep.* 611d6–31).

Although analogical in origin, the final purport of Plato's comparison between the soul and the sea god Glaucus is reasonably clear. He thinks that the account of tripartition in *Republic* 4 does not reveal the soul in its truest nature (*tē(i) alēthestatē(i) phusei*). This in turn places a severe constraint on how we are to understand his attitude to the argument for tripartition in *Republic* 4. The question that then arises, looking back to *Republic* 4 from the vantage point of *Republic* 10, is this: what exactly does his argument for

150   CHRISTOPHER SHIELDS

tripartition in the soul establish regarding the metaphysics of soul? We gain some traction on this question by focussing on Plato's reason for introducing tripartition in the first instance.

III. PLATO'S MOTIVATION FOR INTRODUCING TRIPARTITION

Plato's reason for introducing a tripartite soul into the *Republic* pertains to the overarching goals of that work: Plato wishes to establish the nature of justice and thereby to show why an individual might wish to be just rather than unjust. It was with that end in view that he had originally introduced the edifice of the just *polis*: "We thought that if we first tried to observe justice in some larger things that possessed it, this would make it easier to observe in a single individual" (*Rep.* 434e; cf. 544a–b, 545b, 577c). Although, he says, one cannot know in advance whether the account of justice in the state will apply directly to the individual soul, if state and soul turn out to be the same in structure, differing only in that one is bigger and the other is smaller, then the account of justice should apply to both equally. It is his concern regarding the univocity of justice, and of the subordinate issue of the possible isomorphism of state and soul, that motivates Plato's question about the internal character of the soul:

"A city was thought to be just when each of the three natural classes within it did its own work, and it was thought to be moderate, courageous, and wise because of certain other conditions and states of theirs."

"True," he said,

"Then, if an individual has the same three kinds belonging to his soul,[6] we will expect him to be called by the same names as the city if he has the same conditions (*pathē*) in him."

"That's altogether necessary," he said.

"Then, once again, my good man, we arrive at a rudimentary question regarding the soul: do these three kinds belong in it or not?" (*Rep.* 435b4–c5)

In calling this question rudimentary, or simple, or perhaps even trifling (*phaulon*; cf. *Euthph.* 2c3; *Phaedo* 95e8; *Euthd.* 307c1; *Ion* 532e2), Plato evidently speaks in an irony-tinged earnestness: the question is utterly fundamental but also, as it emerges, fiendishly difficult. It involves him in any number of questions of metaphysical psychology, including the following: Are human souls essentially complex? If so, which are their essential constituents and which, if any, inessential? We already suppose that human beings have beliefs, desires, and thoughts. Does each of these activities eventuate from a faculty discrete from the faculties of the others? And what are these faculties? Mere dispositions of the soul? Or is each a quasi-substance in its own right? If so, can any one of them exist in the absence of the other two?

This last question is not idle. At any rate, the Glaucus passage of *Republic* 10 suggests that the soul in its truest nature might be shorn of the body-sullied "affections and forms present in human life" (*ta en tō(i) anthrōpinō(i) biō(i) pathē te kai eidē*; *Rep.* 612a5). When Glaucon asks where we must look to discover the true nature of the soul, Socrates responds: "To its love of wisdom" (*eis tēn philosophian autēs*; *Rep.* 611e1), a love which Plato clearly houses in the soul's capacity to reason (*Rep.* 581d10-e4) – a capacity which he in turn identifies as that element in the human soul which is simultaneously somehow most divine *and* most human (*Rep.* 588b10–e1, *Rep.* 611e1). So far as *Republic* 10 is concerned, Plato may be thinking of the soul as having one feature or capacity essentially, and the others merely accidentally.

That would be an unsettling view, of course, and may even prove inconsistent with Plato's argument for tripartition in *Republic* 4. If that argument has the result that each human soul is essentially tripartite, then something is deeply amiss with the suggestion that any one element of the soul could exist in the absence of the others. In particular, something would be amiss with the evident purport of the Glaucus passage: that the element by which the soul reasons (*to logistikon*) can exist alone, without the other divisions of soul.

Fortunately, no such contradiction in fact arises for Plato. A careful inspection of his argument for a divided soul in *Republic* 4 shows that it does not commit him to a mereology of souls according to which human souls have *essentially* three parts. Indeed, not only does his argument fall short of establishing any such conclusion, any attempt to strengthen it so as to attain that result distorts his characterization of the ideally just human soul. The harmony of the just soul is not merely the harmonious integration of three antecedently given discrete parts, but rather the complete subordination of all of the soul's tendencies to the direction of its core faculty, reason. An optimally just soul is an optimally rational soul; and the optimally rational soul is a uniform soul. The actual argument offered by Plato for tripartition in *Republic* 4 does nothing to threaten this outcome. On the contrary, Plato himself makes clear that the "parts" of the soul identified in *Republic* 4 neither exclude one another nor exhaust the whole of the soul.

IV. THE LOGIC OF PLATO'S ARGUMENT
FOR TRIPARTITION

Plato's argument proceeds in two stages. First, he establishes that the reasoning element (*to logistikon*) is not the same as the appetitive element (*to epithumētikon*) (*Rep.* 436c–439e).[7] He then turns to the slightly more vexed question of whether there is a third element, reducible to neither the appetitive nor the rational. He argues that there is a third element, a spirited element (*to thumoeides*) (*Rep.* 439e–441c). At the end of this second phase, he declares victory: "Well, then, we have at long last reached dry land, and it is pretty well agreed that the same kinds (*genē*) are in the city and within the soul of each individual and further that they are the same in number" (*Rep.* 441c4–6).

The basic argumentative strategy of the two phases differs: the first appeals directly to a principle of opposition, the precise statement of which must be carefully parsed. The second phase also deploys this same principle, but then, given its additional complexity, needs in addition to appeal to some version of the indiscernibility of identicals, that if *a* has a feature *b* lacks, then *a* is not identical to *b*. This further principle allows Plato to fend off the suggestion that the third element might simply be one of the two established in the first phase, but under a different guise.

The first phase proceeds as follows:

Phase One:
1. If *S* stands in two opposing relations with respect to some object *o*, then *S* must do so in virtue of different internal elements *a* and *b*. (Call this the Principle of Opposing Relations (POR)) (*Rep.* 436b8).
2. Acceptance and rejection are opposing relations, as are pursuit and avoidance (*Rep.* 437b1–5).[8]
3. So, if *S* both accepts/pursues and rejects/avoids *o*, *S* must do so in virtue of different internal elements *a* and *b*. [1, 2]
4. Sometimes one and the same soul *S* both accepts/pursues and rejects/avoids one and the same object *o*. (Call this the Phenomenological Datum (PD).)
5. So, *S* must do so in virtue of different internal elements *a* and *b*. [3, 4]
6. If (5), the soul *S* is complex: it has internal elements *a* and *b*.
7. So, *S* is complex: it has internal elements *a* and *b*. [6, 7]

So far, if sound, Phase One establishes two elements within the soul, but does not characterize those elements intrinsically, even if it recommends characterizations of the parts it establishes. That is, it does not yet establish what sorts of elements are in view; nor does it establish anything determinate regarding the questions of mereology we have posed. Let us, however, for ease of exposition, suppose that *a* is reason (*to logistikon*) and *b* appetite (*to epithumētikon*). We will return to these identifications below.

On that assumption, if sound, Phase One does establish complexity within the soul by showing that souls have as internal elements reason and appetite – at least, that is, for those souls subject to the phenomenological datum (PD). In order to establish not merely bipartition, but tripartition, Plato notes that he must move on to Phase Two (*Rep.* 439e–441c). Here the argument requires more than bare opposition, since in terms of the logic of the argument, (POR) and (PD) alone could never generate more than two parts; any appeal to these two premises could in principle be handled by mere bipartition. Suppose now that we have applied the argument again, and have found a conflict between two mental states. The natural conclusion would be that we had another instance of *a–b* opposition. Unfortunately, contends Plato, in some cases that does not suffice: in some instances, the elements of opposition cannot be identified with *a* and *b*.

The second phase of the argument accepts (1-7), the thesis that the soul has discrete internal elements, as established, and then appeals to another sort of phenomenal datum. The case of Leontius (*Rep.* 439e–440a) represents an instance in which the soul wars with its appetitive element, even though the warring partner cannot be the reasoning element. So, concludes Plato, there must be a third element.

The second phase thus runs:

1. *S* is complex: it has internal elements *a* (*to logistikon*) and *b* (*to epithumētikon*).
2. Sometimes we experience a conflict with *b* (i.e., *to epithumētikon*).
3. (POR)
4. So, there is an element of the soul, *c*, which is distinct from *b*.
5. This element is either identical with *a* (*to logistikon*), or it is a third element in the soul.
6. If this element, *c*, is identical with *a* (*to logistikon*), then, *c* and *a* have all their properties in common. [The Indiscernibility of Identicals]
7. The elements *c* and *a* do not have all their properties in common.
8. Hence, *c* is not the same element as *a*. [5, 6]
9. Hence, there is a third element of the soul, *c*, distinct from both *a* and *b*. [5, 8]

This element Plato calls spirit (*to thumoeides*).

Plato has given good grounds for identifying distinct elements in the soul, provided that the several substantive theses upon which these arguments rest are true. At any rate, as structured, his arguments in both phases are clearly valid. Only the question of their soundness remains.

In that regard, two premises in Phase One merit special consideration: (POR), the Principle of Opposing Relations, and (PD), the Phenomenological Datum.

Plato states (POR) as follows:

It is clear that the same thing will not be willing to do or suffer opposites (*tanantia*) in respect of the same element, in relation to the same thing, at once. Accordingly, should we discover these things occurring in these cases [sc. in the soul], we shall know that this was not the same but many (*Rep.* 436b8–11)

The first thing to notice about (POR) is that it is wrong to characterize it as "the earliest explicit statement in Greek literature of the maxim of Contradiction" (Adam 1905, vol. 1, p. 246). If it were, then the principle would be very secure indeed. The "Maxim of Contradiction," or the Principle of Non-Contradiction as it is more regularly called today, holds that it is not possible for *x* to be both *F* and *not-F* at the same time in the same respect. Since the opposites (*tanantia*) Plato goes on to mention are not contradictories but contraries or opposites, (POR) cannot be an instance of the Principle of Non-Contradiction.[9] Rather, Plato's (POR) is a more complex explanatory principle of some sort, a synthetic principle rather than a logical principle. Unfortunately, it is easier to say what (POR) is not than it is to say what it is.

Although a synthetic principle, (POR) is not merely a *psychological principle*, to the effect that if psychological subjects exhibit contrary tendencies they must be complex. As he takes up objections to (POR), Plato considers two sorts of potential counterexamples: an archer and a spinning top (*Rep.* 436c7–e7, 439b8–c1). Neither of these is rejected on the grounds that it is not the right sort of subject for the application of (POR); neither, that is, is rejected on the grounds that it is not a psychological subject. Rather, suggests Plato, an engaging interlocutor might propose the top as a counterexample on the grounds that the whole of it is moving while the whole of it is standing still.[10] Plato responds by distinguishing the axis (*to euthu*) and the circumference (*to peripheres*; *Rep.* 436e1–2), thus highlighting that something might satisfy demands of (POR) in virtue of non-spatial or abstract features – a response with intriguing consequences regarding his conception of the soul.

The case of the archer is similarly instructive: one might contend that an archer is both pulling and pushing with respect to the same object, in violation of (POR). As his response makes clear, Plato is imagining someone contending that an archer's hands, taken together, are simultaneously pushing the bow and pulling it towards him: "It is not right, I think, to say of an archer that his hands are both pushing the bow away and pulling it towards him, but rather that one hand is pushing it away and the other is drawing it towards him" (*Rep.* 439b10–11). Here one consequence of Plato's procedure comes into view: one might as easily have said that the archer's hands are drawing the string while pushing the bow (*to toxon*; 439b9), thus dividing the object rather than the subject. Yet this would not really have changed anything regarding the force of (POR). The claim is that nothing can be in contrary relations to one and the same object. There is plainly some sense in which the archer and the bow are individual objects; neither can, given (POR), stand in relations of contrariety with respect to *any* one object. It will in fact be a consequence of (POR) that the bow can no more do and suffer contrary relations with respect to the archer than the archer can do and suffer contrary relations with respect to the bow.

Together, these points show that (POR) appeals to opposing relations quite generally. Plato assumes, quite reasonably if not unassailably, that when relations with contrary tendencies show up in a single subject with reference to the same object, then the subject in question must be internally complex. It is not a contradiction to say, e.g., that the archer is both pulling and pushing the bow; but it would be false to insist that the archer is both pulling and pushing the bow simultaneously with precisely the same aspects of himself. Nor is it a contradiction of logic to say that a man is both descending and ascending a mountain at one and the same time; the reason we feel a greater impossibility in such a case is that we are at a loss to specify distinct aspects of this man in which he might be said to be manifesting these opposing tendencies.

This general principle has a psychological application, because various psychological attitudes can be contrary to one another. In virtue of (POR), we find Plato insisting that we must, when we discover opposing tendencies within, look to find aspects, or elements, or parts, in virtue of which those tendencies are manifested. It is a non-trivial matter, of course, to determine precisely when two psychological tendencies qualify as opposing in the sense required by (POR). For instance, if Sigmund loves and hates his mother, we think it applies. Might one, however, despise and envy the God who has interdicted knowledge in the Garden of Eden with the same part of the soul?[11] The relevant relations need to be somehow exclusionary, and given that the forms of exclusion extend well beyond contradiction, it is not always completely clear when the principle applies in psychological cases.

That allowed, one may easily agree with Plato regarding some basic cases. For instance, it seems eminently reasonable to invoke (POR) when we are drawn to drink some cool clear water, but are at once pushed away from drinking that same water, because it is known to be laden with naturally occurring arsenic. The knowledge does not slake our thirst; our appetite for water does not abate when we realize that *this* cool clear water is not to be drunk.

These simple conflicts are continuous with more complex internal conflicts, including those that are more difficult to judge in terms of (POR).

This is especially so in the case of Leontius who, it seems, has an internal conflict of a more indelicate sort. He has an appetite to view corpses.[12] He struggles, and then shrieks that it will be a feast for his eyes to give in to that desire, as he then does; yet he himself finds his own appetite repugnant.

The crucial development in Phase Two of Plato's argument appeals to the thought that the struggle within Leontius' breast is not an opposition between appetite (*epithumia*) and the reasoning faculty (*logistikon*). Nor is it a simple struggle between competing appetites. It is rather a non-rational element seeking to check an appetite. The element at variance with appetite in this example is not plausibly taken to be the rational faculty, he implies, because the struggle does not seem to pit a base desire against a faculty calculating the agent's long-term well-being. Now, it is difficult to suppose that this result can be delivered directly by Plato's phenomenological datum (PD), premise (5) of Phase One of his argument. That is, it strains credulity to suppose that we are immediately aware of a conflict between appetite and some other quadrant of the soul which we know not to be reason. Still, it is a defensible development of Plato's first phase if he holds that the opposing element lacks a feature manifested by reason. For then he is entitled to conclude, as he does in fact conclude, first, that the opposing faculty cannot be identical with appetite, by (POR), and then again, second, that it cannot be reduced to the rational faculty, by the indiscernibility of identicals.

Plato is self-conscious in his appeal to the indiscernibility of identicals in this argument, expressly wondering whether a bare conflict with appetite suffices to establish a third psychic element. Having applied (POR) to the case of Leontius, Plato concludes that there must be *something* in the soul beyond appetite. He then observes that something filled with spirited pride at times contends with appetite, and so asks regarding the element opposing Leontius' insalubrious appetite: "Then is it also different from the rational part, or is it some form of it, so that there are two parts in the soul – the rational and the appetitive – instead of three?" (*Rep.* 440e). He answers that it must be a third part, "as long as it proves to be something different from the rational part" (*Rep.* 441a5–6). This, he says, will not be at all difficult to establish, because conflicts of the sort described show up even in small children, who lack reason, and indeed, to drive the point home, even in non-rational animals (*Rep.* 441a–b). Granting these claims, it is clear that the opposing element cannot be identified with reason; so, since neither is it appetite, it must be a third element.

Plato calls this third element *spirit* (*thumoeides*). Spirit poses some interesting challenges to Plato's interpreters, since it is not at all clear how its various functions and activities unify into a single element. It engages in self-rebuke (*Rep.* 440a); it wells up in anger when it perceives a slight or senses injustice (*Rep.* 441d); it allies itself with reason against appetite, when called to do so, like a dog to a shepherd (*Rep.* 440c–d). In general, it seems to be a psychic element with a reflexive awareness of the self and its social standing, able to combat desires and easily incited to anger when it perceives something as amiss.[13] Because we are at present primarily interested in the logic of the argument, we must set aside these interesting and important questions. The important point to grasp in the current context is that spirit cannot be reduced to reason, since it has features lacked by reason. Indeed, according to Plato, it is not even coextensive with the rational faculty. So, spirit must be a third element in the soul.

In arguing for the third element of the soul in Phase Two of his argument for tripartition, Plato again appeals to (PD), the phenomenological datum; so, he seems to be supposing that the sorts of cases described will be familiar to us all. The experiences he mentions do in fact resonate: we do at times rebuke ourselves; we do at times respond angrily to perceived slights; we do struggle with our appetites in ways that do not directly engage our personal calculations regarding our long-term well-being. It seems perfectly obvious, whatever its ultimate significance from the standpoint of psychic division, that we do experience the kinds of psychic upheaval to which Plato repeatedly appeals in his argument for tripartition. One question investigated below concerns whether we *must* experience such internal discord.

This is because Plato seems to indicate that we can escape such discord by becoming perfectly just. Plato describes the just person as follows:

One who is just does not allow each bit within him to do the work of any other or allow the classes within him to interfere with one another. He structures well what is really his own and rules over himself. He puts himself in good order, is his own friend and comes to be dear to himself, joining in unity what are three, like three limiting notes in a simple musical scale – high, low, and middle. Having bound together all these and any others there may be in between, and from having been many things, he becomes entirely one, moderate and well assembled. Only then does he act. (*Rep.* 443d1–e1)

Plato's ideal human is a fully integrated harmonious soul, someone who has fully harmonized the three elements of his soul and "any others there may be in between" and has thus become "entirely one." This is striking, since Plato's just man emerges as someone to whom (PD) does not apply. Plato's just person is like Aristotle's *phronimos*: such a person acts virtuously well and gladly, without needing to overcome the impediment of internal struggle.

This fact regarding the just person raises a fundamental question regarding the character of Plato's psychic mereology: when the three elements of the soul give way to something which is entirely one, then internal discord abates. If so, then the argument Plato develops to establish the tripartite psychology has no purchase in the case of the just person. (PD) does not apply in his case. If that is correct, then Plato's argument for tripartition seems not to describe a condition of the human soul in general, but of the human soul in its normal suboptimal condition. How, then, can it be taken to establish an essential or even universal feature of the human soul? In light of this question, it becomes necessary to reflect upon what Plato's argument for tripartition does and – more importantly does *not* – establish.

V. FIVE THINGS THIS ARGUMENT DOES NOT ESTABLISH

Plato's argument for tripartition is plainly a centerpiece of his *Republic* as well as a landmark in the history of psychology. Precisely where its significance extends, however, remains an unsettled question. It accordingly behoves us to reflect upon the limits of the argument by focussing in some detail on the matter of what it does *not* establish. Doing so is important not least because the argument has too regularly been taken to establish some theses about the soul it in fact does not establish, including indeed some theses it in fact *could not* establish. These are: (i) that the soul is *essentially* tripartite; (ii) that the parts of the soul are *homunculi*; (iii) that the parts of the soul are individual psychological subjects; (iv) that the division of the soul marked in *Republic* 4 precludes other, competing divisions he might introduce elsewhere; and, finally, (v) that the parts of the soul are indeed "parts" in any sense of "parts" according to which the whole soul is some manner of aggregate. About this last point, it follows that when reflecting on the very real kinds of psychic discord Plato catalogues with such arresting insight in the *Republic* we would do well to follow Plato's own practice by speaking of "parts" only sparingly and in an attenuated sense.

It bears stressing that the limits traced here rely upon the exegesis of Plato's two-phase argument provided in the last section. Naturally, those who think the argument establishes more than is here claimed are at liberty to challenge the reconstruction of the argument provided above. Short of that, however, Plato's argument proves less committal than many of his interpreters have supposed.

(1) The Platonic soul is not essentially tripartite

There is a point regarding the logic of Plato's argument which demonstrates very clearly that he cannot, under pains of committing a modal fallacy, be intending to use his argument to establish three essentially distinct parts of the human soul. The reason is straightforward: the logic of Plato's argument for soul-division does not warrant any such conclusion.

If the human soul's rational, spirited, and appetitive faculties are permanent and essential parts or features of the soul, then they are *de re* necessary. Plainly, however, Plato's argument does not support any such modal conclusion. The reason is the occurrence of (PD), the Phenomenological Datum, which features in both phases. Plato's (POR), the Principle of Opposing Relations, generates a division only if opposite tendencies crop up in the same soul. There is reason to believe that opposite tendencies crop up in the same soul, however, only if we accept, on phenomenological grounds (PD), that one and the same soul undergoes internal strife. Granting that we do in fact experience internal strife on occasion, the question becomes whether we *must* undergo such experiences, at the cost of ceasing to be human beings.

The point here is not merely epistemological – though it is true that we would have no grounds for applying (POR) were it not for (PD). Rather, we would commit Plato to a modal fallacy unless we were regarding him as asserting (PD) as necessary. In its briefest form, in the first phase of his argument Plato infers from (POR) and (PD) that there are at least two elements in the human soul, namely, reason and appetite. To arrive at the conclusion that these two elements belong essentially, and so necessarily, *both* premises must be necessary. That is, from (1) *Necessarily (POR)* and (2) *(PD)*, Plato is not entitled to infer (3) *that the soul necessarily has distinct elements*. That conclusion requires, additionally, a modal version of (PD). (From (1) *Necessarily, if Stanley is married, then he has a spouse*, and (2) *Stanley is married*, it does not follow that (3) *Stanley necessarily has a spouse*. This modal conclusion would follow only on the further, false premise that Stanley is necessarily married.)[14] If, however, Plato's argument fails to establish that divisions of the soul are necessary, then it equally fails to establish that the divisions he marks are essential to the soul.

Given that this is a straightforward modal fallacy, and given that there is no indication in the text whatsoever that Plato is guilty of it, it is difficult to see what could have induced commentators to saddle him with it.

Of course, one could attempt to strengthen the argument Plato actually gives by treating (PD) as a necessary truth. As far as the logic of the argument goes, there would then be a valid argument for the conclusion

160 CHRISTOPHER SHIELDS

that the soul is necessarily divided. It is difficult to see why Plato should wish to accept such a modal premise, however. To begin, his description of the just person provides every indication that he believes that it is within the realm of possibility that a human soul could be strife-free. Indeed, he pretty well asserts just this, later in the *Republic*, when he characterizes the just person as free of internal civil war (*Rep.* 586e–587a). On its surface, this sounds as if he thinks it is actual that some humans escape (PD). If he thinks it is actual, then Plato trivially thinks it possible; and if it is possible that some humans exist strife-free, then it is trivially possible that they do so. It follows, then, that (PD) is not necessary.

To repeat the present, more modest point, however: the argument Plato provides for soul-division in *Republic* 4 does not establish essential divisions within the soul. Since he does not assert (PD) as necessary, he cannot infer that the soul is essentially divided. Fortunately, he draws no such conclusion.

(2) The parts of the soul are not homunculi

It is an attractive metaphor, and one to which various commentators have succumbed.[15] The picture is that each of the three aspects of the soul is a sort of little man, perhaps not fully formed, but each with a wide range of the intentional states and the sort of autonomy regularly ascribed to individual psychological subjects. It is just that one of the small men within is dominated by his appetites and is a beastly sort of man, and another is dominated by his spirit and is a fierce, proud man, insufficiently attentive to his reasoning faculty. By contrast, the rational man within is cool and calculative, tracking the good in his every move. These three jostle with one another, one sometimes dominating and the other receding and then the other coming to the fore in hegemonic fashion. This model explains both the strife we experience within, so often characterized by Plato as a sort of civil war (*Rep.* 586e), and also the phenomenon of *akrasia*; when reason decides on a course of action only to be upended before implementing its desires, the explanation resides in the unruly behaviour of its autonomous near neighbour, appetite.[16]

The picture is reinforced by the thought just introduced, that reason, to take just one example, has its own desires. Plato is in fact free in making such ascriptions.[17] He says that each part of the soul has its own pleasures and desires (*Rep.* 580de3–587e4), and (ii) that each has its own wants and wishes (*Rep.* 437b1–c10, 439a1–d2). More strikingly, he represents the parts of the soul as conversing with one another, sparring even, with each making the case for its own prerogatives (*Rep.* 442b5–d1, 554c11-e5, 589a6–b6). Indeed, each part can engage in at least means–end reasoning (*Rep.* 442b5–d1, 574d12–575a7). Taken together, these sorts of remarks suggest that each soul-part is a little human unto itself.

Of course, any such determination already presupposes that we have distinguished the three components of the soul into discrete parts identifiable independently of the soul whose components they are. It is, however, unclear that we have made any such determination. Indeed, it would be something surprising to learn first that there is a part of the soul serving as the seat of appetite and another serving as the seat of reason, but then also to learn that the first part reasons and the second has appetites or desires – that the *epithumetikon* has its own proprietary reasons and the *logistikon* has its own proprietary appetites or desires. If by contrast we do not think that the argument of *Republic* 4 establishes such discrete components, then we will simply regard these remarks as innocuous from the standpoint of mereology, if consequential from the standpoint of moral psychology.

As regards the mereology of souls, Plato is manifestly not saying that each soul comprises other complete souls (*ad infinitum*?), but only that the single soul, insofar as it has appetites, also reasons in ways coloured by those appetites, and that one and the same soul, insofar it has reason, also has desires pursuant to what it identifies as good for itself (cf. *Rep.* 560a). Plato does not need to postulate committees of little men in order to account for the inescapable fact that we sometimes desire what we believe to be good and sometimes strategize ways to secure the objects of our appetites.

More to the point, nothing in Plato's argument for soul-division licenses any such conclusion: the best we can say is that the argument, if sound, establishes distinct elements within each individual soul. It would be a further matter to establish that these elements had the character of mini-agents.[18] Given this result, we should recognize that talk of *homunculi*, no matter how colorful, comes at a significant price: as we have seen, if taken at all literally, homuncularism ascribes to Plato a truly perplexing view of the human person. This is more fully appreciated by considering the next thesis Plato's argument for soul-division does not establish.

(3) The parts of the soul are not individual psychological subjects

In a fairly clear way, the topic of homunculi with respect to tripartition intersects with a related but logically distinct topic, the question of whether the parts of the soul are individual psychological subjects. By accepting any literal form of homuncularism, we also accept the view that the individual parts of the soul are themselves psychological subjects (since little men, like big men, are psychological subjects). Yet one could in principle hold that the individual parts of the soul are non-derivative bearers of psychological states without also supposing that they manifest a range of states necessary to qualify as intentional agents in their own right. So, the weaker thesis should be treated separately, recognizing that it is a necessary condition of the stronger.

The contention that each individual element in the soul is a psychological subject in its own right is crucially vague. Taken in one way, it is perhaps utterly unobjectionable. After all, if, for instance, each element of the soul is really simply the whole soul characterized under some partial description, then trivially the three elements of the soul will be psychological subjects. Each will simply be the whole soul differently described. So much, indeed, could well follow unproblematically from Plato's argument for triparition.

In order to see what *is* problematic, we need to distinguish two theses:

- Modest Subjectivity: each element of the soul is a bearer of psychological states.

So far, as suggested, the thesis is so weak as to be harmless. To strengthen it, we need to add some further theses:

- Strong Subjectivity: (i) each part of the soul is a non-derivative, discrete bearer of psychological states; and (ii) the entire soul is also a non-derivative discrete bearer of psychological states; and (iii) the entire soul comprises its three parts.

Strong subjectivity is, to say the least, a strange and peculiar doctrine. Its peculiarity Chisholm characterized aptly: "You could want the weather to be colder and I could want it to be warmer; but that heap or aggregate which is the pair of us (that thing that weighs 300 pounds if you and I each weigh 150 pounds) does not want anything at all." [19] Strong Subjectivity vitiates Chisholm's quite reasonable observation.

Needless to say, we would need a powerful argument to commit Plato to any such outlandish thesis. Fortunately, nothing in the argument for tripartition comes anywhere close to committing Plato to Strong Subjectivity. Plausibly, the argument does commit him to Modest Subjectivity; but, as we have seen, there is nothing really unusual about that.

In between Modest and Strong Subjectivity there is a continuum of positions, including, for instance, the thought that each of the three individual soul-parts is a subject in its own right, but that the whole soul is no such thing. The whole soul might be a sort of hollow psychic placeholder, waiting to be occupied by one of its constituent subjects. [20] Again, this would be an odd sort of thesis to foist upon Plato, and it would

Plato's divided soul 163

be one, in any case, which ultimately devolves into a kind of homuncular-ism. As we have already seen, homuncularism lacks any argumentative basis in Plato's text.

(4) Plato's argument is consistent with other forms of soul-division

When we appreciate that Plato's argument for tripartition entails neither homuncularism nor any objectionable form of psychological subjectivity, nor indeed even that the elements of the soul are essentially distinct components of it, then we have come some way towards appreciating the fluidity of his characterization of the divided soul. We have also thereby become equipped to deal with the fact, distressing to some,[21] that Plato also introduces other non-equivalent forms of soul-division within the *Republic*.

One primary example occurs in *Republic* 10,[22] where Plato actually relies on (POR), the same principle of division deployed in *Republic* 4, but now to reach a non-equivalent division of soul:

Very often when the reasoning part has measured and has indicated that some things are larger or smaller or the same size as others, the opposite appears to it at the same time ... And did we not say that it is impossible for the same thing to believe opposites about the same thing at the same time? ... Then that element of the soul forming a belief contrary to the measurements and that forming a belief in accordance with them cannot be the same ... Now, surely the element putting its faith in measurement and calculation is the best element of the soul ... Then, the element that opposes it is one of the inferior elements in us. (*Rep.* 602e4–603a8)

Commentators have worried in several ways about this passage. First, the division of the soul in *Republic* 4 is tripartite, whereas this new division is bipartite. Second, and more substantively, assuming the tripartite division of the soul from *Republic* 4 to be fixed and invariant, they have consequently also wondered how Plato might graft this bipartite division onto his earlier tripartite division.

For instance, if we think the inferior part of the soul in *Republic* 10 comprises both spirit (*thumos*) and appetite (*epithumia*), then we are left with several odd results. Why, for instance, should perceptual illusion, clearly the result of activities in the inferior part of the soul in *Republic* 10, derive from the activities of spirit (*thumos*) or appetite (*epithumia*)?[23] Given that Plato develops his division of the soul in *Republic* 10 as part of his critique of the mimetic arts, it is crucial to his argument that the inferior soul be in a position to generate false *perceptual* beliefs. If we thought that this fell to spirit or appetite exclusively,[24] either individually or in concert, then we would be hard pressed to explain why Plato should think such an odd and peculiar thing.

Again, however, these sorts of worries arise only for those who have assumed that the tripartite division of soul in *Republic* 4 is intended by Plato to be exclusive and exhaustive. As we have seen, however, this misconstrues both what he says in that book and the logic of the argument he uses to establish tripartition. As regards Plato's text, he says very clearly in *Republic* 4 that the just person harmonizes the three elements in his soul "and any others in between" (*Rep.* 443d10), thereby undermining any suggestion that he understands his tripartite division to be exhaustive. More importantly, this is just as we should expect, given the logic of his argument: nothing in either Phase One or Phase Two has the result which has occasioned worries regarding his non-equivalent division in *Republic* 10. That is, the argument does not establish anything incompatible with Plato's offering different, non-equivalent divisions of the soul elsewhere. Indeed, the problem about bipartition in *Republic* 10 only makes acute something which should already be clear: the three parts of the soul discussed in that book leave no obvious room for that "part" of the soul by which the soul perceives. Perception is coextensive with neither appetite, nor spirit, nor reason. Yet in any sense in which the reasoning faculty is a part of the soul, so too is the perceptual faculty.

(5) The parts of the soul are not compositional parts

This brings us around to Plato's conception of *parts*. In the course of discussing Plato's argument for soul-division, we have fallen into the dominant practice of referring to psychic elements as "parts." In one sense, this is in keeping with Plato's own practice. He too refers to the divisions of the soul in *Republic* 4 as "parts" even within that book, albeit in a manner which is "neither recurrent nor emphatic."[25] The word "part" (*meros*) occurs towards the end of *Republic* 4 (442b10, c4, 444b3), long after the argument for soul-division has run its course. Still, he does use the word, and for this reason amongst others there is no reason to avoid referring to the elements of the soul as "parts."

There is, however, plenty of reason to be circumspect about this usage. Generally speaking, talk of "parts" encourages a view of the Platonic soul we have been keen to combat: the view that the soul is somehow an aggregative entity, composed of three separate and discrete parts which might or might not work in concert with one another. The difficulty arises because "part" is ambiguous across a variety of related but distinct meanings. In classical extensional mereology, parthood is transitive: if my elbow is part of my arm, and my arm is part of my body, then my elbow is part of my body. Still, many perfectly ordinary notions of parthood do not respect transitivity, and so are not parts in the sense required by classical extensional mereology: my elbow is a part of me, and you and I, let us say, are parts of a discussion group; but my elbow is not a part of any discussion group.[26] So, when he speaks of the soul's elements as parts, what does Plato mean?

To answer this question, we must first distinguish two notions of part: *compositional parts* and *aspectual parts*. For the notion of compositional parts, we begin with a notion of *overlap*:

- x overlaps y =$_{df}$ there is a z such that z is a part of x and z is a part of y.

Using that notion, we can introduce a notion of compositional parts as follows:

- the x's are compositional parts of y =$_{df}$ (i) the x's are all parts of y, (ii) no two x's overlap (and there are at least two x's); (iii) every part of y overlaps at least one of the x's; and (iv) any given x can exist without y.

In this sense, seven beans compose a hill of beans; every bean is a compositional part of the hill. As (iv) makes clear, a necessary condition of something's being a compositional part of something else is its being detachable from the whole which it partly composes. So, constituent parts are not parasitic on the whole for their identity conditions: a bean counter may decide to remove a bean from one hill of beans and add it to the beans of another. Then that same bean has become a constituent part of a different hill of beans.

This notion of part may be contrasted with a much broader and more nebulous notion of part, namely *aspectual part*:

- x is an aspectual part of y =$_{df}$ for any state of affairs in which a is Φ, being-Φ is part of a.

On this view, if Socrates is curious, then *being-curious* is a part of Socrates; if Athlone is the center of Ireland, then *being-the-center-of-Ireland* is part of Athlone; if the Louvre is a museum, then *being-a-museum* is part of the Louvre; indeed, if the main building of the Louvre has an exterior surface, then *being-an-exterior-surface-of-the-Louvre* is part of that building in the Louvre.

Obviously, this is an extended notion of "part." It is, however, evidently the sort of thing we mean when we say, e.g., "He will always take unnecessary umbrage – that is just part of his psychological make-up." The feature *being-an-unnecessary-umbrage-taker* does not appear to be a compositional part. It is more like the exterior of the Louvre. That surface is not detachable from the Louvre; it could not, for instance, be removed and made to become a constituent part of the Museum of Modern Art in New York. Similarly, *Socrates' wishing that Alcibiades would calm down* is an aspectual part of Socrates. Arguably – though this would perhaps be disputed by some trope theorists – that very wish could not be detached from Socrates and made to be part of Alcibiades himself. Rather, while Alcibiades could in principle wish that Alcibiades would calm down, his wish would not be Socrates' wish, but a different wish with a partially shared content.

To speak of an aspectual part is effectively just to speak of a property or feature. It follows, then, that something's being an aspectual part is not sufficient for its being a compositional part. So, if Plato's soul-divisions are parts only in the aspectual sense, then nothing follows about their being compositional parts. If, indeed, someone objects that aspectual parts are not really parts, if, that is, aspectual parts are deemed not to be parts by fiat, then that will be perfectly acceptable – except in that case Plato's argument for a tripartite psychology will prove not to be an argument for tripartition at all. Supposing that aspectual parts are parts, we may put the question: what sorts of parts are the parts (*merē*) of the soul of which Plato speaks in *Republic* 4 (442b10, 442c4, 444b3)?

Two considerations suggest that Plato's soul-parts are aspectual parts and no more. The first is a point of diction: Plato uses the word "part" (*meros*) in a wide variety of contexts – so wide, in fact, that almost nothing follows from his calling the elements of the soul "parts" (*merē*). Among his many uses:

- He wonders whether the pious is part of justice (*meros to hosion tou dikaiou*; *Euthphr.* 12d5).
- He speaks of the even as part of number (*meros to artion tou arithmou*; *Euthphr.* 12d8).
- He uses the typical locution for fractions, a fifth part, or one-fifth, of the number of votes in Socrates' trial (*to pempon meros tōn psēphōn*; *Ap.* 36b1; cf. *Rep.* 369e6).
- He speaks of doing one's part in endeavoring to destroy the laws (*hēmas epecheirēsas apolesai to son meros*; *Cri.* 54c8).
- He investigates whether a whole always consists of its parts, thus raising the question of whether all parts are compositional parts (*Tht.* 204e1–11).
- A class and a part are different from one another (*eidos te kai meros heteron allēlōn einai*; *Pol.* 263b5), whereas in *Republic* 4 the terms are used interchangeably of the elements in the soul (see n. 6).
- He speaks as one kind of hunting as a part of hunting (*thēreutikon meros*; *Soph.* 220c7) and both wholesale and retail sales as parts of purveying (*Soph.* 2203d).

Plato's divided soul

- He speaks of there being a part of imitation that pertains to painting (*kata tēn zōgraphian touto to meros*; *Soph.* 236b10–c1).
- He speaks of an equal part of an angle (*meros gōnias orthēs*; *Tim.* 53d2–3). This is only a very small sample of the many uses to which Plato puts the word "part." Very clearly, he uses it to cover a wide range of cases, few of which, in fact, qualify as compositional parts. In consequence, if we find him using the word "part" (*meros*) for elements of the soul, little follows regarding his conception of the soul's mereology.

More importantly, nothing in Plato's argument for psychic division in *Republic* 4 entails that soul-parts are more than aspectual parts. In particular, (POR), the Principle of Opposing Relations, the premise which does the greatest amount of work in generating distinct elements in the soul, is silent on the question of the kinds of elements it distinguishes. Indeed, it is exceedingly difficult even to see how the principle could be strengthened in such a way that it required compositional parts. After all, Plato himself applies it to the case of the top, where the parts in question are manifestly not compositional parts. The circumference of a top is, on the contrary, like the exterior of the Louvre: it is an aspectual part.

Taking all that together, we arrive at the conclusion that the parts of the soul (if that is what we wish to call them) introduced in *Republic* 4 are not in any sense compositional parts. They are, rather, mere aspectual parts. For all that the argument for psychic division implies, then, the soul has parts in precisely the sense in which a point has parts. We may say of a point that it is both a terminus of one line and the bisector of another; but this sort of observation does nothing to generate compositional parts for the point. Rather, we appreciate that points, like Platonic souls, are mereological simples.

VI. CONCLUSIONS

This is a welcome result, because it saves Plato from the charge that he "directly contradicted himself on a point of the gravest importance."[27] If he believes that souls are both essentially tripartite and also essentially simple, then Plato embraces an unsustainable contradiction right at the heart of his *Republic*. What gives way is the thesis that the soul is essentially composite. Nothing in Plato's argument for the tripartite soul entails homuncularism; or that each part of the soul is a psychological subject in its own right; or that a soul has anything beyond aspectual parts; or, indeed, that the soul's divisions are in any sense essential to it.

On the contrary, Plato's argument establishes something important and profound, if somehow bewildering, that we can be opaque to ourselves, that one and the same soul can draw upon distinct motivational streams when preparing for a single action. If there is oddness in this conclusion, it is already encoded in the Phenomenological Datum to which Plato appeals: we experience internal strife and mental conflict, even though we are individual agents. It only obscures the peculiarity of this feature of our agency and clouds Plato's contribution to moral psychology to insist that he deals with this phenomenon effectively by denying it; for that is precisely what homuncularism does. The contention that according to Plato's mereology of soul each individual psychological subject comprises three other individual psychological subjects is not only bewildering in its own terms, but also serves to camouflage the phenomenon Plato seeks to uncover and display. Internal conflict is by this device transmuted into garden-variety external conflict; yet we know that conflicts *between* agents are not the same as conflicts *within* agents, since squabbles between neighbors are not in the least peculiar, whereas internal discord, including the sort issuing in akratic behavior, is perennially puzzling. According to Plato, internal discord arises when our motivational streams are not integrated with one another, when and only when we are suffering from psychic disarray. Because we wish not to be in this unhappy condition, we also wish for the enhanced psychic unity characterized by Plato as the enviable state of the just human being.

As Plato insists in response to Glaucon's incredulity in *Republic* 10, when cleansed of its corporeal encrustations, the soul, like the sea god Glaucus, may be a uniform simple. Its being simple is consistent with its having aspectual parts; and its having aspectual parts is all that is required for the moral psychological work Plato's divided soul is introduced to effect in the *Republic*. When he thinks of the three parts of the soul joined in harmony in the case of the just human being, Plato is not thinking of three tiny agents working in concert, as if the divisions of the soul were three little choristers singing in unison from the same hymn sheet. Instead, he is thinking of the just soul as a psychological river, with tributaries seamlessly merged into the course set by its one essential element, that element which is, according to Plato, at once most human and most divine: reason.[28]

NOTES

1. Adam 1905 vol. 2, p. 420 *ad loc.*: "Glaucon regards the originally half-theological doctrine of the immortality of the Soul with the same sort of well-bred incredulity which it inspired in most of Plato's contemporaries ... and is astonished that a well-balanced mind should treat it seriously as a philosophical dogma capable of being established by rational argument."

Plato's divided soul

2. So, Cross and Woozley 1964, p. 120, contend that an essentially tripartite soul in *Republic* 4 generates an "irresolvable contradiction" for Plato.

3. Compare Berkeley, *Principles* 141: "We have shown that the soul is indivisible, incorporeal, unextended; and it is consequently incorruptible."

4. In fact the story of Glaucus is variously told. For some variations, see Athenaeus vii.48; cf. Pausanias 6.10.1, 9.7.22. He is mentioned in Euripides (*Orestes* 362) and there is also a lost play of Aeschylus taking him as its subject. Plato stresses primarily that his true nature is obscured by the encrustations of the sea.

5. Although certainly permissible, it would be preferable in this context to avoid the translation of *eidē* (Rep. 612a5) as "parts," as in Grube, rev. Reeve.

6. In the context, it would be preferable to render *eidē* as "kinds" or "forms" or "types," rather than "parts" in the present context, as Grube, rev. Reeve prefer. The immediate correlate to *eidē* in the current passage is *genē* at *Rep.* 434b3. The divisions of the soul, whatever their status, are variously called by Plato *genē* (441c, 443d), *eidē* (435b, c, and e), and *merē* (442b, c; cf. 439b, c, d). The meaning of the word *merē* is discussed in §V below.

7. I use the word "element" as a neutral term, as picking out indifferently Plato's talk of *eidē* (forms or types), *genē* (kinds), and *merē* (parts), as well as his habit of simply using instrumental datives, e.g. *hō(i) logizetai* (that by which one reasons) at *Rep.* 439d5.

8. Instances of acceptance and pursuit include: appetite (hunger or thirst), willing, and wishing (*Rep.* 437b7–c7); instances of rejection and avoidance are: refusal, unwillingness, and lack of appetite (*Rep.* 437d8–10).

9. Irwin 1995, 381 n. 4, appreciates this point and states it clearly: "From (a) x has a tendency F, and (b) x has a tendency G that is contrary to F, we cannot infer that (c) has a tendency F and not (x has tendency F). If Plato thinks he is entitled to (c), he is seriously confused. There is no need to suppose, however, that he is influenced by this confusion."

10. I diagnose this example in Shields 2001, p. 148. I also agree with the suggestion of Bobonich 2002, p. 529. It is not beyond controversy, but it is reasonable to assume that *to euthu* and *to peripheres* (e1–2) refer to the axis of the top, along which it does not move, and its circumference, along which it does.

11. Milton, *Paradise Lost* V: "And 'O fair plant,' said he, 'with fruit surcharged,' | Deigns none to ease thy load, and taste thy sweet, | 'Nor God, nor Man? Is knowledge so despised?' | Or envy, or what reserve forbids to taste?"

12. It is often said that his appetite is of a sexual nature. It might be, but in fact that conjecture relies not on Plato's text, but on an unstable emendation of a fragment of ancient comedy deriving from Kock 1880, vol. I, p. 739. Cf. Ferrari 2007, p. 182.

13. See Cooper 1984, Annas 1981, and Singpurwalla forthcoming-2.

14. More formally, for clarity: "$\Box$ (p $\rightarrow$ q); p; $\therefore$ $\Box$ q" is fallacious. What is needed is: "$\Box$ (p $\rightarrow$ q); $\Box$p; $\therefore$ $\Box$ q". It is not clear, however, on what basis Plato could assert the second premise as necessary. Surely, in any event, he does not do so in the text of the *Republic*. On the contrary, he seems to deny that it is necessary.

15. Annas 1981 is clearest, most engaging, and most original on this point. See also Bobonich 2001, Shields 2006, Kamtekar 2006, and Stalley 1975.

16. See Shields 2006.
17. See Bobonich 2001, p. 204, for an overview of the relevant textual data in this regard.
18. Price (2009) looks carefully at some of the syntactic evidence regarding whether Plato speaks of soul-parts in agent-like terms. Although his remarks are useful and instructive, in fact little follows regarding agency from Plato's occasional tendency to speak of the divisions of soul in agent-like terms. If we agree that "Maggie's heart yearns for reconciliation but her intellect knows that any attempt in that direction would only be self-destructive," we do not thereby name three agents, Maggie's heart, Maggie's intellect, and Maggie's self. There is only one agent: Maggie. Such quotidian ways of speaking are, from the standpoint of agency, mainly inconsequential.
19. Chisholm 1991, p. 172.
20. This seems one of the possible views considered by Bobonich 2001, p. 254, who, to his credit, recognizes the oddity of this sort of thesis: "The *Republic*'s partitioning theory commits Plato to denying the unity of the person . . . What seems to be a single psychic entity is in fact a composite of three distinct and durable subjects . . . We should not underestimate the conflict between such a theory and our ordinary intuitions. One important sign of this is the near impossibility of imagining what it would be like to be such a compound. It seems that one ends up either imagining possessing all the psychological states simultaneously (thus losing the idea that they belong to different subjects) or one imagines being each of the parts of the soul (thus losing the idea that they form a single person)."
21. So Nehamas 1982/1999 and Annas 1981.
22. I have benefited from the excellent discussion of Singpurwalla (forthcoming-1) in thinking about this issue.
23. So Nehamas: "why should our *desire* tell us that the immersed stick is bent?" (1982/1999, p. 265). This would indeed be a reasonable question if Plato were constrained to map one soul-division onto the other. Similarly, Annas 1981, p. 339, finds cause for criticism on this score: "Plato presumably fails to see that his argument will not work, that desire has nothing to do with optical illusions."
24. Another alternative (for those operating on the assumption that the tripartite division of soul is exhaustive and exclusive) is that the division between inferior and superior is a subdivision within the rational soul alone. This strategy, adopted by Nehamas 1982/1999 and Murphy 1951, is convincingly rejected by Singpurwalla (forthcoming-1).
25. Price (2009, n. 1). As Price observes, the term "part" (*meros*) makes an appearance only late in *Rep.* 4, at 442b10, c4, and 444b3.
26. On the presumed transitivity of the parthood relations, see Johansson 2004.
27. Archer-Hind 1881, p. 128. In the end, Archer-Hind agrees with my final conclusion that Plato is not guilty of this mistake, though our reasons for reaching this conclusion diverge sharply.
28. I am grateful to Rachel Singpurwalla for her incisive and instructive comments on an earlier draft of this essay, and to Graham Oddie, whose effortless and unsettling questions first forced me to rethink some fundamentals of Platonic psychology.

CHAPTER 9

The meaning of "saphēneia" in Plato's Divided Line

J. H. Lesher

Plato's famous comparison of the different forms of human awareness with a line divided into four parts contains many puzzling features. Among the most enduring of these have been whether each of the forms of awareness has its own set of objects (and if so, what objects correspond with *dianoia* or "understanding"); whether the line extends in a horizontal, vertical, or even diagonal direction; whether the equal length of the line's central segments is a matter or some importance or an unintended, perhaps even irrelevant, consequence of the proportions assigned to the other segments; and whether the line merely identifies the various possible forms of awareness or describes a multi-stage process through which each learner must pass on the way to full comprehension. In this essay I touch on some of these questions, but my main aim is to make sense of what I regard as Socrates' most puzzling claim, namely that the different line segments provide a measure of the relative degrees of *saphēneia* and *asapheia* – usually translated into English as "clarity" and "obscurity" – available to human beings. I will argue that none of the usual translations of *saphēneia* provides us with a satisfactory understanding of this remark. I then review the use of *saphēs* and its cognates from the time of the Homeric poems down to the fourth century BCE and argue that the relevant sense of *saphēneia* in this setting is "full, accurate and sure awareness of an object." I conclude by arguing that Plato's simile, properly understood, can be seen to provide not only an explanation of his rationalist conception of knowledge but also a coherent line of argument in support of that set of doctrines.

I. THE SIMILE AND SOME INITIAL PUZZLES

At *Republic* 509d Socrates directs his interlocutor, Glaucon, to represent two different realms, one visible and the other intelligible:

by a line divided into two unequal sections and cut each section again in the same ratio – the section, that is, of the visible and that of the intelligible order – and then

172 J. H. LESHER

as an expression of the ratio of their comparative clearness and obscurity you will have (*kai soi estai saphēneiai kai asapheiai pros allēla*), as one of the sections of the visible world, images. By images I mean, first, shadows, and then reflections in water and on surfaces of dense, smooth, and bright texture, and everything of that kind, if you apprehend.

I do.

As the second section assume that of which this is a likeness or an image, that is, the animals about us and all plants and the whole class of objects made by man.

So I assume it, he said.

Would you be willing to say, said I, that the division in respect of reality and truth[1] or the opposite is expressed by the proportion – as is the opinable to the knowable so is the likeness to that of which it is a likeness?

I certainly would.

Consider then again the way in which we are to make the division of the intelligible section.

In what way?

By the distinction that there is one section of it which the soul is compelled to investigate by treating as images the things imitated in the former division, and by means of assumptions from which it proceeds not up to a first principle but down to a conclusion, while there is another section in which it advances from its assumption to a beginning or principle that transcends assumption, and in which it makes no use of the images employed by the other section, relying on ideas only and progressing systematically through ideas. (509d–510b, Shorey's translation)

In the succeeding passage (510c to 511b) those who employ hypotheses and visual aids are identified as students of "geometry and the kindred arts" (we later learn that these are arithmetic, plane geometry, solid geometry, astronomy, and harmonic theory). By contrast, those who operate at the highest level employ only Forms and proceed all the way to an unhypothetical first principle – almost certainly, though this is not stated, to the Form of the Good. Socrates then directs Glaucon to accept as names for the corresponding states or "affections" (*pathēmata*) in the soul:

... "rational knowledge" (*noēsis*) for the highest, "understanding" (*dianoia*) for the second,[2] "belief" (*pistis*) for the third, and for the last, "perception of images" (*eikasia*) ...

Socrates concludes by directing Glaucon to arrange the four states of awareness in a proportion,

considering that they participate in *saphēneia* (*saphēneias ... metechein*) in the same degree to which their objects participate in reality (*alētheias metechein*) (511d–e)

Despite the extreme brevity and sketchiness of Socrates' presentation, three intended lessons seem clear: (1) that we should regard physical objects as the

The meaning of "saphēneia" in Plato's Divided Line

dependent effects of Forms just as we regard reflections and shadows as the dependent effects of physical objects;[3] (2) that while objects of thought can be securely known, the changeable things in the visible realm can be objects only of belief or opinion; and (3) that since the mathematical sciences (at least as then practiced) employ visual aids and (ultimately) unjustified hypotheses, they fail to achieve knowledge of the best possible kind.

But how should we understand Socrates' assertions: (1) that images, when compared with their physical originals, *provide us with a measure of the degrees of* saphēneia *and* asapheia *achievable within the visible and intelligible realms*; (2) that the four states of awareness *participate in* saphēneia *to the same degree in which their objects participate in reality*; and (3) that the portion of the intelligible realm investigated by dialectic is saphesteron *(that is, more* saphes*) than the objects studied by the mathematical sciences*? Translators have rendered these *saphēs* terms in a variety of ways, with "clarity," "precision" (or "exactitude"), "truth," and "knowledge" (or "knowability") being the most frequent choices.[4] But I think it can be shown that none of these provides a satisfactory understanding of the meaning of Socrates' remarks.

Consider the most frequent choice: "clarity." Socrates asserts in connection with (1) that the images or likenesses of things are inferior to their originals with respect to *saphēneia*. Might this mean that images – shadows and reflections on polished surfaces – have a lesser degree of clarity than the things of which they are images?[5] Perhaps, but it seems a rather obvious fact that images can be either clear or unclear, just as physical objects can be clear or unclear to an observer, depending on the conditions under which they are perceived. In fact, the image of Socrates on a flat and highly polished surface might actually be clearer (i.e., brighter, less distorted, more detailed) than the person Socrates when seen at a distance or in a poor light. So it seems just false to say that images are inherently less *clear* than their originals. Similarly, Socrates holds that the mathematical sciences as currently practiced fall short of philosophical dialectic with respect to *saphēneia*. Might this mean that those who employ visual aids in their inquiries necessarily achieve a less *clear* understanding than those who avoid using such aids? One would normally expect just the opposite to be the case since visual aids, especially those used in mathematical demonstration, typically serve to promote clarity of presentation and understanding rather than to diminish it.[6] It is not obvious, moreover, why a person who employed one or more hypotheses during the course of an inquiry would necessarily have a less *clear* understanding than one who pursued an inquiry all the way to a first principle. In general, hypothetical lines of reasoning can

174   J. H. LESHER

be stated and understood either clearly or unclearly just as non-hypothetical ones can. But to ask a more basic question: Why should we be talking here about *clarity*? Socrates introduces the simile to explain how we will need to reorient our thinking in order to achieve knowledge of the realities as opposed to having mere opinion concerning their dependent effects. Clarity is a good thing, no doubt, but it would be strange if Socrates' main objective here were merely to explain how we can achieve greater and lesser degrees of *clarity*. For a parallel set of reasons, it would also be implausible to suppose that the point of the simile is to illuminate the various possible degrees of "precision" or "exactitude"; that is, this also seems too limited an objective.

Perhaps, then, as some have thought, *saphēneia* means "truth," and the different realm-parts and corresponding states of awareness differ from one another with respect to the degrees of truth present or attainable at each level.[7] As we shall see, *saphēs* did sometimes mean "true" and *saphēneia* was sometimes "the sure truth." But it is implausible to think that Socrates is speaking of the truth of some statement, proposition, or belief when in (3) he characterizes as *saphesteron* (that is, as more *saphēs*) "*the part of reality and the intelligible realm* that is contemplated by the science of dialectic." One "part of reality" may be more or less knowable than another, and we may be able to achieve greater or lesser degrees of truth when we direct our thoughts toward one region rather than another, but the parts or regions cannot themselves be more or less true. Moreover, in his main characterization of the line at 509e, as elsewhere, Socrates sets *saphēneia* in contrast not with *error* or *falsehood* but with *asapheia* – "obscurity" or "indistinctness."

It would also be implausible to equate *saphēneia* here with either knowledge or knowability for the simple reason that in (2) the four realm-parts and their corresponding states of awareness are said to embody *saphēneia* to different degrees, while only two of the realm-parts and their corresponding states of awareness (those above the main divide) are said to constitute *knowledge*. But if we cannot think of the *saphēneia* represented by the different line segments as a matter of clarity, truth, precision, or knowledge, then how should we think of it? Here a brief review of the general use of *saphēs* and *saphēneia* may be helpful.[8]

II. *SAPHĒS AND SAPHĒNEIA*

The original meaning of *saphēs* appears to have been "clear or evident from an objective point of view" – as said, for example, of an object or person located directly in front of an observer.[9] The adjective *saphēs* does not occur in the Homeric epics but Homer uses the adverbial form *sapha* in speaking of those who "say or know clearly, well, or for sure."[10] Typically, what a person knows *sapha* is what he or she has directly experienced. For example, when Ajax comes out from among the ranks to challenge Hector he promises:

> Hector, now indeed you will know *sapha* one on one
> What kind of leaders there are among the
> Danaans. *(Homer, Iliad 7.226–27)*

Conversely "knowing *sapha*" is said to be difficult or impossible when the relevant circumstances lie far off in space or time:

> Nor do we yet know *sapha* how these things will be,
> Whether for good or for ill we sons of the Achaeans
> will return. *(Il. 2.252–53)*

On some occasions one who "knows *sapha*" can perform a task in a "sure or competent manner":

> Since I know *sapha* on my own how to utter taunts . . . *(Il. 20.201)*
> Among them a herdsman who does not yet know *sapha*
> How to fight a wild beast . . . *(Il. 15.632–33)*

Similarly, one who knows how to "speak *sapha*" can convey information to others in a competent and reliable manner. That this involves, at a minimum, speaking truly is evident from the command Sthenelus issues to Agamemnon:

> Son of Atreus, do not lie when you know how to speak *sapha* (*mē pseude'*
> *epistamenos sapha eipein*). *(Il. 4.404)*

And "knowing how to speak *sapha*" can, in turn, rest on knowing the facts:

> Has he heard some news of the army's return, which he might tell us *sapha*, since he
> has previously learned it? *(Od. 2.30–31)*

In the Homeric poems, then, "knowing *sapha*" involves having a full, accurate, and sure awareness of some matter of fact *or* being able to perform a task in a sure and expert manner, in both cases typically on the basis of prior experience.

A number of sixth- and fifth-century writers also use *saphēs* in connection with sure and accurate perception or knowledge. In *The Hymn to Hermes* the old man explains to Apollo how the fading light prevented him from knowing *saphōs* the identity of the person he saw passing by:

> My son, it is hard to tell all that one's eyes sees (*argaleon men, hos opthalmoisin*
> *idoito*), for many wayfarers pass to and fro on this way, some bent on much evil, and

176   J. H. LESHER

some on good: it is difficult to know each one (*chalepon de daēmenai estin hekaston*). However, I was digging my plot of vineyard all day long until the sun went down, and I thought (*edoxa*), good sir, but do not know *saphes* (*saphes d' ouk oida*) that I saw a child, whoever the child was, that followed some long-horned cattle – an infant who had a staff and kept walking from side to side: he was driving them in a backward way, with their heads turned toward him. (201–11)

Similarly, in the *Hymn to Aphrodite* (167) Anchises is described as "not knowing *sapha*" what will happen to him in the future as a consequence of his having slept with a goddess. In Sophocles' *Oedipus Tyrannus* (977–78), Jocasta asks Oedipus "Why should a human being be afraid when chance rules and there is no *saphēs* foreknowledge (*pronoia*) of anything?" Pindar gives voice to the same lament in *Nemean* 11:

> As for that which comes from Zeus, no *saphes* sign
> Attends men, but all the same we embark on ambitious projects . . .
> And streams of foreknowledge (*promatheias*) lie far from us.   (43–46)

In a more positive vein, Herodotus makes a point of describing the measures he took to determine the reliability of reports he received concerning the worship of Heracles:

Moreover, wishing to get clear knowledge (*saphes ti eidenai*) of this matter when it was possible to do so I took ship to Tyre in Phoenice where I heard there was a very holy temple of Heracles. There I saw it (*eidon*), richly equipped with many other offerings. . . . At Tyre I saw (*eidon*) yet another temple of that Heracles called the Thasian. Then I went to Thasos, too, where I found (*heuron*) a temple of Heracles built by the Phoenicians. . . . Therefore, what I have discovered by inquiry plainly shows (*ta men nun historēmena dēloi sapheōs*) that Heracles is an ancient god. (2.44, trans. Godley)[11]

In the *Seven against Thebes* Aeschylus twice links the possession of *saphēneia* with direct observation when the scout promises:

> Eteocles, most noble lord of the Cadmeans,
> I have come from the camp bearing sure word (*saphē*) of things there,
> For I myself am an eyewitness (*katoptēs*) to these matters . . .   (39–41)

> For my part, for the things that are yet to come
> I will keep a trusty eye (*ophthalmon*) on them
> So you, by the sure truth of my account (*saphēneiai logou*),
> Will know (*eidōs*) what is going on and be kept free of harm.   (66–68)

And when the Odysseus of Euripides' *Philoctetes* challenges the wisdom of the seers he asks: "Why, then, seated on your seers' thrones, do you solemnly swear to sure knowledge (*saphōs . . . eidenai*) of the gods' will, you people who are past masters of these sayings? For anyone who claims to know about

The meaning of "saphēneia" in Plato's Divided Line   177

the gods (*theōn epistasthai*) knows no more than how to persuade with words" (fr. 794, Collard trans.).[12]

At some point in the first half of the fifth century BCE the physician Alcmaeon of Croton declared that:

[Concerning things non-evident, concerning things mortal], gods possess *saphēneian* but it is given to mortals to conjecture (*tekmairesthai*) ...[13]

As this remark is usually translated, the gods "see clearly" or "have clear knowledge," perhaps about both mortal and non-evident matters, but it is given to mortals to conjecture (literally: to draw inferences from *tekmar* or "signs").[14] *Why* only the gods should have clear knowledge Alcmaeon does not tell us, but it was a commonplace of early Greek poetry that since the gods are present everywhere they have knowledge of all that happens, while during their brief lifetimes mortals see only a little of the world and know even less. For example, when in Book 2 of Homer's *Iliad* the singer calls on the Muses for assistance he declares: "You, goddesses, are present and know all things, while we mortals hear only a rumor and know nothing" (485–86). In any case, when Alcmaeon credits *saphēneia* to the gods he appears to be crediting them not with *clarity in thought or expression* but rather with having a *direct and sure knowledge of what there is.*

A number of early Greek thinkers shared what appears to have been Alcmaeon's assumption that having sure knowledge requires being in a position to observe the relevant objects, events, or states of affairs. In fragment B34, composed at some point in the early decades of the fifth century BCE, Xenophanes of Colophon distinguishes, so far as we know for the first time anywhere, between knowledge and opinion as well as between knowledge and true opinion, in a way that bears some resemblance to Alcmaeon's claim:

And of course no man has been nor will there be anyone
Who knows the clear and sure truth (*to saphes*)
Concerning such things as I say about the gods and all things.
For even if at best he were to succeed in speaking of what is brought to pass
Still he himself would not know. Yet opinion is fashioned
     for all.   (Sextus Empiricus, *Against the Mathematicians* 7.49.110 = DK 21B34)

Xenophanes does not tell us precisely *why* no mortal has known, or ever will know, "the clear and sure truth," but the scope of the topic as it is given in line 3 – "such things as I say about the gods and all things" suggests that here too being in a position to have direct access to events might have been a relevant factor. Nothing could be at a greater remove from the direct experience of human beings than the actions of the gods, and the nature

178   J. H. LESHER

of things as they exist in all places and at all times (which was the main object of inquiry among Xenophanes' predecessors, the Milesian scientists). So Xenophanes' main point might well have been that since no human being has had or ever will have direct access to divine operations, or to events as they occur at all places and times, then no one has known or ever will know *to saphes*, i.e., "the clear and sure truth" about these matters, although each may have his or her own opinion. The considerations mentioned in lines 4 and 5 would serve to reinforce this negative assessment of the prospects for knowledge by pointing out that even if, in a kind of "best-case scenario," one were to succeed in speaking about an event "as it is brought to pass," that person would still not have sure knowledge concerning non-evident matters. In these remarks, then, Xenophanes appears to have embraced the traditional view of mortal beings as short on direct experience, assumed an intimate connection between having direct experience of events and knowing the clear and sure truth about them, and drawn the logical conclusion.

An additional data point is a set of remarks in the Hippocratic treatise *On Ancient Medicine*. In the course of criticizing those who claim that the medical inquirer needs to use postulates, i.e., cosmological theories, in order to achieve good results, the author declares:

> Wherefore I have deemed that [medicine] has no need of an empty postulate, as do insoluble mysteries, about which any exponent must use a postulate, for example, things in the sky or below the earth. If a man were to judge and declare the state of these, neither to the speaker himself nor to his audience would it be clear whether his statements were true or not. For there is no test the application of which would give certainty (*eidenai to saphes*). (*On Ancient Medicine*, 1.20–27, Jones trans.)

Our author appears to have no objection to the use of cosmological hypotheses as such; indeed, he assigns them some degree of value when one is dealing with matters "above the heavens and below the earth" – the traditional characterization of the subject matter of Ionian natural science. But when one conducts inquiries into non-evident matters, where the use of hypotheses is essential, there can be no *saphes* knowing either for the person himself (perhaps an echo of the phrase "he himself would not know" in Xenophanes B34) or for those in his audience. The fact that our author provides no additional argument in support of this claim suggests that by this point it had become a philosophical commonplace that without direct experience there can be no sure knowledge.

Forms of *saphēs* occur frequently in Plato's dialogues, in four different settings:

The meaning of "saphēneia" in Plato's Divided Line   179

(1) In connection with sense-perception. At *Euthydemus* 271a Crito complains to Socrates: "There was such an enormous crowd about you that I myself, wanting to hear, could not get any nearer or hear anything clearly (*akousai saphōs*)." Similarly, at *Protagoras* 316a Prodicus' booming bass voice "rendered his words indistinct (*asaphes*)." The Athenian of Plato's *Laws* recommends (at 812d) that those who seek to imitate virtue through playing the lyre be limited to producing notes that correspond precisely with those made by the singer's voice: "they must do so for the sake of the *saphēneia* of the notes, and so make their tones concordant with those of the voice." Here *saphēneia* appears to designate the clear (i.e., full and accurate) perception a person can have of an object, or the clarity (i.e., fullness and accuracy) with which some object is perceived.[15]

(2) In connection with clear speaking and thinking. Both Plato and Xenophon depict a Socrates who seeks to gain a correct understanding of the virtues by examining others, often individuals who are "unable to express themselves clearly" (*mēden echōn saphes legein*, *Mem.* 4.6, 13; cf. *Gorgias* 451d–e; *Charmides* 163d, and *Euthyphro* 6d). Socrates also expresses the desire that his own beliefs and statements be clearly understood by others (cf. *ouden gar pō saphes legō* at *Gorgias*, 463e; cf. *Gorgias* 500d, *Euthyphro* 10a, *Hippias I* 300e, *Hippias II* 364c, *Laches* 196c, *Phaedo* 100a, etc.). Typically, what Socrates invites others to state as clearly as they can is the essential nature or "what it is" of one or more of the virtues, as at *Euthyphro* 6d: "Try to tell me more clearly (*peirō saphesteron eipein*) . . . what holiness might be" (*to hosion hoti pot' eiē*);[16] and on many occasions what is either *saphēs* or *asaphēs* is a moral or philosophical question.[17] At *Statesman* 262c the Eleatic Stranger expresses the desire to explain matters more clearly (*saphesteron phradzein*) for the sake of *saphēneia*, where what is being sought is a satisfactory account of the method of division. *Saphēneia* also appears to mean "a clear explanation or understanding" at *Rep.* 524c: "Sight, too, saw the great and the small, not separated but confounded. And for a *saphēneia* of this, the intelligence is compelled to contemplate the great and small, not as thus confounded but as distinct entities."

(3) In connection with sure truth, or knowing the sure truth. At *Phaedo* 69d Socrates states that:

> Whether I was right in this ambition [to philosophize], and whether we have achieved anything, we shall know the sure truth (*to saphes eisometha*), if god wills, when we have reached the other world, and that I imagine will be soon.

180   J. H. LESHER

With Socrates' concurrence, Simmias urges those present to put various views of the nature of the soul to the test even though: "It is difficult if not impossible to know the sure truth (*to men saphes eidenai*) about these questions" (85c). At *Meno* 100b Socrates similarly declares that "we will not know the sure truth" (*to de saphes . . . eisometha*) about how virtue is acquired until we first determine what virtue itself is. At *Phaedrus* 277b Socrates declares that no speech should be credited with *bebaioteta* and *sapheneian*, by which he appears to mean "certainties" and "sure truth."

(4) In connection with precision or exactitude. At *Phaedo* 65b, Socrates' characterization of the body's senses as neither *sapheis* nor *akribeis* follows his assertion that "we neither see nor hear anything precisely (*akribes*)." At *Philebus* 61a, Socrates contrasts grasping the Good *saphos* with grasping it in outline form (*kata tina tupon*).[18] And when (from *Philebus* 55c to 59b) Socrates argues that the arts that most concern themselves with number and calculation are also the ones that achieve the greatest degree of precision, *sapheneia* appears as frequently as *akribeia*. Although we cannot be certain that precision (or exactitude) was associated with *saphes* among earlier writers,[19] this does appear to be the case among classical authors.[20]

To sum up: while *saphes* may have originally designated that which is directly present to an observer, at some point the term became associated with the kind of full, accurate, and sure awareness a person could have of what had been directly presented to him or her. Homer and other early writers often speak of those who can say, know, or do things *sapha* or *saphes*, i.e., "well, clearly, or for sure" on the basis of their personal experience; and a number of early Greek thinkers appear to have viewed direct experience as an essential condition for having *sapheneia* or knowing *to saphes*. Plato also uses *saphes* in connection with speaking and understanding as well as with reference to perception and knowledge that is "full, accurate, and sure" (and, on some occasions, detailed and precise). So while the Greek adjective *saphes* covers the same semantic ground as the English adjectives "clear" and "perspicuous" it additionally designates forms of awareness that are "true" or "accurate" as well as "sure" or "reliable." In Plato, as in earlier writers, *sapheneia* sometimes means "clarity in thought or expression" but it can also connote the full, accurate, and sure awareness persons (or gods) can have of their circumstances. So when we turn to consider the meaning of Socrates' remarks concerning *saphestera* realms of investigation and differing degrees of *sapheneia*, we ought to be alert to the possibility that what is under discussion is not the conditions under which we achieve *clarity in thought*

The meaning of "saphēneia" in Plato's Divided Line   181

or expression, but rather those under which we achieve a *full, accurate and sure awareness of the realities*.

III. *SAPHĒNEIA* IN THE DIVIDED LINE

At 507a–509d (just prior to the introduction of the simile of the line at 509d–513e) Socrates likens the Good that is the cause of intelligible reality and knowledge to the sun that is the cause of the being and visibility of the things in the sensible realm. At 508c–d he likens success and failure in visual experience with success and failure in thought:

> When we turn our eyes to objects whose colors are no longer in the light of day but in the gloom of night, the eyes are dimmed and seem nearly blind, as if clear vision were no longer in them. . . . But when [our eyes] are directed upon things upon which the sun shines (*hōn ho hēlios katalampei*), they see clearly (*saphōs*) and vision appears to reside in them. . . . Apply this comparison to the soul also in this way. When it is firmly fixed on that on which reality and being (*alētheia te kai to on*) shine, it conceives (*enoēse*) and knows (*egnō*) them and appears to possess reason (*echein noun*), but when it focusses on that which is mixed with darkness, the world of becoming and passing away, it has opinion, its edge is blunted, it shifts its opinions this way and that, and again seems as if it lacks intelligence (*noun ouk echonti*).

Thus, in his introduction to the line Socrates identifies the two conditions that make for success in perceiving, thinking, and knowing: directness of approach and maximal degree of reality. Both conditions will figure prominently in the ensuing accounts of the line and cave, as well as in the proposals for reforming the sciences.

As Socrates describes them, the prisoners confined in the cave are physically restrained and unable to look directly at one another's bodies or at the objects being carried along on the pathway located above and behind them (515a–b). They spend their entire lives looking only at "the shadows cast from the fire on the wall of the cave" (515a). Only one who has been released from his bonds will be able to turn around to see the "more real things" (*alēthestera*, 515d).[21] Socrates' point here is not that the images whose movements the prisoners spend their lives tracking are intrinsically less *clear* than their originals, but rather that the prisoners will never achieve a *clear and sure awareness* of *what those higher realities are* unless and until they turn their gaze directly toward them. Seen in this context, a reference to "degrees of *saphēneia*" would naturally be taken to be the claim that just as we cannot gain a full, accurate, and sure visual awareness of physical objects so long as we focus our attention on their dependent effects – on their shadows or reflections – in just the same way we cannot have a full, accurate, and sure knowledge of the realities so long as we focus our attention on their dependent effects – on the things located in the visible realm. Accordingly, we should translate Socrates' otherwise perplexing remark in these terms: "as an expression of the degree to which we can achieve *a clear and sure awareness*, as one of the sections of the visible world, you will have images [and then you will also have the originals of which these are the images]." His assertion at 511d–e that the different forms of awareness participate in *saphēneia* to the degree in which their objects participate in reality should be read as the claim that our *awareness of the nature of things increases in clarity and sureness* to the degree to which we direct our thoughts away from the imperfect and changeable things in the visible realm and toward the things that remain fully and forever what they are.

This view appears with sufficient frequency in the dialogues to be regarded as one of Plato's personal philosophical convictions. We may compare *Phaedo*, 83a–b where Socrates describes the soul operating under the influence of "philosophy" as "trusting nothing but its own independent judgment upon objects considered in themselves (*auto kath' hauto tōn ontōn*), and attributing no truth to anything which it views as indirectly as being subject to variation, because such objects are sensible and visible, but what the soul itself sees is intelligible and invisible." Similarly, at *Cratylus* 439a Socrates implies that learning about the realities through themselves (*di' autōn*) is better and clearer learning (*kalliōn kai saphestera hē mathēsis*) than learning about them through the medium of names. Failing to have one's thoughts focussed on the proper objects, or more specifically, being unable to distinguish between an image and that of which it is an image, links up with one of the most persistent motifs in Plato's writings: the view of ordinary consciousness as a dream-like state.[22]

Lastly, the elements of direct attention and maximal degree of reality figure prominently in Socrates' criticism of current scientific practice. Dialectic, he holds:

makes its way to an unhypothetical first principle, proceeding from a hypothesis, but without the images used in the earlier part, using Forms themselves (*autois eidesi*) and making its investigation through them.

But mathematicians take a less direct approach since:

they use visible forms and make their arguments about them, although they are not thinking about them, but about those other things that they are like. (510d)

The meaning of "saphēneia" in Plato's Divided Line

The second element, invariant reality, surfaces when Socrates describes how scientists employ perceptual aids – in geometry: diagrams; in astronomy: the starry heavens; in music: audible harmonies – thereby importing into their investigations the variability and uncertainty characteristic of all sensible objects (perhaps accounting for the equality of the line's two central segments). So when Plato declared the Forms *saphestera* than the objects of current scientific inquiry, his point was not that the diagrams scientists employ are inherently unclear, or that scientists must inevitably think unclearly whenever they employ hypotheses, but rather that in so far as they focus their investigations on visible shapes, observed movements, and audible harmonies, scientists fail to conduct the kind of inquiry that could provide them with maximal *saphēneia*, i.e., a complete, accurate, and sure awareness of the realities.

IV. EXPLANATION AND ARGUMENT

That there are "degrees of reality," that only objects of thought can be known, and that some beneficent power is the cause of the existence and knowability of the realities – each of these distinctively Platonic doctrines is given expression in the three famous similes put forward in *Republic* 6 and 7. But there is reason to think that in developing these figures Plato was attempting not only to explain his teachings but also to provide reasons to accept them as correct.

It may be helpful to remember that the *Republic*, the dialogue, was itself an extended exploration of a clear comparison case – the nature of justice in the ideal state – sparked by an interest in discovering the nature of justice in the individual (and ultimately, proving that the life of the just person is intrinsically superior to the life of the unjust one). Once it has been established that justice in the state exists when each of its three classes does its own job, as well as the general principle that justice is essentially a matter of "each doing its own" (cf. *archēn te kai tupon tina tēs dikaiosunēs* at 443CI), Socrates concludes that justice exists in the individual when each of the elements in the soul – reason, spirit, and appetite – "does its own and avoids meddling in the business of the others."

Socrates' procedure here near the end of Book 6 displays the same pattern: first identifying a clear case for comparison, then articulating a general principle, then drawing one or more specific conclusions. He begins the process in the sun passage by holding up as a clear case for comparison the kind of *saphes* awareness we enjoy when our faculty of sight is directed toward a fully illuminated physical object. Neither Plato's contemporary readers nor

184   J. H. LESHER

his empiricist-minded predecessors would have had reason or inclination to challenge this starting point. Indeed, as we have seen, for many early writers and thinkers it was precisely when we could have direct experience of the relevant circumstances that it became possible to see, speak, or know *sapha*, *saphes*, or know *to saphes*, and have *saphēneia*. Next, in the simile of the line, Socrates introduces the notion of "degrees of *saphēneia*" when he explains how turning our attention toward a physical object's secondary effects – toward its shadows and reflections – will result in an awareness of what the object is that is less *saphes*, i.e., less complete, less accurate, and less secure than the one we would enjoy were we to focus our attention directly on the object itself. This supports the general principle that the degree of *saphēneia* we are capable of achieving varies in direct proportion to the extent to which our attention is directed toward the primary realities rather than toward their secondary effects. It follows from this principle, first, that so long as scientists concern themselves with imperfect and changeable phenomena rather than with perfect shapes and bodies, exact ratios, and entirely uniform motions, they will never achieve the most complete, accurate, and sure knowledge possible. It also follows that since the things we encounter in sense-experience are inherently less stable and permanent than their essential natures, if we aim to achieve a full, accurate and sure awareness of the realities we must direct our attention toward those superior objects of thought and leave the things in the visible realm alone. That at least is one coherent line of argument Plato develops in and through his famous simile.[23]

NOTES

1. "In respect of reality and truth" is Shorey's translation of *alētheiai*. As will soon become evident, in the passages under discussion here Plato is concerned primarily with "truth in its ontological sense," i.e. where the "true x" = the "real x" (cf. LSJ s.v. *alētheia* I.2: "after Homer also *truth, reality*, opposed to *appearance*"). For a representative selection of the relevant passages in Plato, see the Budé *Lexique* under *alētheia*, "1 ontologique."

2. *Noēsis* and *dianoia* present so many difficulties that translators often choose to leave the terms untranslated. Since *noēsis* is a nominative formed from the verb *noeō* –"think," "perceive," "understand," "plan," "intend," etc., one might expect it to be translated as "thought" or "thinking." But on occasion Plato speaks of knowing the Form as a matter of possessing *nous* (cf. *Rep.* 511d4 and *Timaeus* 51d where *nous* is contrasted with *doxa alēthēs*), and at *Rep.* 533d he identifies the awareness achieved at the highest level of the line as *epistēmē*, a standard "knowledge" term. So some English "knowledge" expression seems mandatory. The point of the adjective "rational" is to mark off *noēsis* as a purely *a priori* form of knowledge, i.e., a knowledge achieved without reliance on

The meaning of "saphēneia" in Plato's Divided Line 185

sense-perception. Since the English "understanding" has both an epistemic and a non-epistemic use (insofar as it is possible to have an incorrect understanding on some point), it is less than a perfect choice for a division within the realm Plato identifies at 510a as the knowable (*to gnōston*). But "understanding" at least conveys the idea that one who studies a science is attempting to grasp the nature of things, rather than resting content with unreflective belief.

3. Cf. Stocks 1932, p. 217: "the essential purpose of the Simile of the Line is to elucidate the dependence of the world of sight upon the world of thought by comparing it to the dependence of a shadow or reflection on the thing shadowed or reflected, and ... this relation of copy to original is the key to the whole exposition." For discussions of the tensions between taking the simile as a set of analogies and taking it as a comprehensive account of cognition, see Annas 1981, pp. 248–56, and Cross and Woozley 1964, ch. 9.

4. Shorey chose "clarity" and "obscurity" to translate the *saphēneia* and *asapheia* at 509d9 but switched to "truer and more exact" for the *saphesteron* in Glaucon's description of the region studied by dialectic at 511c, to "clearness and precision" for the *saphēneias* in Socrates' reference to the four kinds of awareness at 511e3, and "more clear and exact" for the *saphestera* in the reference at 515e to the shadows within the allegory of the cave. Adam took the different levels to represent degrees of truth and knowability. In his personal copy of Adam's commentary, Werner Jaeger drew a line through Adam's "clarity" and penciled in "certainty." Cornford 1945 selected "clearness and obscurity" for the *saphēneia* and *asapheia* at 509d, "greater certainty and truth" for the *saphesteron* at 511c, "clearness and certainty" for the *saphēneias* at 511e, and "clearer than" for the *saphestera* at 515e. By contrast, Lee 1955, Grube 1974, and Reeve 2004 consistently translate in terms of "clarity and opacity" (or "clarity and obscurity"), "clearer than," "clarity" and "clearer than" respectively.

5. As Adam puts it: "we shall have four segments, representing in order of clearness, (1) images and the like ... etc."

6. For an informative discussion of the benefits that accrue to the mathematician from the use of diagrams in mathematics (especially in geometry), see Patterson 2007.

7. In his note on 511c Adam 1902, p. 71, commented: "*saphēs*, originally 'clear', often = 'true'." Reeve 1988 states: "Immediately following the formula of the Line, we are told that '[the visible section] has been divided into parts as far as truth or falsity are concerned' ... More precisely, it is about degrees of truth – or better about the degrees of relative closeness to truth" (p. 79). But Reeve also glosses *saphēneia* as "clarity" and "cognitive reliability" (pp. 78, 80).

8. We have ample warrant for looking to the general use of *saphēs* in order to understand the meaning of *saphēneia*. Even within the confines of the sun and line passages Plato moves from the adverbial *saphōs* to the noun *saphēneia* to the comparative form of the adjective *saphesteron* before returning to *saphēneia*.

9. Chantraine 1968, p. 991, citing the Hittite form *suppi*: "pure, clear," held that *saphēs* and its cognates "exprime l'idée d'évidence, de clarté avec une vue objective."

186   J. H. LESHER

10. *LSJ* compares "know *sapha*" with *eu oida* and translates both as "know assuredly" or "know of a surety" (i.e., "know for sure").

11. For a discussion of the meaning of *saphēs* in Greek historical literature see Scanlon 2002.

12. For other expressions of a religious skepticism voiced in terms of *saphēs*, see the *Helen* (744–54, 1137–1150), *Heracles* (60–62), *Iphigeneia at Tauris* (475–78), *Hippolytus* (189–97), and *Bellerophon* (fr. 304).

13. Following the text and numbering of the fragments of the Presocratics as given in Diels and Kranz 1951. Alcmaeon's dates and the text of B1 are both matters of dispute.

14. For *saphēneia* LSJ gives "clearness," "distinctness," "the plain truth" and "sure knowledge" (citing this passage); and for *saphēnēs*: "the plain truth." By ancient standards, knowledge of "the sure truth" would have been a pleonasm since one who possessed the truth in a sure manner would thereby possess knowledge (see the discussion in Lesher 1994).

15. This use of *saphēs* may explain Socrates' otherwise inexplicable characterization of the eye as "the clearest organ in the body" (*tou saphestatou en sōmati, Rep.* 532c); which is to say, it is the "most clearly aware" organ. Aristotle makes the same claim in *Meta.* A 1: "[Sight] more than any of the other senses makes us know and brings to light many differences between things" (980a).

16. Cf. Xenophon, *Mem.* 1.1.16; 4.6.13; 4.5.1; Plato, *Hippias I*, 286e; *Lysis* 211b; *Euthyphro* 15c–e; *Charmides* 163d; *Euthydemus* 10a; *Laches* 190e; *Gorgias* 457d, and *Meno* 100b; among others.

17. Cf. "Is it clear (*saphes*) that the sophist is a wizard or are we still in doubt? . . . It is clear (*saphes*) that he is one whose province is play" (*Sophist* 235a); "What you are saying is disputable and not yet clear" (*ou pō saphes, Gorgias* 451e), etc.

18. Cf. *Phaedo* 107b where Socrates speaks of the need "to investigate our original assumptions *saphesteron*" as well as at *Sophist* 254 when the Stranger promises to "investigate *saphesteron* the nature of the philosopher."

19. It is possible that the *sapha* at *Il.* 3.89 means "precisely" or "accurately" ("no man can say *sapha* where he died"), but "no man can say for sure" would make equally good sense.

20. Cf. Pindar's remark that "I would not know how to state a *saphē arithmon* for the pebbles of the sea" (*Olympian* 13.45). When in fragment B1 (DK I, 432, 5) Archytas speaks of those who have already made discoveries in the sciences, claiming that "they have handed down a *saphē diagnōsin* of the speed of the constellations and their rising and setting," he appears to be praising earlier scientists for their ability to state the *precise* speeds and locations of the constellations.

21. The meaning of *alētheia* has been the subject of much discussion, much of it inspired by Heidegger's erroneous view that the archaic meaning of *alētheia* was "state of un-hidden-ness" applied to entities come out of hiding. For more defensible accounts of the early meaning of *alētheia* see the studies by Cole, Kahn, and Wolenski.

The meaning of "saphēneia" in Plato's Divided Line 187

22. Cf. *Rep.* 476: "Is not the dream state, whether the man is asleep or awake, just this – the mistaking of resemblance for identity?" It seems virtually certain that Plato here follows Heraclitus (cf. Heraclitus B1, 21, 26, 75, 89). For a useful analysis of the nature of the mistake see the discussion in Harte 2006.

23. I am indebted to many friends and colleagues for helpful comments on earlier versions of this essay: Emily Baragwanath, Rachel Barney, Matthew Colvin, Douglas Frame, David Gallop, Daniel Graham, Samuel Kerstein, Mark LeBar, Georgia Machemer, Patrick Miller, Emese Mogyorodi, John Palmer, Paul Pietroski, David Reeve, Eleanor Rutledge, Kirk Sanders, Tom Scanlon, Rachel Singpurwalla, Nicholas Smith, Peter Smith, and Eva Stehle. I am especially grateful to Patricia Curd for the comments on my paper she presented at the 2008 Arizona Colloquium in Ancient Philosophy.

CHAPTER 10

Plato's philosophical method in the Republic: the Divided Line (510b–511d)

Hugh H. Benson

Plato's image of the Divided Line has captured the attention of his readers for centuries. Much of this attention has been focussed on the nature of the ontological divisions associated with the four sections of the Line, especially the third.[1] This is as it should be since a number of features of the Line point in the direction of ontology. The initial division of the Line into two parts suggests an ontological focus,[2] as does the subdivision of the first part. But when Plato turns to distinguishing the subsections of the second part, his focus becomes a contrast in methodologies.[3] The method of the third section – which I will call the dianoetic method because it results in *dianoia* – is distinct from the method of the fourth section of the line – traditionally called the dialectical method, which results in *epistēmē* or *noēsis*.

I will maintain that the Divided Line passage suggests that these two methods are distinguished less by their formal features than by the manner in which these two methods are carried out. Both methods employ the formal features of the more general method introduced as early as the *Meno* and traditionally called the method of hypothesis.[4] When the method of hypothesis is employed incorrectly it can achieve only *dianoia* and so amounts to the dianoetic method. When the method of hypothesis is employed correctly, one can achieve *epistēmē* and is engaged in dialectic. It is with this feature of the Line – the contrast between the correct philosophical method, dialectic, or the road to the greatest *mathēma*,[5] and its near relative, dianoetic – with which I will be primarily concerned.[6] The former, I maintain, is the correct application of the method of hypothesis; the latter an incorrect application of this same method.

A BRIEF STATEMENT OF THE DIVIDED LINE

The image of the Divided Line is familiar to the readers of Plato. So I will only take a moment to present its basic features.

188

In response to Glaucon's request to continue his explanation of the similarity of the Form of the Good to the Sun, Socrates reminds Glaucon of the two kinds of things – the visibles and the intelligibles – with which he introduced the Sun analogy (507b9–11). He encourages Glaucon to think of these things like a line divided into two unequal parts – La and Lb – which in turn are to be divided into two subsections – L1 and L2 of La and L3 and L4 of Lb – according to the same ratio as the original division. So we get the following image.

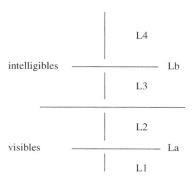

Note: I here make at least the following assumptions in presenting the image in this way: [1] that the line should be displayed vertically rather than horizontally, [2] that the sections of the line increase in size from L1 to L4, and [3] the following ratios and equivalence hold: L1 : L2 :: La : Lb; L3 : L4 :: La : Lb; L1 : L2 :: L3 : L4; and L2 = L3. While there may be some significance in these assumptions for the overall interpretation of the line (see, e.g., Cross and Woozley 1964, p. 204, Fogelin 1971, p. 375, and especially Smith 1996, pp. 27–28), no part of the argument of the present paper depends on these assumptions.

THE INITIAL STATEMENT OF THE DISTINCTION BETWEEN L3 AND L4

After briefly[7] instructing Glaucon to place images in L1 and the original of these images in L2, Socrates offers the following introductory descriptions of L3 and L4. First L3,

[A] In one subsection, the soul, [1] using as images the things that were imitated before (*tois tote mimētheisin hōs eikosin chrōmenē*), [2] is forced to investigate from hypotheses (*zētein anagkazetai ex hupotheseōn*), [3] proceeding not to a first principle but to a conclusion (*ouk ep' archēn poreuomenē all' epi teleutēn*). [510b4–6],[8]

190 HUGH H. BENSON

and then L4

[B] In the other subsection, however, it [1] makes its way to a first principle that is not a hypothesis (*to ep' archēn anupotheton*), [2] proceeding from a hypothesis (*ex hupotheseōs iousa*) [3] but without the images used in the previous subsection, using forms themselves and making its investigation through them (*kai aneu tōn peri ekeino eikonōn, autois eidesi di' autōn tēn methodon poioumenē*). [510b6–9]

This introductory description of the top two sections of the line does not focus on a distinction of objects. Rather the top two sections are distinguished in terms of a method or procedure of the soul. Moreover, while the point is perhaps not explicit in these lines, it is evident that according to Plato the first of these methods or procedures of the soul is in some way inferior to the second.[9] The dianoetic method is in some way inferior to dialectic. Finally, three features are specified for each of the two methods distinguished in these passages.

[A1] Dianoetic uses as images the things that were imitated before

[A2] Dianoetic is forced to investigate from hypotheses

[A3] Dianoetic proceeds not to a first principle (*archē*), but to a conclusion (*teleutē*)

[B1] Dialectic makes its way to an unhypothetical first principle (*archē*)

[B2] Dialectic proceeds from hypotheses

[B3] Dialectic does not use the images used in the previous section, but Forms themselves

[A1] corresponds to [B3], [A3] to [B1], and [A2] to [B2]. We seem to be encouraged to recognize that both dianoetic and dialectic proceed from hypotheses (*ex hupotheseōs*).[10] The surrounding features are meant to distinguish the ways in which the two methods proceed from hypotheses. Dianoetic proceeds from hypotheses not to an *archē*, but to a *teleutē*, while dialectic proceeds from hypotheses to an *archē* that is unhypothetical. In addition, dianoetic in proceeding from hypotheses uses in some way the ordinary objects of L2, while dialectic does not. Dialectic only uses Forms in proceeding from hypotheses. These differences, then, must explain the inferiority of dianoetic to dialectic. They are what distinguish dianoetic from dialectic and so what explain its inferiority. The remainder of the Divided Line passage is devoted to explaining these two differences.

Before looking at the differences between these two methods, let us look at what they have in common. They both proceed from hypotheses. But what is it to proceed from hypotheses?

Plato's philosophical method in the *Republic*

A BRIEF DESCRIPTION OF THE METHOD OF HYPOTHESIS

At *Meno* 86d–e, Socrates famously yields to Meno's request to examine whether virtue is teachable before they have examined what virtue is on the condition that Socrates be permitted to proceed from a hypothesis (*ex hupotheseōs auto skopeisthai; Meno* 86e3) in the manner of the geometers. After a brief explanation of this method (*Meno* 86d3–87b1) Socrates proceeds to practice it in the remainder of the *Meno*.[11] Again, in the *Phaedo* Socrates apparently appeals to this method and uses it as part of his final argument for the immortality of the soul.[12] Indeed, in the run up to Socrates' account of the Form of the Good of which the Divided Line image is a part, Socrates has been made to exemplify this method in response to the question whether Kallipolis is possible.[13] What emerges from these passages is a method consisting of two stages each consisting of two procedures.

In the first, or proof, stage [1a] one seeks to identify a hypothesis from which an answer to the question whose answer one seeks to know can be derived, and then [1b] one shows how the hypothesis entails the answer to the question. In the second, or confirmation, stage one seeks to confirm the truth of the hypothesis, [2a] first by identifying a further hypothesis from which the original hypothesis can be derived and showing how this derivation goes until one reaches "something adequate,"[14] and then[15] [2b] by testing the consequences of the hypothesis to see whether they agree with one another.

Since Robinson, it has been common to describe the method of hypothesis as consisting of both an upward and a downward path,[16] but this is potentially equivocal. Both stages of the method could be plausibly described as consisting of an upward and downward path. The upward paths of both stages would consist in identifying the relevant hypotheses ([1a] and [2a]) from which either the answer to the original question is to be derived ([1a]) or the original hypothesis is to be derived ([2a]). Both stages would also appear to have a downward path. In the case of the first stage the downward path would consist in something like the proof from the hypothesis (or, more plausibly, hypotheses) to the answer to the original question ([1b]), while in the second stage it would consist of testing the consequences of the hypothesis (again, more plausibly, hypotheses) by which one preliminarily confirmed the original hypothesis to see whether they agree with one another ([2b]). But notice that while the upward paths of the two stages are merely different tokens of the same type – both consisting in identifying a higher hypothesis – the downward paths of the two stages are quite different. The downward path of the first stage amounts to providing or displaying a proof of the answer to the original question (the conclusion or *teleutē*),[17] while the downward path of the second stage amounts to a second confirmation procedure of the hypothesis.

The failure to distinguish between these different downward paths partially undermines the otherwise helpful comparison of the method of hypothesis to the geometrical methods of analysis and synthesis.[18] The methods of analysis and synthesis are primarily restricted to the first or proof stage of the method of hypothesis. The method of analysis corresponds to the search for the hypothesis from which the answer to the question can be derived and the method of synthesis corresponds to the exposition of the derivation of the answer from the hypothesis.[19] Nothing corresponding to the second confirmation procedure can be readily found. Consequently if one is to identify Plato's method of hypothesis with the geometrical method of analysis and synthesis one must either omit the second confirmation procedure as part of Plato's method of hypothesis or conflate it with synthesis ([1b]). But this second confirmation procedure should not be omitted from Plato's method of hypothesis. It is explicit in the *Phaedo* 101d3–6[20] and exemplified in both the *Meno* (89c5–96d4) and *Republic* (487a–502c). Consequently, insofar as we understand dianoetic and dialectic both to be employing the method of hypothesis – the former incorrectly, the latter correctly – we should expect to find the procedure represented by [2b], as distinct from [1b].

If this is what it is to proceed from hypotheses, let us look at how dianoetic differs from dialectic.

THE FULLER ACCOUNT

Being told that [L3] differs from [L4] in that the method of [L4] proceeds to an *archē* while the method of [L3] does not, and that the method of [L3] uses ordinary objects while the method of [L4] does not is apparently no less obscure to Glaucon than it is to us. For in response to Socrates' initial statement of the distinction between these two segments of the line, Glaucon announces that he does not yet understand (510b10). In an effort to aid Glaucon's understanding, Socrates offers a more detailed explanation of the dianoetic method ([L3]) from 510c1–511b2 and of the dialectical method ([L4]) from 511b3–c2. The explanation is apparently successful,

Plato's philosophical method in the Republic   193

given Glaucon's ability to summarize the distinction at 511c3–d5,[21] which Socrates endorses in his concluding statement of the ratios at 511d6–e5.[22]

The more detailed explanation of the dianoetic method consists of first an elaboration of the first difference – the movement to a *teleutē* vs. the movement to an *archē* – from 510c1–d4, and then an elaboration of the second difference – the use of ordinary objects vs. the use of only Forms – from 510d5–511a2, followed by a concluding segment that recapitulates the original introductory description – from 511a3–b2.[23] The briefer follow up explanation of [L4] consists of a short redescription of the first difference at 511b3–8 and then a short redescription of the second difference at 511c1–2. Let us begin with Plato's elaboration of the first difference.

THE TREATMENT OF HYPOTHESES

According to Socrates, the practitioners of dianoetic (e.g., geometers, arith-meticians, and the like)[24] make hypotheses (e.g., the odd and the even, the various figures, and the like) as though they knew them (*hōs eidotes*), not thinking it necessary to give a *logos* of them, as though they were clear to all (*hōs panti phanerōn*). Under these conditions, the dianoeticians begin from such hypotheses, validly[25] going through the steps until they reach the *teleutē*, i.e., an answer to the question with which they began (510d2–3).

Plato contrasts the practice of dianoetic in this regard with dialectic at 511b3–8. According to Socrates, dialecticians make their hypotheses not as first principles, but really as hypotheses, like stepping stones, in order to reach the unhypothetical *archē*. Having grasped this *archē* dialectic comes down to a *teleutē* (511b7–8).

Plato does not contrast dianoetic with dialectic on the grounds that the former does while the latter does not proceed to a *teleutē*. On the contrary, both methods proceed to a *teleutē* from the hypothesis.[26] The contrast consists rather in how the two methods treat the hypotheses with which they begin their procedure to a *teleutē*. Dianoetic treats them as *archai*,[27] as already known, as not needing a *logos*, as already clear to all,[28] when they are not, while dialectic does not. Dialectic treats them as the genuine hypoth-eses that they are – as assumptions from which one can derive the *teleutē* but which in order to be known require confirmation up to the genuine *archē* of everything. That is, dianoetic does not treat its hypotheses as requiring confirmation as it should, while dialectic does.

Put in terms of the model of the method of hypothesis in the previous section, dianoetic confines itself to the proof stage, while dialectic embraces both the proof and the confirmation stages (replacing the "something adequate" in the latter stage with the unhypothetical *archē*). Dialecticians recognize, as Plato puts it later, that no "mechanism could possibly turn any agreement (*homologian*) into knowledge when it begins (*archē*) with something unknown and puts together the conclusion (*teleutē*) and the steps in between from what is unknown" (*Republic* 7.533c3–5).[29] So the first difference between dianoetic and dialectic that partially accounts for its inferiority is dianoetic's failure to confirm its hypotheses, as it should. It is an incomplete application of the method of hypothesis and consequently can hope to achieve at most *dianoia*, not *epistēmē*.

The incompleteness of the dianoetic method, however, need not lie in its failure to employ the confirmation procedure at all – although in some extreme cases it may. Rather the incompleteness of the dianoetic method lies in its failure to employ the confirmation process to the extent it should. Most geometers and mathematicians – indeed, especially those of the proto-Euclidean sort around the Academy at the time – propose to confirm their initial hypotheses by deriving them from higher hypotheses[30] concerning the nature of the odd and the even, for example.[31] But insofar as they are practicing dianoetic, at some point in their reasoning they will take as known, as not needing confirmation, as an *archē* what is in fact still a hypothesis in need of confirmation and to this extent their inquiry will remain incomplete.

Plato's point is that the goal of philosophical inquiry – dialectic as opposed to dianoetic – (whatever the objects at which it is directed) is to provide hypotheses from which the answer to the original question can be derived and which are themselves derivable from the unhypothetical *archē*. Moreover, Plato maintains that one cannot rightly claim to know the answer until this goal has been achieved. Short of confirmation from the unhypothetical *archē* one's inquiry remains incomplete.[32] Of course, Plato would concede that few – perhaps none – of us has successfully completed such an inquiry. Much work remains to be done. But the procedure to be followed remains the same. The difference between dianoetic and dialectic lies not in the procedure, but in how each treats its hypotheses. The former takes them to be known and confirmed when they are not; the latter does not.[33] Just so, we find Socrates employing dialectic in attempting to answer whether virtue is teachable in the *Meno*, whether the soul is immortal in the final argument of the *Phaedo*, and whether Kallipolis is possible in *Republic* 5 and 6. The procedure employed is indistinguishable from dianoetic – at least with respect to this first difference. What makes these dialectical inquiries[34] is Socrates' explicit recognition that there is more work to be done.

Plato's philosophical method in the *Republic*

THE USE OF ORDINARY OBJECTS

Thus far we have only addressed one of the ways that dianoetic differs from dialectic – the way in which the two methods treat their hypotheses. But there is a second difference between them. Dianoetic uses ordinary objects – the objects of *pistis* – in some way that dialectic does not. The issues here are more difficult (to my mind) both philosophically and textually, but the model we have been developing thus far will help. Let's look at what Socrates is made to say about this second difference.

In the more detailed explanation of L3 (510d5–511a2), Plato tells us that dianoetic uses ordinary objects as follows. The dianoetic geometers use and make *logoi* about (*peri*) visible shapes, but they do not think about them but rather about the things these shapes are like. That is, they make *logoi* for the sake of (*heneka*) the square itself and the diagonal itself, not for the sake of the squares and diagonals that they draw. Rather they use these squares and diagonals seeking to see the square itself and diagonal itself which cannot be seen except by thought (*tēi dianoiai*).

Notice first that dianoeticians are described as making *logoi* (*tous logous poioumenoi*) contrary to the suggestion just a few lines earlier that they failed to think it necessary to give (*didonai*) *logoi*.[35] Now, of course, the notion of making or giving *logoi* is notoriously equivocal, and a careful reading of the Greek here may indicate that Plato is pointing to a subtle distinction between the things that *logoi* are about and the things they are for the sake of.[36] We will return to this distinction in a moment, but for now what Plato says here reinforces the earlier suggestion that Plato allows that some dianoeticians do engage in the confirmation process. While some dianoeticians simply propose a hypothesis from which an answer to the original question can be derived without seeing the need to provide any *logos* concerning that hypothesis, many (perhaps most) dianoeticians do not. Both dialecticians and dianoeticians (at least for the most part) provide *logoi* of their hypotheses. The difference lies in how they provide *logoi*. The first difference, as we have seen, indicates that dianoeticians fail to provide complete *logoi*, i.e., complete confirmation. But Plato's talk of *logoi* here indicates that the dianoeticians' confirmation process fails in yet another way connected to the use of ordinary objects. Their confirmation process is not only incomplete, but also in some way defective. It is in some way about ordinary sensible objects, while for the sake of the forms. Thus, the second difference between dianoetic and dialectic which accounts for the inferiority of the former also concerns the confirmation stage of the method of hypothesis.

Against this, however, in the more detailed explanation of L4 Plato writes that once dialecticians have confirmed their hypotheses up to the unhypothetical *archē* they turn around coming down to the *teleutē* (i.e., the answer to the original question) "without making use of anything visible at all, but only of Forms themselves, moving on from Forms to Forms, and ending in Forms" (*Republic* 6.511c1–2). The contrast with dianoetic here suggests that dianoeticians use ordinary objects not as part of the confirmation process, but in the downward path of the proof stage ([1b]). They are used in proceeding from the hypothesis to the *teleutē*, while dialectic does not make use of ordinary objects during this procedure. This suggests that the second difference which accounts for the inferiority of dianoetic lies not in the confirmation stage, but in some failure of the downward (or synthesis) portion of the proof stage. Thus, contrary to the conclusion of the previous paragraph, dianoetic somehow employs ordinary objects in the proof stage, while dialectic does not.

Plato has frequently been understood here as appealing to geometry's use of diagrams in its proofs.[37] While something like this is almost surely right, there are at least two difficulties with this suggestion as it stands.

First, it is difficult to see why Plato should find the mere use of diagrams as indicating the inferiority of dianoetic. One might respond by appealing to Plato's general disparagement of sense-perception as a method of knowledge acquisition and appeal to his repeated use of vision terms in the description of the way in which dianoetic makes use of the things that were imitated in the previous sub-section (*tois horōmenois eidesi, idein, idoi*).[38] The idea seems to be that dianoetic uses sense-perception to examine or study things which should be studied by thought or reason. Dianoetic uses sense-perception as a way of studying the Forms. Dialectic does not. But this kind of response is a consequence of a simplistic understanding of Plato's attitude with respect to sense-perception. Plato does to be sure disparage the mere use of sense-perception at the beginning of the *Phaedo*. Knowledge of the Forms is best acquired by a disembodied soul's direct apprehension. But for those of us with embodied souls Plato appears to recognize a useful role for ordinary sensible objects. In his account of the theory of recollection in the *Phaedo* he explains that sensible objects serve as a kind of necessary catalyst, while in his account of the education of the philosopher-rulers in *Republic* 7, he distinguishes between the features of ordinary sensible objects which do not turn the soul toward truth and knowledge and those that do.[39] So it cannot be the mere use of diagrams as ordinary sensible objects that Plato is objecting to. Instead, he must be objecting to the way they are used in dianoetic.[40]

Plato's philosophical method in the Republic

Second, it is difficult to see how understanding the second difference between dianoetic and dialectic as finding fault with geometry's use of diagrams is sufficiently generalizable. Whatever else one thinks about the dianoetic method, it must be applicable to other disciplines besides geometry. It must at least be applicable to the other mathematical disciplines and one would imagine to the propaedeutic disciplines of Book 7.[41] It is, however, not obvious how the use of diagrams is to be employed outside of geometry. Of course, this problem is even worse, if one permits, as the interpretation I am encouraging does, dianoetic inquiries concerning things like virtue, its teachability, the immortality of the soul, and the possibility of Kallipolis. How does one use diagrams in proving the teachability of virtue or the possibility of Kallipolis?

Of course, one might think that the *Republic* itself provides an answer to this last question. The analogue of geometric diagrams in the proof of the nature of justice goes as follows: construct – as a thought-experiment – an ideal city and then examine what justice is. So understood, however, the use of diagrams and their analogues no longer looks plausibly restricted to the downward portion of the proof stage of the method of hypothesis – [1b].[42] But in any case, we are still left with the question why dianoetic's use of ordinary objects, geometry's use of diagrams, or Socrates' use of thought-experiments is problematic. Why does dianoetic's use of ordinary objects make it inferior to dialectic?

Perhaps, the distinction in the more detailed description of L3 between making *logoi* about sensible objects and making *logoi* for the sake of forms will provide some help. This might suggest that Plato is emphasizing the indirect nature of dianoetic. Dianoetic seeks to know or think about the Forms by in some way using or thinking about the things that are images of Forms.[43] Unfortunately, Plato provides very little guidance on the nature of this indirection.

A common way to explain this indirection is by appealing to an incorrigibility or certainty requirement for dialectic.[44] The directness of dialectic as opposed to the indirection of dianoetic is Plato's way of indicating that the unhypothetical *archē* is directly known as a result of incorrigible or certain intuition – viewing, intuiting, believing (directly) the *archē* suffices to guarantee its truth. I can find nothing in the *Republic* – other than the evidence of indirection itself – that explicitly appeals to incorrigible direct intuition. The argument for understanding Plato's appeal to indirection in this way tends to be more philosophical than textual.[45] Nevertheless, the philosophical objections to understanding the appeal to direct intuition as an appeal to some sort of psychological certainty are too numerous to

198   HUGH H. BENSON

rehearse. Understanding the appeal to direct intuition as an appeal to psychological incorrigibility, on the other hand, is philosophically more respectable, but the cost of restricting the sorts of propositions susceptible to a plausible incorrigibility requirement is rather high. The best candidates for such propositions are rather insubstantial claims like "I am in pain now" or more boldly "Nothing is both F and not-F in the same way at the same time relative to the same thing."[46] But neither of these look like plausible candidates for "the unhypothetical *archē* of everything" from which one can derive answers to such questions as whether virtue is teachable, the soul is immortal, or Kallipolis is possible. Consequently, while in the end an appeal to incorrigibility or certainty may be the best we can do in accounting for the second difference between dianoetic and dialectic, we would do well to look elsewhere for help in explaining dianoetic's use of ordinary objects.[47]

DIALECTIC IN BOOK 7

We can get some help with this difference by looking outside the Divided Line passage to the parallel passage at *Republic* 531d–535a. At 533b6–e3, Plato distinguishes between dialectic and the propaedeutic disciplines in a familiar way. The propaedeutic disciplines leave untouched the hypotheses that they use and are unable to give an account of them. Dialectic, on the other hand, destroys its hypotheses and proceeds to the *archē* itself, so as to be secure. We have here the first of the two ways in which Plato distinguishes dianoetic from dialectic in the Divided Line passage – the difference in the way the two methods treat their hypotheses. The propaedeutic disciplines do not attempt to confirm their hypotheses (completely), but treat them as *archai* and proceed to *teleutai*. Dialectic attempts to confirm its hypotheses up to a genuine *archē* and then proceeds to the *teleutē*.

Unfortunately, the second difference is not mentioned explicitly, except perhaps in passing when describing the propaedeutic disciplines by means of the dream metaphor. Socrates explains to Glaucon that "we described [these disciplines] as to some extent grasping what is, for we saw that, while they do dream about what is, they are unable to command a waking view of it" (*Republic* 7, 533b7–c1). Plato here suggests that like dianoetic in L3 the propaedeutic disciplines aim to view, grasp, or think about what is, but manage instead to only view, grasp, or think about it partially. Nevertheless, while the indirectness of the propaedeutic disciplines and dianoetic may be exhibited here, the appeal to the use of ordinary objects is not. Indeed, the indirectness is attributed to dianoetic's incompleteness, i.e., its failure to

Plato's philosophical method in the Republic 199

confirm its hypotheses up to the unhypothetical *archē* rather than to dianoetic's use of ordinary objects.

Fortunately, Plato expands upon the dream metaphor when he describes the knowledge of the good after the second statement of the ratios at 533e4–534b2. Plato writes:

Unless someone can distinguish in an account the Form of the Good from everything else, can survive all refutation (*dia pantōn elegchōn diexiōn*), as if in a battle, striving to judge things not in accordance with opinion but in accordance with being (*mē kata doxan alla kat' ousian prothumoumenos elegchein*), and can come through all this with his account still intact, you'll say that he doesn't know the good itself or any other good. And if he gets hold of some image of it, you'll say that it's through opinion, not knowledge, for he is dreaming and asleep throughout his present life, and, before he wakes up here, he will arrive in Hades and go to sleep forever. (*Republic* 7, 534b8–d1)

We should recall that the Divided Line image was explicitly introduced to further explain the similarity between the Sun and the Form of the Good. But if the Form of the Good is to be found anywhere in the image of the Divided Line it appears to be identified with the unhypothetical *archē*.[48] Consequently, Plato here indicates that the unhypothetical *archē*, the form of the good, is subject to an account (*tōi logōi*), that it must be subjected to refutation (*elegchōn*) and tested (*elegchein*), not according to opinion (*kata doxan*) but according to being (*kat' ousian*), and that one who fails to treat the unhypothetical *archē* this way views it partially or indirectly (grasping an image of it) as though in a dream. Here, then, we have a more detailed description of what it is according to Plato to fail to view or grasp the unhypothetical *archē* directly.

Two things immediately stand out from this description. First, viewing the unhypothetical *archē* does not guarantee its truth, but requires confirmation by avoiding refutation. To know the Form of the Good it is not enough simply to view it, and somehow thereby know it. One must be able to respond in some way successfully to all attempts to refute it. One must test it and give an account of it. Second, the confirmation process and the kind of account that is referred to here is not the confirmation process consisting of looking for higher hypotheses from which the original hypothesis can be derived. By hypothesis, there is no higher hypothesis from which the unhypothetical *archē* can be derived. Rather the confirmation process referred to here looks more like the process of in some way testing the consequences of the unhypothetical *archē*.

We should recall that the method of hypothesis introduced earlier consists of two confirmation processes, only one of which consists in looking for a higher hypothesis from which the original hypothesis can be derived. According to that model, one must not only confirm the hypothesis by deriving it from a higher hypothesis, but one must also examine the consequences of the hypothesis to see whether they cohere with one another. Each hypothesis must be confirmed by being derived from a higher hypothesis *and* by being tested for coherent consequences until one reaches a hypothesis that cannot be derived from a higher hypothesis and cannot be refuted in virtue of incoherent consequences.

Even so, the nature of this second confirmatory process is notoriously obscure. Not the least of its obscurities is that it appears merely to be testing the higher hypothesis for self-consistency.[49] Self-consistency is of course a laudatory goal for a hypothesis, but the odds of postulating a self-contradictory hypothesis from which one derived lower hypotheses or the *teleutē* are rather low.[50] Reading the current passage as a description of this second confirmation process, however, may provide some clarity. For the process described here is reminiscent of the *elenchus* (Kahn 1996, p. 296).

We know from Socrates' use of the *elenchus* in the early definitional dialogues that the *elenchus* too is essentially a test for consistency. But Socrates' use of this method in these dialogues is essentially *ad hominem* (Benson 2000, chs. 2–4). Socrates is concerned to test the interlocutor's knowledge of the definition (or hypothesis), not the definition (or hypothesis) itself. Consequently, what Socrates tests in these dialogues is the consistency of the interlocutor's beliefs. The method of hypothesis, however, is precisely not *ad hominem*. That is why it is introduced when it is in the dialogues. Plato makes Socrates introduce this method in the *Meno* precisely at the point in the dialogue when the object of inquiry is no longer Meno's knowledge but the nature (and/or teachability) of virtue (Benson 2003). Consequently, what must be tested for consistency must be different. The *Phaedo* suggests that Plato describes what is tested for consistency as the consequences of the hypothesis. This is the second confirmation process of the method of hypothesis. But how is this supposed to work?

Our current passage from the *Republic* suggests that dianoetic and dialectic differ with respect to this second confirmation process. The former tests the consequences of its hypotheses *kata doxan*; the latter tests the consequences of its hypotheses *kat'ousian* (see Fine 1990, p. 112 n. 49). This distinction parallels the distinction in the Divided Line between dianoetic's use of ordinary objects (the objects of *doxa*) and dialectic's restriction to the use of forms (*ousiai*). Suppose that Plato has in mind two different sorts of consequences – roughly contingent consequences and essential consequences, as some have thought is suggested by Glaucon's distinction among

Plato's philosophical method in the Republic

three types of goods at the beginning of *Republic* 2.[51] The idea is that dianoetic tests the consistency of what it takes to be genuine or essential consequences, but which are in fact only contingent or artificial consequences of its hypotheses – consequences of its hypotheses in virtue of contingent or artificial features of the world. For example, the consequences of the nature of justice are that it provides one with a good reputation and political power[52] or the consequences of the nature of philosophy are that philosophers are vicious and useless,[53] or perhaps even the consequences of the nature of virtue are that it is not taught. Dialectic, on the other hand, tests for the consistency of the genuine or essential consequences of its hypotheses and can explain away the appearance of inconsistency by explaining how the apparently contrary evidence (the artificial consequences which are at odds with the essential consequences) is not really a consequence of the hypothesis.

If this or something like it is what Plato has in mind here, then the second difference between dianoetic and dialectic with which we struggled while examining the Divided Line can be understood as follows. Dianoetic, in virtue of studying the forms by means of their images (e.g., justice as instantiated, philosophy as instantiated, virtue as instantiated),[54] mistakes what are not in fact consequences of its hypotheses as genuine consequences. It takes features of the Form that follow from the contingent nature of the world – so to speak – as genuine features of the Form and tests them for consistency. It makes its *logoi* about the instances, rather than about the Form for the sake of which its *logoi* are made. Dialectic, by contrast, does not mistake features of instances of Forms for those features that follow from the Form's being or nature. It tests those features for consistency and responds to the contrary evidence of the artificial or contingent consequences. If one can derive the answer to the original question from a hypothesis which itself is underivable and can confirm that hypothesis by checking its consequences for consistency and against contrary evidence, one can genuinely be said to know the answer to the original question.

Perhaps a brief example would help. At *Republic* 5, 471c4–473b3, Socrates considers the question whether Kallipolis is possible. He reduces a positive answer to this question to the hypothesis that political power and philosophy coincide (473b4–e5). He confirms this hypothesis first by identifying a hypothesis concerning the nature of philosophy – roughly that it is the ability to grasp what is always the same in all respects (474c8–480a) – and deriving the hypothesis that political power and philosophy coincide from this higher hypothesis (484a1–487a8). But at 487b1–d5 Adeimantus objects to this confirmation of the hypothesis by maintaining that it follows from the nature of philosophy that philosophers are useless and vicious (contrary presumably to the consequences of the hypothesis that political power and philosophy coincide that philosophers are beneficial and virtuous). Socrates is made to respond by pointing out that the consequence that philosophers are useless and vicious is in fact an artificial consequence – a consequence of instantiations of philosophy given the contingent nature of Athens in the fifth century BCE (487d6–502c8).[55] By means of the Ship of State analogy Socrates explains that genuine instantiations of philosophy are useless in the current climate because they go unrecognized (owing to the blindness of the Demos and the obfuscation of the demagogues). On the other hand, those philosophers alleged to be vicious are in fact not genuine instantiations of philosophy, but rather they have a genuine potential or nature to become a genuine instance but have been corrupted by their education and upbringing. The nature or being (*ousia*) of philosophy is not the cause of these consequences.[56] Even so, Socrates does not take his hypotheses to be other than the hypotheses they are, falling short of being confirmed by the unhypothetical *archē* – the Form of the Good which Socrates fails to know (506a–d). Here then we have dialectic as opposed to dianoetic at work in the dialogues.[57]

CONCLUSION

If something like this is right, then according to Plato the work of philosophy (and, one might speculate, much of Socrates' practice in the dialogues) goes as follows. When faced with a question whose answer they do not know, philosophers look for a hypothesis from which an answer can be derived and show how that answer is derived. But philosophers (unlike dianoeticians) realize that their work has only just begun. Philosophers recognize that the hypothesis from which the answer was derived is in need of confirmation. They will search for higher hypotheses from which this original hypothesis can be derived and they will test its consequences for consistency and against contrary evidence. Philosophers will take care to examine the consequences of the hypothesis that follow directly from the nature of the Forms involved and not from contingent or artificial features of the hypothesis. Moreover, philosophers will recognize that until they have followed this confirmation process all the way to the unhypothetical *archē* and responded, as though in battle, to all of the contrary evidence of its consequences, they cannot be said to know the answer to the original question. They will not have completed the dialectical method.

Plato's philosophical method in the Republic   203

Of course, if we are fully to understand Plato's notion of the work of philosophy there remains much work to be done. For now I simply hope to have advanced the potential benefit of examining Plato's dialectical method with the current model of philosophical inquiry in mind.[58]

NOTES

1. See Burnyeat 1987, p. 217, who calls this "the great question." Smith 1996 offers an excellent discussion of the literature of the twentieth century prior to 1996. Since 1996 see, especially, Burnyeat 2000, Denyer 2007, Foley 2008, and Netz 2003.
2. Although we should note that even here the beings are distinguished in terms of our cognitive access.
3. To be precise, Plato may suggest that the top two sections of the line have distinct objects at 511d6–e5 and 534a5–8. But the vast majority of Plato's discussion of the difference between these sections is focussed on the distinct methodologies. A full account will have to address this passage but for now I, like Plato, will be focussed on the distinct methodologies. See Robinson 1953, p. 194: "we must distinguish a lower and a higher way of getting at the intelligible world. That is the main point of the Line, the two 'ways' or methods of mathematics and dialectic." See also Cross and Woozley 1964, pp. 226 and 232 and Fine 1990, pp. 100–05.
4. See Cross and Woozley 1964, pp. 252–53, Moravcsik 1973, p. 159, perhaps Smith 1996, p. 33, and Bailey 2006, pp. 102–03. *Pace*, e.g., Gonzalez 1998, p. 14.
5. We should recall that the three analogies that occupy the end of Book 6 and the beginning of Book 7 are motivated by an attempt to explain the greatest *mathēma*, or the Form of the Good; *Republic* 6.504a–506e.
6. A potential equivocation is associated with Plato's use of the Greek words that get translated as "dialectic." In the *Republic* 7 passage dialectic is treated more like a fixed state, an *epistēmē* or *technē*, analogous to the propaideutic *epistēmai* or *technai* of arithmetic, calculation, geometry, astronomy, and harmonics, while in the Divided Line passage dialectic is treated more like a method or procedure by which one acquires *epistēmē* or *noēsis* analogous to the dianoetic method or procedure of arithmetic, calculation, geometry, and the rest. This difference between the two passages is not insurmountable and much of what is said about dialectic in the two passages helps to inform the other but it is important to keep these two distinct treatments or ways of referring to dialectic distinct. Throughout the course of the present essay I will be treating dialectic as the method or procedure of acquiring *epistēmē* – the method of philosophy – not as the skill or fixed state one acquires when one acquires *epistēmē* – philosophy itself.
7. Of the eighty lines of the Divided Line passage only fifteen or so are devoted to the distinction between L1 and L2. The remainder of the passage is devoted to explaining the difference between L3 and L4, almost all of which is focussed on a contrast in the method of L3 and the method of L4.

8. All translations of the *Republic* are from Grube and Reeve 1992.

9. The point is made explicitly by Glaucon in his summary of Socrates' distinction at 511c3–d5, which Socrates is immediately made to endorse.

10. [A2] differs from [B2] in three ways: [1] [A2] uses *zētein* while [B2] uses *iousa*, [2] [A2] uses the plural *hupotheseōn* while [B2] uses the singular *hupotheseōs*, and [3] only dianoetic is said to be forced (*anagkazetai*) to proceed from hypotheses. The first two differences are insignificant. The third difference is more significant. See Burnyeat 1987, p. 219.

11. Or at least so I have argued; see Benson 2003.

12. See *Phaedo* 99c ff. Socrates does not use the phrase "proceed from" or "investigate from a hypothesis" in the *Phaedo*, but the method he describes as "hypothesizing (*hupothemenos*) the *logos* that seems best" is essentially the same as the method described as proceeding from a hypothesis in the *Meno* and the *Republic*. See, for example, Bluck 1955, p. 156, Bedu-Addo 1979, pp. 122–24, and Moravcsik 1973, p. 159, *pace*, for example Robinson 1953, p. 121, Weiss 2001, p. 187 n. 10, Scott 2006, p. 204, and Byrd 2007a, pp. 141–42 n. 4.

13. Again, at least so I have argued; see Benson 2008. In what follows I will be using words like "imply," "proof," "derive," "consequences," and "propositions." I do so, however, in full recognition of Annas' salutary comment that "Plato, . . ., actually says little in non-figurative language that implies that knowledge forms a body of truths in which the lower depend on the higher and can be shown to be derivable from them. And this view involves two serious problems. One is that, in a world where Aristotle has not yet begun to codify the forms of valid argument and formalize logic, Plato has no precise terms for 'proposition', 'imply', 'derive', and no explicit distinctions between premises, conclusions, and rules of inference. . . . And, second, on this view the 'unhypothetical first principle' ought to be a proposition, indeed a super-proposition from which all the basic propositions of the special sciences can be derived" (Annas 1981, pp. 288–89). I believe, but will not argue here, that the seriousness of the first problem can be mitigated a bit, and Plato's notion of an "unhypothetical *archē* of everything" is a serious problem in my view regardless of what language we use. In what follows, however, I do not intend the language of "derive," "imply," "proof," etc. to be used in anything other than the relatively figurative sense of Plato's actual language of "consequences," "agreement," etc.

14. This portion of the second stage is simply a repetition of the proof stage directed at the hypothesis identified in [1a].

15. Bailey 2006, p. 102 takes [2b] to temporally precede [2a]. This is evidently the suggestion of *Phaedo* 101d1–102a2, but this is not how the method gets practiced in the *Meno* and the *Republic*. I suspect that the temporal order does not matter. See Benson 2003 and Benson 2008.

16. See Robinson 1953, pp. 160–62.

17. See Annas 1981, p. 292.

18. See, e.g., Cornford 1932, p. 72, Mueller 1992, and Menn 2002.

19. See Mueller 1992, p. 175: "in synthesis one simply writes down the proof discovered by analysis, that is, one goes through the steps of analysis in reverse

Plato's philosophical method in the Republic   205

order"; Menn 2002, p. 195 suggests that synthesis "confirm[s] what has been discovered by analysis." Insofar as synthesis is seen as a further confirmation of the hypothesis, and not simply the writing down of the proof as discovered by analysis, the difference between the method of analysis (and synthesis) and the method of hypothesis I am proposing will be diminished.

20. See Mueller 1992, p. 182 concerning *Phaedo* 101d3–6. See also Mueller 1992, p. 187.

21. See Glaucon's repeated claims to understand at 511b1, 511c3, and 511e5.

22. See Netz 2003, pp. 303–04.

23. "This, then, is the kind of thing that, on the one hand, I said is intelligible, and, on the other, is such that [A2] the soul is forced to use hypotheses in the investigation of it (*hupothesesi d' anagkazomenēn psuchēn chrēsthai peri tēn zētēsin autou*), [A3] not travelling up to a first principle (*ouk ep' archēn iousan*), since it cannot reach beyond its hypotheses (*hos ou dunamenēn tōn hupotheseōn anōterō ekbainein*), [A1] but using as images those very things of which images were made in the section below (*eikosi de chrōmenēn autois tois hupo tōn katō apeikastheisin*), and which, by comparison to their images, were thought to be clear and to be valued as such" (511a3–b1).

24. Plato's reference to the geometers here and at 511b1–2 and 511d3 is significant. It reinforces the earlier suggestion that he has in mind the method of hypothesis which he introduces in the *Meno* as the method practiced by the geometers. It also supports taking the procedure of the propaedeutic disciplines – beginning with number and calculation and ending in harmonics – to be the method of hypothesis as well. Of course, Socrates' point in introducing this method in the *Meno* is not to engage in geometry but to employ it on the question that Meno is insisting on pursuing – whether virtue is teachable? And he does employ it on this question in the last third of the *Meno*. The method, then, is apparently paradigmatically employed in geometry, and mathematics more generally, but it would be a mistake to take it to be confined to geometry (see 511b1–2). While the method can (and presumably often is) employed on geometrical objects like the various figures and angles, it can also be employed on "ethical objects" like virtue and its teachability among other things.

25. *Homologoumenōs* cannot be translated as "consistently" as Shorey does since the *teleutē* is not simply consistent with the hypothesis but is in some way a consequence of the hypothesis, hence I translate "validly" following Grube/Reeve. For a similar difficulty see the translation of *sumphōnein* at *Phaedo* 100a3–100a8; for a helpful discussion see Gentzler 1991.

26. That is, both methods go up to a hypothesis [1a] and then down (see *katabainēi*) to the answer to the question with which one began [1b]; contra Cornford 1932, p. 72 who apparently takes the dianoetic method to represent the downward path and dialectic to represent the upward path.

27. See 511c6–7 in Glaucon's summary.

28. See *Republic* 7.533c1–3.

29. Burnyeat 2000, p. 23 n. 33 takes the use of *homologian* here to indicate "that knowledge or understanding should not depend on an interlocutor's

206   HUGH H. BENSON

agreement; all relevant objections should have been rebutted." I agree that in the wider context (533–34), part of Plato's point is precisely this (cf. pp. 198–202 below), but at 533c this is not Plato's point. Rather Plato's use of *homologian* here is allusion back to 510d where the point is clearly that knowledge (*epistēmē*) cannot be acquired by an argument whose premises are unconfirmed or unsecured – however that confirmation is to be accomplished.

30. And by testing the coherence of their consequences, [2b]. More on this second confirmation procedure below.

31. See Reeve 2003, pp. 40–41, who points out that these mathematicians also give definitions (*logoi*?) of their starting points. Reeve takes this as evidence that *logos* cannot be understood as definition, but must be understood as argument or justification (see Annas 1981, p. 287), since geometers do not fail to give definitions of their starting points but do fail to give arguments for or justifications of them. I doubt that Plato would be much impressed with this distinction, because for him to give a definition is to give a justification and vice versa (or at least so I believe). But the important point for our purposes is that the geometers who do not give *logoi* of their starting points fail to practice dialectic to the extent that they fail to take the *logoi* of their starting points to require confirmation.

32. That Plato views dianoetic as an incomplete version of dialectic is strongly reinforced by Glaucon's suggestion in his summary of the distinction that the things which the dianoeticians do not yet know are knowable once they reach the unhypothetical *archē* (511d2).

33. Consequently, insofar as Plato is critical of contemporary mathematicians it is not because they use hypotheses. As Burnyeat points out, they are forced to. Rather it is because at some point in the process they treat their hypotheses as *archai*. They take what requires confirmation as not requiring confirmation.

34. See n. 43 below.

35. And later in the parallel passage in Book 7 the propaedeutic practitioners are described as unable to either give or receive *logoi* (*Republic* 7, 534b3–7).

36. The suggestion may be that dianoeticians do not think it is necessary to make *logoi* about the square itself, but do make *logoi* about squares, even though the *logoi* that they make are for the sake of the square itself, not for the sake of squares.

37. See Mueller 1992, p. 184, who writes concerning the two differences we have been examining between dianoetic and dialectic: "There is little doubt that Socrates has in mind here two features of mathematics that we associate particularly with geometry: the use of diagrams in arguments and the derivation of conclusions from initial assumptions (synthesis)." Indeed, Plato may even be supposed to have in mind geometry's practice of construction. For the latter see, for example, Mueller 1992, pp. 175–77, and Menn 2002, p. 199.

38. See also *aisthētoi* at 511ci.

39. See Byrd 2007a and 2007b, who dubs the sensible objects or their sensible properties which turn the soul toward truth and knowledge "summoners."

40. I am aware of only one place where the non-empirical nature of dialectic may be highlighted. At 532a1–b3 Plato says that the dialectician "tries through

Plato's philosophical method in the Republic   207

argument and apart from all sense-perceptions to find the being itself of each thing (*hotan tis tōi dialegesthai epicheirēi aneu pasōn tōn aisthēseōn dia tou logou ep' auto ho estin hekaston horman*) and doesn't give up until he grasps the good itself with understanding itself (*mē apostēi prin an auto ho estin agathon autēi noēsei labēi*)." But even here dialectic may be being contrasted with La, i.e., the method of the empirical *technai* (for Plato's reference to these see *Republic* 7, 533b3–6), rather than with L3, i.e., dianoetic.

41. For the identification of the propaedeutic disciplines (at least when not followed to their completion in dialectic) and dianoetic, see 533d1–7.

42. In addition, one will be obliged, I suppose, to understand Socrates' method in this portion of the *Republic* as dianoetic rather than dialectic. See Cooper 1966, p. 67, who sees this as a positive result.

43. See Annas 1981, pp. 280–82.

44. See, for example, Cornford 1932, pp. 73–74, Robinson 1953, pp. 172–76, Cross and Woozley 1964, pp. 252–53, Santas 1980, p. 255, and most plausibly Bailey 2006. Annas 1981, pp. 281–82 does not explain the indirection in this way, but in my view leaves the indirection unexplained.

45. See especially Bailey 2006, pp. 102–03.

46. Bailey 2006, pp. 102–11, plausibly argues that the principle of non-contradiction which Aristotle treats as an unhypothetical *archē* would also be so treated by Plato. Nevertheless, we will need more contentful propositions than the principle of non-contradiction to derive answers to the questions in the subsequent sentence.

47. For others who reject understanding Plato as appealing to incorrigible or certain intuition see, for example, Annas 1981, pp. 283–84, Reeve 1988, p. 77, and McCabe 2006.

48. See, for example, Robinson 1953, p. 139, Baltzly 1996, pp. 164–65 n. 34, and Denyer 2007, pp. 306ff.; *pace*, for example, Bedu-Addo 1978, p. 124.

49. Perhaps Bostock 1986, p. 168.

50. Baltzly 1996 offers an alternative way of understanding the second confirmatory process. Unfortunately, Baltzly's account leaves unrelated the second confirmatory process and dianoetic's use of ordinary objects.

51. See, for example, Foster 1937, White 1984, and Pappas 1995, p. 55.

52. The consequences of justice if it were only a good of Glaucon's third type.

53. See *Republic* 6, 487a–502c and Benson 2008.

54. If one only examines justice as it is in fact instantiated one might conclude that it only results in good reputation and power and not in pleasure; if one only examines philosophy as it is in fact instantiated, one might conclude that philosophers are useless and/or vicious; if one only examines virtue as it is in fact instantiated one might conclude that it is unteachable.

55. Adeimantus is using ordinary objects and examining the consequences of the hypotheses *kata doxan*.

56. Socrates is using Forms alone and examining the consequences of hypotheses *kata ousian*.

57. For a defense of this interpretation of *Republic* 471c–502c see Benson 2008.

58. I am grateful to the audience of the Arizona Colloquium in Ancient Philosophy and a number of individuals, whose comments, questions, and objections have forced me to clarify, if not abandon, my position, especially Dom Bailey, Monte Cook, Ray Elugardo, Lee Franklin, Michelle Jenkins, Rusty Jones, John Malcolm, Andrew Payne, Jerry Santas, Rachel Singpurwalla, Nick Smith, Jan Szaif, and Nick White.

CHAPTER 11

Blindness and reorientation: education and the acquisition of knowledge in the Republic

C. D. C. Reeve

Education is not, according to Socrates, "what some people boastfully profess it to be," when they say they can "pretty much put knowledge (*epistēmē*) into souls that lack it, like putting sight into blind eyes" (518b8–c2). On the contrary, it "takes for granted that sight is there, though not turned in the right way or looking where it should look, and contrives to redirect it appropriately" (518d5–7). Properly conceived, education is the craft concerned with "this very turning around ... with how this instrument [with which each of us learns] can be most easily and effectively turned around, not of putting sight into it" (518d3–5) – where the instrument in question is reason (*logos*) or the rational element (*to logistikon*) (580d8). Together with appetite (439d6–7), spirit (439e2–3, 581a9–b4), and perhaps a few other elements (443d7–8), reason constitutes the embodied human soul. Consequently, education cannot accomplish its task of reorienting reason without reorienting the whole soul, any more than an eye can be turned around except by turning the whole body (518c6–8). Primarily targeted on the reason, Platonic education is thus forced to extend its purview to appetite and spirit. In the *Republic*, this part of education is discussed first, in Books 2 and 3. But, since it does not involve the acquisition of knowledge (522a3–6), we will keep it offstage until the final act, so as to focus on Platonic education's primary target and on the perplexing contrast Socrates draws between reorienting it and curing its blindness.

When first introduced in Book 4, reason's functions seem primarily practical. It is "really wise and exercises foresight on behalf of the whole soul," and so is its proper or appropriate ruler (441e3–5), "guards the whole soul and the body against external enemies ... by deliberating" (442b5–7), and has "within it the knowledge of what is advantageous both for each part and for the whole, the community composed of all three" (442c5–7). By the time we reach Book 9, however, it seems to have become more contemplative or theoretical: reason is "always straining to know where

209

210   C. D. C. REEVE

the truth lies" and is appropriately called "learning-loving and philosophical" (581b6–11).

That it is nonetheless still conceived as a single, indissolubly unified
psychic element (611b1–612a6) seems due, in part at least, to a pair of
doctrines. The first concerns the role of the good in rational choice.
When it comes to good things, we are told, "no one is satisfied to acquire
things that are believed good. On the contrary, everyone seeks the things
that are good. In this area, everyone disdains mere belief," so that what is
really good is "what every soul pursues, and for its sake does everything"
(505d5–9). The second doctrine concerns the subject matter of learning:
"The most important thing to learn about" is the form of the good, since "it
is by their relation to it that just things and the rest become useful and
beneficial" (505a2–4). Reason's putatively theoretical role is thus to learn
about something with such profound practical import that "anyone who is
going to act sensibly in private or public must see it" (517c3–4). Put another
way, the truth reason is always seeking is (or includes) practical truth. That
is why the unhypothetical first principle on which knowledge of it depends
is itself the good (508b12–511e5).

What eventually emerges as the most beneficial thing, however, the one
the *Philebus* calls "the [best] good *in a human being*" (64a1), is the theoretical
activity of knowing or contemplating the good and the other forms, since
the pleasure it provides is the most pleasant one and the philosophical life
around which it is organized, happiest (576d6–588a10). Thus reason's
practical goal is to use its knowledge of the good not just to ensure that
the appetitive and spirited elements get what is advantageous to them, but
to ensure that it itself gets to do the contemplating that is the most
advantageous thing of all (442c4–7, 586e4–587a2).

The knowledge that Socrates thinks cannot be put into the soul, like the
sight blind eyes lack, is a *dunamis* – a power or capacity (477d8–e1). As such,
two different factors determine its identity: what it deals with (*eph' hōi*) and
what it does (*apergazetai*). Powers that share both factors are identical, while
powers that share neither are different (477c6–d5). In the case of knowledge
the two are tersely specified: "knowledge deals with what is (*tōi onti*), to
know what is as it is (*to on gnōnai hōs echei*)" (478a7).[1] Later, when we learn
that belief (*doxa*) is concerned with (*peri*) the visible realm of becoming,
while understanding (*noēsis*), which is identical to knowledge, is concerned
with the intelligible realm of being (534a2–3), the substitution of *peri* for *epi*
suggests that one is simply a stylistic variant of the other. The implication
seems to be that what knowledge (or any other power) deals with is what it
concerns or what its field of operation is.[2]

Our grip on the other element in this definition of knowledge, which specifies what knowledge does, is tightened by Socrates' brief characterization of learning's culmination:

A real lover of learning (*philomathēs*) strives by nature for what is ... He does not linger over each of the many things that are believed to be, but keeps on going, without dulling his erotic passion or desisting from it, until he grasps what the nature is of each thing itself (*autou ho estin hekastous tēs phuseōs*) with the part of his soul that is fitted to grasp a thing of that sort because of its kinship with it. Once he is drawn near to it, has intercourse with what really is, and has begotten understanding and truth, he knows (*gnoiē*), truly lives, is nourished, and – at that point, but not before – is relieved from his labor pains. (490a9–b7)

What the lover of learning grasps is a Platonic form, such as the form of beauty, or beauty itself:

We say that there are many beauties (*polla kala*), many goods (*polla agatha*), and so on for each such thing, thereby distinguishing them in an account (*diorizomen tōi logōi*) ... We also say there is a beauty itself (*auto kalon*) and a good itself (*auto agathon*), and so on for all the things that we then posited as many. Now we reverse ourselves and posit a single form (*idean*) of each, since we suppose there is a single one, and call it what is each (*"ho estin" hekaston*) ... And we say that the former are visible but not intelligible, while the Forms are intelligible but not visible. (507b1–9)

Putting these texts together, then, we see that what the learner begets, having grasped the form of beauty, is an understanding of it that is embodied in a true account or definition of its nature. Hence it is this that must constitute knowing *what is* (beauty) *as it is*.

Belief, which is a different power from knowledge, deals not with the form of beauty, but with those other things, *ta polla kala* (476b4–d8, 478e1–479d8) – which, as far as grammar alone goes, could be either beautiful particulars or kinds or types of beauty. What Socrates says about them is that there is not one that won't also "clearly be an ugly (*aischron phanēsetai*)" (479a6). Glaucon agrees. All of them, he says, "are somehow clearly both beauties and uglies (*kai kala pōs auta kai aischra phanēnai*)" (479a8–b1). Then comes the following summing-up:

SOCRATES: So is each of the manys any more what one says it is than it is not what one says it is (*esti mallon ē ouk estin hekaston tōn pollōn touto ho an tis phēi hauto einai*)?

GLAUCON: No, they are like those double games people play (*epamphoterizousin*) at parties, or the children's riddle (*ainigmati*) about the eunuch who threw something at a bat – the one about what he threw at it and what it was in. For these things, too, play a double game (*epamphoterizein*) and one cannot

understand them as fixedly being or fixedly not being or as both
or as neither. (479a8–c5)

The conclusion Socrates draws is that "the many *norms* (*ta polla nomima*) of beauty and the rest are somehow rolling around between what is not [beauty] and what purely is [beauty]" (479d2–4). A few pages later, he explains why this is so:

Do you think there is any difference, then, between the blind and those who are really deprived of the knowledge of each thing that is, and have no clear paradigm (*enarges paradeigma*) of it in their souls – those who cannot look away, like painters, to what is most true, and cannot, by making constant reference to it, and by studying it as exactly as possible, establish here on earth norms (*nomima*) about beauties, justices, or goods, when they need to be established, or guard and preserve those that have been established? (484c5–d2)

Since the form, which is what knowledge deals with, is a clear paradigm, the corresponding many, dealt with by belief, is presumably an unclear one.

The reference to paradigms and the contrast between manys and unique forms recalls a well-known passage from the *Euthyphro* in which Socrates explains that he is seeking not "one or two of the many pieties (*ta polla hosia*)," but rather "the form (*eidos*) itself, by virtue of which (*hōi*) all the pieties are pieties," so that "by concentrating on it and using it as a paradigm (*paradeigmati*)" he may call "a piety any action of yours or anyone else's that is such as it, and may deny to be a piety whatever isn't such as it" (6d9–e6). What he is seeking is thus a standard or norm that does two things. First, it enables its possessor to judge particular cases correctly. Second, because it is so to speak reality's own norm – the one *by virtue of which* the particular cases are in fact of the relevant sort – it is both justificatory and explanatory.[3]

When someone possesses such a paradigm of beauty, he understands what beauty *is* and can produce a true account or definition of it. One of the masses, by contrast, who possesses instead the unclear paradigm *ta polla kala*, produces an account that at once shares in the defects of the paradigm and is, perhaps, the best guide to them. Euthyphro's first account of piety is a case in point: "I say that what is piety is precisely what I am doing now: prosecuting those who commit an injustice ... Not prosecuting them, on the other hand, is what is an impiety" (*Euthyphro* 5d8–e2). Socrates responds, "But surely, Euthyphro, there are also other manys (*alla polla*) you call pieties" (6d6–7). His point isn't that Euthyphro has cited a particular instance when what was wanted was a type or kind, but that Euthyphro has picked out the wrong type or kind through citing a particular instance as a paradigm that proves unreliable, since some of the actions

Blindness and reorientation 213

it deems pieties are impieties, while some it deems impieties are pieties. The paradigm plays a double game, therefore, and cannot be understood as fixedly being piety or fixedly not being piety or as being both or neither.

It is this that connects *ta polla kala* precisely to belief, making it (or them) the right sort of thing for it to deal with. When Euthyphro uses his paradigm to make judgments about cases, even when he makes no mistakes in applying it, he will sometimes make true judgments, sometimes false ones. His power or capacity to make judgments about piety is therefore fallible. But fallibility is just what distinguishes belief from knowledge (477e7–8): what is believed is sometimes true, sometimes false, whereas what is known is always true. Knowledge is a reliable judgment-making power; belief, an unreliable one.

A major aim of the *Republic*, of course, is to show that a city cannot be maximally just or happy unless it is ruled by philosophers, since they alone have knowledge of forms and the good (473c11–e4, 506a9–b1). But to serve that purpose, the knowledge in question must apparently extend beyond what is to perceptibles and the world around us. When Socrates imagines himself explaining to the philosophers of his own ideal city, Kallipolis, why they must rule, he seems to acknowledge as much:

Each of you in turn must go down to live in the common dwelling place of the other citizens and grow accustomed to seeing in the dark. For, when you are used to it, you will see infinitely better than the people there and know precisely what each image is and also what it is an image of (*gnōsesthe hekasta ta eidōla hatta esti kai hōn*), because you have seen the truth about the beauties, justices, and goods (*kalōn te kai dikaiōn kai agathōn*). (520c1–5; also 402b5–7, 506a4–7)

A few pages later, however, he seems to deny that *epistēmē* of the perceptible world is possible at all: "If anyone tries to learn something about perceptibles ... I would say that he never really learns – since there is no knowledge (*epistēmēn ouden*) to be had of such things (*tōn toioutōn*)" (529b5–c1; also 508d3–8). Moreover, when cognitive powers are canonically relabeled, as we saw, *epistēmē* is identified with *noēsis*, a power that is exclusively "concerned with being (*peri ousian*)" (533e3–534a3) and the intelligible realm of forms (511b2–c2).

There are other texts, however, that seem to countenance the extension of *epistēmē* to the visible or perceptible realm. For example, knowledge (*gnōsis*) of forms and of their visible images is said to belong to "the same craft (*technē*) and discipline" (402b9–c8). Since the most common object of the verb *epistasthai* in Plato is *technē* (which is often itself a synonym of *epistēmē*), the implication seems to be that we can have *epistēmē* of both.[4] That implication seems to be embraced as doctrine, moreover, when

214 C. D. C. REEVE

Socrates asserts: (1) that "the knowledge (*epistēmēs*) that alone among all the other sorts of knowledge (*epistēmōn*)" should be called "wisdom" (*sophian*) is the knowledge that deliberates "about the city as a whole, and about how its internal relations and its relations with other cities will be the best possible" (428c11–429a3), and (2) that "as regards the same manufactured item, its maker . . . has correct belief about its good and bad qualities, while its user has knowledge (*epistēmēn*)" (601e7–602a1).[5]

From the interpretive point of view, then, the *Republic* can itself seem, like the riddles Glaucon talks about, to be playing something of a double game. But this is in part because we have left out a crucial element – namely, the interplay of knowledge with perception-based belief that is required if a reliable paradigm is to be applied correctly in particular cases. Speaking in the voice of the Muses, Socrates attributes the ultimate decline in Kallipolis to the need the philosophers have to employ just such a combination of powers in making judgments: "Even though they are wise, the people you have educated to be leaders in your city, will, by using rational calculation combined with sense-perception (*logismōi met' aisthēseōs*), nonetheless fail to ascertain the period of good fertility and of infertility for your species" (546b1–3). That, indeed, is why "it is natural for practice to have less of a grasp of truth than theory (*lexeōs*)" (473a1–3). Applied is never so exact as pure.

All the same, there are procedures that can increase practice's exactitude or decrease its margin of error, and high on Socrates' list are the ones that involve those other denizens of the intelligible realm – numbers:

The same object, viewed from nearby, does not appear the same size, I presume, as when viewed from a distance . . . And the same things appear bent and straight when seen in water or out of it, or concave and convex because sight is misled by colors, and every other similar sort of confusion is clearly present in our soul . . . And haven't measuring, counting, and weighing proved to be most welcome assistants in these cases, ensuring that what appears (*to phainomenon*) bigger or smaller or more numerous or heavier does not rule within us, but rather what has been calculated or measured or even weighed? . . . And that is the task of the soul's rational element? . . . [And it] believes in accord with the measurements (*doxazon . . . kata ta metra*). (602d6–603e2)[6]

As counting, measuring, and weighing can correct unaided perception, so knowledge of forms can correct unaided perception of their images, enabling the philosopher to see them "infinitely better" than those who have no such knowledge. Once this mixed cognition is recognized as more reliable in this way, however, little of philosophical significance hangs on whether we call it *epistēmē* or not. Plato himself, as we saw, may not be altogether

Blindness and reorientation 215

consistent on the topic. What matters for the *Republic*'s overall argument is simply that, whatever we call it, it should be both as reliable as possible and unavailable to anyone unless he has knowledge of forms.

When Socrates attempts to get across the difference in reliability between powers, it is invariably to the difference between a thing and its likeness or image that he appeals. Those who merely believe are like dreamers who think, "a likeness is not a likeness, but rather the thing itself that it is like" (476c4–5), whereas someone who grasps the beautiful itself and "is able to observe both it and the things that participate in it, and does not think that the participants are it, or that it is the participants," lives in knowledge of the real waking world (476c7–d3). In the allegory of the Cave, which illustrates "the effect of education and the lack of it on our nature" (514a1–22), the progress towards knowledge is represented as a four-stage journey upward in which crude likenesses (shadows of puppets of human beings and other things) are replaced by less crude ones (the puppets that cast the shadows) and finally by the things themselves (real human beings and other things).

One obvious advantage of this appeal is that it allows the abstract notion of cognitive reliability to be understood in terms of the familiar idea of degrees of resemblance or of accuracy of representation. A disadvantage is that it can mislead if it is taken literally – if we forget that cognitive reliability of paradigms is the crucial or target notion, talk of likenesses and originals merely a way of explaining it. The following confident claim is an infamous case in point: "We are adequately assured of this, then, and would remain so, no matter how many ways we examined it: what is completely is completely an object of knowledge (*to men pantelōs on pantelōs gnōston*), and what is in no way at all, is an object of complete ignorance (*mē on de mēdamēi pantēi agnōston*)?" (477a2–4). Taken literally, this sounds like arcane metaphysics. Degrees of existence, of reality, and of truth have all been detected in it. Yet Socrates presents it as something obvious and irresistible even to the mass of people who aren't metaphysicians and know nothing about intelligible forms (476d4–e8). We should expect, therefore, that its literal meaning is somehow leading us astray.

What is *gnōston* (negative: *agnōston*) is what knowledge deals with or is concerned with. Hence, as knowledge of beauty deals with what is beauty, so knowledge *simpliciter* deals with what is *simpliciter* (compare 438c6–e10). The adverb *pantelōs* (negative: *mēdamōs*) belongs not to the language of cognitive reliability, but to that of likenesses and originals, in terms of which the former is explained or communicated. The thought is that because an incomplete or imperfect likeness is an unreliable paradigm, so a reliable one would have to be a perfect or complete likeness. *Pantelōs* thus adds nothing

216 C. D. C. REEVE

to the claim that knowledge deals with what is except a sort of placeholder for the incomplete likenesses that will have real work to do once belief – which is a power lying in-between knowledge and complete ignorance (*agnoia*) in cognitive reliability – enters the picture. Knowledge deals with what completely is, ignorance with what is not, and belief with "what partakes in both being and not being, and cannot correctly be called purely one or the other" (478e1–3).

Though we now understand how to read such claims, it still comes as a bit of a surprise to learn that "what is not is most correctly characterized as not some one thing, but as nothing (*ouch hen ti alla mēden*)" (478b11–c1). Once we recall that we are still speaking the language of likenesses, however, we can see our way forward. Ignorance is a cognitive power that is as opaque as knowledge is clear (478c9–d4). Knowledge is infallible; it always makes true judgments. Ignorance is not (like belief) just fallible, but erroneous: it always makes false judgments. What would it have to deal with – what sort of paradigm would it have to employ – in order to do that? Well, ignorance of beauty would have to deal with what is not beauty, so that whatever was not a beauty would be judged a beauty by it. Hence ignorance *simpliciter* would have to deal with what is not *simpliciter*. Encode that in the language of likenesses and what we get is the clause we left unexamined: "what is in no way at all is an object of complete ignorance."

As persistent as the explanation of cognitively reliable paradigms in terms of likenesses and originals is the association of cognitively unreliable ones, first, with the visible realm and, second, with non-uniqueness or plurality: "The same account applies to just and unjust, good and bad, and all the forms: each of them is itself one thing, but because they appear all over the place in partnership with actions and bodies, and with one another, each of them appears to be many things" (476a5–8; also 402b5–c8). To treat one of these perceptible beauties as if it were beauty itself, therefore, is to make the mistake the masses make of taking an image for an original. Of course, the masses themselves cannot characterize their mistake that way, since they have no access at all to the originals in question (476c1–2). What they *can* be brought to accept, however, is that the paradigm they use to make judgments about beauty does not provide them with knowledge of it (476d7–e2).

We have already poached extensively on the argument Socrates develops for this purpose. Central to it, as we noticed, is the acknowledgement by Glaucon, on behalf of the masses (476e7–8), that none of the many beauties is any more a beauty than it is not a beauty (479a8–b1). We might well wonder how he can be so sure that the masses will acknowledge this. In the

Blindness and reorientation

manner of contemporary experimental philosophers has he perhaps taken a poll? The answer is that if he hasn't, Socrates has. We see an example in the case of Euthyphro. When he is asked what piety is, he cites an example from the perceptible world as a paradigm. His paradigm is then shown by Socrates to play a double game. As a result, Euthyphro acknowledges that his answer does not manifest the knowledge of piety to which he laid claim. Since, in this regard, he is like every other person Socrates has examined, Glaucon's confidence seems well founded. At the same time, Euthyphro is also like Socrates' other interlocutors in that he cannot be led through Socratic questioning to a cognitively reliable account of piety. Presumably, this is the basis for Socrates' own puzzling claim that the masses not only do not believe in the form of beauty, but "would not be able to follow (*hēgētai*) anyone who tried to lead them to knowledge of it" (476c1–2).[7]

Though the mathematical sciences – comprising arithmetic, plane and solid geometry, astronomy, and harmony (525b9–531b7) – constitute an important step on the way to knowledge, they also have cognitive deficiencies that prevent them from reaching that goal by themselves:

I think you know that students of geometry, calculation, and the like hypothesize the odd and the even, the various figures, the three kinds of angles, and other things akin to these in each of their methodical inquiries, as if they knew them (*hōs eidotes*). They make these their hypotheses and don't think it necessary to give any account (*logon . . . didonai*) of them, either to themselves or to others, as if they were clear to everyone. And going from these first principles through the remaining steps, they arrive in full agreement at a conclusion about what they set out to investigate. (510c2–d3)

What giving an account means here, as in the *Euthyphro*, is giving a justificatory explanation. The problem with the mathematical sciences, therefore, is that they leave their various first principles unjustified or unexplained, and so are forced to treat them as hypotheses.[8] As a result, the conclusions they reach have a merely hypothetical status incompatible with real knowledge (533c3–6).

The remedy Socrates proposes for this defect is *dialectic*, which "does not consider these hypotheses as first principles, but as stepping stones and links in a chain enabling it to reach the un-hypothetical first principle of everything" (511b3–6), which is the form of the good and the pinnacle of dialectic's upward path (532a6–b2). Having grasped it, dialectic takes a path down from it, "without making use of anything visible at all but only of Forms themselves" (511c1–2), until it reaches the first principles of the mathematical sciences, so that its un-hypothetical status is somehow

218   C. D. C. REEVE

transmitted to them. Implying that he himself has not reached this pinnacle, and that even his current beliefs about it are "beyond the range of the present discussion," Socrates undertakes to explore "what seems to be an offspring of the good and most like it" (506c2–e1).[9] The result is the complex allegory of the sun.

The first strand in this allegory is epistemological in purport. As the sun gives visible things the power to be seen, so the good gives knowable things – forms – the power to be known (509b1–6). Coupled with the fact that the forms are all "in a rational order (*eis tetagmena*)" (500c3), this suggests that the analogue of the sun's light that the good emits is the ground or basis of intelligibility, which is presumably something like rational order, rational unity, or logical structure.[10] The good itself would then be the form of such order or structure, and so an object of knowledge (508e3). But since there would be no truth, and so no knowledge, without it, it would also be the cause of truth and knowledge (508e2–3), and so would be "other than they" (508e4–5). As the very source of intelligibility, moreover, it would plausibly be thought of as "the brightest of the beings" (518c9), and the most valuable or estimable of them (509a4–5).

The purport of the more opaque second strand in the allegory is metaphysical or ontological. As the sun "provides for the coming-to-be, growth, and nourishment of visible things,"[11] it tells us, so intelligible things owe their "existence and being (*to einai kai tēn ousian*)" to the good, "although the good is not being, but something yet beyond being, superior to it in rank and power" (509b1–9). Again, the hypothesis that the good is the form of rational order helps us see why this might be so. For if there were no rational order, no form could be the being it is, since none could be a truthmaker for – or have the specific sort of rational order captured by – its account or definition. As the source of such order, therefore, the good could be intelligibly thought of as "beyond being" – that is, as a more basic explanatory factor than that of being.

As the form of rational order, it is understandable, to some extent, why the good should be reached (at least in part) from the mathematical sciences, since they are plausibly thought of as dealing with order and structure. By the same token, it is understandable why it should be thought of as a first principle that is deeper or more fundamental than theirs. As the sun is the source of the light that makes everything – including itself – visible, so the good, as the form of rational order, is the source of the rational order that makes the beings – including it itself – intelligible as the beings they are.

Blindness and reorientation

The usual alternative to treating something as a hypothesis is to explain or justify it by appeal to something else. But that is ruled out in the case of an ultimate first principle. Another alternative, Socrates implies, is to refute all the objections that can be raised against it: "in order to avoid going through all these objections one by one and taking a long time to prove them all untrue," he says, "let us hypothesize" that the principle of opposition (a variant of the Principle of Non-Contradiction) is true (437a4–7). Being able to defend the good in this way, moreover, is precisely what is required in order to have knowledge of it:

Unless someone can give an account the form of the good, distinguishing it from everything else, and can survive all examination (*elengchōn*) as if in a battle, striving to examine (*elengchein*) things not in accordance with belief, but in accordance with being; and can journey through all that with his account still intact, you will say that he does not know the good itself or any other good whatsoever. (534b8–c5)

Dialectic thus becomes the philosopher's peculiar craft or science, since it is "the only method of inquiry that, doing away with hypotheses, journeys to the first principle itself in order to be made secure" (533c8–d1).[12] It isn't until astronomers and theorists of harmony "ascend to problems (*eis problēmata aniasin*)," therefore, that their studies are "useful in the search for the beautiful and the good" (531c2–7).

As an obvious descendant of Socratic examination (note the two occurrences of the verb *elengchein* in 534b8–d1, quoted above), dialectic seeks to grasp "what each thing itself is (*ho estin hekaston*)" (533b1) – it seeks the form that is both a reliable paradigm for judging particular cases and explains why they are such cases. Perhaps going beyond the elenchus, however, the grasp it seeks is "methodical (*methodos*) and wholly general (*peri pantos*)" (533b2). A philosopher must be "high-minded enough to contemplate all time and all being (*theōria pantos men chronou, pasēs de ousias*)" and be "always reaching out to grasp all things as a whole (*tou holou kai pantos*)" (486a5–9). The very mark of a dialectician, indeed, is possession of the sort of "unified vision (*sunoptikos*)" (537c6–7) that is partly achieved when the subjects the philosophers "learned in no particular order as children" are brought together, so that "a unified vision (*sunopsin*) of their kinship both with one another and with the nature of what is" is achieved (537c1–7; also 531c9–d3). Though nothing is said directly about what the step involves educationally speaking, the implication seems to be that it consists in defending scientific first principles against objections not in isolation from one another, but all together, so that the accounts of them that survive refutation will all fit together consistently.

220 C. D. C. REEVE

The education of Plato's philosophers is not complete, however, even when, at the age of thirty-five, their five years of dialectical training culminate in this consistent vision of being as a whole. After that, they must spend another fifteen years engaged in practical politics, taking command "in matters of war and the other offices suitable for young people, so that they won't be inferior to others in experience" (539e4–6). If this were simply the occasion on which theory meets practice, we might be inclined to downplay its importance for understanding education and the acquisition of knowledge as such, but that is not Socrates' own picture of the situation:

> In these offices, too, they [the dialectically-trained philosophers] must be tested to see whether they will remain steadfast when they are pulled in different directions or give way . . . Then, at the age of fifty, those who have survived the tests and are entirely best in every practical task and every branch of knowledge (*epistēmais*) must be led at last to the final goal (*telos*) and compelled to lift up the radiant eye-beams of their souls, and to look towards what itself provides light for everything. And once they have seen the good itself, they must use it as their paradigm and put the city, its citizens, and themselves in order (*kosmein*) throughout the remainder of their lives, each in turn. (539e6–540b1)

Dialectic's upward path so crucially involves political practice, therefore, that the good cannot be reached without it. But that means that knowledge – knowledge of anything – cannot be reached without it, either.

The reason for this seems to lie in a doctrine we have already noticed in another context: only the user of a kind of thing (whether it is manufactured or living) has knowledge "about what the good and bad points are in the actual use of the thing he uses," because he "has the most experience of it" (601d8–10). For the kind of thing a philosopher-king uses is surely a city – a community consisting of human beings, other living things, various natural and manufactured items, a geographical location, and so on. That is why he can use the good itself as a paradigm to put his city and himself in order (428c11–429a3, 500b8–501b7). *The* good thus seems to be (or include) the good of a city.

Though cities may initially seem too modest a kind of thing for something as exalted and superior as the good itself to be the good of, this is not so. For the most important constituents of the philosophers' city are its human citizens. In part, they are products of nature – they have first natures; in part, they are cultural products, shaped by years of education and training – they have second natures. But even their first natures (their genetic makeup, as we would say) are not entirely nature's unaided work. Instead, they are in significant part the products of a complex eugenics

Blindness and reorientation 221

program, designed to ensure an adequate stock of excellent future philosophers and guardians. Since "the periods of good fertility and infertility" for humans are governed by esoteric facts about the sun, the seasons, and the structure of the cosmos, this program is one place where the good of a city emerges as involving something rather grand (546a1–547a6).

Another – yet more significant – such place lies in human first nature itself. Unlike appetite and spirit, reason is "akin to what is divine and immortal and always exists," and so is itself simple, immortal (611b5–612a6), and "more divine (*theioterou*)" than they (518d11–e1). Its good, therefore, which is part of the good of the city, is scarcely going to be something narrowly political or worldly. As the good of an immortal, it must be the sort of good that can be available not just for "the entire period from childhood to old age," but for "the whole of time" (486a9–10, 608c6–d3). As more narrowly the good of a *rational* immortal, it must also be a source of "the pleasure of knowing where the truth lies," in which such a being's peculiar happiness consists (581d10). However exalted the good itself may be, then, the good of a city must keep pace with it.

With the grasp of the good, the goal of Platonic education has been finally reached. For education, as we recall, is the craft concerned with turning reason around from the visible to the intelligible realm, "not of putting sight into it." The final clause, much insisted on by Socrates, remains nonetheless puzzling. Once reason is appropriately turned, he seems to think, it will simply see what it is looking at. It is to seeing, indeed, that its operation is invariably likened. Seeing, of course, can be very theory-laden. So we might be tempted to think of Platonic education as providing the theory with which its intellectual equivalent must be laden. Mathematics, dialectic, practical politics would then take on the appearance of a vast theory that reveals or makes visible the good, while the good itself would emerge as the entire structure of forms that is the theory's ontological correlate. Since this theory would alone provide the un-hypothetical cognition required for knowledge, some sort of epistemological holism would result, at least where forms were concerned[13] – although cognition of the visible world of becoming might still be plausibly represented as reliabilist in nature. We know about visible things because, with the holistic theory of *something else* – forms – to hand, we can make reliably true judgments about them.

It is an attractive picture. But, for all that, it seems to miss the main point or hit just beside it. When the philosophers finally see the good itself, they have the infallible, un-hypothetical cognitive grasp of it that is a paradigm of knowledge. But they have no knowledge of anything else until they take the

C. D. C. REEVE

road back down from it, gaining additional infallible, un-hypothetical cognition in the process:

> When the eye of the soul [reason] is really buried in a sort of barbaric bog,[14] dialectic gently pulls it out and leads it upwards, using the crafts we described to help it and cooperate with it in turning the soul around. From force of habit, we have often called these branches of knowledge. But they need another name, since they are clearer than belief and darker than knowledge. (534d1–6)

Hence it is only when philosophers descend from the good, "making no use of anything visible at all," that they have knowledge of any other forms (511c1–2). Apparently, then, they can have knowledge of one form reached in this way, without yet having knowledge of others, so that holism is ruled out. There is ample motivation, therefore, to consider an alternative to the attractive picture.

Imagine an eye that has the power to see, but isn't turned in the right direction. Imagine, too, that it has in it many layers of differently distorting lenses. Now imagine a craft or science that can, first, turn it around until it is facing where it should. This is what training in the mathematical sciences does: it leads reason to look away from the visible world up toward the intelligible one. When reason is looking in the right direction, dialectic enters the picture. What it does is remove the distorting lenses by systematically solving all the puzzles and problems that cloud reason's vision. At that point, practical political training takes over the unified vision that results and imbues it with rich content. What reason will be able to see then isn't a vast structure – a vast rational order – of forms, but the principle of that order, the good that determines it. (That is what makes the sun analogy appropriate rather than misleading or inept. For the sun is not a complex whole constituted by all visible things, but the very source of visibility.) Once the philosophers have that principle in their intellectual grasp, knowledge of other forms becomes possible, but may be piecemeal rather than holistic.

There is not, for that matter, any reason to think that what a philosopher knows in knowing forms is all by itself, so to speak, sufficient for his purposes as king. Users of flutes, who know the good and bad points of flutes, tell the flute-makers what sort of flutes to make. But they themselves do not know, and need not know, how to make flutes. The good and bad points of flutes, moreover, are themselves relative to – or partly determined by – the music that a good city ought to allow and provide training in. And no user of flutes need know what such music is. Even its makers or composers need not know it. For the "harmony and rhythm" of music

Blindness and reorientation 223

must be appropriate to the poems they accompany, and the poems must be appropriate in content to the larger social role of the singers in whose education and later civilized life they figure (398d8–9).[15]

We can already see where this line of thought leads. Eventually, we will reach the designer of the good city's constitution – the philosopher-kings – that Socrates, Glaucon, and Adeimantus are impersonating. How *they* will stand to the poems we have been discussing is something about which Socrates is quite explicit: "You and I are not poets at present, Adeimantus. But we are founding a city. And it is appropriate for the founders to know (*eidenai*) the patterns on which the poets must base their stories, and from which they must not deviate. But they should not themselves make up any poems" (378e7–379a4). The philosophers know the patterns the poets must follow. But these patterns, as the discussion makes clear, are neither poems nor detailed blueprints for them. Thus the poets, though they may not have knowledge, or even reliable cognition, of the subject matter – ethical and otherwise – of their poems, nonetheless have something significant to contribute to the poems the city needs for the education and entertainment of its citizens. If this contribution requires the philosophers' pattern in order for *good* poems – that is poems that contribute to the good of the city and its citizens – to result, it is also true that the pattern requires the contribution. We might think, in fact, that the philosopher could not arrive at his pattern – could not know what the pattern of a good *poem* could possibly be – unless he had learned a lot about poetry from its actual practitioners (see 398e1–400c6). What Plato calls knowledge may require the hypothesis-destroying effects of the good, but what thereby gets transformed is still – like the untransformed mathematical sciences – a huge cognitive achievement on the part of people who may not be philosophers themselves. By the same token, what the philosophers distinctively know emerges as something well short of omniscience of the sort that holism seems, unhappily, to imply.

The self-styled educators, who claim to be able to put knowledge into souls like sight into blind eyes stand revealed now as people who think that the soul does not need an eye (533d2), a divine or god-like element (611b5–612a6), in order to acquire knowledge. Even if the soul were blind, so that it couldn't see the good itself were the two face to face, it could still, by learning everything else the philosopher learns, acquire knowledge. Countenancing the good, however, is a precondition of countenancing any forms. By rejecting it, therefore, these educators reject forms too. In the case of beauty, justice, and goodness, then, they, like the

224 C. D. C. REEVE

masses, must think that the corresponding manys provide reliable standards, adequate for knowledge. It is this that establishes their identity:

None of those private wage-earners – the ones these people call sophists and consider to be their rivals in craft[16] – teaches anything other than the convictions the masses hold when they are assembled together, and this he calls wisdom ... Knowing nothing in reality about which of these convictions or appetites is beautiful or shameful, good or bad, just or unjust, he uses all these terms in conformity with the great beast's [i.e., the masses'] beliefs – calling the things it enjoys good and the things that anger it bad ... Don't you think, by Zeus, that someone like that would make a strange educator? ... But that such things are truly good and beautiful – have you ever heard anyone presenting an argument for that conclusion which was not absolutely ridiculous? ... So then, bearing all that in mind, recall our earlier question: Can the masses in any way tolerate or accept that the beautiful itself (as opposed to the many beautiful things), or each thing itself (as opposed to the corresponding many) exists? ... It is impossible, then, for the masses to be philosophical. (493a6–494a3)

We might have guessed, of course, that any educators in Plato who "boastfully declare" (*epangellomenoi*) that they can teach something important about human values and how to live would turn out to be sophists. But even Socrates admits that if he possessed the craft claimed by the sophist Evenus, of being able to teach virtue and wisdom to human beings, he would boast about it. "I, you see," he says, "would pride myself and give myself airs if I had knowledge of these things" (*ekallunomēn kai hēbrunomēn an ei epistamēn tauta*) (*Apology* 20c1–3). It is not so much the boast that is the problem, therefore, but its epistemological and metaphysical presuppositions.

We noted at the beginning that reason cannot be turned toward the good and the intelligible world of forms unless the larger soul of which it is a part is turned with it. Much of Platonic education has to be directed, therefore, at the reorientation of the soul's appetitive and spirited elements. The problem with the former of these is that, based in the body (585a8–b1) and focussed squarely on the perceptible world where bodily hunger, thirst, and sexual desire find their satisfactions, it can keep reason focussed there too, forcing it to serve as its instrument and slave:

Haven't you ever noticed in people who are said to be bad, but clever, how sharp the vision of their little soul is and how sharply it distinguishes the things it is turned towards? This shows that its sight is not inferior, but is forced to serve vice, so that the sharper it sees, the more evils it accomplishes. However, if this sort of nature had been hammered at right from childhood, and struck free of the leaden weights, as it were, of kinship with becoming, which have been fastened to it by eating and other such pleasures and indulgences, which pull its soul's vision downward – if, I say, it got rid of these and turned towards truly real things,

Blindness and reorientation 225

then the same element of the same people would see them most sharply, just as it now does the things it is now turned towards. (519a1–b5; also 553b7–d7)

Through proper habituation, therefore, the set of appetites must be pruned of its unnecessary or non-beneficial members, while its necessary or beneficial ones are moderated and made harmonious with reason's aims and dictates (558d8–559b6). This habituation is provided to future guardians or philosophers primarily by the Platonic version of *mousikē* and *gumnastikē* – the traditional Ancient Greek education in poetry, song, music, and dance (376e1–3).[17] As its work progresses, Kallipolis, allowed to grow luxurious under the influence of unnecessary appetites (373a4–7, d9–e1), is declared to be undergoing purification (399e4–5).

By nature multifarious, non-unified, body-centered, and downward-focussed, appetite must be fashioned into reason's ally through acculturation. The case of spirit is different: it is "the natural auxiliary of the rational element, provided it has not been corrupted by bad upbringing" (441a2–3). For its love of honor (581a9–b4) naturally orients it toward *to kalon* (the fine, noble, or beautiful), which both attracts honor and is allied with the good. The Platonic version of *mousikē* and *gumnastikē* thus aims to solidify and develop this natural orientation. While it does this primarily by shaping desires and emotions, making them harmonious "through habits" rather than by imparting knowledge (522a4–7), such shaping still has a cognitive as well as a conative aspect. Someone properly trained in *mousikē* and *gumnastikē*, Socrates says, will feel "disgust correctly" and, because he does,

will praise beautiful things, be pleased by them, take them into his soul, and, through being nourished by them, become beautiful and good. What is ugly or shameful, on the other hand, he will correctly condemn and hate while he is still young, before he is able to grasp the reason. And, because he has been so trained, he will welcome the reason when it comes, and recognize it easily because of its kinship with himself. (401e4–402a4)

To hate or be disgusted by the wrong things, therefore, isn't simply to be wrongly motivated, it is to misperceive the world, and so pass on perceptual misinformation to reason. Through *mousikē* and *gumnastikē*, in other words, reason acquires the good-adapted eye it needs to deal reliably with the visible world.

When the vast Platonic educational machine consisting of *mousikē*, *gumnastikē*, the mathematical sciences, dialectic, and practical politics is fully successful, the result is someone possessed of each of the four virtues or excellences Socrates considers: wisdom, courage, temperance, and justice. The rational element in him knows and desires the good; the appetitive and spirited elements see and desire in harmony with reason. The ideal of order embodied by the good in him meets its human exemplar (500b1–d2). But Platonic education is fully successful only in a relatively small number of cases (428e9–429a1): people with the natural capacities required of philosopher-kings are rare (476b9–10, 503d10). In most people, the obstacles nature poses are too great for even the most resourceful education entirely to overcome. The results are the guardians ("ruled" by their spirited element) and the producers ("ruled" by their appetitive one), which Kallipolis also – fortuitously – needs. But though guardians and producers cannot achieve either virtue or the happiness that it alone ensures, with education's help, they can come as close to the two as their natures allow (580b1–c5). Education is "the one great thing" (423e2), therefore, and *mousikē* and *gumnastikē*, which are its foundation, are the guardians' own guardhouse (424c8–d1), the one that, when breached, heralds political decline (546d4–547a6).

A clear boon to everyone *sub specie temporis*, Platonic education is surprisingly more of a mixed blessing *sub specie aeternitatis*. What life will it choose when, at the spindle of Necessity, a soul faces reincarnation? If it has been educated to become a philosopher, it will have "the ability and the knowledge to distinguish a good life from a bad," and so will choose well (618b6–619b1, 619d7–e5). If, on the other hand, it belongs to someone that has "lived its previous life in a rationally ordered (*tetagmenēi*) constitution sharing in virtue through habit but without philosophy," it chooses its next life "without adequately examining everything," and so ends up as the soul of a tyrant, "fated to eat his own children among other evils" (619c1–d1). Since the forms the philosopher looks to in designing the constitution of Kallipolis are also, as we saw, "in a rational order (*eis tetagmena*)" (500c3), the soul in question could be that of any one of its many non-philosopher citizens. For them, then, Platonic education turns out to be something of a disaster in the longer term.

It is a deflationary note, no doubt, on which to end, so let me quickly sound another. Any account of the acquisition of knowledge through education is bound itself to be subject to epistemological scrutiny. Plato's account in the *Republic* is no exception. It is noteworthy, in fact, for offering such scrutiny of so large a target. How, we want to know, does Plato know all that about the soul and the Good and the best way for the one to reach the other? In a particularly candid passage, he has Socrates answer this question. "Only the god," Socrates says, knows whether what the allegory of the Cave encodes about education, forms, and the good is true (517b6–7). It is a bold summing up – reminiscent of the conclusion Socrates reaches

Blindness and reorientation

on his own behalf about the meaning of the Delphic Oracle's pronounce-ment about him (*Apology* 23a5–6) – of a larger theme, in which a contrast is drawn between a "longer and more time-consuming road" and the implic-itly shorter one taken in the *Republic* (435c9–d4; also 504b1–505b3, 531d2–533a5). That the longer road is the upward and downward path of dialectic seems certain. For a succinct description of the shorter one, however, we must turn to the words of Simmias in the *Phaedo*:

> To know the plain truth about such matters is either impossible or extremely difficult in this present life, but to fail to examine what is said about them in every possible way (*ta legomena peri autōn mē ouchi panti tropōi elengchein*), or to give up before one has investigated them exhaustively from every angle, shows utter soft-ness in a man. You see, where these matters are concerned, it seems to me that one must certainly achieve one of two things: either learn or discover how they stand; or, if that is impossible, then at least adopt the best of the things people say, and the one that stands up best to examination, and, carried on it as on a sort of raft, face the dangers of life's voyage – provided one cannot travel more safely and with less risk on the more secure vessel of some divine saying. (85c1–d4)

Though there is, perhaps, a hint that Socrates himself may have sailed on the more secure vessel (496a11-e3), the *Republic* itself is best seen as raft only – a splendid prototype to use in thinking about education, refit it as we will and must.

NOTES

1. It is not entirely clear why knowledge (or any power) cannot differ from another power with respect to just one of these factors.
2. Crafts or science are powers (1 346a2–3), each of which "does its own work and benefits that with which it deals (*eph' hōi*)" (1, 346d5–6). What medicine deals with is the body (1, 342c1–2), however, which is the very thing with which medical knowledge seems to be concerned.
3. Compare *Meno* 97e5–98a8.
4. See Lyons 1963, pp. 139–228.
5. Compare *Meno* 97a9–b7, *Theaetetus* 201a4–c2.
6. I have omitted part of the following passage from the quoted text: "But quite often, when it has measured and indicates that some things are larger or smaller than others, or the same size, the opposite simultaneously appears (*phainetai*) to it (*toutōi*) to hold of these same things . . . And didn't we say that it is impossible for the same thing to believe (*doxazein*) opposites about the same thing at the same time? . . . So the element in the soul that believes (*doxazon*) contrary to the measurements and the one that believes in accord with the measurements could not be the same" (602e4–603a2). What appears to reason certainly conflicts in this case with what reason believes. But this conflict is not the sort that

228   C. D. C. REEVE

necessitates psychic division, since perceiving (*phainesthai*) and believing (*dox-azein*) are not the same psychological relation. An opposing view is defended in Burnyeat 1999, pp. 223–27.

7. Compare *Symposium* 210a6.

8. Here the suggestion is that mathematicians give *no* accounts of their first principles. Later, however, the problem seems to be that the accounts they give are inadequate. "No one with even a little experience of geometry," Socrates tells Glaucon, "will dispute that this science is entirely the opposite of what is said about it in the accounts of its practitioners . . . They give ridiculous accounts of it, though they can't help it. For they speak like practical men and all their accounts refer to doing things. They talk of 'squaring,' 'applying,' 'adding,' and the like, whereas the entire subject is pursued for the sake of . . . knowing what always is, not what comes into being and passes away . . . [Hence geometry] can draw the soul toward truth and produce philosophical thought (*philosophou dianoias*) by directing upward what we now wrongly direct downward" (527a1–b10). What mathematicians do wrong, apparently, is speak of the abstract triangle itself, for example, as if it were the sort of thing that can be moved or changed. They treat it, in other words, as if it were a perceptible triangle, like the triangles they draw in their diagrams – part of the visible world of becoming rather than of the intelligible world of being. As a result, the accounts they provide are inconsistent with the epistemological claims of the mathematical sciences themselves to provide knowledge of "what always is."

9. This is a nice example of a form being an object of belief.

10. In the *Philebus*, the good itself resides "somewhere in the area of measure" (66a6–7). In the *Timaeus*, the god "desiring that all things should be good, . . . took over all that is visible . . . and brought it from disorder into order, since he judged that order was in every way the better" (30a2–6). In the *Gorgias*, Callicles' immoral advocacy of "advantage-taking" (*pleonexia*) is diagnosed as a consequence of his having neglected geometry, which would have shown him that it is "geometrical [or proportionate] equality" not advantage-taking that makes "this universe a world-*order* . . . and not a world-*dis*order" (507e6–508a8).

11. At 516b9–c2, the latter debt is explained as follows: "the sun provides the seasons and years, governs everything in the visible world, and is in some way the cause of all the things that he [the one ascending from the cave] used to see."

12. Compare Aristotle's "demonstration by refutation" of the Principle of Non-Contradiction in *Meta.* Γ 4.

13. See Reeve 1988, pp. 80–95; Fine 1999, pp. 228–29.

14. See 519a7–b5.

15. It is a nice irony, apparently lost on Glaucon and Adeimantus when music is returned to in Book 10, that this leads to flutes, their users, and their makers being altogether outlawed from Kallipolis (399d3–5).

16. I.e., rivals in the craft of teaching virtue. See *Apology* 24c–25c, *Protagoras* 317e–328d.

17. It may be provided to producers by training in a craft. See Reeve 1988, pp. 176–78, 186–91.

CHAPTER 12

Music all pow'rful

Malcolm Schofield

I. INTRODUCTION

I've been checking out the word "music" in indexes to some standard works in English on the *Republic* and to some recent "companions" to the dialogue. No mention in the index to Cross and Woozley's *Philosophical Commentary* of 1964, nor in that to Annas' *Introduction* of 1981. This isn't a deficiency in the indexing. Music doesn't figure in the texts either very much. Of course, both these books were written BBE: before the Barker era, i.e., before the publication of Andrew Barker's revelatory two volume *Greek Musical Writings*.[1] But things are not much different with Santas's *Blackwell Guide* of 2006 (no reference to music in the index, nor to Barker in bibliographies), or Ferrari's *Cambridge Companion* of 2007 (his index does capture a couple of passing references, to music as an ingredient in the education for the guards set out in Books 2 and 3, but in discussions which mainly have other fish to fry). There's actually more about music in Gabriel Richardson Lear's chapter on the beautiful in Santas, and in the discussion there of "musical-poetic education," although Ferrari's massive 627-item *bibliographie raisonnée* lists the section entitled "Musica e carratere nella *Reppublica* di Platone" in Barker's more recent *Psicomusicologia nella Grecia antica* (2005), as well as to two or three other pieces – none in English – on the topic.

Anglophone students might conclude that music plays no central role in the argument of the *Republic*: would they be right? In this chapter I shall be arguing for the centrality of music in Plato's conception of education in the *Republic* – in his developmental psychology and in his social and political theory alike. I shall start by looking at some of the key passages in Book 3 where Socrates explains the importance of music for fostering our capacity for philosophy (section 2), before turning to his discussions of what sort of music is appropriate for training the city's guards and how musical *mimēsis* works (section 3). Then I shall consider why it is that poetry looms much

230   MALCOLM SCHOFIELD

larger than music in most accounts of the dialogue's teaching on art and
culture. Here I shall be devoting particular attention to the treatment of
mimēsis in Book 10's critique of poetry as imitation, and to ways in which it
diverges from the treatment in Book 3 (section 4). There follows a sketch of
the role of music in the later *Laws*: something seldom mentioned or
discussed when people think about Plato on art. But as well as containing
material that is compelling in its own right, the *Laws* clearly develops further
the cultural agenda of the *Republic*, and in doing so leaves the critical
importance of music for the health of society in no doubt whatsoever
(section 5). I offer some final remarks in a brief conclusion (section 6).

2. MUSIC AND THE SOUL

I start with a passage from Book 3 at 401d–402a (Text 1):

Now Glaucon, I said, is upbringing in music of pre-eminent importance for the
following reasons? Because rhythm and harmonic mode (*harmonia*) slip their way
into the inner regions of the soul, and take the most powerful hold on it, bringing
grace with them, and make a person graceful – that is, if someone is brought up
correctly, but if not, the opposite? And because anyone who has been brought up in
music as he should will have the most acute perception of what's missing [sc. in
products of artistic craftsmanship] and what's not been crafted beautifully or not
grown beautifully; and quite rightly feeling distaste for them, will praise what is
beautiful, and taking delight in them and absorbing them into his soul, he will be
nourished by them and become a fine, good person; and the ugly he will quite
rightly criticize and hate while still young:– until he is able to take in reason,
and when reason comes the person who has been brought up this way will welcome
it more than anyone does, recognizing it because of its kinship [sc. its beauty is
akin to the products of artistic craftsmanship with which the soul is now familiar:
cf. 401c–d].
   It's certainly *my* view, he said, that an upbringing in music is to be undertaken
for these sorts of reason.

Before we try to engage with the extraordinarily ambitious claims the
Platonic Socrates makes for music in this passage, some comments on the
translation are needed. I follow most of the translators I've consulted in
rendering *mousikē* at the beginning and end of the extract as "music."
Instead of "my upbringing in music," however, Tom Griffith both times
has "musical and poetic education."[2] What his version attempts to capture
is the point that the notion of *mousikē* so far in play in the account of the
education of the guards has quite explicitly included the sung or spoken
word (*logos*) as well as rhythm and mode (cf. e.g. 376e, 398b); and it is a key
Socratic thesis in Book 3 of the dialogue that mode and rhythm must be in

line with *logos*, not as in the chromatic "new music" of late fifth-century Athens[3] the other way around (mode and rhythm dictating, *logos* tagging along behind). On the other hand, the ingredient in *mousikē* which is the explicit focus here is of course what one might call something wholly *musical*, or *wholly* musical, music *in senso stretto* (Barker): mode and rhythm – though pre-eminently mode and rhythm as used in song (and dance). And something the passage brings home to us is that the *core* of *mousikē* for Plato is music: the core, that is, for the purpose of its use in education, which is to shape the soul.

As Socrates explains, it is above all the effect of mode and rhythm on the soul that makes it graceful, if of course they are the right sort of mode and rhythm. I say "mode and rhythm": Barker, in translating the words here in *Greek Musical Writings*, adds a note suggesting that *harmonia* in this context is to be taken in a wider sense of "patterns of order exhibited by movement and melody." But our passage is only the latest phase in the ongoing stretch of argument about "style in song and melody" which started at 398c. We must surely suppose that *harmonia*, coupled here as so often with *rhuthmos*, carries just the same sense of "mode" that it has borne since the notions were introduced in tandem at 398d (anticipated at 397c–d). Socrates certainly broadens his discussion at 401a–d to emphasize how important it is for the environment in which children are brought up to surround them with beautiful artifacts (and indeed natural creations) of every kind, but so far as I can see "gracefulness and want of grace" are the terms he applies to these, not *harmonia* and *rhuthmos*.

Plato's original readership would have taken it for granted that the core of *mousikē* is music *in senso stretto*, at any rate in an educational context. Descriptions of a typical Greek aristocratic education in other fourth-century texts usually imply a tripartite scheme: reading and writing (*grammata*), physical training (*gumnastikē*), music (*mousikē*), says Aristotle in the *Politics* (8.3 1337b24), although unhappy as he is unless he can as usual get a quadripartite division, he adds that there is a case for making drawing a fourth element. Xenophon has essentially the same triad, with "activity in the wrestling school" substituting for "physical training" (*Lac. Pol.* 2.1) and placed third after music; the pseudo-Platonic *Theages* likewise has reading and writing, playing the *kithara*, and wrestling (*Theag.* 127e). The same sequence is implied by *Charmides* 159c, which has "playing the *kithara*" for "music," as also in Protagoras' great speech at *Prot.* 325d–326c, much the most interesting passage for our purposes (so when Socrates at 376e in the *Republic* makes music precede physical training in his educational programme, he is proposing nothing out of the ordinary).

Protagoras emphasizes that the writing teacher has an ethical purpose in mind, and will make his students read and learn the poems of good poets (one imagines he is thinking in the first instance of Homer and Hesiod), and the *kithara* instructor will likewise teach them the poems of other good poets, lyric poets (like Anacreon and Simonides, presumably), and compel the children to assimilate rhythms and modes in their souls, so that shaped by rhythm and harmony they may become "useful for speaking and acting." No wonder Glaucon doesn't take much persuading in our *Republic* passage of what Socrates says about mode and rhythm. It sounds as though the general idea was already in vogue in aristocratic circles of the time: which indeed is suggested by Aristophanes' *Frogs*, where the chorus of initiates links the virtues of a good citizen with an upbringing in "wrestling schools, and choruses, and *mousikē*" (*Frogs* 727–30).[4]

In the *Republic*, it is true, Socrates sweeps up what one might call the higher functions of the writing teacher, i.e., the teaching of poetry that isn't sung, like Homer and Hesiod, under *mousikē*. I'll comment on that presently (in the *Laws* the implication seems to be that this activity will be returned to the writing teacher: 809e–812a). For the moment my point is that it was the common cultural and linguistic assumption that an education in *mousikē* involved in the first instance singing and playing *music*. The *Republic*'s incorporation of Homer and Hesiod (eventually, of course, to be expelled from Kallipolis) into discussion of education need not signal renunciation of the assumption. Many discussions of art and the arts in the *Republic* might leave the impression that *poetry* is what's most important. Socrates does insist that mode and rhythm must match the words. The words – the right kinds of words – come first. It is striking, however, that it's not the consciously understood words (*logoi*) that are cited as the influence which will do most to shape the soul (and – as we shall see – to nourish its capacity to appreciate reason), but the music *in senso stretto* that is designed to match them. Unconscious assimilation is for Plato more important in the process than conscious understanding; and the mode in which the right content is assimilated is more powerful than the content itself – that is why *mimēsis* ends up taking center stage in Plato's theory of art.[5]

The passage we are discussing offers a cameo study of how the shaping takes place: of the way music powers aesthetic, ethical, and intellectual habituation. From unconscious beginnings there is a progression through conscious perception and assimilation of beauty until finally, at a point in human development when someone becomes capable of reason, they want to *be* rational because they respond to *reason*'s beauty (readers of the

Symposium will not find the sequence surprising). As the child learns to sing and play music, its rhythms and modes "slip their way (*kataduetai*) into the inner region of the soul." Socrates had emphasized in what immediately precedes the way the character of artefacts produced by painters, builders, and the like gradually day by day has its unconscious effect on the soul (he twice uses the verb *lanthanein* in developing the point). Without its awareness "some one great evil" (or in a good moral and aesthetic environment, by parity of reasoning a great good) may constitute itself there (401b–d). But none of these arts – he now implies – exerts so powerful a hold as music. Socrates' entire discourse on music (broadly conceived) reaches its goal when it shows how music brings the soul to passionate love of beauty (403c) – and nothing is more effective at that than music *in senso stretto*.

When Socrates talks of mode and rhythm reaching the "inner" region of the soul, he doesn't explain what they might meet when they get there. The obvious candidate is what Socrates calls "the learning-loving element" (*to philomathes*). Other passages in Book 3 indicate that, while physical training is primarily what is needed to develop the "spirited" element in the soul (*to thumoeides*), the development of the "learning-loving" or philosophical (*to philosophon*) element is the special province of music. This is not to deny that music works on the *thumoeides* too. Indeed, the need for a "mixture" of training and music to make the spirited and learning-loving elements harmonious or concordant is emphasized. Thus when Socrates rounds off the whole treatment of the guards' education he has been working through for much of Book 2 and most of Book 3, he stresses that proper development of the *thumoeides* requires music as well as physical training. Training strengthens it, but without music it is likely to become hard, dangerous, uncivilized, without grace or rhythm. Music will soften it, but leave it enfeebled if physical training is neglected (410c–411e).

The scenario Socrates envisages if music were to be omitted from a person's upbringing makes it evident, however, that he associates it particularly with philosophy and the soul's learning-loving element. He begins by imagining some one who "has nothing to do with music or philosophy," "absolutely no association with the Muse" (411c–d). He continues (411d, Text 2):

Even if he did have some love of learning in his soul, then given that he is getting no taste of topics of learning and enquiry, and is not involved in rational argument nor in any form of music, the learning-loving element becomes weak and deaf and blind – because it is not being aroused or nourished, with the person's senses not getting thoroughly cleaned out.

234   MALCOLM SCHOFIELD

In fact such a person becomes a hater of rational argument, and positively *un*musical. He lives his life "in ignorance and stupidity, without grace or rhythm" (411e).

Plato isn't here *equating* music and philosophy – although "association with the Muse" is a compendious way of including engagement with both under a single heading: what we might call "culture." He seems to see them as points on a single spectrum. The characteristic activity of the learning-loving element within us *when that is fully-fledged* is philosophy, Socratically conceived: argument, reasoning, focussed on inquiry and the acquisition of knowledge. Its cognitive potential, however, is something music *in senso stretto*, as well as the right poetic content, can begin to develop long before there is the active adult capacity for reasoning or argument. That we have such potential before we are able to "take in reason," as Text 1 puts it (402a), is provocatively indicated way back in Book 2, where Socrates identifies a disposition he describes as naturally philosophical and learning-loving in *dogs* – which define friends and enemies on the basis of whether they know them or not. Humans, too, need to have that same natural disposition if as guards of the city they are to behave with appropriate gentleness towards the citizens (375e–376c). And of the two ingredients in the education Socrates now goes on to expound – music (including words as well as mode and rhythm) and physical training – it must obviously be music that will have the job of fostering our cognitive capacities.

When in Text 2 Socrates suggests that association with the Muse "arouses" and "nourishes" the learning-loving element, he certainly has in mind the effects of philosophical argument, as the brief recapitulation of the passage in Book 4 confirms. He speaks there of the way music (presumably not or not solely *in senso stretto*) "tones up and nourishes" the soul "with fine *logoi* and subjects of study" (441e).[6] But that talk of nourishment in Text 2, and of the cleansing of the senses (presumably from their passions, fears, fantasies, and physical appetites: cf. *Phaedo* 64c–67b), also recalls the way music *in senso stretto* is represented in Text 1 as nourishing a person and heightening sensory awareness of the beautiful *before he or she is able to "take in reason."* The conjecture that there, too, *to philomathes* is what Socrates has in mind is supported by the detail of the account he gives of the response the soul makes to music. That response is characterized in cognitive terms throughout. The growing child – if properly nurtured – develops through exposure to mode and rhythm an acute perception both of beauty and of faulty craftsmanship, as one would expect of a creature whose senses are cleansed and whose learning capacity is fostered. Then on developing the

Music all pow'rful 235

full capacity for reason the soul welcomes it, as it has now been enabled to do, as something to which it is already akin.[7]

Why should it be the learning element that music helps develop? What is significant here is that it isn't the sounds of music as such that are the sole focus, but just as importantly rhythm and mode: music's audible structure. It is of course debatable how far that structure will in Plato's view have reflected the same kind of mathematical structure as he believed the proper study of harmonics should take as its concern (see Book 7, 530c–531c; cf. 528e–530c, on astronomy).[8] If we allow ourselves to call in evidence the late *Philebus*, it looks as though he never ceased thinking that in practice musicians found concords not by "measure" but by practiced conjecture (*Phlb.* 55e–56a; cf. *Rep.* 530e–531b). Nonetheless in the idealizing vein that runs through Text 1 and its immediate context, it looks as though music as experienced is being regarded as approximating rational structure, with that structure giving it its ordered beauty, and possessing therefore something requiring reason for its full appreciation. It will be through sensory perception of structure that music *in senso stretto* primes the cognitive and potentially rational element in the soul for reason itself.

3. "BUILDING A GARRISON IN MUSIC"

If education in music plays a crucial role in the *Republic*'s developmental psychology, no less important is its social and political role. When Socrates starts to bring to an end his discussion of what instructions the guards must follow if they are to preserve the city in unity, he insists on one thing: they must preserve the system of education and upbringing (423d–424b). He gets more specific (424b–d, Text 3):

They must not allow any radical innovation in exercise regime or in music such as would contravene the system, but must stand guard over them so far as they can. They should get alarmed when anyone says:

> The latest song, fresh from the singer's lips,
> Has most appeal to men

– in case all too often it be thought that the poet is talking not of new songs, but a new style of song, and in case that might be applauded. It's not the sort of thing that should be applauded, nor the way to take the poet. Preventing change to a new form of music is something requiring precautions – change in music presents a global threat. Nowhere do you get perturbations in styles of music without perturbation in the most important social and political *nomoi*: as Damon says, and I believe him.

Include me among the converted, said Adeimantus.

So it looks as though the guards must build their garrison here, I said, in music.

236   MALCOLM SCHOFIELD

The figure of Damon, associate of Pericles, seems to stand behind quite a lot of Plato's thinking about music in the dialogue.[9] For the ethical theory of "which types of rhythm imitate which lives" Socrates refers to Damon by name as able to supply expert opinion (400a–c). And at the present juncture in Book 4 he subscribes to Damon's theory that with change in musical styles, political turmoil is inevitable. Once again music *in senso stretto* is what is at issue, as the pun on *nomoi* makes plain. As in music *nomoi* were the songs canonically sung on specific occasions and in specific genres, so Socrates here talks of the consequences for *political nomoi* (in many contexts the adjective would be otiose), i.e., laws and customs. Adeimantus volunteers the thought that slackening the rules in music makes lawlessness seep into character and behavior, and then into business dealings – and once that happens laws and social and political systems are threatened with wanton disregard. Socrates' response is non-committal: "Oh. So that's how it is?" (424d–e).

I think his remark about the sort of garrison the guards must build indicates that from the perspective he has been articulating throughout Books 2 and 3, he would see a different route from musical revolution to political catastrophe. If the guards are to be the city's garrison, they can be so only if they have in their own souls a garrison which makes and keeps *them* the people they must be (*quis custodiet ipsos custodes?* was exactly the right question). That garrison within is the character shaped above all by an upbringing in the right sort of music. Without the garrison within there can be no garrison for the city. There will be nothing to stop the guards starting to behave like wolves instead of the sheep dogs they *should* resemble (416a–b). Adeimantus is wrong to think that the political rot will start with the commercial transactions of the economic class. The more fundamental problem is that the ruling class will cease to be capable of doing its job, on which everything else of moral importance in the city turns.

The means by which guards are to be educated in music and become musical is of course *mimēsis*. *Mimēsis* is what has to carry the huge burden of expectation that the *Republic* asks its readers to place upon music for the prospects of developmental psychology and political order alike. By the time it reaches styles of music *in senso stretto*, Book 3 has already been devoting discussion to right and wrong forms of *mimēsis*. What Socrates has in mind in the first instance is assimilating oneself to someone else by copying them through the way one creates and enacts a poetical/musical performance: through "making music," as we might say (393c). Apprentice guards are to imitate the *appropriate* models: "brave, *sōphrōn*, god-fearing, free – that sort

Music all pow'rful

of thing" (395c), and to imitate in a simple style the good person's manner of speech (398a–b). The content – the words (*logoi*) – should be the sort of content such a person would utter, and (as we have already noted) mode and rhythm must match the words.

But when Socrates specifies the only two modes he is willing to have used in musical education, a further conception of *mimēsis*, more difficult to understand, comes into play. Here is the relevant passage (399a–c, Text 4):

I don't know about the modes, I said. Just leave me the mode which would appropriately imitate[10] the notes and cadences of someone who is courageous in battle and in every activity forced on a person, or who is not succeeding or facing wounds, death, or some other misfortune, and who in all these circumstances stands up to what befalls him steadily and patiently. Leave me also another mode: appropriate for someone who is engaged in a peaceful action, not forced upon him but voluntary, such as persuading somebody of something and making a request (whether it be a god in prayer or a human being by instruction and exhortation), or, by contrast, holding oneself back when someone else tries to instruct one or get one to change one's mind – and who as a result acts intelligently, and does not behave arrogantly but in all these circumstances acts in a *sōphrōn* and measured way, and is content with the consequences. Leave me, then, these two modes, a forcible and a voluntary one, which will best imitate the tones of the unfortunate and the fortunate, the *sōphrōn* and the courageous.

One thing that strikes one immediately about Text 4 is the complex set of contrasts it employs. The basic opposition is between music appropriate to action under duress and music suited to voluntary activity. But these are further correlated with misfortune and good fortune, and again with courage (conceptualized in a remarkable stoical manner) and judiciousness (*sōphrosunē* here certainly includes self-control, but that is not the keynote of the scenario or the virtue envisaged). Passive endurance is the hallmark of proper behavior under duress, whereas what Plato has Socrates focus on at rather greater length in voluntary behavior is broadly speaking *argumentative* activity of various kinds (persuading, requesting, instructing, exhorting, etc.), and intelligence and judiciousness in performing it or in responding to it, and in coping with its outcomes. It is tempting to see a further contrast: between music that imitates behavior expressive of the *thumoeides*, and music that imitates activity characteristic of the learning-loving element's developed capacity for rationality: the practical rationality required of the ruler of a city, or of someone on the receiving end of instruction or persuasion in the assembly – simultaneously a matter of character and intellect (like Aristotelian *phronēsis*).

238 MALCOLM SCHOFIELD

What we have to envisage seems to be something like this. The singer playing on the *kithara* sets to music the sort of words that are characteristically used by courageous or judicious people in situations that call forth their courage or their judgment – employing one mode for courage, another for *sōphrosunē*: the words someone uses when coping with misfortune or injury (cf. 390d), or again when giving someone else thoughtful advice (cf. 389e) or responding to instruction or a request. That way he imitates the courageous or the *sōphrōn* person by assimilating himself to them. But what enables him to achieve this is the way the modes in question (which Glaucon identifies as Dorian and Phrygian) *themselves* imitate the notes and cadences characteristic of such speech. The same will be true *ceteris paribus* of the kinds of rhythm Socrates will countenance. Good rhythm follows fine or beautiful speech by *assimilation* (*homoioumenon*, 400d). But this is imitation of speech not in parrot mode, but *as expressing thought or character*.[11] That is the more fundamental sense in which mode and rhythm are *mimēmata*. When Socrates sums up the whole theory a little later, he describes goodness in mode and rhythm as "close relatives and imitations of good and *sōphrōn* character" (401a; cf. 400e).[12] We naturally want to ask *how* music could represent intellect or character. Here the suggestions I made earlier about musical structure may be helpful. Towards the end of Book 4 Socrates will compare the well-ordered soul explicitly with musical structure. The virtuous person tunes the three elements of the soul "just like the three fixed points in a musical attunement – top, bottom, intermediate"; indeed, if there turn out to be more elements, all of them have to be tied together in a well-attuned self-disciplined unity (443d–e; cf. 412a). We might accordingly infer, as Andrew Barker proposes, that in musical *mimēsis* it is the concordant structure that constitutes courage or *sōphrosunē* in a person's soul which gets expressed in the structure of their speech, as represented in the structure of the Dorian or Phrygian mode in which the singer sings and plays a particular melody.[13] Underlying this is a reciprocal causal process. Learning to sing and play in such rhythms and modes will gradually shape the soul into concordant structures, which will then find expression in such music.

That must help to explain music's exceptional power. It isn't just that it represents and expresses conditions – virtuous or vicious – of the soul itself, which is not true of painting, weaving, building and similar arts, mentioned just before Text 1 as similarly influencing the unconscious mind.[14] It is also that *the way in which* it expresses virtue corresponds in its audible structure to the concordant structure of virtue itself.

Music all pow'rful   239

4. THE POWER OF MUSIC AND THE POWER OF POETRY

If the argument of sections 2 and 3 is on the right lines, music *in senso stretto* is in the *Republic*'s view the most powerful of the influences which can shape the young soul. Yet that may well not be the impression you get if you read the literature on the dialogue's theory of art. Poetry, not music, is what usually figures in this capacity and certainly gets the lion's share of attention.

There are some obvious reasons for this. For one thing, music doesn't take up nearly so much space in Plato's treatment of *mousikē* in Books 2 and 3 as do epic and dramatic poetry. There are around eighteen Stephanus pages on poetry, just four on music. In Book 10 the topic is actually introduced as *poiēsis*, and its scope further specified by the subsequent reference to "the poets of tragedy and all the others engaged in imitation" (595a–b). The Book 10 discussion runs for a bit over thirteen Stephanus pages, and the poetic material it engages with is mostly and most memorably Homer and tragedy. It is hard to avoid concluding that whatever the importance Socrates is made to claim for music, poetry is a more significant preoccupation in the *Republic*. Book 10 in particular seems designed to leave us registering the sense that philosophy has one enemy more dangerous than any other: not the "new music," but poetry. So what we need from the theory of art is a *critique* before anything else. And although there are very occasional references to music in Book 10, a critique of poetry and its power is what Socrates puts center stage.

Plato has at least a rhetorical problem in the *Republic*. He wants to make a strongly Damonian thesis about music – rejecting what he sees as new music's degenerate enthusiasm for the *aulos* (it is at just this juncture that he has Socrates claim to have purged luxury from the city: 399c–e), and its enslavement of word to mode and rhythm, and appropriating the basis Damon had worked out for an ethics and politics of music. But at the same time he wants to put up front in his treatment of *mousikē* something else: his own extended and distinctive and presumably in many ways novel development of Xenophanes' attack on Homer and Hesiod, reducing the standard tripartite division of education to a bipartition in the process (there isn't total silence about reading and writing, but it's treated as something so preliminary as to need no real discussion in this context: e.g., 402a–b). The radical message most prominently conveyed by Books 2 and 3, to be reinforced yet more strongly in Book 10 by exploitation of the psychology of Book 4 and the metaphysics of the central books, is that Homer, Hesiod, and the tragedians have just as powerful and almost wholly corrupting and

240   MALCOLM SCHOFIELD

destructive impact on human character as ever did the new music (which is after all only briefly and allusively mentioned at all).

What sticks in the mind are passages like 378a–e, rehearsing a sequence of gruesome tales about hatred and warfare in heaven, with its conclusion that telling young children stories designed to promote virtue is of the highest importance; the repeated insistence that stories about the gods that terrify children or make them *not* god-fearing – with vivid examples – are to be eliminated (e.g. 381e, 383c, 391e); Book 3's opening onslaught on passages in Homer that inculcate the fear of death; and Book 10's argument (605c–606d) about poetry's corrupting manipulation of our feelings – comedy as well as Homer and tragedy. The conclusion at 606d generalizes the point to "sexual urges, emotion, everything in the soul that is appetitive and bound up with the painful and the pleasurable." The effect of poetic imitation is to feed and water these when they ought to wither away. It makes them our rulers. If we want to be better and happier, we should be ruling them.

Socrates *could* have gone on to write half a page on modes and rhythms, adding as the culminating consideration that if the poet casts his words in the modes and rhythms of lamentation or sexual indulgence (the different variants of the Lydian mode, for example: 398d–e), the grip on the soul is as vicelike as it can be. But he doesn't. It's actually rather striking that the one reference to meter, rhythm, and mode in Book 10 occurs in a passage in which Socrates identifies words and phrases as the poet's palette for imitation, whose colors enable him to exercise "a kind of powerful bewitchment." Meter (significantly put first on the list: the element most pertinent to epic and tragic speech), rhythm, and mode seem to be mentioned only as the vehicles for language, or the matter that it informs (601a–b). So it is not easy to resist the thought that – in the rhetoric of the dialogue, at least – poetry, mostly epic and tragic, is what the *Republic* is interested in where *mousikē* is concerned. For music *in senso stretto* Plato turns in Book 3 briefly and belatedly to Damon, only to turn quickly away again.

One might go further, and argue that the difficulty is not just one of rhetoric. It might be thought that Plato faces a theoretical and philosophical problem in advancing the claims he wants to make for music. In her contribution to the Ferrari *Companion*, Jessica Moss suggests that according to the theory of Book 10, imitative poetry "caters to the appearance-responsive, non-rational soul, while poets who present 'quiet and moderate' characters, like painters who present true proportions, fail to present things as they appear and thus fail to engage this part of the soul."[15] Moreover, it does what it does in a particularly compelling way. It captures the

Music all pow'rful

241

complexity and variety of human life as it appears to be, including its conflict and what we have come to call its tragedy. That way it exercises its control over our sympathies. What Plato wants from good art, by contrast, is simplicity: "a protagonist," to quote Moss again, "who accepts imminent death calmly, and spends his last hours in quiet, rational persuasion." She comments: "This last makes for excellent Platonic dialogue – but does it give even the most highbrow among us what we want from art?"[16]

I take it one thing she means is: morally uplifting and intellectually intriguing though the *Phaedo* may be, does that sort of thing have the *power* of art? I don't think the example need embarrass Plato on that ground. My mother's Latin teacher used annually to devote the last class of the school year to a reading of the final scene of the *Phaedo*. It was a much anticipated occasion, which regularly reduced reader and audience to tears. Just the reason why Socrates was wise to send Xanthippe away at the beginning of the dialogue, you might say. But the reaction was a reaction to a piece of theater. And painters over the centuries have thought the scene ideal for representation. It would seem odd to refuse acknowledgment of the power of what was designed to be a work of art. But if we do want to say that what Plato would count as good art has its own power, Moss is surely right to ask: *how* on his Book 10 theory of art *can* it have power?

It's a difficulty about good art for Plato that a definition of *mimēsis* as imitation of things as they appear, not as they are, leaves us paradoxically with no logical space for representation of courageous and judicious character as it is, and no possibility in consequence of such a representation exercising any power over us. So when we go back to Socrates' specification in Book 3 of the musical modes he wants the guards to be able to learn and employ, their imitation of the notes and cadences of speech to express steadfastness and reasonableness can't count as imitations as conceptualized in Book 10, and can't accordingly exercise the power of *mimēsis*. In short, only bad art is really art, and only bad art has the power of art.

At this point there's obviously a temptation to introduce some distinction that will allow Plato to count both good and bad art as mimetic and as art. There is a sense in which Moss herself thinks this needn't be much of a problem. Book 3 recognizes a form of *mimēsis*, she suggests, that copies not appearances but realities.[17] This could be connected with the *Sophist*'s distinction (*Soph.* 235a–236c) between "likeness-making" (which imitates things as they really are, preserving the original proportions and so forth), and "appearance-making" (which imitates them as they appear) as coordinate species of the art of producing *mimēmata*. Then both "the poetry [and – though she does not say so – the music] that survives censorship in

242 MALCOLM SCHOFIELD

Books 2 and 3 and the hymns to the gods and eulogies of good men that survive in Book 10" would fall under the first of these two categories.[18]

In another sense, the distinction doesn't seem to help with the main problem which concerns her and us: why and how good art could exercise *power* over us. For that we would need some account of its effect on the soul. Does good art, too, appeal to the emotions and appetites, or to something else, and how, and what kind of appeal is it? If we turn back to Book 3, and to *its* account of the impact of music on the soul, then we do have at least a sketch of an answer to these questions. Music principally appeals to *to philomathes*, it does so by prompting perception of audible structure, and such perception is a cognitive response to beauty, prefiguring the response of reason once that develops. But these answers we can extract from Book 3 material don't help to complement the theory of *mimēsis* developed in Book 10.

If the arguments of the last few pages are on the right lines, the impression that despite the claims made for it in Book 3, music *in senso stretto* is *not* at the heart of Plato's main theory of art in the *Republic* isn't just a difficulty created by the rhetoric of the dialogue. A more fundamental problem is that Book 3's description of the power music exercises through *mimēsis* suggests an explanation of the phenomenon quite different in character and scope from the theory of mimetic art Book 10 develops to confirm and underpin the treatment of Homer and Hesiod in Book 3. We do seem to have two not readily compatible conceptions of *mimēsis*.

5. MUSIC IN THE *LAWS*

Not only do people who write about art in the *Republic* not often say much about music. They seldom say anything about the treatment of art in the *Laws* either. From the perspectives we have been developing on the *Republic* so far, there are things of immediate interest in what the *Laws* has to say, primarily in Books 2 and 7. First, the *Laws* devotes very little attention to Homer, Hesiod, and tragedy (a short but celebrated passage at 816d–817d dismisses comedy and tragedy). Second, it works out an account of *mimēsis* that exploits a number of the ingredients Plato had incorporated in his theory of *mimēsis* in *Republic* Book 10. Third, the performance of music is central to its program for education and indeed the whole conduct of life in a well-ordered society. Above all, the *Laws* turns the importance of music for the health of society that the *Republic* had now and again asserted into a subject for sustained treatment, leaving readers in none of the doubt they might have been left in by the *Republic*.

The *Republic* had expelled the honeyed Muse, but the hymns to the gods and encomia of good men that were to be admitted into the city (607a) now in the *Laws* come into their own. The music appropriate for them is discussed on several occasions and in Damonian terms. If we look back at the *Republic* from the vantage point of the *Laws*, the central role Book 3 of the *Republic* accords to music is reaffirmed as forcefully as it could be, and the mimetic theory of Book 10 accordingly adapted to positive ethical purposes. Polemical critique of epic and tragedy, on the other hand, so prominent in the *Republic*, begins to look as though it been a ground-clearing exercise, not needing repetition, and not the enduring core of the dialogue's treatment of art.[19]

That is not to say that the *Laws'* discussion of art has no critical edge. The Athenian Stranger is not very far into his account of the basis for "the correct education" (653a) before he confronts the fact that some people enjoy choral dancing that is depraved (655c). A subtle examination of their mindset ensues. The Athenian suggests that such a person won't say that the dancing he relishes is good. People wouldn't stand for that – it would be regarded as blasphemy (655d). He will be like someone who associates with bad people of depraved habits, and accepts and enjoys their lifestyle. He criticizes them – but as a sort of game, aware of his own wickedness in a dreamlike way. He's bound to assimilate himself to what he enjoys, even if he's ashamed actually to applaud it (656b). The root of the problem is that most people say that the standard of correctness in music is its power to provide souls with pleasure (655c–d). In other words, where music is concerned it's not that the ethical has no hold on their minds at all (it certainly retains it over their tongues), but that compared with pleasure the purchase it has on them is rather weak.

As often in the *Laws*, and in this so unlike the *Republic*, Plato is prepared to work with the grain of the culture. The Athenian finds something helpful in the common opinion. After further discussion, he suggests that correct use of the music and play in choral performance should be based on the recognition that we enjoy ourselves when we think we're prospering, and we think we're prospering when we're enjoying ourselves (657c). That shouldn't mislead us into thinking that prizes for music should go to performers who give the most enjoyment to the greatest number (657e). Nonetheless competitions to reward musicians who give us pleasure aren't wholly misconceived in their assumption that music should be judged by the pleasure it gives (e.g., so far as the Athenian and his elderly interlocutors are concerned, rhapsodes performing the *Iliad* or *Odyssey* or some Hesiod: 658d–e). The question is rather: who should be the judge? It's not just

244   MALCOLM SCHOFIELD

anyone's pleasure that should count. What delights "the best people and those adequately educated" should be regarded as "the loveliest Muse" (658e–659a).

Like much in the *Laws*, that sounds distinctly Aristotelian. There's also a clear relationship with something that might have sounded merely counterfactual or embryonic in Book 10 of the *Republic*. There too Plato made pleasure and pain key to the power poetry and above all tragedy exert over the human psyche. Pleasure is the benefit people think they get from tragedy (606b) – in reality "slow poison" as Myles Burnyeat described it.[20] If the honeyed Muse were allowed residence in Kallipolis, pleasure and pain would be twin kings instead of law and whatever is generally agreed to be the best *logos* (607a). However, poetry and *mimēsis* aimed at pleasure would gladly be admitted if they could show that they are beneficial for social and political systems and human life (607c–e). That is precisely the basis on which they are countenanced in the *Laws* – except that the Stranger explicitly applies the idea to music *in stretto senso*.

Music saturates the cultural thinking of the *Laws*. The Stranger's account of the test of good music (658e–660a) provokes Cleinias into a tirade against novelties in music (660b), applauded by the Athenian, who will present a full-blown Damonian jeremiad, reminiscent of Socrates' remarks in Book 4 of the *Republic* (424b–c), on the political degeneration caused by degenerate music in the famous theatocracy passage in Book 3: you can't contravene *nomoi* in music without triggering *paranomia* in the social and political sphere (700a–701b). In Book 7 this theme is linked with theory about right and wrong modes, in a passage (799e–802e) presenting interesting material on male and female modes (cf. also 812b–e). What the Athenian proposes by contrast is a highly regulated musical regime integrated into the educational system from the outset. Penelope Murray sums it up succinctly in her contribution to a fine collection of essays on music she edited in 2004 with Peter Wilson:[21]

In Plato's Cretan city the entire educational system is based on *mousikē*, and it is through choral performance that citizens will learn to acquire *aretē*, the virtue on which a just and harmonious society depends. All members of the community must sing and dance, hence three choruses are set up, the first consisting of children, the second of those under 30, and the third of those between 30 and 60, sacred to the Muses, Apollo, and Dionysus respectively. The third of these choruses, the "finest element in the city" (665d), is not to be a chorus like the others,[22] but will act as moral arbiters, dedicated to the mastery of "a music that is nobler than the music of the choruses and the theatres" (667a–b). As expert judges

Music all pow'rful

members of this chorus will decide on the repertoire that is to be performed by the city at large.

As in the *Republic*, musical performance is a matter of *mimēsis*. In fact the Athenian claims everyone would agree that all musical productions consist in *mimēsis* and representation (or "effecting a likeness," *apeikasia*: 668c, cf. 668a). But the *Laws* doesn't appear to see anything intrinsically problematic in this: here it is more like Book 3 than Book 10 of the *Republic*. The *Sophist's* distinction between production of likenesses and appearances is apparently dropped. Nor is there any suggestion as in Book 10 of the *Republic* that art can only represent the appearances of things, or feed only those elements in us which ought to wither away – although the *Laws* agrees that while composers must have knowledge of mode and rhythm, they won't necessarily know whether the imitation (*mimēma*) they produce is good or not (670e, 801b–c: cf. 802b–c). But knowing whether it is a *mimēma* of what is good or fine is crucial for judgment as to its acceptability (668a–b). And the Athenian goes on to lay down the requirements for sage criticism of any representation (*eikōn*) in music or any of the arts. A judge must know "what is being represented, whether it is represented correctly, and whether the representation is good" (669b).[23] As in Books 3 and 4 of the *Republic*, the view is taken that someone who goes wrong in music will suffer particular damage – and the *Laws* adds that the damage it inflicts is very difficult to detect (669b–c). There follows another impassioned denunciation of the "new music" (669c–670a).

The whole system of choral performance is grounded in a theory about human nature that does more to explain our attraction to art than anything Plato offers us in the *Republic*. The theory is first introduced in Book 1 of the dialogue, and then rearticulated in the form most relevant to an account of education at the beginning of Book 2. The idea is that in children the first sensations are pleasure and pain. Accordingly it's in pleasure and pain that virtue and vice first present themselves to the soul, i.e., in whether pleasure and pain are handled and educated rightly (653a–c). Like any other young animals, children "can't keep still [cf. Ar. *Pol.* 1340b29] – neither their bodies nor their voices – so they are always wanting to move and make sounds, jumping and skipping as though dancing with pleasure and making a game of it, and uttering noises of all kinds." But where they're different from other animals is in their capacity to perceive order and disorder in their motions, i.e., what we call *harmonia* and *rhuthmos*, mode and rhythm: as in the *Republic* (Text 1), perception is stressed (653e; cf. 664e). So the gods have given us "rhythmic and harmonic perception bound up with

246   MALCOLM SCHOFIELD

pleasure" – expressed in the choral performance (here Plato allows himself an etymological pun on *choros*, dance, and *chara*, joy) of singing and dancing (653d–654a). The *Laws* doesn't offer any account of the deep structures underlying the causal processes involved. But I imagine that isn't because Plato has renounced the sort of theory it looked as though Books 3 and 4 of the *Republic* might be presupposing (the *Timaeus* and the *Philebus* suggest that he became increasingly attracted to such forms of explanation in his latest period), but because the *Laws* is not a dialogue written to satisfy scientific curiosity.

6. CONCLUDING REMARKS

I could have gone on to explore the way Aristotle, too, in the eighth and last surviving book of his *Politics*, similarly makes music *in senso stretto* the major focus of his whole discussion of the upbringing and education appropriate for citizens. In the key chapter 5 he leans heavily on the treatment of music in Book 2 of the *Laws*; and (though some commentators have tried to read him differently)[24] any preoccupation with poetry as such is hard to find. But pursuing Plato into Aristotle would take us too far away from the *Republic*. For now, I hope it will be enough to have suggested that if we too take our cue from the *Laws*, we shall get a better sense of why the few pages on music in the *Republic* give us a keener insight into its theory of the shaping of the human soul than anything else in the dialogue.

I don't think Plato's theory of musical education in the *Republic* has ever been better explained than by Nettleship in the lectures on the dialogue he delivered 125 years ago. So I will finish by quoting a relevant extract from the version subsequently published, where the author writes at one point as if he is drawing on the *Laws* as well as (primarily) our Text 1:[25]

We must notice further that thus learning to read the sensible world [i.e. through *mimēsis*], or the world as it presents itself in ordinary experience, is a preparation for learning to read the world in another way. A man who has been educated thus will have an instinctive sense of what is beautiful and ugly, and will love the one and hate the other, before he is able to frame in his mind a reason for loving or hating them. But when reason comes, a man so nurtured will recognize it and welcome it from natural kinship with it, that is to say, because his own feelings are already in accord with it. Plato conceived that there was a real continuity between the education of art and the education of science and philosophy, which he afterwards requires should follow it up. In childhood the soul of man is completely subject to the senses, its perceptions are all disordered. Gradually it frees itself from the tumultuous influences of sense, and establishes order and connection in what it

Music all pow'rful 247

perceives and thinks. The great agents by which this process can be helped are, first, the education in *mousikē*, and, second, the education in science and philosophy. In both Plato would say there was reason (*logos*); in its earlier, sensible form it shows itself as rhythm, harmony, and shape; in its later, it shows itself as principles or laws, which are apprehended by the intelligence (understood, not seen or heard or felt).[26]

NOTES

1. Barker vol. 1 (1984), vol. 2 (1989).
2. In Ferrari and Griffith 2000.
3. For which see e.g. Barker 1984, ch.7, or West 1992, pp. 356–72.
4. I am grateful to Stephen Halliwell for drawing my attention to this passage.
5. The contrast between content ("what") and manner ("how") is quite explicit; see 392c, 394c.
6. Both at 411d (in Text 2) and at 441e I take Socrates to be anticipating the account of philosophy to be given in the central books, not to be implying that the education in *mousikē* (broadly conceived) described in Books 2 and 3 already includes exposure to argument and studies (*mathēmata*) in the sense he intends (cf. 522a–b).
7. My argument in section 2 runs parallel to that in Brancacci 2005. See also on 401e–402a Gill 1996, pp. 270–71. Socrates' emphasis on the perception of beauty and ugliness fostered by mode and rhythm makes Irwin's identification of the element of the soul which registers them as appetite appear eccentric: Irwin 1995, pp. 217–18. In Irwin 1977, p. 330 n. 28, commenting on 403c, he had seen *kalon* (the beautiful or admirable) as appealing to the philosophical part of the soul.
8. Greek musical theorists like Archytas were already in Plato's day making modal relationships the subject of a technical science of harmonics: see Huffman 2005, Barker 2007, ch. 11.
9. On Damon see e.g. Barker 1984, ch. 10 appendix B; Wallace 2004.
10. Here as elsewhere I translate *mimeisthai* here as "imitate," but as the discussion that follows brings out, "express" is the particular form of representation that seems to be at issue in this passage.
11. That *mimēsis* here shifts from impersonation to expression is well noted and discussed in Halliwell 2002, pp. 131–32.
12. Well discussed by Brancacci 2005, pp. 99–103: "the true cast of mind [*dianoia*] consisting in a character which is well and beautifully constituted."
13. Barker 2005, pp. 28–38.
14. A contrast put to me by Antony Hatzistavrou.
15. Moss 2007, p. 441.
16. Moss 2007, p. 442.
17. Moss 2007, p. 437 n. 36.
18. Moss 2007, p. 421 n. 12.
19. See further Halliwell 2002, pp. 61–71.
20. Burnyeat 1999, p. 319.

248   MALCOLM SCHOFIELD

21. Murray 2004, pp. 376–77.
22. A contestable interpretation: there is clear indication that the chorus of Dionysus will succumb to the "medicine" of wine, and renew their youth in dance (665b) and song (666b–d; cf. also the summing up at 670c–671c). See Prauscello 2010.
23. For discussion see Hatzistavrou forthcoming.
24. For an excellent recent discussion, see Ford 2004. The conception of musical *mimēsis* in play in *Pol.* 8.4–7 is explored in Halliwell 2002, pp. 237–49.
25. Nettleship 1901, pp. 115–16.
26. My thanks are due to audiences in London, Tucson, and Edinburgh, where I read versions of this essay in 2008; to Tom Cheshire and Lucia Prauscello for some enjoyable discussions, and for showing me work in progress of their own; and to Antony Hatzistavrou, Stephen Halliwell, and James Wilberding, for some challenging email correspondence. This revised version incorporates the outcome of reflection on many of their thoughts. Andrew Barker tells me that he has revised his views on Damon, and has an idea why Glaucon calls Phrygian the mode he so designates: we await publications.

Bibliography

Adam, J. 1905. *The* Republic *of Plato*. 2 vols. Cambridge.
  1963. *The* Republic *of Plato*. 2 vols. 2nd edn. Cambridge.
Adkins, A. W. H. 1960. *Merit and Responsibility: A Study in Greek Values*. Oxford; rpt. Chicago.
  1971. "*Polupragmosune* and 'Minding One's Own Business': A Study in Greek Social and Political Values." *Classical Philology* 71(4): 301–27.
Albinus, L. 1998. "The Katabasis of Er." In *Essays on Plato's* Republic, ed. E. N. Ostenfeld. Aarhus.
Allan, D. J., ed. 1993. *Plato:* Republic I. Bristol.
Annas, J. 1981. *An Introduction to Plato's* Republic. Oxford.
  1982a. "Knowledge and Language: The *Theaetetus* and the *Cratylus*." In *Language and Logos*, ed. M. Nussbaum and M. Schofield. Cambridge, 95–114.
  1982b. "Plato's Myths of Judgment." *Phronesis* 27: 119–43.
  1999. *Platonic Ethics Old and New*. Cornell.
Anonymous. 1963. *Prolegomena to Platonic Philosophy*, trans. L. G. Westerlink. Amsterdam.
Archer-Hind, R. 1881. "On Some Difficulties in the Platonic Psychology." *The Journal of Philology* 10: 120–31.
Aronson, S. H. 1972. "The Happy Philosopher Problem – A Counterexample to Plato's Proof." *Journal of the History of Philosophy* 10: 383–98.
Bailey, D. T. J. 2006. "Plato and Aristotle on the Unhypothetical." *Oxford Studies in Ancient Philosophy* 30: 101–26.
Balot, R. 2001. *Greed and Injustice in Classical Athens*. Princeton.
Baltzly, D. 1996. "'To an Unhypothetical First Principle' in Plato's *Republic*." *History of Philosophy Quarterly* 13: 149–65.
Barker, A. 1984. *Greek Musical Writings*, vol. 1. Cambridge.
  1989. *Greek Musical Writings*, vol. 2. Cambridge.
  2005. *Psicomusicologia nella grecia antica*. Naples.
  2007. *The Science of Harmonics in Classical Greece*. Cambridge.
Barnes, J. ed. 1984. *The Complete Works of Aristotle*. Princeton.
Barney, R. 2001a. *Names and Nature in Plato's* Cratylus. New York.
  2001b. "Platonism, Moral Nostalgia, and the 'City of Pigs'." *Proceedings of the Boston Area Colloquium in Ancient Philosophy* 17: 207–27.

250 *Bibliography*

2004. "Callicles and Thrasymachus." In *Stanford Encyclopedia of Philosophy.* (http://plato.stanford.edu/entries/callicles-thrasymachus).

2006. "Socrates' Refutation of Thrasymachus." In Santas 2006, 44–62.

Beatty, J. 1976a. "Plato's Happy Philosophers and Politics." *The Review of Politics* 38: 545–75.

1976b. "Why Should Plato's Philosopher Be Moral, and Hence, Rule?" *The Personalist* 57: 132–44.

Bedu-Addo, J. T. 1978. "Mathematics, Dialectic and the Good in the *Republic* VI–VII." *Platon* 30: 111–27.

1979. "The Role of the Hypothetical Method in the *Phaedo.*" *Phronesis* 24: 111–27.

Belfiore, E. 1983. "Plato's Greatest Accusation Against Poetry." *Canadian Journal of Philosophy* 9: 39–56.

Benardete, S. 1989. *Socrates' Second Sailing: On Plato's Republic.* Chicago.

Benson, H. H. 2000. *Socratic Wisdom: The Model of Knowledge in Plato's Early Dialogues.* New York.

2003. "The Method of Hypothesis in the *Meno.*" *Proceedings of the Boston Area Colloquium in Ancient Philosophy* 18: 95–126.

2006. "Plato's Method of Dialectic." In *A Companion to Plato*, ed. H. Benson. Oxford, 85–100.

2008. "Knowledge, Virtue, and Method in *Republic* 471c–502c." *Philosophical Inquiry* 30: 1–28.

Berry, E. G. 1940. *The History and Development of the Concept of THEIA MOIRA and THEIA TUCHÊ Down to and Including Plato.* Chicago.

Blondell, R. 2002. *The Play of Character in Plato's Dialogues.* Cambridge.

Bloom, A. 1968. *The* Republic *of Plato.* New York.

Blössner, N. 1997. *Dialogform und Argument: Studien zu Platons "Politeia".* Stuttgart.

2007. "The City–Soul Analogy." In Ferrari 2007, 345–85.

Bluck, R. S. 1955. *Plato's* Phaedo. London.

Bobonich, Christopher. 2001. "Akrasia and Agency in Plato's Laws and Republic." In *Essays in Plato's Psychology*, ed. E. Wagner. Lexington; originally published in *Archiv für Geschichte der Philosophie* 76 (1994): 3–36.

2002. *Plato's Utopia Recast: His Later Ethics and Politics* (Oxford: Clarendon Press).

Bodéüs, R. 1993. *The Political Dimensions of Aristotle's Ethics.* Albany.

Bostock, D. 1986. *Plato* Phaedo. Oxford.

Brancacci, A. 2005. "Musique et philosophie en *République* 2–4." In *Études sur la République de Platon*, vol. 1, ed. M. Dixsaut. Paris.

Brann, E. 1967. "The Music of the *Republic.*" *Agon* 1: 1–117.

2004. *The Music of the Republic: Essays on Socrates' Conversations and Plato's Writings.* Philadelphia. First published as: "The Music of the *Republic.*" *St. John's Review* 39 (1989–90): 1–103.

Brickhouse, T. C. 1998. "The Paradox of the Philosophers' Rule." In Smith 1998, vol. 2, 141–52.

Brisson, L. 1992. *Platon, Timée–Critias.* Paris.

1998. *Plato the Myth Maker.* Tr. G. Naddaf. Chicago.

Broadie, S. 2001. "Theodicy and Pseudo-History in the *Timaeus*." *Oxford Studies in Ancient Philosophy* 21: 1–28.

2005. "Virtue and Beyond in Plato and Aristotle." *Southern Journal of Philosophy* 43: 97–114.

Brown, E. 2000. "Justice and Compulsion for Plato's Philosopher-Rulers." *Ancient Philosophy* 20: 1–17.

2004. "Minding the Gap in Plato's *Republic*." *Philosophical Studies* 117: 272–302.

Burkert, W. 1985. *Greek Religion*. Harvard.

Burnyeat, M. F. 1977. "Examples in Epistemology: Socrates, Theaetetus and G. E. Moore." *Philosophy* 52: 381–98.

1987. "Platonism and Mathematics: A Prelude to Discussion." In *Mathematics and Metaphysics in Aristotle*, ed. A. Graeser. Stuttgart.

1999. "Culture and Society in Plato's *Republic*." *Tanner Lectures in Human Values* 20: 215–334.

2000. "Plato on Why Mathematics is Good for the Soul." In *Mathematics and Necessity*, ed. T. Smiley. Oxford, 1–81.

Byrd, M. 2007a. "Dialectic and Plato's Method of Hypothesis." *Apeiron* 40: 141–58.

2007. "The Summoner Approach: A New Method of Plato Interpretation." *Journal of the History of Philosophy* 45: 365–81.

Calvo, T. and L. Brisson, eds. 1997. *Interpreting the* Timaeus–Critias. Sankt Augustin.

Chantraine, P. 1968, 1970, 1975, 1977, 1980. *Dictionnaire étymologique de la langue grecque*. Paris.

Cherniss, H. 1971. "The Sources of Evil According to Plato." In *Plato: A Collection of Critical Essays*, ed. G. Vlastos. Garden City, 244–58.

Chisholm, Roderick. 1991. "On the Simplicity of the Soul." *Philosophical Perspectives* 5: 167–81.

Clay, D. 1994. "The Origins of the Socratic Dialogue." In *The Socratic Movement*, ed. P. A. Vander Waerdt. Ithaca, 23–47.

1997. "The Plan of Plato's *Critias*." In *Interpreting the* Timaeus–Critias, ed. T. Calvo. Sankt Augustin, 49–54.

1999. "Plato's Atlantis: the Anatomy of a Fiction." *Proceedings of the Boston Area Colloquium in Ancient Philosophy* 15: 1–21.

Clay, D. and A. Purvis. 1999. *Four Island Utopias*. Newburyport.

Cole, T. 1983. "Archaic Truth." *Quaderni Urbinati di Cultura Classica* 64: 7–28.

Collard, C., M. J. Cropp, and K. H. Lee. 1995. *Euripides: Selected Fragmentary Plays, 1*. Warminster.

Collard, C., M. J. Cropp, and J. Gilbert. 2004. *Euripides: Selected Fragmentary Plays, 2*. Warminster.

Cooper, J. 1984. "Plato's Theory of Human Motivation." *History of Philosophy Quarterly* 1: 3–21.

1997a. "The Psychology of Justice in Plato." Rpt. In *Reason and Emotion*. Princeton. First published in *American Philosophical Quarterly* 14 (1977): 151–57.

ed. 1997b. *Plato: Complete Works*. Indianapolis.

forthcoming. "Political Community and the Highest Good." In *Being, Nature, and Life: Essays in Honor of Allan Gotthelf*, ed. R. Bolton and J. Lennox. Cambridge.

Cooper, N. 1966. "The Importance of *Dianoia* in Plato's Theory of Forms." *Classical Quarterly* 16: 65–69.

Cornford, F. M. 1945. *The Republic of Plato*. London and New York.

1965. "Mathematics and Dialectic in *Republic* VI–VII." In *Studies in Plato's Metaphysics*, ed. R. E. Allen. London.

Cross, R. C., and A. D. Woozley. 1964. *Plato's* Republic: *A Philosophical Commentary*. London.

Dahl, N. O. 1991. "Plato's Defense of Justice." *Philosophy and Phenomenological Research* 51: 809–34.

Davies, J. 1968. "A Note on the Philosopher's Descent into the Cave." *Philologus* 112: 121–26.

De Jong, I. 2004. "Narratological Theory on Narrators, Narratees, and Narrative." In De Jong et al. 2004.

De Jong, I., R. Nünlist, and A. Bowie, eds. 2004. *Narrators, Narratees, and Narratives in Ancient Greek Literature*. Leiden.

Demos, R. 1964. "A Fallacy in Plato's *Republic?*" *Philosophical Review* 73: 395–98.

Denyer, N. 2007. "Sun and Line: The Role of the Good." In Ferrari 2007, 284–309.

Diels, H., and W. Kranz. 1951. *Die Fragmente der Vorsokratiker*. 6th edn. Berlin.

Dobbs, D. 1985. "The Justice of Socrates' Philosopher Kings." *American Journal of Political Science* 29: 809–26.

Dodds, E. R. 1951. *The Greeks and the Irrational*. Berkeley.

Dorion, L.-A., trans., comm. 1995. *Aristote: Les Réfutations Sophistiques*. Paris.

Dorter, K. 2003. "Free Will, Luck, and Happiness in the Myth of Er." *Journal of Philosophical Research* 28: 129–42.

2006. *The Transformation of Plato's* Republic. Lanham.

Douglas, M. 2007. *Thinking in Circles: An Essay on Ring-Composition*. New Haven.

Eliot, T. S. 1944. "Little Gidding." In *Four Quartets*. London.

Ellis, R. 1998. *Imagining Atlantis*. New York.

Else, G. 1972. "The Structure and Date of Book 10 of Plato's *Republic*." *Abhandlungen der Heidelberger Akademie der Wissenschaften*. Heidelberg.

Feeney, D. C. 1993. "Towards an Account of the Ancient World's Concept of Fictive Belief." In Gill and Wiseman 1993.

Ferrari, G. R. F. 2003. *City and Soul in Plato's* Republic. Sankt Augustin.

2008a. "Glaucon's Reward, Philosophy's Debt: The Myth of Er." In *Plato's Myths*, ed. C. Partenie. Oxford.

2008b. "Socratic Irony as Pretence." *Oxford Studies in Ancient Philosophy* 34: 1–33.

Ferrari, G. R. F., ed. 2007. *The Cambridge Companion to Plato's* Republic. Cambridge.

Ferrari, G. R. F., ed., and T. Griffith, trans. 2000. *Plato: the* Republic. Cambridge.

Fine, G. 1990. "Knowledge and Belief in *Republic* V–VII." In *Epistemology*, ed. S. Everson. Cambridge, 85–115.

1999. "Knowledge and Belief in *Republic* 5–7." In *Plato 1: Metaphysics and Epistemology*, ed. G. Fine. Oxford, 215–46.

Fogelin, R. J. 1971. "Three Platonic Analogies." *Philosophical Review* 80: 371–82.

Foley, R. 2008. "Plato's Undividable Line: Contradiction and Method in *Republic* VI." *Journal of the History of Philosophy* 46: 1–23.

Ford, A. 2004. "Catharsis: The Power of Music in Aristotle's *Politics*." In *Music and Muses*, ed. P. Murray and P. Wilson. Oxford.

Forster, M. 2007. "Socrates' Profession of Ignorance." *Oxford Studies in Ancient Philosophy* 32: 1–35.

Foster, M. B. 1936. "Some Implications of a Passage in Plato's *Republic*." *Philosophy* 11: 301–08.

1937. "A Mistake in Plato's *Republic*." *Mind* 46: 386–93.

Frede, D. 1996. "Plato, Popper, and Historicism." *Proceedings of the Boston Area Colloquium in Ancient Philosophy* 12: 247–76.

Frede, M. 1992. "Plato's Arguments and the Dialogue Form." In Klagge and Smith 1992, 201–19.

Gallop, D. 1965. "Image and Reality in Plato's *Republic*." *Archiv für Geschichte der Philosophie* 47: 113–31.

Gentzler, J. 1991. "*Sumphonein* in Plato's *Phaedo*." *Phronesis* 36: 265–77.

Gifford, E. H. 1905. *The* Euthydemus *of Plato*. Oxford.

Gill, C. 1977. 'The Genre of the Atlantis Story." *Classical Philology* 72: 287–304.

1979. "Plato's Atlantis Story and the Birth of Fiction." *Philosophy and Literature* 3: 64–78.

1980. *Plato, the Atlantis Story* (Timaeus *17–27*, Critias). Bristol.

1993. "Plato on Falsehood – not Fiction." In Gill and Wiseman 1983, 38–87.

1996. *Personality in Greek Epic, Tragedy, and Philosophy*. Oxford.

Gill, C. and T. Wiseman, eds. 1993. *Lies and Fiction in the Ancient World*. Exeter and Austin.

Gonzalez, F. J. 1998. *Dialectic and Dialogue: Plato's Practice of Philosophical Inquiry*. Evanston.

Gosling, J. C. B. 1973. *Plato*. London.

Griswold, C. L. 1986. *Self-Knowledge in Plato's* Phaedrus. New Haven.

Grube, G. M. A. 1992. *Plato's* Republic. Indianapolis.

Guthrie, W. K. C. 1950. *The Greeks and Their Gods*. London.

1971. *Socrates*. Cambridge.

1975. *A History of Greek Philosophy*, vol. 4: *Plato, The Man and His Dialogues: Earlier Period*. Cambridge.

Hall, D. 1977. "The *Republic* and the Limits of Politics." *Political Theory* 5: 293–313.

Halliwell, S. 1988. *Republic 10*. Warminster.

2002. *The Aesthetics of Mimesis*. Princeton.

2007. "The Life and Death Journey of the Soul: Interpreting the Myth of Er." In Ferrari 2007, 445–73.

Halperin, D. M. 1992. "Plato and the Erotics of Narrativity." In Klagge and Smith 1992, 93–129.

254   *Bibliography*

Harte, V. 2006. "Beware of Imitations: Image Recognition in Plato." In Herrmann 2006, 21–42.

Hatzistavrou, A. 2006. "Happiness and the Nature of the Philosopher-Kings." In Herrmann 2006, 95–124.

Forthcoming. "'Correctness' and Poetic Knowledge: Choric Poetry in the *Laws*." In *Plato and the Poets*, ed. P. Destrée and F. G. Herrmann. Leiden.

Herrmann, F.-G. 2006. *New Essays on Plato*. Swansea.

Hitz, Z. 2005. Review of K. Raaflaub's *The Discovery of Freedom in Ancient Greece*. *Journal of Philosophy* 102: 594–601.

Hornblower, S. 2004. *Thucydides and Pindar*. Oxford.

Höschele, R. 2007. "Garlands in the *Garland*: Meleager's Poetics of Entanglement." University of Toronto, 2007. University of Virginia, 2007.

2010. *Die blütenlesende Muse: Poetik und Textualität antiker Epigrammsammlungen*. Tübingen.

Howland, J. 1993. *The* Republic: *the Odyssey of Philosophy*. New York; rpt., Philadelphia. 2004.

Huffman, C. A. 2005. *Archytas of Tarentum: Pythagorean, Philosopher and Mathematician King*. Cambridge.

Irwin, T. H. 1977. *Plato's Moral Theory*. Oxford.

1995. *Plato's Ethics*. Oxford.

Johansen, T. 2004. *Plato's Natural Philosophy: A Study of the* Timaeus-Critias. Cambridge.

Johnson, R. R. 1999. "Does Plato's Myth of Er Contribute to the Argument of the *Republic*?" *Philosophy and Rhetoric* 32(1): 1–13.

Kahn, C. 1972. "The Meaning of Justice and the Theory of Forms." *Journal of Philosophy* 69: 567–579.

1987. "Plato's Theory of Desire." *Review of Metaphysics* 41: 77–103.

1996. *Plato and the Socratic Dialogue: The Philosophical Use of a Literary Form*. Cambridge.

2003. *The Verb "Be" in Ancient Greek*. Indianapolis and Cambridge.

Kamtekar, R. 2001. "Social Justice and Happiness in the *Republic*: Plato's Two Principles." *History of Political Thought* 22: 189–220.

2006. "Speaking with the Same Voice as Reason: Personification in Plato's Psychology." *Oxford Studies in Ancient Philosophy* 31: 167–202.

Karasmanis, V. 2002. "Dialectic and the Good in Plato's *Republic*." *Cahiers de Philosophie Ancienne*. Ousia.

Kayser, J. R. 1970. "Prologue to the Study of Justice: *Republic* 327a–328b." *The Western Political Quarterly* 23: 256–265.

Keyt, D. 2006. "Plato and the Ship of State." In Santas 2006, 189–213.

King, D. 2005. *Finding Atlantis: A True Story of Genius, Madness and an Extraordinary Quest for a Lost World*. New York.

Kirkwood, G. 1982. *Selections from Pindar*. Chico.

Klagge, J. C., and N. D. Smith, eds. 1992. *Oxford Studies in Ancient Philosophy*, suppl. vol.: *Methods of Interpreting Plato and His Dialogues*. Oxford.

Bibliography

Klosko, G. 1981. "Implementing the Ideal State." *Journal of Politics* 43: 365–89.

Kock, T. 1880. *Comicorum Atticorum Fragmenta*, vol. 1. Leipzig.

Kraut, R. 1973. "Egoism, Love, and Political Office in Plato." *Philosophical Review* 82: 330–44.

    1991. "Return to the Cave: *Republic* 519–521." *Proceedings of the Boston Area Colloquium in Ancient Philosophy* 7: 43–62.

    1992. "The Defense of Justice in the *Republic*." In *The Cambridge Companion to Plato*, ed. R. Kraut. Cambridge, 311–37.

Laks, A. 2000. "The *Laws*." In *The Cambridge History of Greek and Roman Political Thought*, ed. C. Rowe and M. Schofield. Cambridge.

Lear, E. 1862. *A Book of Nonsense*. London.

Lear, G. R. 2006. "Plato on Learning to Love Beauty." In *The Blackwell Guide to Plato's* Republic, ed. G. Santas. Oxford, 104–24.

Lear, J. 1992. "Inside and Outside the *Republic*." *Phronesis* 37: 184–215.

    2006. "Allegory and Myth in Plato's *Republic*." In Santas 2006, 25–43.

Lee, H. D. P. 2001. *The Republic*. London.

Leroux, G. 2002. *Platon, La République*. Paris.

Lesher, J. 1994. "The Emergence of Philosophical Interest in Cognition." *Oxford Studies in Ancient Philosophy* 12: 1–34.

Liddell, H. and R. Scott. 1848. *A Greek-English Lexicon*. 9th ed. rev. H. Jones and R. McKenzie, with 1968 suppl. Oxford.

Long, A. A. 1977. "Chance and Natural Law in Epicureanism." *Phronesis* 22: 63–88.

Lorenz, H. 2006. *The Brute Within*. Oxford.

Lyons, J. 1963. *Structural Semantics: An Analysis of Part of the Vocabulary of Plato*. Oxford.

Mahoney, T. A. 1992. "Do Plato's Philosopher-Rulers Sacrifice Self-Interest to Justice?" *Phronesis* 37: 265–82.

Mara, G. M. 1983. "Politics and Action in Plato's *Republic*." *The Western Political Quarterly* 36: 596–618.

McCabe, M. M. 2006. "Is Dialectic as Dialectic Does? The Virtue of Philosophical Conversation." In *The Virtuous Life in Greek Ethics*, ed. B. Reis. Cambridge.

McPherran, M. 2003. "Socrates, Crito, and Their Debt to Asclepius." *Ancient Philosophy* 23: 71–92.

Menn, S. 2002. "Plato and the Method of Analysis." *Phronesis* 47: 193–223.

    2006. "On Plato's *Politeia*." *Proceedings of the Boston Area Colloquium in Ancient Philosophy* 21: 1–55.

Merriman, F. V. 1915. "The Rise and Fall of the Platonic Kallipolis." *Mind* 24: 1–15.

Miller, M. 1985. "Platonic Provocations: Reflections on the Soul and the Good in the *Republic*." In O'Meara 1985, 163–93.

Moors, K. 1988. "Named Life Selections in Plato's Myth of Er." *Classica et Medievalia* 39: 55–61.

Moraux, P. 1968. "La joute dialectique d'après le huitième livre des *Topiques*." In *Aristotle on Dialectic: the* Topics, ed. G. E. L. Owen. Oxford.

Moravcsik, J. M. E. 1973. "Plato's Method of Division." In *Patterns in Plato's Thought*, ed. J. M. E. Moravcsik. Boston.

Morgan, K. 1998. "Designer History: Plato's Atlantis Story and Fourth Century Ideology." *Journal of Hellenic Studies* 118: 101–18.

2000. *Myth and Philosophy from the Presocratics to Plato.* Cambridge.

2004. "Plato." In De Jong *et al.* 2004.

Morgan, M. L. 1990. *Platonic Piety.* New Haven.

1992. "Plato and Greek Religion." In *The Cambridge Companion to Plato*, ed. R. Kraut. Cambridge.

Morrison, Donald. 2001. "The Happiness of the City and the Happiness of the Individual in Plato's Republic." *Ancient Philosophy* 21.1: 1–24.

2007. "The Utopian Character of Plato's Ideal City." In Ferrari 2007, 232–55.

Morrison, J. S. 1955. "Parmenides and Er." *The Journal of Hellenic Studies* 75: 59–68.

Moss, J. 2007. "What is Imitative Poetry and Why is it Bad?" In Ferrari 2007, 415–44.

2008. "Appearances and Calculations: Plato's Division of the Soul." *Oxford Studies in Ancient Philosophy* 34: 35–68.

Mueller, I. 1992. "Mathematical Method and Philosophical Truth." In *The Cambridge Companion to Plato*, ed. R. Kraut. Cambridge, 170–99.

Murphy, N. R. 1951. *The Interpretation of Plato's Republic.* Oxford.

Murray, P. 2004. "The Muses and Their Arts." In *Music and the Muses*, ed. P. Murray and P. Wilson. Oxford, 365–89.

Myres, J. L. 1932. "The Last Book of the *Iliad*." *Journal of Hellenic Studies* 52: 264–96.

Nehamas, A. 1982/1999. "Plato on Imitation and Poetry in *Republic* X." In *Virtues of Authenticity: Essays on Plato and Socrates.* Princeton; originally published in *Plato on Beauty, Wisdom and the Arts*, ed. J. Moravcsik and P. Temko. Totowa, 47–78.

Nettleship, R. L. 1897. *Philosophical Lectures and Remains of Richard Lewis Nettleship*, ed., with a biographical sketch, by A. C. Bradley and G. R. Benson. London and New York.

1901. *Lectures on the* Republic *of Plato.* 2nd edn. Oxford.

Netz, R. 2003. "How Propositions Begin." *Hyperboreus* 9(2): 295–317.

Notomi, N. 1999. *The Unity of Plato's Sophist.* Cambridge.

Notopoulos, J. A. 1951. "Continuity and Interconnection in Homeric Oral Composition." *Transactions of the American Philological Association* 82: 81–101.

Ober, J. 1989. *Mass and Elite in Democratic Athens.* Princeton.

1996. *Political Dissent in Democratic Athens.* Princeton.

O'Connor, D. K. 2007. "Rewriting the Poets in Plato's Characters." In Ferrari 2007, 55–89.

Ostenfeld, E. 1996. "Socratic Argumentation Strategies and Aristotle's *Topics* and *Sophistical Refutations*." *Methexis* 9: 43–57.

Ott, W. 2006. "Aristotle and Plato on Character." *Ancient Philosophy* 26: 65–79.

Otterlo, W. A. A. van. 1944. *Untersuchungen über Begriff, Anwendung und Entstehung der griechischen Ringkomposition.* Amsterdam.

1948. *De Ringcompositie als Opbouwprincipe in de Epische Gedichten van Homerus.* Amsterdam.

Pangle, T., ed. 1987. *The Roots of Political Philosophy: Ten Forgotten Socratic Dialogues.* Ithaca.

Bibliography

Pappas, N. 1995. *Plato and the* Republic. New York.

Parry, R. 1996. *Plato's Craft of Justice*. Albany.

Patterson, R. 2007. "Diagrams, Dialectic, and Mathematical Foundations in Plato." *Apeiron* 40: 1–33.

Popper, K. 1962. *The Open Society and its Enemies,* vol. 1: *The Spell of Plato.* Princeton.

Prauscello, L. 2010. "Patterns of Chorality in Plato's *Laws*." In *Music and Politics in Ancient Greek Societies*, ed. D. Yatromanolakis. New York and London.

Price, A. W. 2009. "Are Plato's Soul-Parts Psychological Subjects?" *Ancient Philosophy* 29: 1–15.

Race, W. H. 1997. *Pindar.* 2 vols. Cambridge.

Randall, J. H. 1970. *Plato: Dramatist of the Life of Reason.* New York.

Reeve, C. D. C. 1988. *Philosopher-Kings: The Argument of Plato's* Republic. Princeton.

2003. "Plato's Metaphysics of Morals." *Oxford Studies in Ancient Philosophy* 25: 39–58.

2004. *Plato:* Republic. Indianapolis.

Richardson, H. 1926. "The Myth of Er (Plato *Republic* 616b)." *Classical Quarterly* 20: 113–33.

Robinson, R. 1953. *Plato's Earlier Dialectic.* 2nd edn. Oxford.

Roochnik, D. 2003. *Beautiful City: The Dialectical Character of Plato's* Republic. Ithaca.

Rosen, S. 2005. *Plato's* Republic: *A Study.* New Haven.

Rowe, C. 1999. "Myth, History and Dialectic in Plato." In *From Myth to Reason? Studies in the Development of Greek Thought*, ed. R. Buxton. Oxford, 263–78.

Rushdie, S. 1996. *The Moor's Last Sigh.* New York.

Ryle, G. 1966. *Plato's Progress.* Cambridge.

Sachs, D. 1963. "A Fallacy in Plato's *Republic*." *Philosophical Review* 72: 141–58. Rpt in Smith 1998, vol. 2, 206–19.

Sallis, J. 1975. *Being and Logos: The Way of Platonic Dialogue.* Pittsburgh.

Santas, G. 1980. "The Form of the Good in Plato's *Republic*." *Philosophical Inquiry* 2: 374–403.

2001. "Plato's Criticism of the 'Democratic Man' in the *Republic*." *Journal of Ethics* 5: 57–71.

Santas, G., ed. 2006. *The Blackwell Guide to Plato's* Republic. Oxford.

Saxonhouse, A. 1978. "Comedy in Callipolis: Animal Imagery in the *Republic*." *American Political Science Review* 72: 881–901.

Scanlon, T. F. 2002. "'The Clear Truth' in *Thucydides* 1. 22. 4." *Historia* 51: 131–48.

Schein, S. 1997. "The *Iliad*: Structure and Interpretation." In *A New Companion to Homer*, ed. I. Morris and B. Powell. Leiden.

Schils, G. 1993. "Plato's Myth of Er: The Light and the Spindle." *Antiquité Classique* 62: 101–14.

Schofield, M. 1972. "A Displacement in the Text of the *Cratylus*." *Classical Quarterly* 22: 246–53.

2006. *Plato: Political Philosophy.* Oxford.

2007. "The Noble Lie." In Ferrari 2007, 138–64.

Bibliography

Scott, D. 2000. "Plato's Critique of the Democratic Character." *Phronesis* 45: 19–37.

———. 2006. *Plato's* Meno. Cambridge.

Sedley, D. 2007. "Philosophy, the Forms, and the Art of Ruling." In Ferrari 2007, 256–83.

Shields, Christopher. 2001. "Simple Souls." In *Essays on Plato's Psychology*, ed. E. Wagner. Maryland, 137–56.

———. 2006. "Unified Agency and *Akrasia* in Plato's *Republic*." In *"Akrasia" in Ancient Philosophy*, ed. C. Bobonich and P. Destrée. Leiden, 61–86.

Shorey, P., ed. and trans. 1930. *Plato:* Republic, vols. 1 and 2. Cambridge.

———. 1963. "The *Republic*." In *The Collected Dialogues of Plato*, ed. E. Hamilton and H. Cairns. Princeton.

Singpurwalla, R. 2006. "Plato's Defense of Justice." In Santas 2006, 263–82.

———. Forthcoming-1. "The Tripartite Theory of Motivation in Plato's *Republic*." *Blackwell Philosophy Compass*.

———. Forthcoming-2. "Soul Division and Mimesis in *Republic* X." In *Plato and the Poets*, ed. Pierre Destrée and Fritz-Gregor Herrmann (Brill Academic Publishers).

Smith, N. D. 1996. "Plato's Divided Line." *Ancient Philosophy* 16: 25–46.

Smith, N. D., ed. 1998. *Plato: Critical Assessments*, vol. 3. London.

Smith, R., trans., comm. 1997. *Aristotle:* Topics Books I and VIII. Oxford.

Solomon, J. 2001. *The Ancient World in the Cinema*. New Haven.

Sparshott, F. 1982. "Aristotle's *Ethics* and Plato's *Republic*: A Structural Comparison." *Dialogue* 21: 483–99.

Stalley, R. F. 1975. "Plato's Argument for the Division of the Reasoning and Appetitive Elements within the Soul." *Phronesis* 20: 110–28.

Stanford, W. B. 1983. *Greek Tragedy and the Emotions*. London.

Stauffer, D. 2001. *Plato's Introduction to the Question of Justice*. Albany.

Stemmer, P. 1992. *Platons Dialektik*. Berlin.

Stewart, J. A. 1905. *The Myths of Plato*. New York.

Stocks, J. L. 1932. "The Divided Line of Plato *Republic* VI." In *The Limits of Purpose and Other Essays*, ed. J. L. Stocks. London.

Strauss, L. 1964. *The City and Man*. Chicago.

Szlezák, T. 1985. *Platon und die Schriftlichkeit der Philosophie*. Berlin.

Taft, R. 1982. "The Role of Compulsion in the Education of Plato's Philosopher-King." *Auslegung* 9: 311–32.

Taylor, A. E. 1939. "The Decline and Fall of the State in the *Republic* VIII." *Mind* 48: 23–38.

Taylor, C. C. W. 1999. "The Atomists." In *The Cambridge Companion to Early Greek Philosophy*, ed. A. A. Long. Cambridge, 181–204.

Thayer, H. S. 1988. "The Myth of Er." *History of Philosophy Quarterly* 5(4): 369–84.

Thesleff, H. 1993. "Looking for Clues: An Interpretation of Some Literary Aspects of Plato's 'Two-Level' Model." In *Plato's Dialogues: New Studies and Interpretations*, ed. G. Press. Lanham, 17–46.

Thionville, E. 1983. *De la Théorie des Lieux Communs dans les Topiques d'Aristote*. Paris (1855).

Bibliography

Tonsfeldt, H. W. 1977. "Ring-structure in *Beowulf.*" *Neophilologus* 61: 443–52.

Tracy, S. V. 1997. "The Structures of the *Odyssey.*" In *A New Companion to Homer*, ed. I. Morris and B. Powell. Leiden, 360–79.

Vegetti, M. 1999. "L'autocritica di Platone: il *Timeo* e le *Leggi.*" In *La Repubblica di Platone nella tradizione antica*, ed. M. Abbate and M. Vegetti. Naples.

Vernezze, P. 1998. "The Philosophers' Interest." In Smith 1998, 153–73.

Vidal-Naquet, P. 1964. "Athènes et l'Atlantide." *Revue des Etudes Grecques* 77: 420–44.

2008. *The Atlantis Story: A Short History of Plato's Myth.* Exeter.

Vlastos, G. 1954. "The Third Man Argument in the *Parmenides.*" *The Philosophical Review* 63(3): 319–49.

1971. "Justice and Happiness in the *Republic.*" In *Plato II: Ethics, Politics, and Philosophy of Art and Religion; A Collection of Critical Essays*, ed. G. Vlastos. Notre Dame, 66–95.

1977. "The Theory of Social Justice in the *Polis* in Plato's *Republic.*" In *Interpretations of Plato*, ed. H. North. Leiden.

1981a. "Isonomia politikê." In *Platonic Studies*, 2nd edn., ed. G. Vlastos. Princeton, 164–203.

1981b. "Justice and Happiness in the *Republic.*" In *Platonic Studies* 2nd edn., ed. G. Vlastos. Princeton, 111–39.

1991. *Socrates: Ironist and Moral Philosopher.* Ithaca.

Wagner, E. 2005. "Compulsion Again in the *Republic.*" *Apeiron* 38: 131–45.

Wallace, R. W. 2004. "Damon of Oa: A Music Theorist Ostracized." In *Music and the Muses*, ed. P. Murray and P. Wilson. Oxford.

Waterlow, Sarah. 1972–73. "The Good of Others in Plato's *Republic.*" *Proceedings of the Aristotelian Society* 72: 19–36.

Weiss, R. 2001. *Virtue in the Cave: Moral Inquiry in Plato's* Meno. Oxford.

Wekselbaum, C. 2006. "Keeping Up Appearances: A Pattern of Degeneration in Plato's *Republic.*" *Washington University Undergraduate Research Digest* 2(1): 23–46.

Wenskus, O. 1982. *Ringkomposition, anaphorisch-rekapitulierende Verbindung und Anknüpfende Wiederholung im Hippokratischen Corpus.* Frankfurt.

West, M. L. 1992. *Ancient Greek Music.* Oxford.

White, N. P. 1984. "The Classification of Goods in Plato's *Republic.*" *Journal of the History of Philosophy* 22: 393–421.

1986. "The Ruler's Choice." *Archiv für Geschichte der Philosophie* 68: 22–46.

2002. *Individual and Conflict in Ancient Greek Ethics.* Oxford.

Whitman, C. 1963. *Homer and the Heroic Tradition.* Cambridge.

Wilberding, J. 2004. "Prisoners and Puppeteers in the Cave." *Oxford Studies in Ancient Philosophy* 27: 117–39.

Williams, B. 1973. "The Analogy of the City and Soul in Plato's *Republic.*" In *Exegesis and Argument: Studies in Greek Philosophy Presented to Gregory Vlastos, Phronesis* suppl. vol. 1, ed. E. N. Lee, A. P. D. Mourelatos, and R. M. Rorty. Assen, 196–206.

Wolenski, J. 2004. "*Alêtheia* in Greek Thought until Aristotle." *Annals of Pure and Applied Logic* 127: 339–60.

Wolin, S. S. 1960. *Politics and Vision*. Boston.

Worthington, I. 1991. "Greek Oratory, Revision of Speeches and Historical Reliability." *Classica et Medievalia* 42: 55–74.

   1993. "Two Letters of Isocrates and Ring Composition." *Electronic Antiquity*. (http://scholar.lib.vt.edu/ejournals/elant/vini/worthington.html)

Index of passages

Anonymous, *Prolegomena to Platonic Philosophy*
  26.6–7 104
Aeschylus
  Seven Against Thebes
    39–41 176
    66–68 176
Aristophanes
  Frogs
    727–30 232
Aristotle
  Eudemian Ethics
    1246b31–35 37
  Nicomachean Ethics
    1095a–b 41
  Politics
    1316a20–b14 104
    1316b15–27 105
    1337b24 231
    1340b29 245
  Topics
    111b32–33 26
    155b29–157a7 25
    156b10–11 26
Euripides
  Philoctetes 177
  Helena
    267–69 139
  Troiades
    469–71 139
Herodotus
  History
    2.44 176
Hippocrates
  On Ancient Medicine
    1.20–27 178
Homer
  Iliad
    2.252–53 175
    2.485–86 177
    4.404 175
    7.226–27 175

    15.632–33 175
    20.201 175
  Odyssey
    1.32–41 133
    2.30–31 175
Homeric Hymns
  Hymn to Aphrodite
    167 176
  Hymn to Hermes
    201–11 176
Pindar
  Nemean
    11.43–46 176
Plato
  Apology
    20c1–3 224
    23a5–6 227
    36b1 166
  Charmides
    153b 18
    155b–157c 34
    155c–d 18
    155c–e 12
    159c 231
    163d 179
    169d 12
    175a–176a 34
  Cratylus
    383b 35
    384a–385e 36
    384c 35
    385b–d 36
    385e–387b 36
    387b–427d 36
    387d–391a 36
    391c 36
    407e–408b 36
    427d–433a 36
    432e 36
    433a–435e 36
    439a 182

262 — Index of passages

Plato (cont.)
  Cratylus (cont.)
    439b–440d 36
    440e 36
  Critias
    48a–49e 135
    108e4–109a2 56
    110c3–d4 54
    121b7–c2 56
  Crito
    54c8 166
  Euthydemus
    271a 179
    290e 18
    307c1 150
  Euthyphro
    2c3 150
    5d8–e2 212
    6d 179
    6d6–7 212
    6d9–e6 212
    10a 79
    11e–12e 74
    12d5 166
    12d8 166
    15e 14
  Gorgias
    451d–e 179
    463e 179
    464d3–465a2 107
    474a–c 14
    486d 14
    500d 179
    511a2 149
    518d–519b 55
    522b–523a 133
    523a–527e 133, 141
    525b–526b 133
    562d–527c 133
  Hippias Major
    300e 179
  Hippias Minor
    364c 179
  Ion
    532e2 150
  Laches
    179a–180a 35
    196c 179
    200a–201c 35
  Laws
    653a 243
    653a–c 245
    653d–654a 246
    653e 245
    655c 243

    655c–d 243
    655d 243
    656b 243
    657c 243
    657e 243
    658d–e 243
    658e–659a 244
    658e–660a 244
    660b 244
    664e 245
    665d 244
    667a–b 244
    668a 245
    668a–b 245
    668c 245
    669b 245
    669b–c 245
    669c–670a 245
    670e 245
    700a–701b 244
    731c–d 140
    743c 79
    799e–802e 244
    801b–c 245
    802b–c 245
    809e–812a 232
    812b–e 244
    812d 179
    816d–817d 242
    860d–861b 140
    903b4–d3 59
    904c6–905c4 59
  Lovers
    132d 12
    133c 12
    135a 12
  Lysis
    210e 12
    213d 12
    218c 12
    223a–b 13
  Meno
    100b 180
    70a 34
    86d3–87b1 191
    86d–87c 42
    86d–e 191
    86e3 191
    89c5–96d4 192
    99e–100b 34
  Phaedo
    64c–67b 234
    65b 180
    68c–69a 70
    69d 179

Index of passages

78c1–4 148
80b2 148
83a–b 182
85c 180
85c1–d4 227
95e8 150
100a 179
100a4 42
100b 42
101d6–e2 42
101d8 42
107c 133

Phaedrus
227b 14
228d 19
245c–257b 133
263e–264a 19
277b 180

Philebus
55c–59b 180
55e–56a 235
61a 180
64a1 210

Politicus
262c 179
263b5 166

Protagoras
316a 179
325d–326c 231
331a–b 74
345e 140

Republic
327a 38
327a1–3 1
327b 23
328a 1
328d–331b 39
330d1–331a6 147
330d–331a 132
331e–332a 70
332a–b 27
332c 26
334b 27
334b–e 70
335b–d 70
335e–336a 27
336b 23
337a 24
338d–339e 65
342e 23
343b 108
343c 65
343d–344a 108
344b3–5 108
346e3–347d8 84

350d 23
354c3 87
357a 13
357b1–2 83
357b3 83
358a1–3 65
358b 39, 68
358b–c 65
358c–d 27
359a–b 65
359c–360d 40
360d–362c 39
361e 68
362d–363e 132
362e–363e 132
362e–367e 73
367a–b 27
368b–c 14
368c 16
368c–369a 105, 148
368c–369b 7
368c7–369b4 55
368e–369a 65, 67
369a 77
369b–372d 65
369e6 166
371c–d 12
371e 77
372e 12, 77
373a4–7 225
373d9–e1 225
375e–376c 234
376c–402a 65
376d 77
376e 230, 231
376e1–3 225
377a–b 68
377d–e 71
377d–383a 73
378a–e 240
378b 71
378c 74
378d–e 71, 133
378e7–379a4 223
379a 71
380c 71
380c6–10 133
381e 240
383a 71
383c 240
388d 71
389e 238
390a–b 71, 114
390d 238
390d–e 74

Index of passages

Plato (cont.)
  Republic (cont.)
    391a 74
    391e 71, 240
    391e1–2 133
    392a 76
    392a–c 73
    392c–d 19
    392d 20
    392d–394d 44
    393a–394a 20
    393b–c 47
    393c 236
    393d 20
    393d–394b 46
    394b 21
    394b–c 20
    394d 44
    394d–398b 46
    395c 237
    397c–d 231
    397d–398b 44
    398a–b 237
    398b 230
    398d 231
    398d8–9 223
    398d–e 240
    398e1–400c6 223
    399a–c 237
    399c–e 239
    399e4–5 225
    400a–c 236
    400d 238
    400e 238
    401a 238
    401a–d 231
    401b–d 233
    401c–d 230
    401d–402a 230
    401e4–402a4 225
    402a 234
    402a–b 239
    402b5–7 213
    402b5–c8 216
    402b9–c8 213
    402c 78, 79
    403c 233
    403c–412b 65
    407c7–e2 93
    410a2–3 93
    410c–411e 233
    411c–d 233
    411d 114, 233
    411d–e 114
    411e 234

    412a 113, 238
    413c6–7 94
    416a–b 236
    416e–417a 114, 115
    417a 115
    419–420a 76
    419a1–420c4 84
    420b 72
    420b5–421c6 92
    420b–c 77
    423d–424b 235
    423e2 226
    424b–c 244
    424b–d 235
    424c8–d1 226
    424d–e 236
    427e 65
    427e–429a 41
    428c11–429a3 214, 220
    428e9–429a1 226
    429b8–c2 94
    430b–c 70
    432c–433a 16
    433a 17
    433a–b 79
    433c 66
    433e–434a 75
    434a3–d1 92
    434e 150
    435b4–c5 150
    435c–441c 66
    435c9–d4 227
    436b8 152
    436b8–11 154
    436c–439e 152
    436c7–e7 154
    436e1–2 154
    437a4–7 219
    437b1–5 152
    437b1–c10 160
    437b–439e 7
    438c6–e10 215
    439a1–d2 160
    439b10–11 154
    439b8–c1 154
    439b9 154
    439c–441c 7
    439d6–7 8, 209
    439e2–3 8, 209
    439e–440a 153
    439e–441c 152, 153
    440a 157
    440c–d 157
    440e 156
    441a2–3 225

Index of passages

441a5–6   156
441a–b   156
441c–442b   66
441c4–6   152
441d   157
441d–e   79
441e   234
441e1–2   91
441e3–5   209
442b5–7   209
442b5–d1   161
442b10   164, 166
442c2–3   94
442c4   164, 166
442c4–7   210
442c5–7   209
442d10–443a10   85
442d10–443b2   91
442d10–443b3   91
442e–443b   66, 69
443c1   183
443c9–444a2   85
443d10   164
443d1–3   92
443d1–e1   157
443d7–8   8, 209
443d–e   238
444b3   164, 166
444c–445b   66
444e–445a   72
445a–d   105
445c   28, 104
449a   79
450a   104
450a–451b   14
450b   14
457e   14
460a   136
463b5   93
465e4–466c5   84
465e–466b   77
466e1–471c3   55
471c–472a   69
471c–473b   14
471c–473d   106
471c4–473b3   201
472b–c   69
472c–e   106
473a1–3   214
473b4–e5   201
473c   106
473c11–e4   213
473d   106
474c8–480a   201
476a5–8   216

476b4–d8   211
476b9–10   226
476c1–2   216, 217
476c4–5   215
476c7–d3   215
476d4–e8   215
476d7–e2   216
476e7–8   216
477a2–4   215
477c6–d5   210
477d8–e1   210
477e7–8   213
478a7   210
478b11–c1   216
478c9–d4   216
478e1–3   216
478e1–479d8   211
479a6   211
479a8–b1   211, 216
479a8–c5   212
479d2–4   212
484a1–487a8   201
484b   28
484c5–d2   212
485b–487a   68
485d–486b   72
486a5–9   219
486a9–10   221
487a–502c   192
487b1–d5   201
487e7–489c7   107
488b3–4   107
488b6–8   107
488c3–4   107
488c4–7   107
488e3–489a2   107
490a9–b7   211
492a   142
492e–493a   142
493a6–494a3   224
493a6–c8   107
496a10–e2   86
496a11–e3   227
496c3–e2   147
497c   113
498d25   147
500a   28
500b1–d2   226
500b8–501b7   220
500c3   218, 226
500c–d   68
503a   15
503d10   226
504a–b   79
504b1–505b3   227

Index of passages

Plato (cont.)
Republic (cont.)

504b–c	78	517b6–7	226
505a2–4	210	517c3–4	210
505d5–9	210	517c7–d2	96
506a–d	202	517c8–9	83
506a4–7	213	517d4–e2	97
506a9–b1	213	518a1–b4	97
506c	78	518b8–c2	209
506c2–e1	218	518c6–8	8, 209
507a–509d	181	518c9	218
507b1–9	211	518d	8
507b9–11	189	518d3–5	209
508b12–511e5	210	518d5–7	209
508c–d	181	518d11–e1	221
508c3	218	519a1–b5	225
508d3–8	213	519b–520e	95
508e2–3	218	519c8–d7	83
508e4–5	218	519d	77
509a4–5	218	519d8–9	83
509b1–6	218	519e1–520a4	92
509b1–9	218	519e1–520a5	84
509d	171	519e–520a	72, 77
509d–510b	172	520a–c	71
509d–513e	181	520a6–c6	86
509e	174	520a9	88
510b4–6	189	520a9–c3	86
510b10	192	520c	79
510b–511a	78	520c1–5	213
510b–511d	8	520c2–6	97
510b6–9	190	520d–e	75
510c–511b	172	520e1	5, 86
510c1–511b2	192	520e2	94
510c1–d4	193	521b1–11	84
510c2–d3	217	521b9–10	93
510d2–3	193	522a3–6	209
510d5–511a2	193, 195	522a4–7	225
511a3–b2	193	524c	179
511b2–c2	213	525b9–531b7	217
511b3–6	217	528a–b	21
511b3–8	193	528e–530c	235
511b3–c2	192	529b5–c1	213
511b4–6	41	530c–531c	235
511b6–c2	42	530e–531b	235
511b7–8	193	531c2–7	219
511c1–2	193, 196, 217, 222	531c9–d3	219
511c3–d5	193	531d–535a	198
511d–e	172, 182	531d2–533a5	227
511d6–e5	193	532a	78
514a1–22	215	532a6–b2	217
515a	181	533b1	219
515a–b	181	533b2	219
515d	181	533b6–e3	198
516e3–517a6	97	533b7–c1	198
517a8–c5	96	533c3–5	194
		533c3–6	217
		533c8–d1	219

Index of passages

533d2   223
533e3–534a3   213
533e4–534b2   199
534a2–3   210
534b8–c5   219
534b8–d1   199, 219
534d1–6   222
537c1–7   219
537c6–7   219
539e2–540a4   95
539e4–6   220
539e5–540a2   97
539e6–540b1   220
540a4–5   95
540a4–b1   95
540b4–5   96
544a   104, 105
544a–b   150
545b   150
545d   110
546a   109
546a1–547a6   221
546a4–b3   109
546b1–3   214
546b2   109
546d   113
546d4–547a6   226
546e   112
547b   112
547b–c   114
547d   114
547e   119
547e–548a   110
548a   112, 114, 119
548a5–b2   112
548b   114
548c   110
549d–550a   123
550e–551a   119
550e4–551a10   112
551b   110
551c   120
551d–e   119
552a   105, 116
552d   116
552e   115, 116
553a–b   123
553b7–d7   225
554a   111
554b   115
554c   115, 116, 118, 119
554c–d   116
554c11–e5   161
555a   119
555b   110, 112

555c   105, 118
557a   110, 120
557b   110, 112
557e–558a   116
558b   116
558c   120
558d8–559b6   225
559d–e   123
560a   118, 161
560b–e   119
561a   111
561b   111, 119, 120
561b–d   112
562b   110
562e–563c   117
565a   117
565b–c   117
566a   112
566e–567c   112
567c   120
568a–c   44
571b   112
571d   120
572b   112
572b10–d3   117
572d   120
572e   111
573b   120
573e   112
574d   112
574d12–575a7   161
575a   111
575b–576a   112
576d6–588a10   210
577c   150
580a–588b   39
580b1–c5   226
580b5–c4   89
580d   8
580d3–587e4   160
580d8   209
581a   112
581a9–b4   8, 209, 225
581b6–11   210
581d10   221
581d10–e4   151
582a–e   72
585a8–b1   224
586e   160
586a–587a   114
586e–587a   160
586e4–587a2   210
587b   28
588b   39
588b10–e1   151

Index of passages

Plato (cont.)
  Republic (cont.)
    589a6–b6 161
    591b–592b 69
    592a–b 106
    592b 106
    595a 47
    595a5 44
    595a–b 44, 45, 239
    595c 28, 44
    596a–598b 45
    598b–600e 45
    598d 44
    601a–602b 45
    601a–b 240
    601d8–10 220
    601e7–602a1 214
    602c–605c 45
    602d6–603e2 214
    602e4–603a8 163
    605b 45
    605c 44
    605c–606d 240
    605c–607a 45
    605d 47
    606b 244
    606e–607a 45
    607a 243, 244
    607b 44
    607c–e 244
    608c–612a 6, 132
    608c6–d3 221
    608d2–5 147
    611a10–612a6 112
    611a10–b2 149
    611b1–612a6 210
    611b4 148
    611b4–6 147
    611b5–612a6 221, 223
    611b10–c2 149
    611d2–4 149
    611d6–31 149
    611e1 151
    611e2 148
    612a–614a 132
    612a3–4 149
    612a4–5 149
    612a5 151
    612d–e 132
    612e–613b 132
    614a–621a 132
    614b 22
    614b–621d 1, 39
    614b–d 38
    614d–616b 140

    615c–616b 133
    616a 140
    617d 38
    617d–618b 133, 136
    617d–621b 40, 134
    617d2–3 135
    617e–618a 139
    617e–619b 139
    617e3 135, 140
    617e5 135
    618b–619a 133
    618b–619b 141
    618b3 135, 140
    618b6–619b1 226
    618c–d 140
    618d 137, 141
    619a7–b1 89
    619b 137, 139
    619b–c 134, 136, 139, 140
    619c 139
    619c–d 40, 133, 136
    619c1 134, 140
    619c1–d1 226
    619c5 138
    619d7–e5 226
    619e 133, 137
    619e–620d 137
    620a 136, 140
    620a–b 137
    620c 141,
    620e–621c 134
    621a 137
    621a–b 140
    621b 38
    621b–d 133, 134
  Seventh Letter
    341a–345c 36
    341a–b 36
    341b–c 36
    341c 36
    341d–e 36
    342a–343b 36
    343c–d 36
    343e–344b 36
    344c 36
    344d–345c 36
  Sophist
    217a–236e 35
    220c7 166
    223d 166
    235a–236c 241
    236b10–c1 167
    237a–241d 35
    241d–251a 35
    251a–256d 35

Index of passages

256d–259e 35
260a–264b 35
264d–268d 35
Symposium
223b 37
223d 14, 37
Theaetetus
146c–d 35
147a 35
147b 35
204e1–11 166
210a 35
Theages
127e 231
Timaeus
18c1–4 58
19b–c 56
19c8–20b7 53
24d6–e1 56
25c3–6 56
25c6–d6 56
42b3–d2 58
53d2–3 167
86d–e 140

87b 140
90d1–7 58
90e6–91d6 58
Plutarch
Life of Lycurgus
17.1–4 115
18.1 115
Life of Solon
32 62
Sophocles
Oedipus Tyrannus
977–78 139
977–978 176
Thucydides
History
2.37 121
2.81–85 103
7.69 121
Xenophon
Memorabilia
4.6.13 179
Polity of the Lacedaemonians
2.1 231
2.5–9 115

Index of names and subjects

Academy 21, 194
Achaeans 175
Achilles 32, 33, 46, 74
Adeimantus 12, 15, 16, 17, 19, 21, 23, 25, 27, 28,
    39, 43, 65, 67, 68, 73, 76, 77, 132, 201, 223,
    235, 236
Aeschylus 144, 169, 176
Agamemnon 32, 137, 175
Ajax 46, 137, 175
Ajax 21
Alcibiades 30, 166
Alcinous 22
Alcmaeon of Croton 177
Alia 61
Anacreon 232
Anchises 176
Annas, J. 66, 132, 229
Antiphon 19, 21
Antisthenes 21
Apollo 32, 74, 175, 244
Apollodorus 19
Apology 35
appetites 103, 105, 106, 107–09, 111–12, 136, 140,
    142, 151, 152, 156, 210, 221, 224, 240
archē 193, 194, 197, 198, 199
Aristodemus 37
Aristophanes 232
Aristotle 25, 26, 29, 34, 36, 37, 41, 47, 67, 75, 93,
    104, 105, 119, 157, 231, 246
Athena 142
Athenian Stranger 243, 244, 245
Athens 53, 54, 55, 56, 57, 58, 59, 60, 61, 62, 103,
    108, 110, 120–21, 202, 231
Atlantis 52–62
Atropos 134

Barker, A. 229, 231, 238
Beethoven 34
Beowulf 33, 34
Bolivia 60
Brann, E. 38

Brickhouse, T. C. 91, 95, 96, 97
Britain 60
Broadie, S. 40
Brown, E. 95, 96
Brunschwig, J. 38
Burnyeat, M. F. 38, 244

Cadmeans 176
Caesar's Palace 61, 62
cave, allegory of 28, 39, 78, 83–98, 104, 181,
    215, 226
Cebes 148
Cephalus 11, 23, 39, 132, 133
Chaerephon 18
Charmides 18, 103
Charmides 11, 18, 19, 34
Chisholm, R. M. 162
choice of lives 105, 132–43
Chryses 19, 32
city of pigs 12, 16, 109
Cleinias 244
Cratylus 35
Cratylus 35, 37
Critias 52, 54, 56, 103
Critias 52, 54, 60, 61
Crito 18, 179
Crito 35
Cronus 71
Cross, R. C. and A. D. Woozley 229
Cyprus 61

daimōn 135
Damon 235, 236, 239, 240
Danaans 175
death 142, 240
degenerate regimes 103–24,
    236, 244
Delphic Oracle 227
Demiurge 58
democracy 107–09, 110–12, 116–17,
    118–21

270

Index of names and subjects

dialectic   25, 27, 41, 173, 182, 217, 220
dianoia   171, 188–203
Dionysius   36
Dionysodorus   18
Dionysus   244
Disney   61
Divided Line   28, 41, 43, 78, 171–84, 188–203
Dorter, K.   38, 142
Douglas, M.   36, 38, 48
drama   20
dunamis   210

education   113–17, 209–27
Eleatic Stranger   179
elenchus   200
Eleusis   134
Eliot, T. S.   33
Er   38, 133, 134, 135, 142
Er, myth of   22, 38, 39, 40, 132–43, 226
Erlingsson, U.   61
Eroticus   21
Eteocles   176
Eucleides   19
eudaimonia   87, 89
Eudemian Ethics   36, 37
Euripides   139, 169, 176
Euthydemus   18
Euthydemus   18, 19
Euthyphro   212, 213, 217
Euthyphro   217

Ferrari, G. R. F.   229
Forms   42, 43, 94, 172, 211–12

Gadrius   61
Gamla Uppsala   60
Garden of Eden   155
Garland   33
geometry   172
Gibraltar   61
Gill, C.   55
Glaucon   12, 13, 14, 15, 16, 17, 23, 25, 27, 28, 39,
   40, 43, 44, 57, 65, 66, 67, 68, 72, 74, 77, 83,
   84, 85, 86, 87, 90, 96, 106, 141, 147, 148, 149,
   151, 168, 171, 172, 189, 192, 198, 200, 211, 214,
   216, 223, 230, 232, 238
Glaucus   149, 151, 168
gods   133–43
Good, Form of   78, 83, 89, 95–98, 134, 172, 180,
   181, 189, 199, 210, 217, 218, 220, 221
Gorgias   21, 107
Gorgias   14, 29, 54
Greece   44
Griffith, T.   230
Gyges   40

Hades   73, 199
Heaven   134, 137
Hector   32, 175
Heracles   176
Hermes   36
Hermocrates   55
Hermogenes   35
Herodotus   34, 176
Hesiod   21, 71, 74, 232, 239, 242, 243
Hippothales   12
Homer   19, 20, 21, 22, 44, 47, 71, 175, 177, 180,
   232, 239, 240, 242
hypothesis, method of   42, 188–203

ignorance   216
Iliad   19, 20, 32, 33, 34, 48, 177, 243
irony   24
Islam   121
Isocrates   21
isonomia   110, 121

Jocasta   139, 176
justice   17, 134
   defense of   65–79, 90
   in the city   65, 76, 150
   in the soul   65, 72, 92
   rewards of   85, 132
   Thrasymachean   65

Kallipolis
   possibility of   201
katabasis   38, 40
knowledge, definition of   35
Kundera, M.   132

Laches   34
Lachesis   134, 135, 136, 138, 139
Las Vegas   61
law   105, 114, 115, 117
Laws   53, 54, 58, 59, 105, 230, 242, 245,
   246
Lear, G. R.   229
Lear, J.   142
Leontius   153, 156
Leroux, G.   38
liberty   110, 111, 112, 116–17, 121
lottery   133
Lovers   11
Lysias   19, 21
Lysimachus   35
Lysis   11, 13

Magnesia   54
Marathon, battle of   53
mathematics   173, 182, 193, 217

272 · Index of names and subjects

McPherran, M. 35
Meleager 33
Melesias 35
Menexenus 53
Menn, S. 49, 67
Meno 34, 37, 42, 194
mimēsis 44–47, 163, 232, 236, 238, 241, 242, 245
Moss, J. 240, 241
Murray, P. 244
Muses 45, 114, 177, 214, 233, 234, 243, 244
music 157, 179, 222, 225, 229–47
myths 132–43

Necessity 134, 135, 141
Nettleship, R. L. 117, 246
Nicomachean Ethics 36, 75
non-contradiction, principle of 154, 198, 219

Odysseus 22, 141, 142, 143, 176
Odysseus 21
Odyssey 22, 30, 48, 133, 141, 243
Oedipus 176
oligarchy 103, 104, 109, 110, 111, 119
Orpheus 136, 137
Ouranos 71

Palamedes 21
Parmenides 19, 138
Peloponnesian War 54, 55, 103
Pentateuch 34
Pericles 76, 236
Phaedo 35, 42, 191, 194, 196, 200, 241
Phaedrus 19
Phaedrus 19, 21
Philebus 210, 246
Phoenice 176
piety 179, 212, 217
Pindar 21, 34, 176
Piraeus 22, 38
Plutarch 62, 115
poetry 19, 44, 134, 136, 223, 225, 229, 232, 235, 239, 246
Polemarchus 16, 23, 26, 27
Politeia 67
Politics 104, 105, 246
Poseidon 62, 142
Priam 32, 33
problem of evil 135
Proclus 30, 80, 104
Prodicus 179
prophet 138–39, 141
Protagoras 231, 232

reason 103, 105, 113–22, 136, 140, 142, 151, 156, 209–11, 234

recollection, theory of 196
Rist, J. M. 38
River of Forgetfulness 134, 137, 140
Robinson, R. 191
Rudbeck, O. 60
Ryle, G. 27

Sachs, D. 67–72
Santas, G. 229
Sappho 21
Schofield, M. 36, 66
Seventh Letter 36, 38
Sherlock Holmes 27
Ship of State analogy 103, 107–09, 202
Sicily 55
Simmias 180, 227
Simonides 26, 232
Sirens 134
Solon 56
Sophist 35, 37, 245
soul
  analogy to city 66
  immortality of 147–48, 191
  and music 114, 230–35
  nature of 137
  parts of 43, 106, 147–68
  spirited part 93, 113, 136, 140, 142, 152, 156, 210, 221, 224, 233
Sparta 54, 103, 115, 121
Spartel 61
Sthenelus 175
Strauss, L. 15, 25
subjectivity 162
sun, allegory of 28, 78, 189, 199, 218, 222
Sweden 61
Symposium 19, 37, 68, 232
Szlezák, T. 15, 25

Tartarus 137
Tetralogies 21
Theaetetus 21, 35
Theaetetus 19, 35, 37
theia moira 142
Thera 60
Thesleff, H. 38
Thetis 32
Thrasymachus 12, , 17, 23, 24, 25, 39, 65, 66, 67, 69, 72, 77, 79, 103, 104, 107, 108, 142
Thucydides 34, 103, 108, 121, 138
Timaeus 52, 58
Timaeus 52, 53, 55, 58, 59, 61, 62, 246
timocracy 104, 109, 111, 112, 114, 117–18
Topics 25, 27
tragedy 244

Index of names and subjects

Troy   22, 50, 60, 61
Tübingen School   15, 25
tuchē   136, 138, 143
tyranny   103–04, 110, 111, 120
Tyre   176

unwritten doctrines   15, 25

Vidal-Naquet, P.   55
virtues   66, 73, 103, 118–20, 191
   psychology of   69

Vlastos, G.   138

Wilson, P.   244

Xanthippe   241
Xenophanes   177, 178, 239
Xenophon   21, 115, 179, 231

Zeus   32, 56, 57, 71, 142,
   176, 224
Zoroastrian Gathas   34

Lightning Source UK Ltd.
Milton Keynes UK
UKOW06f2010300815

257765UK00008B/193/P